Vision and Calculation

Sheng Hong

Vision and Calculation

Economics from China's Perspective

palgrave
macmillan

Sheng Hong
Unirule Institute of Economics
Beijing, Beijing, China

ISBN 978-981-15-2897-2 ISBN 978-981-15-2898-9 (eBook)
https://doi.org/10.1007/978-981-15-2898-9

This Palgrave Macmillan imprint is published by the registered company Springer Nature Singapore Pte Ltd
The registered company address is: 152 Beach Road, #21-01/04 Gateway East, Singapore 189721, Singapore

Preface to Vision and Calculation

As an author who has published several books, I have always felt that publishing books is amazing. Suddenly one day, a person will say to you, "I read a book of yours many years ago, and it had a great impact on me." In reality, this situation is very rare. More often, you do not know who reads your book and what impact it had on him or her. For instance, I have read the books of the human sages. They have passed away and do not know what kind of impact they have had on me, how they have inspired my thinking, and how I wrote out those inspired thoughts and shared them with others. However, this is the mysterious mechanism of the development of human culture.

This book, ***Vision and Calculation***, is a collection of my papers. The papers were originally written in Chinese, and now they have been collected and published in English. Although I have published several books in English, they have all been research reports for the Unirule Institute of Economics. It is only because I am the leader of the research team and the main writer that I use my name and the name of the collaborator as the authors' names for those reports. However, this book is composed of all of my own papers. This gives me the feeling of facing my English readers directly. I will not know who reads my book or what magical results it will have for them. However, I feel obliged to make it easier for my English readers. Therefore, herein, I'd like to introduce my own academic and cultural background and explain what I think ordinary English readers may find difficult.

The title of this book, taken from one of the articles, is called "Vision and Calculation." Economics has always posited that people are rational economic people and that they will make rational judgments through cost-benefit comparisons. However, we often see irrational behavior. In 2010, a sensational event occurred in China. A young man, Yao Jiaxin, hurt a woman while he was driving. Instead of saving her, he killed her with a knife. This, of course, was morally reprehensible. Nevertheless, from an economic point of view, it was also wrong according to rational calculation. Yao Jiaxin's reason for killing the woman was that the injured women would pester him. Nonetheless, there was a high probability of his crime being uncovered by police and of him being sentenced to death.

There have been many explanations given in psychology and economics about calculation errors. My explanation is that the calculation is wrong because of the limited field of vision. A person's calculations depend on the information that he or she obtains. The more comprehensive the information, the more accurate the calculation. Additionally, the amount or comprehensiveness of the information depends on the field of vision. The larger the field of vision of space and time, the more abundant and comprehensive the information and the more accurate the calculation. In this regard, I quote a Chinese idiom that says, "The mantis stalks the cicada, unaware of the oriole behind." This idiom comes from a story from the Spring and Autumn period (770–221 BC). The story tells that the King of Wu wanted to attack the state of Chu and refused to listen to criticism. At this time, a young man went several times to the garden behind the palace with a slingshot. The King of Wu asked him curiously what he was doing. The boy said, "I saw a cicada chirping in the tree, but it did not know that there was a mantis behind it; the mantis wanted to catch the cicada, but it did not know that there was an oriole behind it; and the oriole wanted to eat the mantis, but it did not know that I wanted to shoot it down with a slingshot." After hearing this, King of Wu decided not to attack Chu. This story vividly illustrates the importance of vision to calculation.

Therefore, why are people (let alone other creatures) limited in their field of vision? The first reason is that it takes attention resources to observe and pay attention to external things, and natural evolution makes creatures save their resources as much as possible. For most of the millions of years of evolution, humans were hunter-gatherers. They only needed to pay attention to the range of a few hundreds of meters and the current time. Beyond this range, the direct threat to their survival was greatly diminished. Thus, applying more observation and attention was a waste of scarce attention resources. Thus, nature automatically limits human attention to a smaller area. The second reason that people are limited in their field of visions is that when people and other creatures find a beneficial target (such as prey), they are more likely to focus on this target and automatically ignore other targets. This is what I call a "win a little game, lose a big game" mistake. However, with the rapid development of human civilization in the most recent thousands of years, the cooperation between human beings has made the factors that affect a person's costs or benefits far beyond his or her physiological field of vision, which may be at the other end of the earth or in another period of time. This requires that people's vision extend beyond the past. Nevertheless, when the psychological structure cannot be quickly evolved and adjusted, overcoming the mistakes of having too small of a vision depends on learning, education, religion, and other cultural traditions.

The subtitle of this book is ***Economics from the Viewpoint of China***. I think there are two difficulties for ordinary English readers. The first is "economics," and the second is "China." Regarding the difficulty of understanding "economics," my book can be regarded as a collection of economics papers. Because my academic major is economics, I am myself an economist. Generally, economics is not hard to read, but I have included some papers herein that contain many mathematical formulas and geometric charts. Their interpretation will not be a problem for readers with an economics background, but they may bring difficulties to ordinary readers. However, I would like to say that these formulas and charts are not the most important part of these papers. If you find it difficult to interpret them, you can skip them and only look at nonmathematical parts and conclusions. I included mathematics in this book mainly because I was influenced by some examples of neoclassical economics and because my research at the Unirule Institute of Economics required the inclusions of some numbers to express judgment and persuade readers; thus, I developed a slight habit of using mathematics.

As an economist, I can be regarded as an economic liberalist. My academic background is mainly in new institutional economics. I think that I inherited the tradition ranging from Adam Smith to Friedrich Hayek. I can still remember the excitement of reading Hayek for the first time. To date, I am still studying Hayek's ***Law, Legislation and Liberty***. Obviously, there is no mathematical formula in Hayek's book. The so-called new institutional economics refer to the economics tradition created by Ronald Coase. In the late 1980s, I read Coase's "The Nature of the Firm" and "The Problem of Social Cost." I not only applauded his theoretical insights but also clearly realized how powerful his theory is in explaining and the practical value of the market-oriented reform in China at that time. I later corresponded with Professor Coase and edited and organized the translation of his selected work ***The Firm, the Market and the Law***. When we heard that Professor Coase had won the Nobel Prize in economics in 1991, the Chinese version of the selected work had just been published.

In 1993, I was invited by Professor Coase to be a visiting scholar at the University of Chicago Law School. For half a year, I had discussions with Professor Coase almost every week. I had read Professor Coase's main articles before I went to Chicago, so what I learned while I was there was more about his thinking methods and academic style. Regarding his thinking methods, he urged me to pay attention to experience and oppose "blackboard economics." He once took me to the Chicago Board of Trade to see trading scenes and told me to "learn the real world." Regarding his academic style, he encouraged me to form academic concepts and theories by using communication and argument. For example, when I asked him to define "institutions," he said that the definition should be formed by the interaction and competition of different definitions. Additionally, he had excellent intuition and the proper judgment of unfamiliar things. He did not come to China, but when we talked about China's rural reform, he said that China's success was due to the fact that there were still families remaining after the dissolution of the people's communes, while Russia's failure in a similar reform was due to there being only individuals left after the dissolution of the collective farms.

Then, I did not see Professor Coase for 14 years. In 2008, he proposed to hold an academic conference on China's 30 years of reform and opening up at the University of Chicago. He used his Nobel Prize to fund the conference attendance of dozens of Chinese economists, entrepreneurs, and officials, and he invited me to attend. "To struggle for China is to struggle for the world," he said in his closing speech. In 2010, Professor Coase organized another academic conference in Chicago. This time, he did not need to fund the travel of the Chinese attendants. On December 29, 2010, to celebrate his 100th birthday, we held a large-scale academic conference in Beijing called "Coase and China" and invited Professor Coase to give a speech via the Internet. "Just as China has Confucius, Britain has Adam Smith," he said. In 2013, while he was planning to visit China, he unfortunately fell ill and died. I cannot help but feel sorry for him when I think that he once said, "I intend to set sail once again to find the route to China, and if this time all I do is to discover America, I won't be disappointed."

Professor Coase founded two schools of thought by himself. In the field of law, it is called "law and economics," while in the field of economics, it is called "new institutional economics." I am an economist, so I am closer to the new institutional economists, such as Professor Douglas North. His ***Structure and Change in Economic History*** helped me to understand Coase's theory. Professor North visited China many times, and he also attended the Chicago conferences organized by Professor Coase in 2008 and 2010. Therefore, I have had many opportunities to meet and discuss with Professor North. The other new institutional economist to whom I am close is Professor Harold Demsez, who, either together with Professor Armen Alchian or independently, published papers on property rights, which are important classics through which we can understand the theory of property rights. When I met Professor Demsez in Chicago in 2008, he was a humorous old man. In addition, I heard Oliver Williamson's lecture on "transaction cost economics" at the Institute of Industrial Economics at the Chinese Academy of Social Sciences in 1988. Another person I should mention is Steven Cheung. Compared to Coase, in terms of age, he is a next-generation scholar. However, his contributions and influence are so great that he could inspire Coase himself, as well as North and others. More importantly, he is Chinese. Cheung introduced new institutional economics to China and attracted the attention of new institutional economists to China. I first read his paper "The Contractual Nature of the Firm," and then later, I read his doctoral dissertation ***The Theory of Share Tenancy*** and his other early papers. I increasingly feel that his theory is one that can explain the Chinese phenomenon better by using new institutional economics.

Therefore, it can also be said that my economics papers are mainly those of new institutional economics. For example, "When Public Goods Become Private Goods" is a chapter that further studies the theory of property rights. In 2002, when I was commissioned by the Ministry of Water Resources to study water rights, I found that the default allocation principle of river water resources in traditional China is that whoever has the ability to dig the canal has the right to the water. However, in modern society, the cost of digging canals has greatly decreased, and there is no water distribution rule established for rivers. In fact, all regions compete for water resources by digging canals, which is known as the "upstream first" principle; this approach resulted in the total reservoir capacity of the middle and upper reaches of the Yellow River exceeding the annual runoff of the Yellow River, which, in turn, resulted in the scarcity of water resources in the Yellow River Basin as a whole. Thus, the Yellow River was cut off for several years. I think that when the cost of obtaining a certain resource is quite high, it may not be a scarce resource because scarcity means that the demand is greater than the supply. What determines demand is not only the scarcity of resources themselves but also the cost of their acquisition. Thus, when the cost of obtaining resources is lower than a certain extent, the resources that are not scarce will become scarce. Only when resources are scarce is it necessary to establish property rights. Therefore, with the development of technology, it seems necessary to establish water rights for water resources without original property rights.

The institution of property rights is related to the physical characteristics of resources. Water is a liquid that flows and is boundary-changeable. To establish property rights, it is more difficult to define the physical boundaries of water than it is those of solid objects. From solid to liquid to gas, to sound, to landscape, and to intangible assets, such as digitality and creativity, they can be considered as a continuous pedigree. An effective property right, first of all, must be "held" by its owner and then must be "exclusive." However, if you want to hold this right, you have to pay the cost or the "exclusive cost." The physical characteristics of a resource will affect its exclusive cost. A liquid is more difficult to hold than a solid, and a gas is more difficult to hold than a liquid. Only when a solid container, such as a reservoir, a bottle, or a balloon, has been created can a liquid or gas be effectively held. Regarding idea-related products, due to the development of printing and the Internet, it is difficult to define their physical boundaries, which can only be protected by an artificial property right system, that is, the intellectual property system. Thus, the concrete form of the institution of property rights, in a dimension, is related to the physical characteristics of resources.

Regarding the difficulty of understanding "China," I include several aspects. The first aspect is China's reform and opening up. This is the field in which I have invested much energy in the past years, and I think it is also the focus of my English readers. The second aspect is the history of China, especially the economic history. Understanding this is necessary to understanding China, including modern China. The third aspect is Chinese culture. This is an important aspect of understanding why Chinese people think in the ways that they do and why China is different from the English-speaking world. The fourth aspect focuses on the problems present in China, which is an important reason why Chinese scholars put forward such problems. The fifth aspect is looking at what has happened in foreign countries from the perspective of China and to give an explanation for these events from the perspective of China.

Let us talk about my cultural background first. Although I am a Chinese, in the early years of my education, I basically did not touch the traditional Chinese culture, which herein mainly refers to the Confucian and Taoist culture. In the middle and late periods of the Cultural Revolution (1966–1976), I worked as a worker in a factory. What I know about "Confucian culture" is a few words of Confucius that were criticized in the movement of "criticizing Lin and criticizing Confucius." After I was admitted to the People's University of China in 1979, I mainly studied economics. In addition to Marxist economics, I also studied western economics. I think that culturally, I am a citizen of the world. However, ironically, it was my first visit to the United States in 1987 that made me feel connected to Chinese culture, because the United States is not a country without cultural color. At the same time, Chinese in the United States also respect Confucius. After returning to China from the United States, I began to read many books about Chinese culture, including Feng Youlan's ***History of Chinese Philosophy***, which was recommended by Mr. Li Shenzhi, and Hou Jiaju's ***Free Economic Thought of Confucianism in the Pre Qin Period***. Of course, the most important thing was to read the original scriptures, including ***The Great Learning***, ***The Doctrine of the Mean***, ***The Analects of Confucius***, ***Works of Mencius***, and ***Tao Te Ching***.

In the tradition of Confucianism and Taoism, what I first agree with is a thought similar to those found in economic liberalism. Confucius said, "Does heaven speak? Yet the four seasons run their course and all things come into being. Heaven does not speak!" Lao Tzu said, "Tao often does nothing but does everything." This kind of expression of natural order philosophy seems more wonderful than Smith's "invisible hand." There are still "hands" in Smith's theory, but there is no "mouth" in Confucius' theory. When I was at the University of Chicago, I borrowed Lewis Maverick's ***China: A Model for Europe*** from the library. This book includes an English translation of Quesnay's ***Despotism of China*** and the author's own description of how European missionaries' letters about Confucianism affected Quesnay and Smith. Later, I read Zhu Xi's collection of Confucian maxims in the Song Dynasty, ***Jinsilu*** (Reflections on Things of Hand), and Wang Yangming's ***Chuanxilu*** (Instructions for Practical Living) with conscience as the core value; influenced by Jiang

Qing's ***Introduction to Gongyang Theory***, I paid attention to the political system of traditional China. Because of the consideration of the problems after the rise of China, I also paid attention to the thought resources about cosmopolitanism in the Confucian literature and to the Confucian ideas and traditions about family, including the ***Book of Filial Piety***. Having comprehensively combed the Confucian literature, I thought that I could use economics to give a reasonable explanation of them, and I began to teach a course called "Economic Explanation of Confucianism" at Shandong University in 2008, and I published the revised lecture notes in 2015. I can call myself a Confucian.

Understanding Chinese history and culture, it is easy to find the key differences between China and the west, such as the attitude toward the family. There are families in the west, but there is "familism" in China. In my chapter "On Familism," I put forward that familism mainly refers to the economic calculations based on the family. This is very different from calculations based on individuals. There are at least two differences between the family and the individual. The first difference is that the individual has a limited life, while the family has an unlimited life, in theory. The second difference is that individualistic individuals are independent of each other, while familial individuals are dependent on each other. Once economics changes the basic research unit, the conclusion may be quite different. For example, a family-oriented society is more inclined to sustainable development because the family life is infinite and its discount rate is zero. If we start from the maximization of family welfare, then succession is more important than the current interests because, if the family is terminated, no matter how great the current interests, the family's utility is zero. As Mencius said, "There are three ways of being unfilial, and the worst one among them is having no descendant." Moreover, because the interests of family members depend on each other, their individual decision-making cannot be independent. However, if we look at the Chinese family tradition from the perspective of individualism, we will mistakenly think that the individual's behavior in the family is very irrational.

Another misunderstanding is about the institution of property rights in traditional China. Among the foreign scholars whom I have contacted, some believe that China has no property rights tradition at all. Many Chinese scholars agree. This belief is caused by the long-term misunderstanding of Chinese intellectuals. Since modern times, especially after the Opium War between China and Britain, China's military failure has led to the extreme emotions of many Chinese intellectuals. When they criticize the Chinese tradition, they believe that nothing is right in China, that is, "everything is inferior to other nations." This naturally includes the institution of land property rights. In my article "How Should the Institutions Change?," I noted that China has had a formed institution of land-free sale since at least the Han Dynasty. After the Song Dynasty, and until the Ming and Qing Dynasties and the Republic of China, the land property rights institution became increasingly mature, forming permanent tenancy. Regarding the permanent tenancy, I made a more detailed discussion of this concept in another chapter, "The Economic Nature of the Permanent Tenancy." The right of permanent tenancy not only refers to the forever tenancy right but also includes some property rights. This is the inevitable result of permanent tenancy and fixed land rent. Therefore, the land property right can be divided into two levels, namely, the surface land right and the undersurface land right. Moreover, these two types of rights are both independent and complete property rights. When either of them is sold to a third party, the consent of the other party is not required.

It is strange that this kind of perfect land system, which is close to textbook, has been the object of Chinese Revolution since modern times. Why is this so? I have made a preliminary discussion in the article "How Should the Institutions Change?" Advocates of the Agrarian Revolution believed that the land was too concentrated at that time. For example, Mao Zedong thought that approximately 70–80% of the land was concentrated in the hands of landlords. However, later researchers posited that he also regarded public land as land owned by the landlords, so he thus overestimated the land concentration. Du Runsheng, another Communist, thinks that the land concentration is only 40%. Zhao Gang's research notes that the Gini coefficient of the land distribution in the period of the Republic of China is only 0.3–0.5. If the surface land right is also regarded as a property land right, then the land distribution is more average. The second accusation of the advocates of the Agrarian Revolution is that the landlords seriously exploited the peasants. However, this was also denied by later research. For example, Gao Wangling's research notes that since the Ming and Qing Dynasties, the paid-in-rent ratio had been continuously reduced from 80–90% to 50–60% in 250 years because the landlords did not have the compulsory means to collect the land rent, and the government did not intend to help the landlords collect the rent. Therefore, the nominal rent rate had been adjusted downward several times.

In "How Should the Institutions Change?," I also compared the land institutions and their changes in England. In the period of the Industrial

Revolution, Britain's land system was still the land tenure system established by William the Conqueror. If a person wanted to buy a piece of land from a peasant, he had to replace the peasant's serfdom status and be loyal to the Lord when he received the land; thus, a land transaction costs 3–5 years of land revenue. Therefore, the land resource reallocation at that time mainly depended on land leasing with convenient procedures, thus completing the transfer of land resources to industries and cities during the Industrial Revolution. In China, the Agrarian Revolution deprived landlords of their land by violence. After land was distributed to the peasants, it was then concentrated in the hands of the government through collectivization. The Agrarian Revolution destroyed the better allocation between the land and the farmers, and because the people's communes were allocated agricultural resources by the government; thus, there was no incentive. Consequently, from 1952 to 1978, China's agricultural labor productivity never exceeded that of the 13th year of Guangxu (1887), and the year of the most severe famine in three years (1961) was only 67% as productive as that of the 13th year of Guangxu; additionally, this period did not promote industrialization or urbanization. This comparison tells us that China's mistake was not only the wrong judgment regarding the nature of the land institutions but also the mistake of the format of the institutional change, that is, the institutional change promoted by violence.

Thus, even if the direction of a reform is correct, the key factor for the success of that reform is whether it can take a peaceful form. This is exactly what happened when China began its reform and opening up in 1978. After three years of famine, Mao Zedong made a small concession, that is, he allowed farmers to have a small amount of private land. Later, it was found that the yield per *mu* of the private plots was four, five, or even ten times that of the collective lands. This was clearly the result of the incentive. This message was brought to the top of the Communist Party by Du Runsheng, who later became known as the father of China's rural reform. The choice the officials faced at that time was whether they could change the so-called collective land into private land. If the property rights institution should be changed, then the law should be changed. The ideological inertia formed in the Mao era made China not have the political conditions to change the law at that time. Later, the actual choice made was a "land household contract system." The implementation results were obvious to all. From 1978 to 1988, China's agricultural output value increased by an average of 15% per year. Interestingly, the success of this institutional change can be explained by the Coase Theorem and other institutional economics theories. In my chapter "Contracts Matter: Toward a More Developed Explanation of History," I discussed this issue in detail.

The Coase Theorem states that if a judge makes an arbitrary decision regarding property rights, then as long as the transaction cost is zero, the parties can optimize the allocation of resources through free transaction. An extension of this theorem that is close to the fact is that "even if the mistakes of government intervention cannot be corrected temporarily due to political or ideological factors, people have a way to correct them. This is the way of contract, which avoids the difficulty or cost of correcting the mistakes of government at present." This suggests replacing property rights reform with contract reform. The contract theory is Steven Cheung's greatest contribution to the new institutional economics. In his ***Theory of Share Tenancy***, he noted that different contracts would bring different efficiencies in the same situation under the same property rights institution. Changing contracts changes efficiency. The institution of property rights can be resolved into contractual rights, that is, the right of use, the right of income, and the right of transfer. The key to the success of China's rural reform is the changing of the contract between the farmers and the state and the collective from fixed wages to fixed taxes and fixed rent without changing the land property rights institution. The former means that, no matter how hard they try, the income of the farmers will remain unchanged; the latter means that as long as farmers pay a fixed amount of tax and of rent, the output increased by their efforts will belong to the farmers themselves.

Another explanation for the success of China's reform made by Professor Steven Cheung is described in his paper entitled "The Economic System of China" presented at the 2008 Chicago conference. He noted that the success of China's reform mainly depends on competition among county governments. The object of competition is capital and human resources. The means of this competition is the reduction of the price of land. To win firms' investment in locality, land price can be reduced to zero or even negative values. The county government's revenue depends on taxes. In 2011, Steven Cheung held a conference on the "Economic System of China" in Shenzhen. My chapter "On the Homology, Separation, and Substitution of Tax and Rent" was written for this conference. I appreciate Professor Steven Cheung's deep understanding of the relationship between rent and tax. I think this understanding is probably related to his permanent residence in Hong Kong, because Hong Kong is a zero tariff-low tax-high land price area. The local government's finance mainly depends on the income from land leases. If an economic agent is both the landowner and the tax collector, there will be some substitution made between rent and tax. A low tax rate means a high rent rate. If the county governments in mainland China have both land rights and tax power, it is a reasonable choice for them to reduce the land price and seek taxes. However, Professor Steven Cheung has made a small mistake here, that is, according to the constitution, rural land is not owned by the government, and the low-cost land provided by the county government to enterprises has been seized from the hands of farmers by force. When the property rights institution is destroyed, the price of land is distorted, and his theory appears as a miscalculation.

The other two important phenomena leading to China's miracle are the emergence of specialized markets and urbanization. I have discussed these phenomena in two chapters, "The Economic Logic of Specialized Markets" and "Transactions and Cities." The specialized market is especially developed in Zhejiang Province. I have been to Haining's leather clothing market, Taizhou's plastic small furniture market, Yongjia's bridgehead button market, Liushi's electrical appliance market, and the like, which are all specialized markets covering the whole country of China; the market radius of Yiwu's small commodity market extends beyond China's borders. Why can specialized markets exist? It is because a specialized market is specialized in selling a certain kind of good, so that various designs, styles, varieties, and brands of this kind of good can be sold in one market. This will bring consumers the utility of variety, that is to say, the selection range of commodities will be increased so that they can be closer to the consumers' own preferences. For this extra utility, consumers are willing to go further to visit markets. This is the main reason for the existence and development of specialized markets. Due to the huge demand brought about by the specialized market, enterprises gather around the market for production so that the specialized market drives the industrial development of the surrounding areas. This is one of the important characteristics of the economic development in Zhejiang Province.

The development of China as a whole is an enlarged version of this specialized market model. Large cities along the coast and in mainland China are formed by the aggregation of many specialized markets, whose market radius is as large as the world. The huge demand flowing into the huge cities attracts a large number of Chinese and foreign enterprises to invest in these cities and their surrounding areas, which in turn drives the expansion of these cities. Therefore, with China's decades of economic take-off, this is a rapid urbanization process. The urbanization rate (the proportion of urban population to the total population) has increased from 30% in 1996 to 60% in 2018, with an average of 17 million farmers entering the cities every year. According to William Lewis, urbanization is one of the two main driving forces of modern economic development, and the other is industrialization. Urbanization brings a huge demand for municipal infrastructure investment and housing investment; it also brings a substantial increase in the income of rural residents after they become urban residents, and it brings important changes in their consumption habits to form a new permanent consumption demand. According to my estimation, in recent years, China's annual investment in the municipal infrastructure has been approximately 2.5 trillion yuan. If the target of China's urbanization rate is 80%, then the promotion of urbanization to China's economic growth will still last for more than ten years.

In 2010, the Qianhai Cooperation Zone of Shenzhen invited us to develop urban industrial planning, which enabled me to think more deeply about this issue. In this regard, Krugman and Masahisa Fujita are pioneers. They believe that the scale economy of production makes people gather into cities. However, there seems to be a gap. In my opinion, cities are based on transactions. Because the trade brings the trade dividend, people will gather for the trade and then bring the market network externality; that is, the growth of the trade opportunity is faster than that of the population density, which will bring more trade dividends and further promote the agglomeration of people. Therefore, the process circles and repeats in this manner. At the same time, agglomeration will also bring the external costs of congestion. The trade dividends minus the external costs of congestion is considered the "agglomeration rent." When the population density reaches a certain degree, the agglomeration rent reaches the maximum value, and the size of the city is also determined. Here, the transaction is the basic unit of research. Coincidentally, institutional economics is also based on using transactions as the basic unit of research; thus, here, spatial economics and institutional economics connect with each other. According to this principle, I have developed a planning model that combines spatial economics and institutional economics, which is a general equilibrium model considering spatial and institutional factors. It can not only help local governments plan but also test institutions and policies.

This kind of city-based research model can also be used in research on the Internet. The two aspects have a common feature, that is, the gathering of people. On the Internet, this is seen as virtual agglomeration. The rise of Internet giants such as Alibaba and Tencent after 2000 is the continuation of the Chinese miracle on the Internet. However, their business models have some puzzling points. Specifically, the marginal cost of online transactions or social platforms is zero, so according to the microeconomics doctrine, the price of their services should be zero; however, according to this method, they will have no money to earn. This is very similar to the "utility pricing problem" discussed by Coase many years ago, which stated that the marginal cost of public utilities with the nature of natural monopoly is lower than the average fixed cost. Thus, if such goods are priced according to the marginal cost, they will bring losses. Harold Hotelling advocated that the government should subsidize the loss, while Coase proposed two-part pricing, that is, consumers should pay both the marginal cost and the average fixed cost. Still, there is no subsidy from the government, and the ordinary consumers of Taobao or WeChat have not paid a cent for their services. Thus, how can Alibaba and Tencent make money?

I explain this in the chapter "Zero Marginal Cost and Virtual Rent." When Alibaba and Tencent provide free services to consumers, then these consumers gather, of course, within the virtual space of the Internet. However, that is enough. As long as they can communicate with each other's willingness to buy and sell and actually close deals, then they have an experience similar to meeting in the real market, but the congestion externalities are almost gone. The previous discussion has noted that as long as people gather, there will be agglomeration rent. Because the agglomeration is created by Alibaba and Tencent's free services, they have reason to collect rent. The objects of rent collection are those who want to occupy a more central position in the virtual space; the formats of rent collection can be platform royalties, transaction commissions, bidding for a more central position, and so on. As it turns out, the rents they receive not only offset the costs but also generate surpluses. This is their business model.

There are some additional papers that I also think are very valuable. However, I think the Preface should not be too long, so I would like to talk about them briefly. Not counting the recent trade war, in the process of China's marketization, there are two relatively large external influences: the Asian financial crisis and the American financial crisis. In my two chapters, "Hedge Funds, Financial Markets, and Nation-States" and "The Institutional Factors of the Financial Crisis in the United States," I discussed these crises from the perspective of China. It is worth emphasizing that I put forward "loss equilibrium" in my later chapter to describe the situation in which people are willing to accept losses to obtain the possibility of huge profits.

In my chapter "A General Theory of Rent-Seeking: Rent Dissipating, Rent Keeping, and Rent-Seeking," I mainly discussed the rent brought about by government regulation in China and the various ways that people, enterprises, or government officials try to retain rent when they see that the rent values may dissipate. Another chapter, "Medical Insurance Paradox: A Hypothesis on Medical Price Increases in Proportion to Copayment Rate Decreases and Verification in China," is a byproduct of my research at the Unirule Institute of Economics. We found that the rapid growth of medical expenses in China seems to be closely related to the popularity of medical insurance; thus, we put forward a hypothesis that the price of medicine is inversely proportional to the copay rate. Our research generally supports this hypothesis.

The last two chapters, "Religious Person and His or Her Implication in Institutions" and "On the Theological Coordinate of Economics," are two chapters that go beyond the scope of economics. The real world must be beyond the scope of economic explanation. In the past two decades, some masters of economics have also paid attention to this problem. For example, when discussing the constitution, James Buchanan proposed that the term of the rational economic person alone could not explain why the U.S. Constitution drafters would consider the interests of future generations, and he explained it with "ethics of constitutional citizenship." The Santa Fe School proposed that a society would collapse if there were only economic persons and no strong reciprocators. Compared with economic men, religious men do not care about interests; thus, they either are strong reciprocators of society or have ethics of constitutional citizenship. By God's measure, even if human beings no longer existed, He would still be doing something toward the rebirth of human beings or intelligent creatures similar to human beings hundreds of millions of years later. This is a matter that can only be understood if we get rid of the current utilitarian computing. If we only see the immediate utility, then human beings could have neither become human beings nor developed today's civilizations. In contemporary China, familism has disintegrated, but most of the people we see are individuals without faith. Only when a group of elites has emerged consisting of those who have transcended utilitarianism and who firmly believe that the natural order is good under any circumstances can Chinese civilization be truly revived.

Beijing, China
November 16, 2019

Sheng Hong

Contents

List of Figures

List of Tables

CHAPTER 1

On Familism

Contents

While comparing China with the western world, people often go to two kinds of extremes. Some think that China is totally different from the western world, while others don't think that there is much difference between them. The correct answer obviously lies in between. But the key question is what their similarity is and what their difference is.

I would love to extend my thanks to Mr. Xu Dianqing, for whose family story inspired me to write this thesis and his agreement on my relating of the story in this thesis. My thanks also go to Mr. Wang Dingding, Zhang Xianglong, Jiang Qing, and Zhang Yan for their constructive suggestions on the revision of the thesis, and also Mr. Ye Hang and Chen Zhiwu for their insightful comments.

Sheng Hong, *Vision and Calculation*,
https://doi.org/10.1007/978-981-15-2898-9_1

At an early stage, western economics had a history of interaction with Chinese cultural tradition (Maverick 1946; Tan Min 1992). From this point of view, they share the foundations of rationalism and the philosophy of natural order. “Rationalism” refers to man’s capability to calculate costs and benefits. Despite lofty moral ideals, the Confucian scholars often used the reason “this is good for you” to persuade people to do something. Western economics itself is about cost-benefit analysis. As to the philosophy of natural order, it can be seen in “Does the God speak? The four seasons shift, and plants and animals grow” by Confucius, and “Do nothing, and everything is accomplished” by Lao Tzu; it can also be found among the Physiocrats,[1] the pioneers of western economics. Based on this philosophy, Chinese cultural tradition and western economics both developed toward economic liberalism, advocating economic freedom and limited government.

So what’s the difference?

1.1 A Family Model

My friend, Prof. Xu Dianqing, once told me a story: when his family first arrived in North America, they were caught in a dilemma: to establish residency, it was crucial for a member of their family to obtain a diploma from a local university, but they could not afford tuition for all of them. So they held a family meeting and decided that his two children and he would go to school while his wife went to work to support them.

Upon hearing the story, I immediately asked if the decision was made in a dictatorial way or a democratic way. Was it “dictatorial” because he, as the male patriarch, made the decision; or “democratic,” because his two children and he, as the majority, made the decision. But to my great surprise, Prof. Xu said: “You are wrong. It’s my wife’s decision.” So what did I miss?

Suppose there are three persons in a family and each person has a fortune of ¥ 100. However, an investment in human resources will cost them ¥ 120. If they insist on individualism, none will make such an investment. But they make a decision to spend ¥ 240 on such an investment for two of

[1] Tan Min: “Physiocratie is the French original of the word physiocratism, which is a combination of the Greek words, nature (φ’υσις) and domination (κρατ’οω), meaning the rule of nature, thus deriving the meaning that human society must obey the laws of nature in order to seek the highest welfare” (1992, p. 103).

them. Besides losing the opportunity, the third person suffers the loss of ¥ 40. Generally, the income generated by the ¥ 40 is for now being lost. For example, if the yearly interest rate is 5%, then ¥ 2 is lost every year.

Again, suppose a person without human resources investment earns ¥ 10 every year, while a beneficiary of the investment earns ¥ 40. The individualist family ("Family B" hereafter) made no investment and its members earn a total of ¥ 30 in a year; while the familist family ("Family A") made the investment and will earn a total of ¥ 90. If we divide the payment among the family members, even the person who "sacrifices" will soon be paid back and even profit. See the following Table 1.1 for more details.

Obviously, Family A's decision is better than that of Family B, because no matter for the whole family or for the individuals in the family, the income of the former is higher than that of the latter. Since the family consists of family members, the family assets measured by the market are mainly represented by the human capital of family members. The increase of family income is mainly the result of the increase of the human capital productivity of family members. If we capitalize it and then imitate the concept of "enterprise value," we can say that "family value" is increased.[2]

The mode of Family A works only because its members trust each other not to leave the family, so the one who "sacrifices" will be paid back.

But isn't there any other way of financing for Family B? For example, two of the family members each can borrow ¥ 20, from the third person and then return the money once they complete their education. But borrowing and lending requires certain conditions, such as the existence of courts and financial markets. Without courts, it is more likely for people to break the agreement, and without financial markets, it is hard for people to agree upon the price of borrowing, which would dramatically increase the costs and the risk of failure of the deal. Therefore, in the early stages of human society when there were no courts or financial markets, the advantage of Family A's mode was more obvious. And this family mode, once formed, profoundly influenced the development institutions in the society.

Even when there are courts and financial markets, Family A's mode is still useful, because of the many costs associated with these two

[2] Suppose that the average working life is 40 years and the discount rate 5%. Then the human capital value of a member of the family with the yearly income of RMB 10 is RMB 180.17, while that of a member of the family with the yearly income of RMB 40 is RMB 720.68. With only human capital calculated, the "family value" of Family B is RMB 540.51, while that of Family A is RMB 1621.53.

Table 1.1 Comparison of resources allocation and income between the individualistic family and the familist family

Family	*Member*	*Original wealth*	*Wealth allocation*	*Yearly income*	*Distribution 1*	*Distribution 2*	*Distribution 3*	*Distribution N*
A	1	100	120	40	30	60	90	$30 \times N$
	2	100	120	40	30	60	90	$30 \times N$
	3	100	60	10	30	60	90	$30 \times N$
B	1	100	100	10	10	20	30	$10 \times N$
	2	100	100	10	10	20	30	$10 \times N$
	3	100	100	10	10	20	30	$10 \times N$

Note Family A and Family B are shown in this table. Each family has three members, represented by "1," "2," and "3." The two families have the same original wealth of ¥ 100. However, in Family A, out of the ¥ 300, ¥ 240 is equally divided between Members 1 and 2 to invest in education, with ¥ 60 left for Member 3, while in Family B, the wealth of ¥ 300 is equally divided among the three members. Since there are two members in Family A who have invested in human capital, their yearly income is ¥ 90: ¥ 40 + ¥ 40 + ¥ 10, while that of Family B is ¥ 30: ¥ 10 + ¥ 10 + ¥ 10. According to the principle of equal distribution among family members, each member of Family A will receive ¥ 30 in the first year (Distribution 1), accumulatively each member will receive ¥ 60 in the second year (Distribution 2), and in the *N*th year, each member will receive ¥ 30 × *N*. Each member of Family B will receive ¥ 10 in the first year and ¥ 10 × *N* in the *N*th year. For the sake of convenience, the interest income of the original wealth is not taken into account

institutions, such as distance to the court, direct expenses and time put in the law suit, possible mistakes and errors in judicial rulings, bank interest, risks of the securities market, the adverse selection and moral hazard of the insurance industry, and so on.

Besides, family is full of special contractual relationships, including not only the responsibilities and obligations regarding resource allocation but also the sexual relationship, fostering children, and providing for senior members. The composition of all these relationships will in turn reinforce and secure each and every relationship in it, establishing a stronger and more reliable relationship between family members without any interference from the market or law and their costs. This is why Prof. Xu's family made the decision as I have mentioned at the beginning of the chapter.

We call Family A's mode the mode of "familism," and Family A is a "familist" family, in contrast with Family B, which is an "individualist" family. **"Familism," as we define it, uses the whole family but not individuals in the family as a unit in cost-benefit calculations**. It is not only thus perceived by people outside the family but also agreed by family members. Inside the family, the distribution of wealth or income is based on the principle of family interest maximization and individual needs. The above-mentioned example shows us that in some cases, familism is superior to individualism.

1.2 The Maximization of Family Interests

As an economic agent, a family is greatly different from individuals. Family is based on marriage. Men and women marry not only to satisfy their sexual needs, but also to rear children. If the purpose of marriage were simply sexual satisfaction, they could just cohabit without getting married. Because of the genetic transmission from parents to children, and the love parents develop for their children through raising them, parents usually regard their children as the continuation of their own lives. In such cases, as long as the life of any member of the family continues, the sense of utility and the judgments about cost and benefit will also live on.

That is to say, if the family persists, utility will increase; if it dies out, there won't be any utility for no matter how much wealth. Since life can continue for generations through fertility, given fixed utility per unit time, utility will also keep increasing as life continues. Therefore, as a unit, family is superior to individual in terms of both space and time. The life of an individual is limited, while theoretically, that of a family is limitless.[3]

If we believe that genetic transmission is the "purpose" of fertility, half of each parent continues to exist in the body of their children, and the both parents share the child's entire life. The more children a couple has, the more their own lives continue. However, because of limited resources, the couple has to balance between having more children and providing more resources for each child (Becker 1987, pp. 116–127). Given limited resources, most parents have to invest a large portion of them in human capital in order to improve the children's ability to acquire more resources.

The idea of including offspring in utility is very close to that of a dynastic utility function proposed by Becker.[4] The difference is that Becker considers the latter to reflect the altruism of parents toward children and the degree of a parent's altruism toward his or her whole posterity is formed by transmitting altruism indirectly from every generation as parents toward the next generation as children (Becker and Barro 1986), while the former internalizes the utility of children as parental utility, extending utility to cover all generations.

Since family members are connected by marriage or blood, their utility functions cannot be separated from those of others in the family. The utility of one family member may be shared by another member, which makes their relationship more complicated. For example, since the wife's benefits may increase that of the husband, costs paid by the husband in order to increase the wife's benefits will be offset, and there might even be net benefits. Again, since the costs of children are also shared by parents, if children reduce their costs, the utility of their parents will be increased. Furthermore, the utility of a family member might be affected by the interaction between other two or more members. For instance, the relationship between a mother and daughter-in-law will greatly affect the welfare of the son/husband. It is impossible for family members to be totally independent from each other, for they are interdependent. That is to say,

[3] Qian Mu once said, "Life is an idea of big totality. Every living individual will die eventually. However, if life is carried on through generations, then it will become eternal" (in Zhou Jie 2004, p. 153).

[4] The basic equation of dynastic utility function is $U_0 = \sum_{i=0}^{\infty} A_i N_i v(c_i)$. U_0 represents the utility of a parent, *Ai* is the degree of altruism of the parent toward each descendant in the *i*th generation, *Ni* is the number of descendants in the *i*th generation, *Ci* is the consumption of descendants in the *i*th generation, and *v* is a utility function of consumption (Becker and Barro 1986).

the behavior or even the existence of one family member will generate an externality for other members. Therefore, based on the principle of "seeking the consent of the one whose interests are involved," every member in the family has, to some extent, the right to decide for others and also the obligation to be decided for. In other words, no member of a family can be totally independent from other members.[5]

The family possesses the above-mentioned characteristics which distinguish it from an individual, that is: **(1) the "life" of the family can be eternal; (2) the costs and benefits of family members cannot be totally independent from each other**. Therefore, for the family, maximum utility is not simply the sum of maximized utility of each family member or the maximization of the total wealth or income of the whole family, but rather the maximization of family utility based on the interactions of family members and the quantity and quality of genetic transmission with guaranteed life quality of descendants and the improvement of the ability to accumulate wealth. Given adequate information and data, it should be possible to find an optimal solution.

By far the largest difference is the limitless utility available to an immortal family. Over the very long term, ever very poor quality of life can sum to an infinite amount. **As long as the net utility of living is positive, other sources of utility would pale into insignificance compared with the continuity of generations**. That's why Mencius said, "there are three ways of being unfilial, and bearing no descendant is by far the largest." For instance, one might accumulate a lot of wealth in an unjust way at the expense of others, so as to bear more descendants, which in turn serves as the bane of the family and causes the destruction of the next generation. Hence, the goal of the maximization of family interests should above all guarantee the maximization of wealth and the quantity of genetic transmission on the condition of generation continuity.

Since the costs and benefits of family members are interdependent, their calculation is based on a different theory from that of calculation for

[5] In the book *A Treatise on the Family*, Gary Becker discusses the issue of the interinfluence of costs and benefits of family members, yet from a slightly different perspective. For example, he points out that the variation of the wife's utility will affect that of the husband: $\partial Uh/\partial Uw > 0$. ∂Uh is the variation of the husband's utility and ∂Uw is that of the wife's utility (1987, p. 196). However, he calls the husband's expense for the wife "donation" and categorizes it as "altruism," which is inconsistent logically. It seems that his analysis in the eighth chapter "Altruism in the Family" can be explained by Egoism.

individuals with individualism. Based on Becker's studies, their difference can be expressed in the following equations:

The relationship between individuals of individualism: $\partial Ui/\partial Uj = 0$;

The relationship between individuals of familism: $\partial Ui/\partial Uj > 0$; $\partial Uj/\partial Ui > 0$;

Ui and *Uj* are the utility of any individual *i* and any individual *j*, who are members of a family when they are familist individuals. In this case, $Uj = f(G, Ri, Ro)$; *G* is the consumption of material goods, *Ri* is the relationship with the family member *i*, and *Ro* is the relationship with other family members. Likewise, $Ui = f(G, Rj, Ro)$. With both $\partial Ui/\partial Uj > 0$ and $\partial Uj/\partial Ui > 0$, the increase of utility is a two-way interaction. Not only does a wife's happiness increase her husband's utility, the latter's happiness also increases the former's utility.

This set of equations implies that between individuals with familism, the variation of one member's utility will affect the utility of another member and such variation can be either positive or negative, while there is no such influence between individuals with individualism. With further observation, we will find that **the utility increased as the result of utility interaction between individuals with familism is mostly positive**; negative utility mainly results from assumed damage or damage from outside of the family, which in turn will stimulate family members to help each other.

It is hard for people outside the family to notice the complex cost/benefit relationship between family members, who themselves also find it difficult to explain. The two-way interaction of increasing utility can be repeated unlimitedly between two members of the family. For example, the husband will make the wife happy if he gives his resources to her, which in turn will make himself happy too. And the happiness of the husband will in turn increase the utility of the wife. The process can keep going on. Therefore, the utility of several individuals will greatly increase once they join the same family; **the total utility of the family is much larger than the sum of utility of individuals without family.**[6] It seems that it is more proper to use the family not the individual as the economic agent.

[6] Zhao Tingyang: "The only effective principle of happiness, harmony or peace is to provide a community or interpersonal system, which must meet the following requirements: (1) the completeness of the community is the general condition for every member's happiness or interests; (2) the overall interests of the community are in proportion to the interests of every member, in other words, the community interests are closely related to individual interests. Therefore, there is no reason for any member to object another. According to the standard of perfect community, the mode of family is the most qualified" (2005, p. 69).

The maximization of family interests is not just the maximization of the current wealth or income of the family. Maintaining the continuity of a family bloodline is a more important goal than increasing current material interests, which means the goal of maximizing family wealth is often in conflict with that of maximizing individual interests, because the realization of the former might come at the expense of the latter. The maximization of family interest will in turn augment individual interests, because if generational continuity is regarded as the increase of one's own utility, then a family which produces generation after generation will increase all its member's interests.

1.3 The Reinforced Family Institutions of China

Compared with the other institutions of human society, the institution of family is the most natural, for it is formed on the basis of human sexual desire and instinct for reproduction. Since it is not in conflict with human nature, it is a natural and most effective institution. It possesses several characteristics: first, family is the oldest institution in human society; which means, secondly, that family has less requirements in terms of external conditions; unlike some modern institutions, it does not rely heavily on other institutions, as market institutions, for example, depend on property rights; third, the costs of the family institution are relatively small. All these characteristics contribute to its vitality among all kinds of institutions.

However, the family institution is not perfect. Throughout human history, the family institution of Han people in China is the most mature and successful, while in other societies, the family institution is not so well-developed due to factors such as nomadic lifestyle, war, cross-ocean trade, and religion, which means that mobility, accidents, and the pursuit of afterlife will weaken the stability of family and thus damage the institution. For example, a survey conducted in the 1940s shows that 55.4% of the Tibetan households in China are "incomplete families" (Li Anzhai 1998, p. 131).

Besides external factors, some characteristics of human nature might also cause "family failure." One partner might be attracted by someone else and have an extramarital affair, which will break the commitment to the spouse; what's worse, the extramarital child would destroy the family property institution and inheritance system. Even between parents and children who are connected through blood, since children first enjoy their rights and then perform their duties, it is likely that children will neglect the duties to provide for their aged parents. All these cases will cause the failure of "family contract."

Generally speaking, a "failing" family is less efficient than a healthy family and will decline and eventually disappear in the competition with many other families. Therefore, the family organization needs to be reinforced so that the family will expand and prosper. First of all, **the concept of family should be reinforced**. In fact, anyone in the world is linked by blood to their ancestors, without the awareness of which the "family" we talk about here won't exist. To reinforce the concept of family is to give a certain family a symbol or name in order to distinguish from other families and record all the generations of the family. Surnames and family trees are for the same purpose, based on which, Han people in China also developed a concrete system, mainly including two related components: (1) ancestor worship; (2) family ancestral temples.

Ancestor worship involves a series of ceremonies. In several parts of China, there are four days in a year for ancestor worship: the 1st day of the 1st lunar month, April 5th, the 15th day of the 7th lunar month, and October 1 (Zhou Jie 2004, p. 86). Ancestor worship ceremonies reinforce one's idea that one is the continuity of one's ancestors' lives and at the same time instill a sense of responsibility to carry on the lineage. The celebrant will pay more respect to living senior members of the family and prefer stable marital relationships, which will help him/her better perform the duty of carrying on the family line.

An ancestral temple is a set of buildings built by several related families to worship their common ancestors, and also the family organization formed by these families. Centered around ancestor worship, an ancestral temple offered a variety of public goods within these families, such as mediation of disputes within member families, supporting widows, widowers, orphans, and the childless, educating children, supporting family members to go to the capital to take the national exam, and building public facilities and defense. Such "clan public goods" benefit and stabilize the cohesion of the unit.

In order to address the asymmetry between children and parents in performing the family contract, the culture of filial piety emphasized respect, obedience, and the duty to support aged parents and arrange for their burial. In order to address disloyalty to the "marriage contract," a comparable culture of virginity emphasized the loyalty of the wife to the husband. Beyond the simple fact that men in China were able to impose an unequal system, these asymmetric requirements for men and women probably reflect the view that an unfaithful wife might cause more serious consequences by jeopardizing the legitimacy of family members or inheritors.

In this familist culture, the family was also reinforced with the coercive powers of the government. For example, in ancient China, it was stipulated in the law that for the same crime, the punishment varied depending on whether the crime was committed against one's parents or not.

Other institutions reinforce the natural family and reduce the phenomenon of family failure. Thus, family members can enjoy confidence in family stability and the loyalty of other members, allowing them to rely on their family for resource allocation, which is more efficient than individual.

1.4 The Moral Education of Familism and Transcendence Beyond Beyond Life and Death

People steeped in familist cultures regard themselves as a link of the family line, allowing themselves to consider their lives infinite, which will significantly influence one's behavior. According to studies of game theory, given a finitely repeated game, a player will be motivated by opportunism and pursue benefit via non-cooperation or at the expense of others, because it is likely that the player will quit the game before others can take revenge. As Louis XV once said—"After me, the deluge!" However, given an infinitely repeated game, one can never quit and non-cooperation or aggressive behavior will be avenged. Therefore, self-interest recommends that one should adopt the strategy of cooperation at all times. According to individualism, life is finite, while according to familism, it is limitless, so the latter will restrain people and make them cooperate with others and society.

The limitless enlargement of one's life utility generated by the concept of familism can be used to persuade people to accept moral codes. There is an old Chinese saying: "the family who does good deeds will leave happiness for their descendants while the family who commit evil deeds will leave trouble and disaster for theirs," meaning that one should do good and accumulate merit for the sake of one's descendants. In the *Book of Filial Piety*, family or clan interests such as "desire to preserve nobility for a long time," "desire to preserve riches for a long time," "preserving the altars of land and grain," "preserving ancestral temples," and "preserving ancestor worship" are used to persuade people, especially princes and high officials, to accept the codes of morality. The word "long" refers to a long period of time over generations. And the bottom line of "morality" is not to harm others.

In practice, the ancestor worship ceremony directly links ancestor worship with moral education. First of all, the ancestors to be worshiped are selected according to moral standards. The reason for the clan to worship a certain ancestor is because the ancestor observed moral codes and made correct decisions, such as improving technology or reforming institutions so that the clan prospered and expanded. Descendants also have the right to choose in ancestor worship, as showed in the system of "the emperor supporting the virtuous" summarized by Zhang Yan: the emperor selects those ancestors who "have made remarkable contributions to the people" and who "have displayed unparalleled virtue" as "examples to be followed by later generations" and to be worshiped. The ancestor worship ceremony combines the memory of ancestors and the learning of ancestors' spirit. That's why we say "worship is the root of education" (Zhang Yan 2004, pp. 247–248). In the ancestor worship ceremony, the ranking is arranged according to ages and also whether the behavior of the ancestor is in line with moral standards, so as to reward the virtuous and punish the vicious. The blessings of ancestors depend on whether descendants observe the ancestors' moral principles, that is, "纯佑秉德" (Zhang Yan 2004, pp. 250–257). The close relationship between ancestor worship and moral education can be seen in the fact that the Chinese character for education (教) consists of characters for filial piety (孝) and culture (文).

The ancestral temple of the clan can also directly enact "clan regulations" or "family teachings," such as the famous Zhu Family Instructions and the Family Instructions of Yan Clan. The purpose of laying down clan regulations or family instructions is to maximize the current interests of the clan, with the condition that the continuity of the clan is secured. Therefore, their codes of conduct are inevitably formed from the perspective of infinite time, which is in accord with basic moral principles, mainly including the organizational structure of the clan, order, and ceremonies, the arrangement of the clan property, the life style of its members, the codes of conduct toward outsiders, and the support provided to the disadvantaged within the clan (ed. Fei Chengkang 1998, Chapter 3).

Individuals are fearful of death. In a monotheist society, belief in the soul not only educates people morally, but also provides comfort in face of inevitable death. In a familist culture, life continues through generations, accomplishing the same goals through different means. It is one of the important functions of religion to make people see beyond life and death and the ancestor worship ceremony is also regarded as the "religious" aspect of the clan (Zhou Jie 2004, pp. 149–156). Furthermore, since the dead are thought to enter the world of gods, death is regarded as a bridge between man and god. Remote ancestors especially are regarded as gods (Zhao Cheng 2000[7]; Zhang Yan 1995, pp. 60–92), not only because they have entered the divine world, but also because their technological and institutional innovations have benefited and expanded the clan. They are worshipped as gods of technology and institutions.

1.5 The Border of Family and Competition Between Families

The familist mode of resource allocation depends upon a condition: one who sacrifices in the present must be sure that they will be paid back in the future, with profit. As the family expands, its ability to ensure this condition becomes weaker and weaker.[8] In a nuclear family, it's trivial. However, as the border of family expands, for example, in the case of two nuclear families whose parents are siblings, despite the blood relationship the children are more remotely connected and have less trust in each other. Therefore, though the two families will, to some extent, help each other, it is not expected that their sacrifices for each other will be compensated. For their children's children, the connection is even weaker and it is harder to practice the principles of familism. After several generations, members of the two families won't regard themselves as belonging to the same clan and the family ends. This can be expressed mathematically:

$$\partial Ui/\partial Uj \rightarrow 0;$$

At the point at which changes in one's utility no longer affect one's relative, familism is indistinguishable from individualism.

In different societies, there are different cultures about family values, different family functions and influence, so family borders are different. Generally speaking, the family in other societies is not as large as that of the Han people, for they don't have the same institutional structures to reinforce the concept of family. In Chinese Han society, the traditional

[7] Zhao Cheng pointed out that according to the analysis of oracle bone inscriptions, the ancestors, kings, and even old officials of Shang Dynasty had some kind of divine power, so they were both ancestor gods and natural gods. The Shang Dynasty even called their ancestors and kings "emperors," which means "God" in oracle bone inscriptions (2000, pp. 46–50).

[8] Generally speaking, the term "clan" is used by scholars to refer to the extended family. But there is no conclusion about where is the border between "family" and "clan." Therefore, the border is neglected in this chapter.

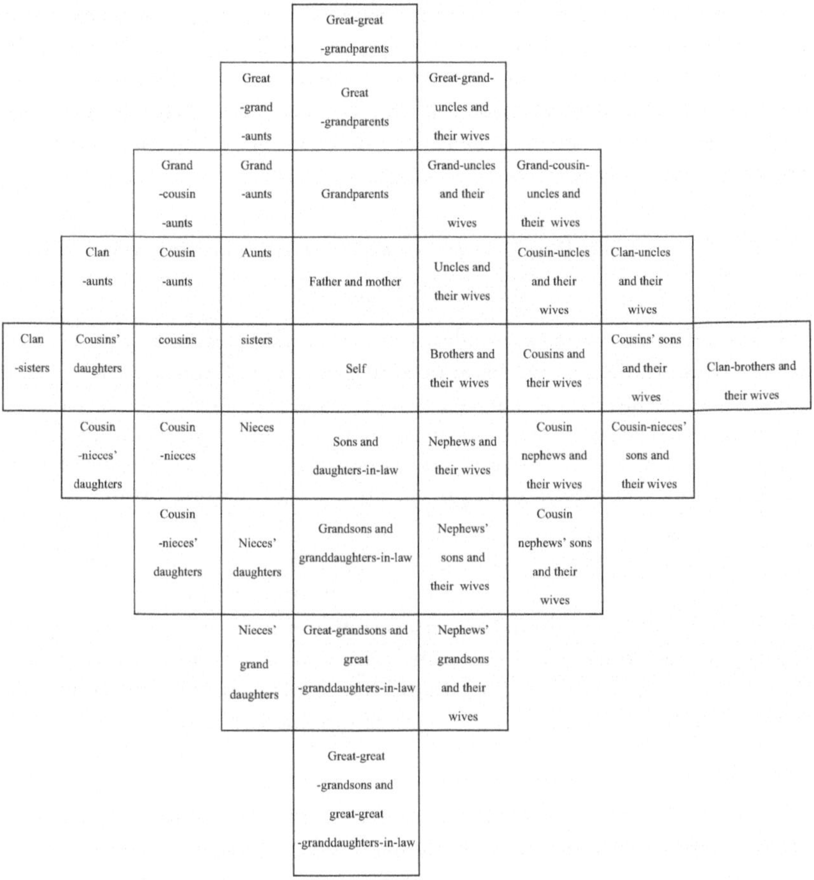

Fig. 1.1 Family borders of Han people in China. (Source: http://www.5fangs.net/gb/)

family border is determined by the duties of ancestor worship, which are called *wufu* (五服), the five kinds of clothes.[9] Each person and their four generations above them are obliged to worship their common ancestor and thus belong to the same clan (see Fig. 1.1); more distant relatives do not have the obligation to worship the ancestor and nor do they belong to

[9] In ancestor worship ceremony, one chooses from five kinds of clothes to perform different levels of mourning according to his relation with the deceased.

the same clan. This natural family border is formed probably for two reasons: first, it is also the border of the blood relationship. Between all the children of fifth generation, the most remotely connected two persons share only about 3.125% of their genes, which is almost equal to that of strangers; second, the population of the clan is so big that the cost of family organization is too high and offsets the benefits of economies of family scale.[10] What's more, the benefits of economies of family scale are not distributed equally within the clan. The closer to the border you are, the less benefits you receive. The benefits marginal members receive from the clan may be outweighed by costs, such as being required to participate in ancestor worship.

Domestic rules do not apply to affairs outside the family. Resource allocation between different families is affected by factors such as the market, religion, government, and war. Fertility is the main purpose of the existence of the family, which requires resources and benign relationships with other families. When it comes to competing for resources, one family has to compete with other families; but if a benign relationship with other families can guarantee the family's continuity and prosperity, then creating such relationships is also a means of competition.

Market, religion, the government, and war are also means of interpersonal competition for resources. Here we will focus on the differences between interfamily competition and interpersonal competition. On the face of it, the individual and the family are only two different subjects in the market. In the market, the individual or the family can achieve their interests without hurting others or other families. But the family is likely to be more committed to the market system than the individual, because the latter will withdraw from the games in the market when life ends but the former will never leave the market. Therefore, the family does not want to advance its interests at the expense of others, for it can expect revenge sooner or later. The second difference is that it is much easier to form production teams in the family based on family structure, because the interaction between family members will increase utility and thus make them more willing to cooperate with each other. However, it is

[10] If a couple has 3 children, then after 4 generations, there will be 81 children in the family; and if there are 3 generations living in the world, then the family will have about 135 members. Though girls will marry to someone outside the family, but boys will marry too, so the total number is fixed. According to studies on totem tribes in Australia, there are averagely about 600 persons within a tribe, which includes 1–12 clans, with over 100 persons each.

difficult to form a team of unrelated individuals, because interaction between them will produce at the most a neutral result.[11] Only with other institutional arrangements in recent times has it become easier for individuals to constitute an enterprise. Another difference is that because of the eternal life of the family, the discount rate of the family is zero, while because of individual mortality, the discount rate of the individual is positive. Therefore, the family and the individual differ greatly in judging the value of resources or assets, which will in turn affect their market behavior. The family emphasizes long-term investments and appreciates the long-term values of the resource or asset. Viewed from generations afar, such an investment policy is more efficient and closer to the approach of sustainable development.

Religion is also a voluntary means of resource allocation. But the individual and the family use different means to advance their interests through religion. The individual obtains interests by competing for position in a religious organization, while it is more likely for the family to use the means of creating "religious products." As I have mentioned before, after a long period of time, an ancestor will be transformed into a god; although there are family borders, people outside the border of the five clothing system still share the same ancestors, which is a way of maintaining extended family ties; as time passes, people are more remotely connected and their common ancestor will become an ancestral god or totem, and might eventually become a god. Ancestor worship and god worship both require resources, including sacrifices and donations. The more influential and "efficacious" a god is, the more sacrifices or donations will be offered. All these sacrifices and donations ultimately go to the living, that is, the families who create and own the god. The efficacy of a god is therefore related to the degree of prosperity of the family worshiping the god, which is determined by which institutions and technology the family uses in the name of the god. Therefore, interfamily competition in religion is competition for improving internal institutions and technology. Religious competition is competition between different gods; the result is either that one

[11] Because in the individualistic interpersonal relationship, "one's utility won't affect another's utility" ($\partial Ui/\partial Uj = 0$); therefore, one will not accept the team cooperation plan which means net loss to himself, while in the familistic relationship, "the increase of one's utility will have positive influence upon another's utility" ($\partial Ui/\partial Uj > 0$), so one might accept the team cooperation plan which will damage his own interest, for as long as the plan is good for other family members, it will in turn increase his own utility to offset the damage. Obviously, the familistic individual has more choices than the individualistic individual.

god wins the most followers in the society, or that gods are ranked according to their degree of efficacy, which in turn decides where sacrifices and donations offered to gods go. For example, in ancient China, there existed a hierarchy of worship known as "ji" (积). All tribes had to offer sacrifices to higher-level gods and their own gods, which were placed in the capital of the kingdom, so they had to transport their sacrifices to the capital (Zhang Yan 1999, pp. 238–254). Though the son of Heaven (天子), a Chinese term of emperor, returned some of these resources to the princes, on the whole he earned a profit.

The government's allocation of resources is realized in two ways: one is through salaries paid to government officials; the other is through political resources owned by officials. The family as a unit competes for resources allocated by government with other families. After the hereditary system prevalent in early China collapsed, it was replaced by investment into political human capital and relationships with officials. In China, this competition mainly centered on the hereditary political resources in the pre-Zhou period, and after the Qin and Han Dynasty, the focus was shifted to the investment into politics-oriented human resources. At the beginning of this chapter, we argued that the family is more prone to human capital investment. Since the Confucian school had become dominant since the reign of Emperor Wu in the Han Dynasty, Chinese families spent more on the Confucian-style education of family member, creating the "scholar-gentry class." Since the imperial examination system was implemented in the Tang and Song Dynasty, rich families would generally plan to educate male youngsters in the family and provide financial support to them to take the imperial examination. The participants would compete for rank in the imperial examination, and later for positions in the government and political status.

War is a means of resource allocation at the expense of the interests or even life of others. For those who have advantages in armed force and like to take risks, this is a low-cost way to obtain resources. However, for most people, war is hard to predict and very risky. A family wants to continue to exist for generations. If it loses a war, the whole family may be destroyed; even if they win, it is inevitable that later generations will be avenged by the loser and the family line will also be broken. Therefore, those who believe in familism are reluctant to accumulate wealth by means of war.

In short, families prefer peaceful and voluntary means in the competition for resources, which brings out two distinguishing characteristics of interfamily competition: first, it focuses on self-improvement; second, it emphasizes the observation of moral principles in the interaction with other families. Families invest more in institutions, technology, and human capital in order to gain advantages over other families in peaceful competition, especially in the fields of the market, religion, and politics. They also for others' interests and feelings and altruism toward others in order to win the favor of other families and social reputation for virtue.

Thus there emerges "moral competition," which is rarely seen in interpersonal competition. Generally speaking, respect for and altruism toward others will win the praise and return of others. The praise will develop into a family reputation, which will make it easier for the family to get along with other families, make it better liked, or help it to be entrusted with political power. Other families will in return favors, especially when the first family is faced with setbacks or crisis. Such returns might be given to the current generation or a later generation. Unlike the individual, the family can better enjoy the benefits associated with reputation because of the family's scale. In contrast with the individualism's view of limited life, familism's unlimited view of time places more value upon praise and reputation, because the benefits of reputation can last for a longer time and it is possible for later generations to benefit from the good deeds of their ancestors, thanks to the unlimited life of the family. So the continuity of a family won't be easily stopped by accidents or disasters and it is more likely to realize the purpose of the family: to have numerous generations.

This moral competition between families can also be used to compete for political power, especially in ancient societies where violence was more primitive, such as in the Stone Age. At that time, stone weapons were not enough to form a broad deterrent force, and thus became the basis of violence for larger political entities. People also began to "disenchant" from primitive religions. The moral prestige of a family was an important resource to gain political power. That is why there is a Chinese say that "competition in ancient times was about morality" (Chen Ming 1999). Because of moral competition for political power, clans tended to elect the virtuous as leaders, such as King Tang of Shang, King Wu of Zhou, and the Duke of Zhou. The development of moral systems and the moral competition outside the family were also encouraged, such as the hundred schools of thought in the Spring and Autumn Period and the Warring States Period (770–221 BC). Superior moral systems were eventually accepted by families engaged in moral competition, such as the mainstream status granted to the Confucius school in the Han Dynasty.

Due to the interfamily competition, some families expanded and prospered, while others declined and disappeared. The families which survived the competition adopted more efficient institutions and technologies, and thus acquired more resources from the market, the religion, and the government, so as to produce more descendants. And because they could live in peace with other families, they suffered fewer man-made disasters and thus faced less risk of being extinguished. On the other hand, families which are in an inferior position in the competition might learn from the winners and accept their technology, institutions, and culture. It is even possible for them to change their family names into those of the successful families. The family name structure in today's China is the result of interfamily competition. About 28% of common family names[12] and about one-third of population[13] are related to the family names Ji and Jiang, which were respectively the parental and maternal family name of the clan of Zhou. The clan of Zhou and the Zhou laid the foundation of the Confucian culture, which later became mainstream in China. The first leaders, King Wen of Zhou, King Wu of Zhou, and the Duke of Zhou, enjoyed popular support and were respected by later generations for their political achievements and virtues. Therefore, the clan of Zhou was the most successful clan in China.

1.6 The Family-Based Political Structure

Like interpersonal trades, the interfamily market can also malfunction. And without doubt, someone has to provide the public goods for families. However, compared with an individualistic society, in a family-based society, the government is formed in a different way and possesses a different political structure.

In individualistic societies, there are normally two ways of forming a government: one is through a social contract—that is, everyone in the society votes for a government. The other is through war—that is, some people who have advantages in armed strength force others to give part of their wealth to them, and for their own sake, they will provide public goods such as protection of property (Olson 1993). However, in a familist society, the relationship between people is neither independent nor equal.

[12] Estimated based on the materials in ***A Brief Study of Surnames*** by Wang Jinsheng.

[13] Estimated based on the data of ***Tracing the Root of Surnames in China*** (2004) by Yang Fujun.

They are, first of all, relatives and their rights depend on their rank in family order. Members have asymmetric rights and obligations toward each other (e.g., the father should be kind and the son should be filial). Outside the nuclear family, order is also established within the clan on the model of domestic order. For example, the family of senior members is the head of the clan.

On the other hand, the larger clan itself will constitute a gens or tribe, which is a small-sized society. Since the family relationship is a natural social relationship, it is hard for clan members to explore and try other new social orders. Therefore, it is hard to implement the voting system of "one man, one vote" in such a society.

The first public goods were those of the clan. The characteristics of family, domestic principles of resource allocation, and the culture of familism assured family members that their costs will be repaid, and made sure that the provision of the public goods would not be undermined by free riding. The basic public good of the clan is ancestor worship, whose purpose was not only to worship a common ancestor but also to identify family members and their status. By reinforcing status relationships within the clan, ancestor worship makes it less likely that members will shirk their duties. Of course, these relationships were structured to maximize clan interests.

In a one-clan society, society expands as the family grows. In fact, the population of the society is "produced" by the family.[14] As time passes and our model society grows, within five generations it will have many members without close family relationships. However, since the society was formed based on the principle of familism, it will set up social structures that maintain bonds between families connected with weakening blood ties. The fact that family distance grows slowly allows such structures to evolve gradually.

Even if a society contains a number of clans without any blood ties, as long as the clan which provides the public goods is significant enough in the society, Mancur Olson's theory of public goods predicts that the

[14] Suppose that a couple has 3 children and each of the children marries someone outside the family and then has 3 children, under normal circumstances—that is, without catastrophes such as war and epidemics and without limits on resources, the family will have 243 members after 5 generations, 59,049 after 10, 14,348,907 after 15, and 3,486,784,401 members after 20 generations. If one generation equals 20 years, then 5 generations equal 100 years, 10 generations 200 years, 15 generations 300 years, and 20 generations 400 years, which is not a long period in the human history.

interests of the clan will cover most interests of the society, and the clan will have motivation to provide public goods for the society. At this point, the political head of the society is the head of the family or clan; the head of family is not elected but naturally selected: that is, it is the senior member of the core family and the elder or the more capable among the brothers.[15]

While the political head of a familist society is an individual, it is the clan that provides public goods.[16] Over time, the clan which first provided public goods is likely to specialize in government, as other clans specialize in other professions. When a clan specializes in providing public goods, it becomes a government, with its members staffing the administration. The family's quasi-immortality makes it better suited to governance than an individual king. For one thing, it provides stability; for another, the

[15] Selecting the eldest living member as the head of the clan is advantageous not only because of his rich experience but also because of his position in the family/clan line, which makes him more closely related to the family/clan than any junior member. For example, if a grandfather has three children and each child has three children of their own, then the welfare of all the children and grandchildren is related to his welfare because any child or grandchild is capable of passing down his genes. The more children and grandchildren he has, the more likely it is for his genes to be passed down. In other words, his utility is in line with the utility of the family/clan. At the same time, theoretically speaking, all his children and grandchildren are equal before him, for each child has half of his genes and each grandchild has a quarter of his genes. Therefore, he will treat all the family members fair and square. But the children, not to mention the grandchildren, will place their own children before the children of their brothers and sisters. The interests of their own family are in conflict with those of the large family. Therefore, it is reasonable in terms of economics that "naturally" the senior will become the head of the family.

It is not hard to imagine that the Chinese perception of "gong" (公) is derived from the concept of clan. The character "gong" first appeared in the Shang Dynasty, meaning the male ancestor. Later it could be used to refer to the male and also the senior. The reason for the male senior to be the head of the clan is because the male have advantages over the female in terms of power and strength and defence is the first "public goods" of the clan (Chang 1999, p. 143); since the family members share the same ancestor, ancestor worship is a "public" affair of the clan; other "public goods" are developed from the ancestor worship; later "gong" could also refer to the king or the nobility and thus reflected the transformation from clan leader to political leader. And the basic requirement for the political leader is to be "fair" and "just."

[16] Zhu Fenghan: in the Shang and Zhou Dynasties, "though members of the ruling class participated in politics as individuals, yet one's status and political influence are determined by the power of one's clan" (2004, p. 2). He Huaihong: "The key figures in the Spring and Autumn Period are all supported by some clan. The individuals and the clan are closely related to each other. Therefore, our deepest impression of the history in the Spring and Autumn Period is about the clans rather than the individuals" (1996, p. 101).

long-term perspective of familism makes the family more capable of making decisions for the long-term benefit of society.[17] The "hereditary system" refers to the passing down of political power between generations. Due to the large number of members within a political clan, the rules for selecting political leaders have a number of possible forms, ranging from selection among senior members of the clan to direct inheritance by an eldest son or eldest brother. It is still disputable which way is better: "selecting the eldest" or "selecting the most capable and virtuous." Therefore, every transfer of political power has to be determined via an internal decision-making process.[18] In the "hereditary" political system, it is the family rather than an individual that rules the institution. The former is superior to the latter based on the above analysis.[19]

As political power inevitably relies on force, interfamily competition for the supreme political power often takes the form of war. But winning the war does not necessarily mean winning supreme political power. The successful family has to not only justify itself in the moral competition, rely on the cultural and political elites, and establish a set of institutions and policies which are efficient and good for the social prosperity, but also keep the balance between several other large clans.

The family-based political framework extends domestic order to the political structure. The political leader entrusted by the family owns supreme power, which means that they, representing the family, have the power to collect taxes and the obligation to provide public goods (including defense, protection of property, maintaining order, justice, etc.). At the same time, in the form of land sequestration (as well as the population

[17] Olson once pointed out that considering the limit of life, the king had the motive by the end of his life to discount earlier his benefits which generate behind he dies, so damage the property rights system and market order (Olson 1993).

[18] Family leaders dethroning political leader happened a lot throughout the Chinese history. As early as in the Shang Dynasty, Tai Jia (太甲) was exiled by Yi Yin (伊尹). According to some analysis, Yi Yin was probably the younger brother of Cheng Tang (成汤) and became the head of the family after the death of the latter (Zhao Cheng 2000, pp. 96–97).

[19] Edward Gibbon, the author of *The History of the Decline and Fall of the Roman Empire*, once said that the hereditary title as "the superior prerogative of birth, when it has obtained the sanction of time and popular opinion, is the plainest and least invidious of all distinctions among mankind. The acknowledged right extinguishes the hopes of faction, and the conscious security disarms the cruelty of the monarch. To the firm establishment of this idea we owe the peaceful succession and mild administration of European monarchies" (1962, Vol. 1, p. 100). He would have presented cases of those successful dynasties in China if he knew more knowledge of Chinese history.

on the land), tax collection rights and the obligation to provide public goods are allocated to important members of the family, generally his brothers and sons, to form a vassal state. The princes have full autonomy, but they have the duty to defend, pay tribute, and obey the dispatch of the Emperor.

Outside the core family and clan members, the family in control of political power also seeks interfamily or interclan alliances by various means, the most important of which are marriage and political cooperation. Besides the members of the clan, the monarch can also enfeoff members of other clans, including in-laws, people with remarkable military or political contributions, and the descendants of previous royal families.[20] For example, in China's Zhou Dynasty, history records the creation of 204 dukedoms, including 53 bearing the Zhou clan surname Ji (姬), and 22 bearing the surnames of in-laws of the royal family: Jiang (姜), Si (姒), Gui (妫), and Ren (任), constituting the majority of dukedoms (He Huaihong 1996, pp. 10–11). The rest of dukedoms were given to families who provided either political cooperation or political influence. Inside Zhou dukedoms, the land could also be divided in the same way. Only the eldest son could inherit the title of duke, while other sons could only be given the title "da fu" (大夫). The political order of the whole society was established according to this domestic order.

There is another advantage of the family-based political structure: that is, it can achieve more with less. As the family expands, blood ties are gradually weakened, and the clan acts like an expanding interest group centered on the chief family. According to Olson's theory of collective action, the core family, with a smaller population than the extended family, is like an interest group with a small number of people, and since its members are most closely connected, it has the strongest cohesive force to act collectively. The more members a family has, the weaker the blood ties and cohesive force are, and the less likely the members will act collectively. However, as they are still more or less connected with the core family by blood, they will be affected by the collective action of the core family. When the first circle of clan members around the core family observes the original costs of collective action which is good for themselves, they will join the collective action; so will the second circle be motived, and the

[20] He Huaihong: in the Western Zhou Dynasty, "the land was given to mainly members of the Ji family and relatives, officials who had rendered outstanding service, old friends and descendants of late saints" (1996, p. 4).

third circle and then the fourth … A clan is like a multi-level holding company. Despite the small number of members, the core family plays the decisive role in mobilizing collective action. The superiority of the clan over the holding company is that people are independent from each other in the latter, while in the former people are connected by blood, so it is easier for the former to take collective action.

However, the familist political structure is limited from the perspectives of time and space. On the one side, as the titles of the emperor and duke are passed down through primogeniture, the blood ties between their descendants will be gradually weakened and eventually they will become strangers and the rules of familism won't work for them, for the foundation for the enfeoffment system has collapsed. The system of alliance through marriages, which was stable for a long time, can address the issue of weakening blood ties, for it can preserve blood ties between different political clans for a longer period of time, as seen in long-term alliances through marriages between the Ji family of the patriarchal gens and the Jiang family of the matriarchal gens of the Zhou clan, the alliance between Qi (齐) and Lu (鲁) and that between Qin (秦) and Jin (晋) in the Spring and Autumn Period, and the Manchu-Mongol alliance in the Qing Dynasty. But due to the effects of polygamy and the early death of legitimate sons, it can only put off, not stop, the weakening process of blood ties. This is probably the reason why even the most excellent dynasty could not last over 30 generations.

On the other hand, as territory expands and the population increases, the number of family members will also increase, but it is impossible for actual domestic order to expand boundlessly. Therefore, a more efficient political integration technique and operation system must be introduced into the family-based political framework, such as the transformation from the enfeoffment system to the system of monarchial centralization of power in addition with the system of prefectures and counties. Accordingly, the hereditary system of official titles was transformed from selecting official candidates from scholar-gentry clans and then to the imperial examination system. As society expands, the family in control of political power has to deal with more and more common families without any kinship relationship to the chief clan, instead of only a few large families. If the ruling family cannot treat the large number of other families without any kinship fairly, there will be a "revolution" to replace the family with a new ruling family. In the field of culture, in Chinese history, the mainstream culture had also transformed from the Confucian culture emphasizing "rites" (礼) in the pre-Qin period to the neo-Confucian school emphasizing "heavenly principles" (天理) in the Song and Ming Dynasties.

1.7 The Familist Constitutional Framework

As the most natural and original basic institution in a society, the family enjoys certain priority in the institutional structure of society. Though the domestic order cannot be extended to the whole society, it is possible to generalize the principles of familism and extend it to constitutional framework of the society. It includes the following aspects: (1) family as the basic unit of society; (2) applying domestic rules to other aspects of society; (3) abstracting the basic principles of familism into the constitutional principles of the society; (4) establishing general principles for interpersonal relationships based on the principle of familism.

Making the family the basic unit of the society places family values in the most important position of the society, even before other several seemingly critical institutions. For example, in the case of someone stealing the sheep from others, Confucius thought that a son should not testify against his father.[21] As the unit of cost/benefit calculation and decision-making, the family cannot and should not testify against itself, just as one would never testify against oneself. Once the son is allowed to testify against his father, he believed, the domestic order would be overthrown and the basic institution of society would be destroyed, removing the foundation for government to rule society.[22] According to this principle, domestic order is placed prior to the property rights system and governmental institutions. Though the property rights system is also very important, it pales into insignificance in front of the institution of family. The family is not only a way of allocating resources, but also an organization for moral education and religious services and the foundation of the political structure. In a familist society, the government's rule is based on domestic order and the interfamily relationship. The family's priority over governmental

[21] *The Analects of Confucius*: "The Duke of She said to Confucius, 'in our clan, a man who behaves with honesty would testify against his own father for stealing a goat.' Confucius said, 'in our clan, an honest man is different. A father would shield his son and a son would shield his father. Then there is honesty.'"

[22] Of course, there is a limit of it, because if without the ability of self-correction, a family continues wantonly to violate the interests of other families, it will be avenged, which is harmful to the family itself.

institutions and the property rights system is an element of familistic constitutional structure.

The most commendable domestic principle is filial piety, emphasizing the respect and love shown by children to parents. The principle of filial piety is not only effective from the physical view, but also metaphysical, which makes it a general rule beyond regional limits.[23] Though the interpersonal relationship outside the family is different from that among family members, the former can assimilate and extend the latter both based on the basic domestic relationships and the feelings one cherishes for one's own families. For example, generally one can extend his filial piety toward one's parents to show respect toward seniors outside the family, loyalty toward one's lord (superiors), and trustworthiness toward friends; the ways of domestic governance can also be applied to public governance.[24,25,26]

This extension of the code of conduct is based on the solid foundation of utilitarianism with its "low cost and high profits." On the one hand, there is no need of massive education, for it is not hard for people to understand "filial piety," which comes naturally from the love of relatives. Neither is it hard for people to understand the more general code of conduct (toward teachers, superiors, and friends), so "the teachings of the sages were successful without being severe, and their governance was effective without being rigorous."[27] This is why its cost is low. On the other hand, since one's parents, one's elder siblings, one's lord, and one's superior should be revered, showing respect toward others' parents, elder siblings, lords, and superiors will make them happy and win their favor.

[23] Zhang Xianglong: "The awareness of filial piety and love is the source of morality" (2007, p. 266). As Kant said, morality is a kind of "absolute order" disregarding any costs or benefits. Filial piety toward one's parents is the original state of the scenario. The love parents show to you is a sunk cost and the investment into parents will not produce any return in the future. Showing filial piety toward one's parents is just something one "should" do.

[24] *The Book of Filial Piety*: "Therefore when they serve their ruler with filial piety, they are loyal; when they serve their superiors with reverence, they are obedient."

[25] *The Analects of Confucius*: "The Master said, 'In the home, the young should behave with filial piety, and out in the world, with brotherly love. They should be prudent and trustworthy. They should love all people and be close to the benevolent. Having so done, their remaining strength should be used to learn literature.' Zi Xia said, 'To revere virtue instead of beauty, to devote all strength to serving parents, to be willing to die in serving the lord, to speak with trustworthiness in dealings with friends.'"

[26] *The Book of Filial Piety*: "The Master said, 'His governance of his family may be transferred as good governance in any official position.'"

[27] "The Governance of the Holy Ruler," the ninth chapter of *The Book of Filial Piety*.

"The reverence paid to one man makes thousands and myriads of men pleased. The reverence is paid to a few, and the pleasure extends to many."[28] This is why its benefits are large. Thanks to its low cost and high benefits, this code of conduct is widely supported and promoted and has become a general principle.

To elevate the principle of filial piety, which is the core of familism, is to generalize it and extend it to interpersonal relations, especially to the relationship between the government leader and the people. Once it becomes the basic code of conduct, the society will like a big family and every member of it will benefit from the value increase brought by familism. Confucius said, "He who loves his parents will not dare [to incur the risk of] being hated by any man, and he who reveres his parents will not dare [to incur the risk of] being condemned by any man. When the love and reverence [of the Emperor] are thus carried to the utmost in the service of his parents, the lessons of his virtue affect all the people, and he becomes a pattern to [all within] the four seas. This is the filial piety of the Emperor."[29] If the head of government is filial toward his parents, he will not dare to treat the common people badly; the best way of loving the common people is to teach them to be filial toward their parents and turn filial piety into the politeness and respect toward other people as a general. It is the filial piety of the Emperor to turn it into a general moral principle, make people respect each other and the society harmonious.

Of course, it is implied that peace and social prosperity will make the royal family last forever.[30] For the continuity of the family, the Emperor should regard following the "will of providence" and the "Mandate of Heaven" as the most important forms of filial piety. It is said in the *Book of Filial Piety* that "In filial piety there is nothing greater than the reverential awe of one's father. In the reverential awe shown to one's father there is nothing greater than the making him the correlate of Heaven. The Duke of Zhou was the man who (first) did this. Formerly, the Duke of Zhou at the altar in the suburbs sacrificed to Hou Ji as the company of Heaven,

[28] "Amplification of the All-Embracing Rule of Conduct," the 12th chapter of *The Book of Filial Piety*.

[29] "The Son of Heaven," the second chapter of *The Book of Filial Piety*.

[30] Confucius has pointed it out clearly that "In ancient times, when the intelligent kings by means of filial piety ruled all under heaven, they did not dare to receive with disrespect the ministers of small states. How dare they do so to the dukes, marquises, counts, and barons! Thus the king obtains joy of thousands states, for serving his royal predecessors." The family of Emperor made thousands states joyful, the latter in return support the former.

and in the Brilliant Hall he honored King Wen and sacrificed to him as the company of God. The consequence was that from [all the states] within the four seas, every [prince] came in the discharge of his duty to [assist in those] sacrifices." Regarding "accompanying Heaven"[31] —one is worthy of the Mandate of Heaven for his virtues are good for the common people—as the most important filial piety is to directly connect the political legitimacy with filial piety. Since "God sees from our people's eyes; God hears from our people's ears"[32] and "Heaven will obey the will of the people,"[33] political legitimacy, to a large extent, depends upon the satisfaction of the people. Therefore, the basic logic of familistic constitutional principle is to place "filial piety" as the highest social principle. The head of government (the Emperor) should follow and implement the principle, that is, to carry out "the filial piety of the Emperor" and the most important "filial piety of the Emperor" is to win the Mandate of Heaven for his reign. "Heaven has no relatives, but only helps those virtuous." An important way of winning the Mandate of Heaven is to win the support of people by treating them benevolently and restraining one's conduct with moral principles.

"Filial piety," as a familist constitutional principle, can also be further extracted into a more general concept. With the ability of identifying with others, people can "love other's elder as I love mine; love other's youth as I love mine;" and "people love not only their relatives and their own children." With the ability of loving one's family, one is also capable of loving others. Such love is called "benevolence." At this point, the specific "filial piety" has been transformed into the general "love" and the specific "rites" (domestic order) into the general "righteousness." Furthermore, the familistic principle of "filial piety" can even be applied universally. Regarding nature as the parents and all the livings things as the children,[34] man will have each other as siblings and all the other living things as companions.[35]

[31] So-called "matching Heaven" means to worship one's ancestor as the honored company of Heaven when worshiping Heaven.

[32] "Wan Zhang," (万章) *The Book of Mencius*, qtd. from "The Great Declaration" (泰誓).

[33] "The 31st Year of the Reign of Duke Xiang," *Chronicle of Zuo*, qtd. from "The Great Declaration."

[34] In *The Western Inscription* (西铭), Zhang Zai remarks: "Heaven is the father; earth is the mother."

[35] *The Western Inscription*: "The people are my siblings, and all things are my companions."

Compared with individualism's general moral principles such as freedom, equality, and philanthropy, this general moral principle, derived from the ethics of familism, will facilitate friendship and cooperation between strangers, for it still implies that "the increase of one's utility will increase that of the other" ($\partial Ui/\partial Uj$). In fact, the culture of familism generates the culture of universalism, while the culture of individualism gives birth to the culture of nationalism.[36] The culture of universalism of "looking on all under the sky as one family," and regarding "all within the four seas as brothers with each other" can become a constitutional principle around the world.[37]

1.8 Conclusion: The Research Approach on Familism and Individualism

The history of economics shows us that the creation of any initial concept (such as transaction costs), or redefinition of an existing concept, or the change of a basic assumption (such as the change from fixed scale return to increasing scale return), might cause a theoretical revolution. The concept of familism is no exception. At the level of definitions, the difference between familism and individualism is that they have different subjects of calculation and action; the former takes the family as the unit while the latter takes the individual as the unit. They generate two different kinds of theoretical frameworks, corresponding with two different kinds of social systems or institutional structures.

The above analysis shows that the most important difference between the family as the economic agent and the individual as the economic agent is that, theoretically, the life span of the family is limitless and the continuity of family line is the family's most important goal. Therefore, the economic agent's view of time and its assessment of costs and benefits also differ from those of individuals, as do decisions and actions based on rational calculation. If we take only the assumption of individualism for granted, we will find decisions made according to the assumption of familism hard to imagine and vice versa.

[36] Mr. Liang Shuming once commented that China emphasized the family and the universe, while the western world emphasized the individual and the nation (1992, pp. 331–332).

[37] Zhao Tingyang: "Since we suppose that familism is the full expression of human nature, then the principle of familism should be the general principle in dealing with all kinds of social, national and universal problems" (2005, p. 68).

If the interpersonal market has what Hayek calls "spontaneous order," so does family-based organization. The organization of a family is the result of human being's sexual desires and instinct of fertility, and the leader of the family is naturally selected—that is, the senior member of the family, without any form of election or any external interference. This kind of family organization remains basically intact after tens of thousands of years of competition among families, which shows that the family, like other "spontaneous" institutions, is effective. It is neglected only because people are used to this kind of spontaneous order.

Another important difference between familism and individualism is that the individualist approach assumes that individuals are independent from each other and equal, without any kind of involvement in any relationship; while the familist approach supposes that individuals are connected by kinship and that there are various ranks or levels naturally formed by genetic relationships. These two assumptions represent two extreme cases in the real world. As far as the extreme case of familism is concerned, with the expansion over generations, the kinship within the family will be weakened and ultimately reduced to an independent relationship equivalent to that predicted by individualism. As far as the extreme case of individualism is concerned, the more interpersonal relationships one frequently engages in, the stronger one will feel the special kinship between people instead of independent and equal relationship. Between individualist and familist relationships, there are a large number of other kinds of interpersonal relationship (see Fig. 1.2).

Obviously, the development of Chinese society basically followed the path of familism, while that of the western world followed the path of individualism.[38] The extreme case of familism or individualism is only the starting point of a society, and during the process of development, China and the western world continuously created new institutions and absorbed the institutional resources of their opposites, in order to overcome the institutional weakness based on its own starting point. For example, during the process of weakening kinship and massive social transformation, China changed its institutional structure from an enfeoffment system to

[38] According to Lewis Henry Morgan, "The experience of mankind has developed but two patterns of government. ... The first and most ancient was a *social organization*, founded upon gentes, phratries and tribes. The second and latest in time was a *political organization*, founded upon territory and upon property" (1964). He thought that since the Greek period, the western world had managed to transform from the first one into the second one (1964, Chapter X).

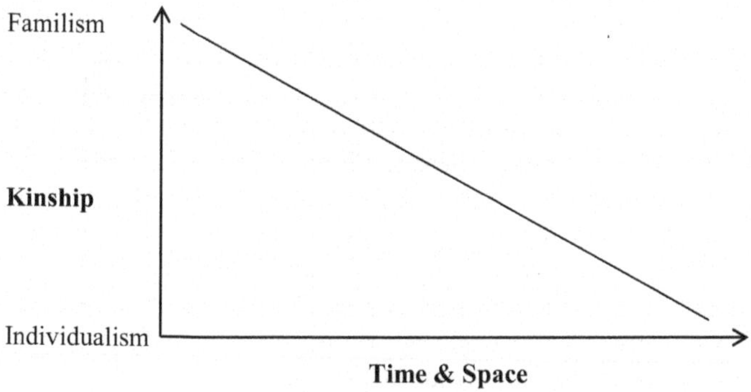

Fig. 1.2 The changing spectrum of familism and individualism
Note: the vertical axis in the picture represents the degree of kinship. The stronger the kinship is, the closer it is to familism; the weaker the kinship is, the closer it is to individualism. The horizontal axis represents the duration of the family line and the space of social expansion. The longer the time and larger the space is, the weaker kinship will be

the system of prefectures and counties, from the hereditary system to the imperial examination system; the revolution in modern China was characterized by individualism, a response not only to the challenges from the west but also to the problem of the large number of families and the dramatic increase of population. In the western world, individualistic people did not have a perspective beyond their own life until their conversion to the monotheistic religion of Christianity, and the problem of moral education and spiritual comfort was thus settled. The church, to some extent, is an alternative to the ancestral temple of the clan.

Because of path dependency, the society with individualism as the starting point tries to integrate all the aspects of the society with the principle of individualism, while that with familism as the starting point tries to integrate all the aspects of the society with the principle of familism. To some extent, these two approaches both succeed. However, in reality, interpersonal relationships are not either familist or individualist. Attempting to integrate all kinds of social relations with the principle of familism might suppress the individuality can ultimately lead to the resistance against the system of the clan; attempting to integrate all kinds of social relations with the principle of individualism might ruin the family, at the expense of familial affection and the irreplaceable functions of education and mutual aid. On the contrary, if the culture of individualism is introduced into a society with the cultural tradition of familism without any matching institutions of the individualistic society, such as Chinese liberation of individuals from the clan system without the support of the religious tradition of monotheism, there might be a large number of "unreligious individuals"—individuals without the view beyond over time limit—and it might cause moral degeneration and spiritual terror. However, if the ancestor worship ceremony is introduced into the individualistic society, there won't be any familial organization to implement it and it will cause controversies with monotheism, such as the "Chinese Rites Controversy" in Early Modern Europe.

Since the familist society is based on the "existing" familial order with slight modification, its "cost of foundation" is small and makes effects soon. That's why in most of the premodern period, the Chinese familist society led other societies[39]; without the support of an existing familial order, individualistic society for a long time had a difficult time. Not until institutions such as Christianity, the constitutional democracy, and nation state were established could it better govern the individualist relationship and lay the foundation for the recent rise of the western world. At the same time, the weakness of familist society in the east was highlighted with its success: that is, the weakening blood ties over generations and the breaking up of the familial order due to excessive population made the Chinese society more and more individualistic. The family-based political structure could not mobilize enough public resources to resist the military power of the democracy-based nation states, such as the United Kingdom. Furthermore, in contrast to the system of democracy, the familist political structure seemed less legitimate politically. At this point, not only could individualist polities challenge and defeat familistic societies, but the individualistic system, as a solution to the social problems associated with familism, became one of the development trends of China's institutions. However, there are also some negative effects of the individualistic society's winning over the familistic society. The former, preferring the means of war, not only directly benefited from the changes in approaches to

[39] In his "The World Economy: A Millennial Perspective," Angus Maddison pointed out that from the year of the first year to 1870, China's economic aggregate has always been ranked number one in the world. In 1870, almost a century after the start of the industrial revolution in Britain, China had already experienced two Opium Wars and Beijing had been looted by the British and French allied forces. In 1820, before the outbreak of the Opium War, China accounted for 33% of the world's GDP (2003, 261st pages).

wealth distribution in the west and the east, but also indirectly benefited from the scientific and technological advances promoted by war. The world would be worse if familistic society turns to war, following the example of western society. We should also observe that the positive discount rate of the individualistic society speeds up the economic growth in the modern society, but at the same time, the modern people might consume the resources which are better saved for later generations.

In general, this chapter provides an approach which will greatly expand our research vision, provide a theoretical framework for the researches on familist society, enable us to further understand the basic logic and phenomena of such societies, and offer a new way of comparing the societies in the east and the west. It is my expectation that this approach will inspire a new interpretation of world history, including the history of China, and provide more choices for people to improve the social institutional structure.

References

贝克尔，加里，《家庭经济分析》，华夏出版社，1987; (Translated from Becker, Gary. *A Treatise on the Family*, Harvard University Press, 1981).

Becker, Gary, and Barro, Robert, "Altruism and economic theory of fertility", *Population and Development Review*, Vol. 12, Supplement: Below Replacement Fertility in Industrial Societies: Causes, Consequences, Policies. (1986), pp. 69–76.

陈明，"《唐虞之道》与早期儒家的社会理念"，载《原道》第5辑，贵州人民出版社，1999; (in Chinese; Chen Ming. "Tang Yu Zhi Dao and the Social Ideology of early Confucianism". *Originated Way*. Vol. 5. Guizhou People's Press, 1999).

费成康主编，《中国的家法族规》上海社会科学出版社，1998; (In Chinese; Fei Chengkang. ed. *Family Disciplines and Clan Regulations in China*. Shanghai Social Science Press, 1998).

Gibbon, Edward, *The Decline and Fall of the Roman Empire*, Abridged by D.M. LOW, Washington Square Press, Inc., 1962.

何怀宏，《世袭社会及其解体》，生活•读书•新知三联书店，1996; (In Chinese; He Huaihong. *The Hereditary Society and Its Disintegration*. SDX Joint Publishing Company, 1996).

李安宅，《德格之历史与人口》，载于《西康户政通讯》；转载于孙怀阳和程贤敏主编，《中国国藏族人口与社会》，中国藏学出版社，1998; (in Chines; Li Anzhai, "The History and Population of Dege." *The Journal of the Civil Affairs in Xikang*. Quoted by The Tibetan Population and Community in China. Sun Huaiyang & Cheng Xianmin. Ed. China Tibetology Publishing House, 1998).

梁漱溟, 《梁漱溟学术论著自选集》, 北京师范学院出版社, 1992; (In Chinese; Liang Suming. *A Personal Anthology of Academic Works by Liang Suming*. Beijing Normal University Press, 1992).

麦迪森, 安格斯, 《世界经济千年史》, 北京大学出版社, 2003; (Translated from Madison, Angus. *The World Economy: A Millennial Perspective*. OECD, 2001).

Maverick, Lewis A. *China—A Model For Europe*, Paul Anderson Co., 1946.

摩尔根, 路易斯•享利, 《古代社会》, 商务印书馆, 1997; (Translated from Morgan, Lewis. H. *Ancient Society*, The Belknap Press of Harvard University Press, 1964).

Olson, Mancur, "Dictatorship, Democracy, and Development", *American Political Sciences Review*, Vol. 87, No. 3 September, 1993.

谈敏, 《法国重农学派学说的中国渊源》, 上海人民出版社, 1992; (In Chinese; Tan Min. *The Chinese Origin of French Physiocracy*. Shanghai People's Press, 1992).

杨复竣, 《中华万姓同根》, 中州古籍出版社, 2004; (In Chinese; Yang Fujun. *Tracing the Root of Surnames in China*. Zhongzhou Ancient Book Publishing House, 2004).

张光直, 《商代文明》, 北京工艺美术出版社, 1999; (Translated from Chang, Kwang-Chih, *Shang Civilization*. Yale University Press, 1982).

张祥龙, 《思想避难:全球化中的中国古代哲理》, 北京大学出版社, 2007; (In Chinese; Zhang Xianglong. *The Haven of Thought: Ancient Chinese Philosophy in the Era of Globalization*. Peking University Press, 2007).

张岩, 《图腾制与原始文明》, 上海文艺出版社, 1995; (In Chinese; Zhang Yan. *The Totem System and The Primitive Civilization*. Shanghai Literature and Art Publishing House, 1995).

张岩, 《[山海经]与古代社会》, 文化艺术出版社, 1999; (In Chinese; Zhang Yan, *《The Classic of Mountains and Seas》 and Ancient Society*. Culture and Arts Publishing House, 1999).

张岩, 《从部落文明到礼乐制度》, 上海三联书店, 2004; (In Chinese; Zhang Yan, *From Tribal Civilization to the Ritual System*. SDX Joint Publishing Company, 2004).

赵诚, 《甲骨文与商代文化》, 辽宁人民出版社, 2000; (In Chinese; Zhao Cheng. *Bone Inscriptions and the Culture of Shang Dynasty*. Liaoning People's Press, 2000).

赵汀阳, 《天下体系——世界制度哲学导论》, 江苏教育出版社, 2005; (In Chinese; Zhao Tingyang. *Institutions in the World—A Philosophical Introduction to the World Institutions*, Education Publishing House of Jiangsu, 2005).

周洁, 《中日祖先崇拜研究》, 世界知识出版社, 2004; (In Chinese; Zhou Jie. Research on the Ancestor worship in China and Japan. World Knowledge Press, 2004).

朱凤瀚, 《商周家族形态研究》 (增订本), 天津古籍出版社, 2004. (In Chinese; Zhu Fenghan, *Research on the Clan Patterns of the Shang and Zhou Dynasties.* (Revised and enlarged edition). Tianjin Ancient Books Press, 2004).

CLASSICAL LITERATURE

《尚书》; (In Chinese; The Book of History).
《孝经》; (In Chinese; Classic of Filial Piety).
《论语》; (In Chinese; Analects of Confucius).
《孟子》; (In Chinese; The Works of Mencius).
《左传》; (In Chinese; Chronicles of Zuo).
《西铭》; (In Chinese; The Western Inscription).
《百家姓考略》. (In Chinese; A Brief Study of Surnames).

(Translated from The Review of New Political Economy (《新政治经济学评论》), Volume 4, Zhejiang University Press, 2008).

CHAPTER 2

Vision and Calculation

Contents

Economics assumes that people are rational. One would, at least, not do things to harm oneself. But this assumption is often far from the truth. For example, in the incident of Yao Jiaxin that shocked China, Yao knocked down a woman while he was driving and simply killed her in order to avoid paying future compensation. Even if Yao didn't know that the clear-up rate for homicide cases in mainland China is as high as 87%, he should have been aware that this ratio is quite high. He still chose to kill the woman, which placed him at a great risk of being sentenced to death. This is clearly not a rational choice. In fact, rationality does not prevent people from making mistakes. People calculate expected costs and benefits, and often there is a gap between the expected and the actual situation. This is not just because the future is uncertain, but also because of the information and data that form the basis of calculation. Information and data is used only within a certain scope. A different scope of information and data

Sheng Hong, *Vision and Calculation*,
https://doi.org/10.1007/978-981-15-2898-9_2

leads to different calculation results. In general, the greater the scope, the more complete, comprehensive, and informative the information and data is, and the closer to correct the result is. However, the scope of a person's concerns is related to their vision.

2.1 The Scope and Results of Calculation

Scope can be understood in two dimensions: space and time. Time has length, and space has size. In general, the longer the time is, and the larger the space is, the more the information contained is complete, comprehensive, and extensive enough to make the calculations closer to correct.

Mancur Olson gave an example: if a king knows he has only a year of life, he would violate his agreement with people in order to maximize benefits and raise taxes as much as possible to use up his wealth before death. But if he expects to live long enough, he will consider long-term interests and impose an appropriate tax rate on people to provide them with a sustained impetus for economic activities, in order to realize a long-term stable and sizable income (Olson 1993). The latter approach would bring more benefits to society in the meantime.

In general, when a period B is longer and contains a period A, it would contain more information than the shorter period. From the perspective of economic calculation, it contains more information about costs and benefits. The more information we have about a behavior, the closer our assessment of it is to be accurate. In order to gather more information, we need to observe this behavior's influence for a longer time. For example, how do you evaluate the result of a new product launch? If you only look at a 100-day period A, it clearly contains less information than the overlapping 200-day period B. Therefore, in order to determine the performance of the new product, the information from time period B would be more accurate than that from the time period A. See Fig. 2.1 below.

In reality, the costs or benefits arising out of an action may not be visible immediately. In some cases, costs must be paid in order to reap benefits in a very long time, such as investment activities; in other cases, benefits could be obtained before costs are paid, such as drinking or taking drugs.

Most human actions are interactive; that is, they represent transactions or interaction between people. One of the features of such action is that it has impact on the costs or benefits of others, and inspires reactions, which in turn influence the costs and benefits of the original actor. For example, a person who rakes in wealth by harming others, such as theft, robbery,

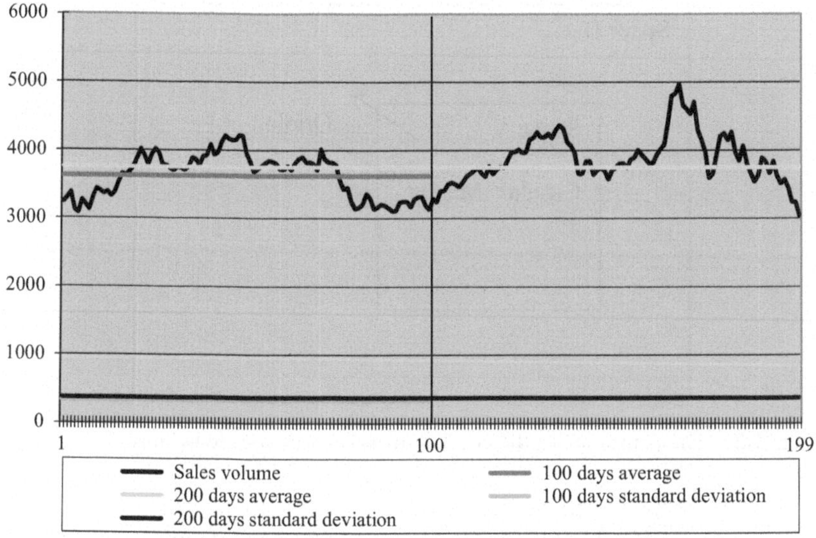

Average volume in 100 days	Average volume in 200 days	Standard deviation in 100 days	Standard deviation in 200 days
3620.35	3752.81	328.16	370.56

Fig. 2.1 Sales volume for a new product
Note: as is shown in the figure, the mean value and standard deviation of time period A (100 days) is different from those of time period B (200 days), and time period B covers time period A, so a more accurate judgment could be drawn according to time period B

cheating, or monopoly, will suffer revenge by someone else, and a person who often helps others is more likely to get gratitude.

The lag time for others to react could be long or short. They may respond immediately, or after ten years or decades. For example, Gou Jian (520 BC–465 BC), the king of Yue State, captured the capital of Wu State and forced Fu Chai, the king of Wu State, to commit suicide, 21 years after he was badly beaten and humiliated by Fu Chai (528 BC–473 BC). Thus, when one person interacts with others, the costs and benefits of his action take a long time to be fully revealed. Therefore, the longer the time period considered—the vision farther of the actor—the more likely closer they are to form a correct judgment.

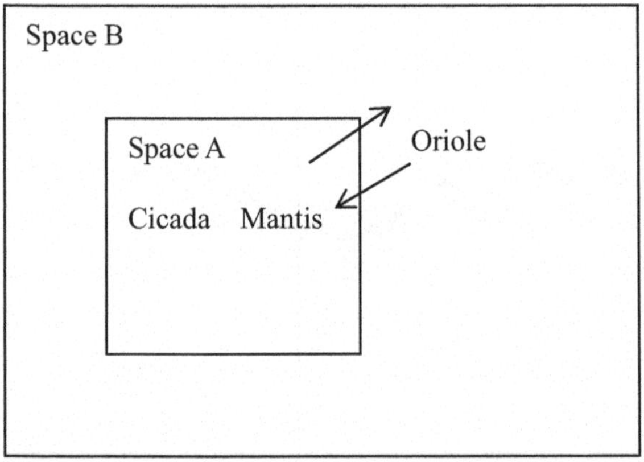

Fig. 2.2 The mantis stalks the cicada, unaware of the oriole behind

People respond to gratitude and resentment across generations. According to He Huaihong, the reason the Zhao family was able to develop and survive during the Spring and Autumn period is because their family leaders helped several other key figures. For example, in the 17th year of Duke Jing of Jin, the Zhao family suffered a big disaster, and almost every one of the family was exterminated. Zhao Wu was saved thanks to Gongsun Chujiu and Cheng Ying, two of the family's disciples. They were able to re-establish the family because of Han Jue's recommendation to the Duke Jing, a combination of different people expressing gratitude. Han Jue was brought up from childhood by Zhao Dun, Zhao Wu's uncle (He Huaihong 1996, pp. 130–140). Therefore, in China there has always been a saying "A family with charity will enjoy joy; a family with evil intentions will suffer calamity."

So it is with space. "The mantis stalks the cicada, but behind them lurks the oriole," this Chinese saying means a larger space can have an effect on a small space. In this idiom, the impact is the threat of the oriole. The mantis has a limited vision as far as its eyes can reach, so it is not aware of the existence of the oriole, but the latter does have a decisive influence on the fate of the mantis.

In general, if there is a space A and a space B, the latter is greater than and contains the former; space B will definitely contain greater information than space A, as in the following Fig. 2.2. The cicada, the mantis, and the oriole can be substituted by any living creature. We can even assume that the living creatures are in space A, then the "oriole" in space B is not necessarily the living creature, but non-living creatures such as water and gas. Climate change in a larger space will also have impact on the cost and benefit of the small living creatures in a smaller space.

To put it in another way, the larger space is the "environment" of the smaller space. The environment and the small space are isolated and independent from each other, while constantly exchanging energy and information. Thus the larger space will inevitably affect the smaller and also includes useful information for the living creatures in the smaller.

Therefore, the conclusion is that rational biological calculation depends on the observed spatial and temporal range. In the case of the same rational ability, the information of calculation which results from a larger spatial and temporal range will be more accurate than those resulting from a smaller spatial and temporal range.

2.2 Why Is Vision Bounded?

Why don't people always try to enlarge their vision and collect and absorb as much information as possible, in order to make more correct decisions? First of all, because of people's rationality, and of course, all biological creatures' rationality is bounded.

The concept of "bounded rationality" contains a lot of meaning, first and foremost the physiological limitations of operations on information. In other words, the biological sense organs to obtain information, such as eyes, ears, mouth, and nose, as well as brain processing information, have costs in observing, watching, obtaining, judging, memorizing, summarizing, processing, and reflecting information. We may call these "information costs" generally.

Existing economic theories come across information costs. Herbert A. Simon first put forward the concept of "bounded rationality" in his *Administrative Behavior*, and analyzed the rationality using method of economics. He argued that, due to limited rationality, "the administrator" does not pursue the "best solution" as long as there is a "satisfactory solution" (1988, pp. 19–21). Kenneth Arrow, in his *Information Economics*, proposed the concept of "information costs" and took information as an object of economic study. It is actually the study of how human beings allocate resources efficiently to maximize the information obtained (1989). It goes without saying that information is an important prerequisite for maximizing benefit.

But it seems that neither Simon nor Arrow directed their research of bounded rationality and information costs clearly enough to temporal and spatial dimensions, although Arrow is more interested in time, particularly future time. In this regard, there might be more studies in psychology. It is just not analyzing in economic terms and raising issues from an economic perspective. However, at the very least, psychology provides plenty of resources worth of thought to economics. One of the manifestations of bounded rationality is bounded vision.

First of all, observation is an activity with costs, that is, physical and mental strength. Attention must be paid to get valid information. "Everybody's attentional capacity is limited," and memory has a cost, too (Eysenck and Keane 2009, p. 171). So is judgment, thinking, and decision-making. All in all, on the one hand, the more information we obtain, the more capable we are of considering and processing information so as to get more accurate results; on the other hand, all biological resources for obtaining and processing information are limited. We need to select in order to manage more information with bounded physical and mental resources choice.

Naturally, people invest their limited resources in the most valuable information. Therefore, to obtain and process information, you need to first determine which is worth having. That is, to establish criteria, paying attention to some information and turning a blind eye to others. In fact, the concept of "attention" itself refers to the ability of paying attention to some things while ignoring others so as to save mental resources (Gazzaniga 2011, p. 426). At the basic level of psychology, it was natural to respond to screaming, strange shapes, and bright colors, because perverse things might pose risks to people.

Another important approach is that people divide space and time into different regions. They only pay attention to information within that region. Typically, they would choose the nearest scope of time and space. In the time dimension, it is choosing the time frame most close to "the current state"; in the spatial dimension, it is choosing the space scope most closely to where "I" am. This is natural. In the very long time of human evolution, information from the temporal and spatial scope closest to the biological subject has biggest impact on the subject.

Therefore, the fact that people pay more attention to time and space closest to themselves is an efficient allocation of scarce physical and mental resources. They pay more attention to information in this scope and intend to ignore information outside. After millions of years of evolution, this

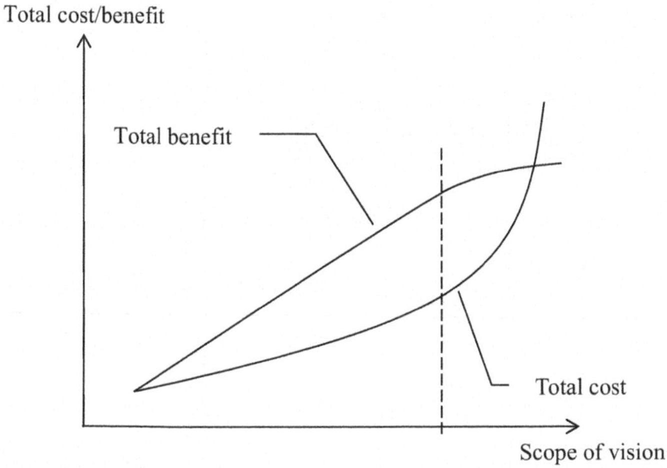

Fig. 2.3 Total cost and benefit of vision scope

method of saving mental resources almost becomes biologically instinct. People act like this subconsciously instead of deliberately.

The question is: how big is the temporal and spatial scope for the instinctive attention? Is there a recognizable boundary? The question can be addressed both by psychological research and by economic reasoning. A broadly empirical assumption is that, along the border of awareness, the marginal cost of psychological resources for obtaining and processing information increases, while the marginal profit for gains from obtaining more information decreases. The volume of information corresponds with the scope of vision. Therefore, this problem is not much different from a general economics question.

Figure 2.3 illustrates changes in the total cost and benefit of information along with the expansion of vision. Because there is an upper limit for a person's mental resources, costs rise significantly when the consumption of resources is close to or reaches the upper limit.

Figure 2.4 shows changes of the marginal cost and revenue of information with the expansion of vision.

A basic conclusion is that the instinctive default scope of vision should end at the point at which the marginal cost of information equals the marginal benefit, likely a region or a border zone.

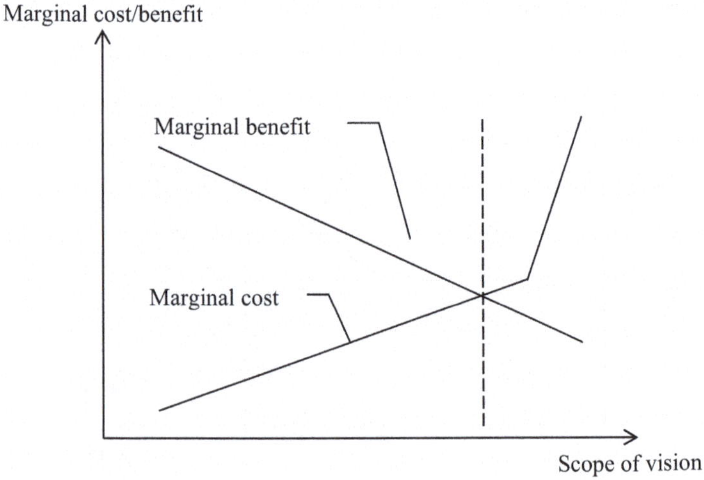

Fig. 2.4 Marginal cost and benefit of vision scope

2.3 Big Games and Small Games

In practice, the spatial and temporal scopes of vision are not independent and separate from each other. Often they constitute a unit of time and space together. Here, we call this unit a "game."

A game has a time limit, such as the 60 minutes of a football game; a spatial boundary, such as a football field; there are also game rules determining who wins and who loses. Once people enter the gaming situation, they are absorbed and barely notice information outside the game. Directing one's attention toward defined games has advantages: it sets the scope of information with temporal and spatial boundaries and replaces the complex or hidden rules of the total environment with simpler and clearer rules. This allows limited rational resources to be more effectively used.

Not only games defined intentionally, such as sports or everyday consumption, act as games—most of human activity is in game mode. For example, jobs are generally designed as games, defining the time, place and scope of work, tasks, rewards and punishment, and so on. Even if you are self-employed, you probably act in game mode. For example, a stock trader has to be in the market hours and at the trading floor or another special location to trade financial securities, and to comply with trading rules. Almost all other human activities, such as culture, education, art, tourism, and even politics, are consistent with the mode of game. In China, there is even a saying "The world is a big theatre, and the theatre is a small world." Therefore, it could be said that human is a species adapted to games.

As noted previously, due to the boundaries of game time and space, people tend to invest their limited mental resources only within the confines of the game, without concerning themselves about things outside of the game. However, no single game can include all human activities. Human activity is thus a series of games, as well as structures made up of big and small games. For example, the first year of primary school is a game, and the winning or losing of this game is determined by the end of year exams; the next game is the second year. For a professional football player, a single match is a game, but signing with a football club is a bigger game.

In general, a big game is made up of a group or series of small games. Winning each small game may mean winning the big game. But in some cases, winning small games does not lead to the winning of big games. It may even be the cause of losing the big game. For example, a student who cheats at an exam may win this small game, but if he or she gets a job on the basis of their false scores without acquiring real skills they will probably be dismissed because of poor performance. A company may increase short-run profits by violating a long-term contract after market prices change, but it would damage its reputation as a result. Furthermore, an official who embezzles a sum of money using his power will probably be reported and end up in jail. More broadly speaking, a government might raise taxes in order to increase present revenue, but in the long run, alienate its people and lose political legitimacy.

In reality and history, there are always cheating students, defaulting businessmen, corrupt government officials, and money-grubbing governments; these persons or institutions almost always lose the big game: students will be expelled, businessmen are defeated in market competition, corrupt officials will be reported sooner or later, and the money-grubbing government will eventually collapse. If we follow the logic of economic rationality, why do people end up in doing things that hurt themselves?

As is stated earlier, people are thinking and determining their actions within games. A person faces the smallest unit of the game when he is taking action, because it is the closest and the most intuitive. When a person enters into a small game, he will tend to think only within the framework of this game. His vision is therefore limited and does not include costs and benefits outside the small game. This will cause calculation errors. Although a lot of people can see through the small game and perceive the big game with acquired learning and education (see discussion in the next section), this human instinct still leads a considerable number of persons to make the error of "winning small games and losing the big one."

2.4 Treat Vision as a Variable

Therefore, is there a way to overcome these flaws? Certainly. Vision can be extended by artificial inspiration—say cultivation or education.

Generally speaking, education can make people smarter. IQ is mostly natural and can hardly change by human efforts. What cultivation or education alters is the person's vision. For example, in education we often talk about "consider others point of view," which means expanding spatial vision; we also speak of "having a long-term plan" or "long-term perspective," that is, to extend time vision. As mentioned earlier, people's calculations change if they have a broader and longer-term vision, because they have more information and thereby can determine outcomes more accurately.

Education and cultivation cause people to learn and inherit the cultural traditions of a society, which is a summary of the experience of generations and implies a longer and wider horizon. Two kinds of knowledge are generally included: One is historical fact; another is the refinement of historical facts into cultural principles. Historical fact is intuitive and easy to understand; cultural principles extracted from history what the correct behavior should be looking from a perspective of bigger space—more people's point of view—and longer term. It can correct the shortcoming of considering problems from within the limits of one's own vision and of smaller games.

For example, there is the maxim "Profits must be integrated with righteousness" in the *Book of Changes*; Mo Tzu said "Righteousness can yield rewards." Chen Huanzhang explained in his *Finance of the Great Confucians* that "righteousness" can be read as "profit," or a long-term and overall "benefit" (2009, p. 58). In fact, the Confucian idea of "righteousness" is a calculation of benefit in a longer and broader vision. More generally, in terms of its external expression, Confucianism is not a religion looking beyond individual life, but rather a set of theories of long-term and rationalistic vision. In persuading others, Confucians also often take the long-term view. As in the *Classic of Filial Piety* (《孝经》), they refer to "keeping noble status for a long time," "holding wealth for a long time," "preserving the ancestral temple," and "preserving sacrifices to the ancestors" to convince the princes, bureaucrats, and knights at all levels to comply with ethical principles. These reasons are the benefit of taking a longer and broader vision.

When it comes to "preserving the ancestral temple" and "preserving sacrifices to the ancestors," we should note that these goals go beyond the length of a person's life and extend across generations. This shows that humans share concerns beyond the length of their own lives. For example, they care about children and grandchildren. Taking advantage of that, education or cultivation can inspire people to have temporal vision beyond one generation. The vision of this range is longer than the vision within a person's life, and thus leads to more accurate decision-making. This is because that the pros and cons of some dimensions of human society, such as political and economic systems, can only be judged after hundreds of years or even thousands of years. When the length of the vision is across generations, its width is beyond regions. Because of the longer time frame, a family is likely to disperse over a broad area.

Finally, a person's vision can completely shake off his body and exist only in his imagination. This is the religious and philosophical approach. One's life is limited, but his imagination can transcend time and space. Rationality can develop "eternal" concepts, exploring the root cause of the universe and picturing best situations for all, as well as natural principles that are universally applicable. Philosophical thinking can bring people beyond their vision.

Although logically less rigorous than philosophy, religion gives a transcendent vision mostly through a sensible explanation of the universe. Master Cheng Yen, the founder and leader of Tzu Chi Merit Society in Taiwan, once said that the Chinese character "智"—*zhi*, meaning wisdom—consists of "知"—*zhi*, meaning knowledge—and "日"—*ri*, meaning the sun—which together mean to "illuminate" (Pan Xuan 2009, p. 56). According to Cheng Yen, knowledge alone is not enough; the illumination of Buddha-light is also needed. Pitch-black time and space need to be illuminated so that people can see the time and space that they don't know. This metaphor is actually the basic content of religion. For example, in Christianity, the word "enlighten" means "lightening." This means a person who is not religious walks in the dark. He will gain great insight once he believes in religion.

A study in experimental economics has proved that more educated people are more patient; this means that their temporal vision becomes longer (Burks et al. 2012). This confirms our previous discussion. Here the "education" we refer to not only means more knowledge about nature, but also a culture of getting along with others. Thus, humans create some forms and systems to get rid of smaller vision determined by natural evolution, and obtain more information about human society, so that they can make more correct decisions.

2.5 Vision, Human Instinct, and Human Society

The discussion above tells us that the boundaries of human vision from the evolution are in most cases effective habits to save limited attention. However, this habit is also in conflict with wider and longer society. This may be because, in the long history of evolution, humans are in most times situated in smaller-scale social settings.

A small social scale does not require a larger vision; personal behaviors do not have a long-term effect and thus are unlikely to produce a long vision. In ancient times, the lack of organization of human society made people more dependent on individuals or small organizations. At this time, it was reasonable and effective for individuals to pay more attention to the nearest places.

With the expansion and organizational improvement of the society, economic efficiency has also improved. This also shows that the welfare of a person or a family also depends on a time and space which is larger than those of traditional settings. At this point, the vision of small games that people have got used to cannot effectively cover every aspect that affects people's interests. If they are not interested in bigger games, it is possible that they win small games but lose big ones. If a person only has the vision of the "family," they will make effort only toward maximizing the benefits of their own family, which may contravene the social and political order.

At this time, "there is a stone-age brain in a modern man's skull"—people cannot change instincts that limit attention formed over millions of years (Ye Hang 2007, p. 10). This instinct, as neural economics describes it, plays a role in decision-making by an automatic process. In this theory, human beings are not only rational, but also emotional; when making decisions, they exhibit a controlled process—that is, rational responses—and also automated processes—that is, instinctive reactions. Decision-making is the result of the interaction between controlled processes and automatic processes (Camerer 2005, p. 58). Therefore, to correct the instinctive defect of too-small vision, we need to change the scale of vision through acquired effort such as education or cultivation, the nature of which is to establish advantages of rationality over instinct by strengthening the rational cognition to support longer and wider vision. That is why every mature society or civilization is accompanied by the development of education.

Of course, as far as civilizations have developed, none have attained universal education for all members to the same level. Even if it is possible to do so, not all educated people can expand their visions to the same length and width. In fact, in the early stage of many societies, only some people had the opportunity of becoming educated and accessing the corresponding resources. Those who were educated were mostly socially significant, and generally had high status in politics or the economy.

In fact, it is not necessary that all people receive equal education, or that they form the same length of vision. This is because, while the scope of people's interactions already covers the globe, in most cases, social institutions that established through communication enable people to make the right decisions while relying only on local information. For example, the costs and benefits of a clothing entrepreneur will be influenced by the behaviors of competitors, suppliers, or customers thousands of miles away, but they can make a decision based only on local product and price information. In this case, demand for education that expands vision is not that strong.

However, there is need for a cultural elite with transcendent vision to form a government and other social organizations. Therefore, public intellectuals and people who work in key sectors that organize the society need to have greater vision. Political groups also need people that have broader and longer vision, so educating their children is an important goal for them. When the political caste system was broken, education or cultivation became an important prerequisite for those who are interested in public service. As long as these people have a broader and longer vision, they can assume the work of social organization.

Any individual living in a modern society can rely on local and current information most of the time and for most decisions. But from time to time, each person needs to have transcendent vision. They will encounter a situation in which market prices are unable to communicate the distant information they need to make a decision. For example, consider environmental issues, elections, disputes with others, and compliance with laws.

When a person's education and self-cultivation fail to convince them to form a long and broad vision and follow reason rather than instinct, instincts will make them ignore the bigger game outside the small game, which leads to blunders like that of Yao Jiaxin.

2.6 Conclusion

Many of what we think of lack of sense is often actually caused by insufficient vision. We can also view vision as an element of reason. Limited rationality is a consequence of limited vision. Sometimes it is not wrong calculations, but limited vision, that lead to a lack of access to adequate information.

Because limited vision evolved to save limited psychological resources, human instincts developed over tens of millions of years cannot respond to the requirements of highly organized, large-scale societies that have developed in the last few thousand years. In mature societies, humans have pursued education, cultivation, and religious enlightenment, aiming at expanding and extending people's vision to adapt to the needs of large-scale society.

However, due to limitations of resources and human endowment, education or self-cultivation cannot expand or extend the vision of all people to the same level. Lots of people are still affected by limitations of vision and make wrong decisions. That is one of the key reasons why rational people make mistakes.

References

阿罗，肯尼思，《信息经济学》，北京经济学院出版社，1989; (Translated from: Kenneth J. Arrow, *The Economics of Information*, Basil Blackwell Limited, 1984).

艾克森和基恩，《认知心理学》，华东师范大学出版社，2009; (Eysenck, M. W., & Keane, M. T. (2005). *Cognitive psychology: A student's handbook* (5th ed.). New York, NY, US: Psychology Press).

Burks, Stephen; Carpenter, Jeffrey; Gotte, Lorenz; Rustichini, Aldo; Which measures of time preference best predict outcomes: Evidence from a large-scale field experiment, *Journal of Behavior and Organization*, Volume 84, Issue 1, September 2012.

陈焕章，《孔门理财学》，中国发展出版社，2009; (Chen Huanzhang, *The Economic Principles of Confucius and His School*, China Development Press, 2009.)

卡麦勒等, "神经元经济学: 神经科学如何为经济学塑型?" 载汪丁丁、叶航、罗卫东主编《神经元经济学: 实证与挑战》; 上海世纪出版集团, 2007。(Translated from: Camerer, Colin; Loewenstein, George; Prelec, Drazen; Neuroeconomics: How Neuroscience Can Inform Economics? *Journal of Economic Literature*, Vol. 43, No. 1, March 2005 (pp. 9–64)).

《认知神经科学》, 中国轻工业出版社, 2011; (Translated from: Gazzaniga, Michael; Ivry, Richard; Mangun, George; *Cognitive Neuroscience: The Biology of the Mind*, 3rd Ed., W. W. Norton & Company; (July 11, 2008)).

何怀宏, 《世袭社会及其解体》, 三联书店, 1996; (He Huaihong, the Hereditary Society and its Disintegration, SDX Joint Publishing Company, 1996).

Olson, Mancur, Dictatorship, Democracy, and Development, *The American Political Science Review*, Vol. 87, No. 3 (Sep. 1993), pp. 567–576.

潘宣, 《琉璃同心圆》, 天下远见出版有限公司, 2009. (Pan Xuan, *The Concentric Circle in Colored Glaze*, Commonwealth Publishing Ltd, 2009).

西蒙, 赫伯特, 《管理行为》, 北京经济学院出版社, 1988. (Translated from: Simon, Herbert, *Administrative Behavior*, The Free Press, 1976).

叶航, "科学与实证: 一个基于神经元经济学的综述", 汪丁丁, 叶航, 罗卫东主编《神经元经济学: 实证与挑战》"导读"; 上海世纪出版集团, 2007. (Ye Hang, Science and Empirical Studies: A Literature Review on Neuroeconomics, the Forward of *Neuroeconomics: Empirical Studies and Challenges*, edited by Wang Dingding, Ye Hang, Luo Weidong, Shanghai Century Publishing Ltd, 2007).

Chinese Classical Documents

《周易》(The Book of Changes).

《墨子》(Mo Tsu).

《孝经》(The Book of Filial Piety).

(Translated from The Review of New Political Economy (《新政治经济学评论》), Volume 24, Zhejiang University Press, 2013).

CHAPTER 3

When Public Goods Become Private Goods

Contents

In economics, goods are divided into "public goods" and "private goods" to facilitate discussion; there is no clear boundary. More generally, even the concept of "scarcity"—which defines the boundary of economics—is not absolute. In the real world, there is a continuous spectrum between two seemingly opposing concepts. The discussion of this middle will facilitate our understanding of concepts at both ends and allow us to avoid replacing reality with concept, or tilting at conceptual windmills.

Besides corresponding to government and market, the concepts of "public goods" and "private goods" also have meaning in property right systems: private goods are appropriately owned via personal and exclusive property rights, while public goods are not. There is no clear line, but factors that determine economic goods become public or private goods will inevitably affect the nature of the property rights that can be exercised

Sheng Hong, *Vision and Calculation*,
https://doi.org/10.1007/978-981-15-2898-9_3

over it. We can even imagine that there is a transition zone between the two: when these factors change, goods can change from being public goods to private goods, or vice versa.

Debate on whether public property rights or personal ones are better often fails to examine the conditions under which an item becomes public goods or private goods; it also ignores the existence of many intermediate forms. It is difficult—and unnecessary—to strictly define public property or personal property. When we have a better grasp of the scope and boundaries of public and private goods and the transition zone between them, we will be able to establish personal property in a more proper situation and depend on public power in places which are inappropriate for private property. We can abandon the jargon which often gives rise to ideological emotions, and talk about property right arrangement in a more objective fashion.

3.1 Another Reason for Scarcity: Harvesting Costs

When incorporated into the study of economics, both public goods and private goods are first of all economic goods: that is, they are scarce. Scarcity occurs when demand exceeds supply at zero price. However, scarcity is not set in stone. As the human population grows, and we grab more resources from the natural world, we find that resource scarcity or abundance is also changing. The general direction is that scarcity increases: resources that were not scarce become scarce. For example, before Europeans came into America, wild animals were not scarce; it was the European's fur trade that made the native population begin to divide their hunting areas. Even more striking is the change of water resources. Water was considered an inexhaustible natural gift until industrialization; but after that, people gradually began to feel water scarcity. In the late twentieth century, many rivers have gone dry, forcing people to consider water a scarce resource.

The simplest explanation for this change is that water supply is fixed, while human demand for water continues to grow. Once total demand for water exceeded the total supply, it became scarce (see Fig. 3.1). This is of course an explanation, but not a comprehensive one.

The process of obtaining a natural resource has two requirements: one is the resource itself, another is action taken to obtain that resource. The

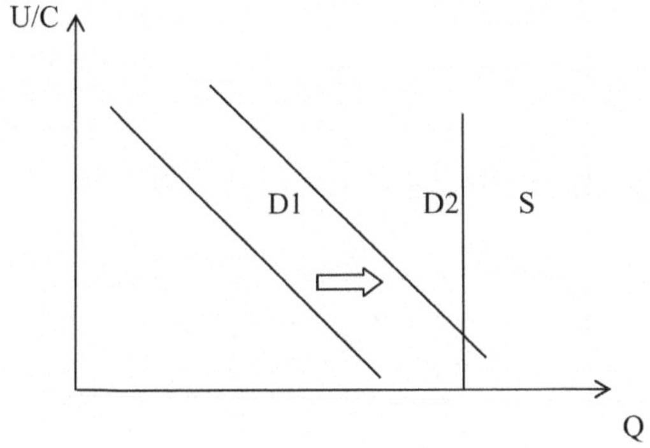

Fig. 3.1 Increased demand for water producing scarcity
Note: Because the supply of water is fixed, the supply curve is a vertical line S; the aggregate growth in total demand is shown as the demand curve moving from D1 to D2. The intersection of D2 and S indicates that at zero price total demand is greater than total supply, producing scarcity

feeling of scarcity thus does not arise simply from the fact that overall human demand is greater than absolute supply of nature. The first part is influenced by pure supply and demand for resources; the second part is influenced by the cost of actions to access resources. Intuitively, if a person wants to obtain a product by buying it, he needs to do two things: One is to buy this product at the store; another is to get the product home. The price of the product corresponds to its scarcity; the freight corresponds to the scarcity of resources expended by transportation. **Thus, even if a resource is scarce, as long as the costs of obtaining this resource are sufficiently high, the resource may not be scarce**. Here, the scarcity of resources can be understood as the price of the resource determined by supply and demand under the condition that harvesting cost is zero (Fig. 3.2).

Suppose there are ten people and five apples, and everyone wants an apple. Apples are apparently scarce. But if these 5 apples are placed 1 kilometer away from the 10 people, it would appear less scarce, for some people might prefer not to eat an apple rather than walk the distance. Strictly speaking, they think that the cost of walking a kilometer is greater than the utility of an apple. The distance here is symbolic: its length represents the cost of access to resources.

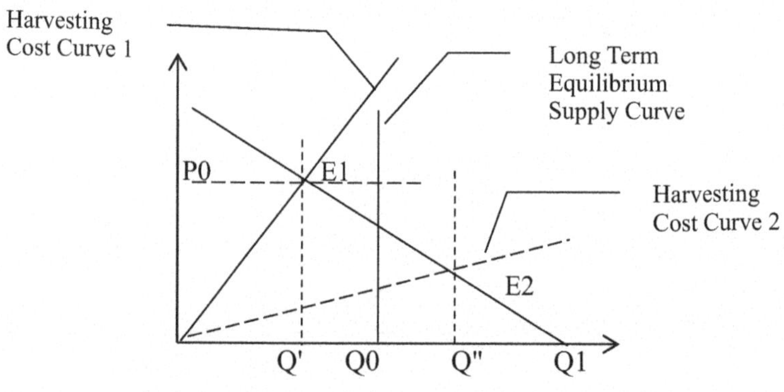

Fig. 3.2 Harvesting cost and scarcity
Note: When the cost of drawing water is high (see harvesting cost curve 1), the water supply amount Q' intersected by curve 1 and the demand curve is below the long-term supply equilibrium of Q0. When the cost of drawing water is lower (see harvesting cost curve 2), the water supply amount Q" intersected by curve 2 and the demand curve is above the long-term equilibrium supply Q0. This illustration can be also used to illustrate the apple example. Q0 represents the supply of 5 apples, and 10 people's demand for apples is 10 (Q1). If these apples are placed one kilometer away, the harvesting cost exists. As harvesting costs differ for different people, their synthesized cost curve is equivalent to harvesting cost curve 1. This curve intersects at E1 with the demand curve; on the right side of E1, people are unwilling to get apples as the harvesting costs are higher than apples' utility. Therefore, the demand for apples is at Q', which is lower than the supply amount Q0, and thus it does not look scarce. When these 10 people have vehicles, the harvesting costs fall (see harvesting cost curves 2), and the equilibrium amount Q" intersected with the demand curve at an amount greater than the supply of five apples (Q0), there is scarcity. P0 is the extent of scarcity of that resource (water or apple)

Such situations are very common in the real world. For example, before reform and opening, Beijing's streets were not as crowded as today, not because there was a small population, but because the cost of using streets—buying a car—at the time was beyond the reach of the average person. From traditional society to the early industrialization, the reason why people don't perceive macroscopic scarcity of water resources may not be that people's total demand for water was not big enough to exhaust the supply (in the predominantly agrarian Qing dynasty, China already had 400 million people, and agriculture is still the biggest water user today), but because of the high cost of access to water resources: dams, reservoirs, and irrigation canals were much harder to build, so scarce engineering resources suppressed demand for water. In locations close to natural bodies of water, people had much easier access to water resources; in these circumstances it was not water that became scare but locations with good access to water. Conversely, compared with China's famous—and famously overcrowded—mountains Huangshan and Mount Emei, Mount Everest is not any less attractive. It is the high costs of climbing up Mount Everest that makes it less overcrowded than the former two. If fishing boats were expensive enough, fish resources would not be depleted even if people love eating seafood.

Therefore, using the extent of scarcity of a resource as a standard and supposing there are harvesting costs, if the harvesting cost is higher than the scarcity of the resources at the equilibrium of supply and demand, the resource can be seen as **an unscarce natural resource**; if the former is lower than the latter, it can be seen as a **scarce public resource**. Or, use the absolute supply of this resource as a standard and suppose there is harvesting cost, when demand at the equilibrium of supply and demand is lower than the absolute supply of the resource, the resource is not a scarce natural resource; when higher, it is a scarce public resource. If the scarcity of the resource is P0, the absolute supply is Q0; harvesting cost at equilibrium is Pg, and corresponding demand is Qg. If the resource is natural and not scare, then $Pg \geq P0$ or $Qg \leq Q0$; if the resource is scarce, then $Pg < P0$ or $Qg > Q0$ and it may be considered a public resource. When a resource is not scarce, it means that there is no tension between resource and human, and no tension and conflicts exist between men, and thus it has no public character, just as no one regards the air as a public resource. Provided they are not scarce, resources are the thing-in-itself and they are "natural"; as long as there is scarcity, there will be conflicts between individuals. To resolve the conflicts is a matter for public life.

In fact, harvesting cost—the key factor that decides whether or not a resource is a "non-scarce natural resource" or "a scarce public resource"—is a variable. With the development of human technology, the cost of access to resources is decreasing. Consider the example of the remote apples. Now assume that those who want to eat have cars and it takes them less than 1 minute to drive 1 km. The reduction of harvesting costs clearly means that more people will try to eat the apples—and 5 apples will seem scarce for 10 people. When the cost of access to a resource falls below a certain point, the scarcity of resources used to obtain the first resource will be lower than the scarcity of the resource itself. At this time, the scarcity of first resource is revealed. "Non-scarce natural resource" will become "scarce public resources." This is common in modern society. With the development of shipbuilding and electronic detection technology, unit fishing costs have been significantly reduced, which contributes to depletion of inshore fish stocks in many countries. With the development of engineering technology, unit costs for water diversion projects have also been reduced. Lots of large water diversion projects supported by the state have been built across rivers and reservoirs, one after another, each with a significant impact on the rivers' water volume. When the unit cost of the water diversion project fell below the scarcity of water resources itself, the macro-scarcity of the water resource appeared. In the absence of public control and effective property rights, there will be overuse of water resources and drying up of rivers.

This phenomenon is clearly a paradox of human society: People pursue technological progress in order to be more efficient and save costs, but the decline of harvesting costs brought by technology makes resources scarce. In the absence of appropriate institutional arrangements, the resource depletion caused by competition for scarce resources is not efficient.[1]

3.2 Labor Costs and the Nature of Property Rights

The word "resources" is used here to refer to natural resources, which means no human behavior is necessary for the resource to exist. "Access to resources" is understood as all human activities imposed on natural resources, which is what we usually call "work." From the perspective of inputs, there is no essential difference between "activities to obtain resources," "activities to use resources," and "activities to process resources"—all require human physical and mental work. There is no essential difference between them if viewed from the perspective of results: all make resources suitable for human consumption. In this sense, fetching an apple from 1 km away, sowing in spring and harvesting in fall, heating ore to get metal, or processing resources physically, chemically, or mechanically to create a product, amounts to the same thing.

Although "resources used to obtain resources" also include resources other than labor, such as capital resource or other natural resources, they

[1] This apparently can be a theme of another work.

can be reduced to natural resources and labor. Therefore, we can take all economic activities as a combination or complementation of natural resources and labor. Rather than the usual practice of listing natural resources and labor in parallel, in this chapter, **it is assumed that it is only through labor that people can obtain natural resources**. This argument is right in most cases with only two exceptions: one is air, the acquiring of which generally does not need any labor. Another is labor which does not involve any natural resources, such as transactional activity, the object of which is another person. If we distinguish trading activities and production activities, "labor" here refers to production activities.

Since natural resources can only be obtained through labor, labor can be considered a specific means to possess resources. The nature of labor itself and its scarcity will affect the means of ownership and legal relationships with natural resources. The biggest difference between natural resources and labor—also a resource—is that labor has a natural owner and natural resources do not. Labor originally belongs to the one who performs it—the laborer. Laborers are individuals, which means individual is the basic unit of cost or utility. Thus, activities obtaining resources through labor have a natural logic, which lays the foundation for a legal form in which resources are possessed by individuals.

However, for different natural resources, or different uses of natural resources, the cost of labor is different. This will also affect the nature of the property rights over natural resources. Let's continue with the story of the apples. This time, the apples grow on trees, which have no owner. If an apple tree has no owner, two people living nearby will compete to pick apples, and will pick the tree clean before any of the fruits ripen. This is a typical "tragedy of the commons" scenario. More strictly speaking, it is the result of scarce public resources in the absence of property rights or common control. However, let's say that our tree grows—one meter, then two, then three, then four, and so on. As the tree grows, it becomes harder for people to pick the apples, until it becomes so troublesome to pick the highest apples that at least one apple is left on the tree. At this point, apples are no longer scarce for the two people, and there will not be a "tragedy of the commons"—both will wait until the apples ripen.

What is the reason? First, as mentioned in the previous section, when the difficulty of obtaining the resource is higher than the scarcity of the resource itself, people do not feel the resource is scarce; there is no "tragedy of the commons" for non-scarce resources. The second reason is that, in most cases, obtaining resources through labor naturally forms the basis of possession. You own the apple you picked. There is no ambiguity. Even in the absence of a formal property rights system, the two sides can live together peacefully. In fact, it could be just such a situation that naturally formed the later property system. Labor, as an important fact that forms the basis of property rights and provides a source of legitimacy, has rarely faced suspicions. The formal legal system is just a confirmation of this natural ownership.

In this way, two kinds of economic objects and their corresponding concepts are divided by their labor costs. If the labor cost is higher than a certain threshold, it is a scarce natural resource and its possession and subsequent property rights will form naturally through labor; if lower, then this natural resource becomes a scarce public resource. In this case, the labor involved obtaining the resource will be overcrowded, resulting in the loss of efficiency for the whole society, and thus it does not naturally form lawful possession of the resource, nor legal property rights. This threshold scarcity of labor equals the scarcity of the resource, or to put it in another way, the threshold occurs where the marginal cost of labor is equal to the marginal utility of this resource. This also shows that the right to possess natural resources not only comes from labor; **in addition, the fact that the cost of labor itself is large enough to make a scarce resource not worth exhausting, preventing inefficient "tragedy of the common"-type outcomes, is an important condition for the legitimacy of this right**. Conversely, if the cost of labor is low compared to the scarcity of the natural resource, the natural resource appears scarce, and labor itself does not constitute the basis for the legitimacy of the possession of the resource.[2] For example, gold mining is complicated labor, but

[2] In the real world, things are not that simple. People often use other natural resources in order to obtain some natural resource. For example, people first occupied waterside land so as to access to water resources. We can still use the above methods to analyze whether the land is "a non-scarce natural resource" or "a scarce public resource," as well as whether it is proper for establishing personal property. But more importantly, we can use the method of "which is scarcer" for making judgment. More generally, suppose there is a natural resource A, if the scarcity of the resource to obtain resource A is higher than the scarcity of the resource A itself, the natural resource A generally belongs to the owner of the resource which can obtain resource A, no matter this obtaining resource is labor or other natural resources. Therefore, in traditional societies, water rights belong to investors of the water diversion project, or as the cum-rights of riparian land rights (i.e., riparian rights). Certainly, this tends to arouse people's illusions—they think the constraint on resource supply caused by the scarcity of resources to obtain that resource is caused by the scarcity of the resource itself. They mistakenly take the rights to resources obtaining the resource for the rights to own the resource itself, just as they call the right to water from a headwater channel "water right."

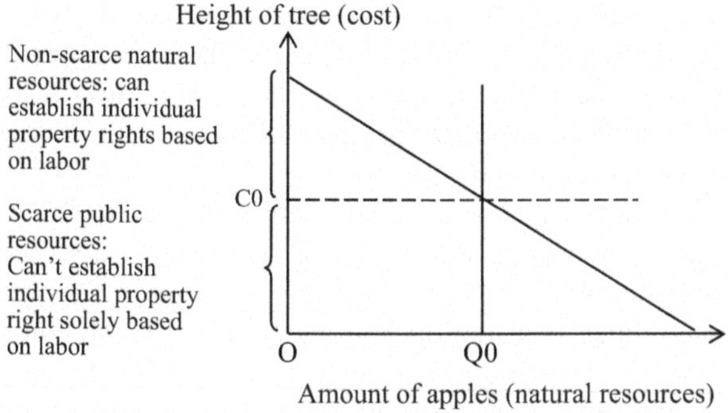

Fig. 3.3 Nature of scarcity and property rights based on labor
Note: For simplicity, assume that the marginal cost of picking apples is constant, and thus the cost curve is a horizontal line. Q0 is the quantity of apples on the tree, or the amount of natural resources. When C0 is the marginal cost of climbing for a person, the cost of picking Q0 apples cost C0 is just equal to the marginal utility of apply Q0 for him. When marginal cost of picking apples is less than C0, the marginal cost of an apple Q0 is lower than the marginal utility from that apple. Therefore, people will pick more apples. However, at this time all apples will be picked, so apples are scarce. If individual property rights to apples are based solely on labor, apples will be overexploited. When the marginal cost of picking apples is higher than C0, the marginal cost of an apple Q0 is already higher than the marginal utility; therefore, people will not pick more than Q0 apples, so it does not appear scarce. At this point, individual property rights can be established based on labor

the scarcity of labor of gold mining is generally lower than the scarcity of gold itself. Therefore, the gold mine is a scarce public resource; free access to the gold mine will make it overcrowded (Fig. 3.3).

When natural resources are not scarce, obtaining resources based on labor can make people live together peacefully and achieve efficient results, and establishing property rights based on the rule of labor is natural. By "natural," we mean that there are no conflicts between people and the cost is very low, and that there is no need for the intervention of a government. Government intervention occurs only because, after the

But this "water right" has nothing to do with the scarcity of water resources itself. Similarly, with the decline in the cost of water engineering, water resources become scarce, at this point, the rule of "he who invests owns water rights," or "he who occupies the river bank owns water rights" is no longer efficient.

formation of property rights, collisions may occur based on the property rights, such as theft, robbery, or fraud. Conversely, if the government does not acknowledge the labor principle in the case of non-scarce natural resources and establishes another property rights system, its costs will be greater than the system based on labor.

But for scarce public resources, labor cannot be used as the sole basis of establishing property rights. What kind of rule is more appropriate? One way is through negotiation. For at least two reasons, this method is not universally used. First, negotiation frequently fails to reach consensus, and in the absence of authority, people may choose other means, including violence, to obtain resources. Second, when the amount of people competing for scarce public resources is considerable, negotiation becomes even more unlikely. In some cases, people may use the same resource without meeting, such as those living upstream and downstream on the same river. In fact, in the absence of a superior authority, negotiation has an important prerequisite: the balance of the parties. In the absence of this prerequisite and in an anarchic world, people tend to use violence. We see this very often in history: tribes or states start wars to fight for land or other resources. Oil, the key strategic resource of the world today, is also an important cause of war. It is for the above reasons that, in the case of scarce public resources, government is involved in establishing property rights. Firstly, when parties are unable to reach an agreement, the government can give an at least ostensibly impartial decision, so that more people are willing to solve the issue through negotiations. Secondly, when the number of competitors for resources is large, government can reduce the cost of negotiations as an initiator, organizer, or core negotiator, to make sure negotiations can actually be achieved. Thirdly, as organization that wields legitimate violence, government can replace illegal violence because of its impartiality and its improvement of social efficiency.

3.3 Forms of Natural Resources, the Human Senses, and Exclusiveness Costs

Shepherding on public land is the *locus classicus* of the tragedy of the commons. However, if the sheep did not immediately consume the grass they live on, the tragedy might not happen. There are times when people "obtain" natural resources and do not immediately consume them; instead they "hold" them for a period. If natural resources are used as assets and people look forward to their production and proliferation, we must hold it permanently. There is a cost for this "holding." Holding costs and harvesting cost are different: the former in the broad sense is a kind of transaction cost, arising from a relationship between people; while the latter reflects the relationship between mankind and nature (e.g., how high is the tree we need to climb). We want to "hold" resources to prevent other people from taking them.[3] The "exclusiveness" we often speak of in economics is related to holding costs. Clearly, the lower the holding cost, the stronger the exclusiveness. Therefore, holding cost can also be called an "exclusiveness cost."

There are several factors that affect exclusiveness costs. First is the holding time. Other conditions being equal, the longer you hold something, the more it costs. Back to the shepherding on public land story: The sheep eat grass directly from the ground, and there is almost no time between "obtaining" and "consuming." So the holding time is almost zero, and the cost is very low. If the sheep snap off the grass, put it on the ground until it dries to a certain level, and then eat it, the holding cost will increase. To prevent the other sheep from eating their grass from its place on the ground, the sheep or the shepherd will have to watch the grass. This will significantly reduce the amount of grass the sheep eat. The increase of exclusiveness costs is comparable to the increase of harvesting costs; at some point the sheep, or the shepherd, think that the marginal cost of holding the grass is higher than the marginal utility of the grass itself, and thus reduce the amount of grazing. Considering that sheep are ruminants is very interesting. To put some resource into one's stomach establishes ownership of that resource, no matter what the legal provisions are. But sheep eat not because they are hungry, nor do they digest immediately after eating. Instead, they store food in their stomach, and enjoy them at an appropriate time. This biological structure clearly lowers holding costs, which enables the sheep to enjoy more grass. Animals can use their stomach to store food not only for themselves. Most birds store food and spit it out for their children when they get home.

From another perspective, to put the natural resource into the stomach is apparently the most secure way of holding resources naturally. It also reveals two other factors affecting the exclusiveness cost: the nature of

[3] Here, the harvesting cost does not include the cost of obtaining resources from others, thus the holding cost does not include the cost of preventing others. For simplicity, we remove the factor of pillage in this article.

holding objects and subjects. The nature of the object is the main body for the natural resource itself. Broadly, natural resources not only take the form of visible solids, they may also be flowing liquid, fizzy gas, invisible waves, abstract text or numbers, or even information. These different physical and non-physical forms have a significant impact on harvesting costs and exclusiveness costs.

Visible solids have definite borders, which makes it easy to identify and define them, and easy to control them. This makes the exclusiveness cost low. In contrast, liquid flows have no clear boundary, and thus they are more difficult to define and control. The usual way is to put the liquid into a solid container, such as a beverage bottle, box, or water storage reservoir. Containers also make liquids available for use. From an institutional perspective, a container is the holding mechanism of the resource. Manufacturing containers is a kind of activity or labor that facilitates holding resources and the liquid in the container is the resource itself. Moving along the spectrum, it is impossible to define and control borders for air. Although, in general, air is not scarce, it can still be used by manufacturing containers, such as balloons or other inflatable balls. The example of air shows that, even if a resource is not scarce, if there are exclusiveness costs, the end use of the resource can still be scarce. For invisible waves (such as electromagnetic spectrum) and digital resources (such as a phone number) that do not even have a physical form, the problem is even more serious, because there are no containers for waves or numbers.

Finally, there is intellectual property. Using the dichotomy of "natural resources" and "labor," natural resources are infinite for knowledge. They are the universal things and social phenomena that people can perceive. But the labor that processes this natural resource is costly, because the skills required are extremely scarce. The original owner of knowledge—the product of labor—is very clear, that is, the "laborer" themselves. However, as a kind of natural resource, information lacks boundaries, and the knowledge that results from processing information is still a form of information. Although the processor of the information has exclusive control of knowledge at the moment of its conception, if he or she wants to benefit from this very valuable product, the knowledge must be spoken out or written. Once that happens, its border is very hard to defend, because the cost of replicating knowledge products is very low.

Another factor affecting exclusiveness costs is the manner of consumption. Resources are largely consumed by human sense organs. Different sense organs consume different resources and different amounts of resources, and thus have different exclusiveness costs. For those that can directly consume resources, such as consumption of food through the mouth and solid items through the hand, exclusiveness costs are low. Other sense organs such as eyes and ears enjoy natural resources mainly through watching and hearing. This does not preclude other people from watching and hearing, and one person's watching or hearing does not harm other persons' watching and hearing. People can obtain sights and sounds at a low cost, but they cannot hold sights and sounds. In other words, the exclusiveness cost is very high.

Like harvesting costs, when the exclusiveness cost is low, it will produce a tragedy of the commons, just like the sheep grazing. But when the exclusiveness cost is high enough—that is, when the marginal cost is greater than or equal to the marginal utility of the resource—the natural resource will appear to be less scarce. At this time, if the harvesting cost is lower than the scarcity of the resource, effective individual property rights cannot form naturally. This is because the exclusiveness cost is too high. Although individuals may be able to obtain a resource at a low cost, it is hard for them to hold a resource in a natural state without others taking it away. A typical example is radio spectrum. In "The Federal Communications Commission," Professor Ronald Coase describes the scene of the crowding of the radio broadcasting spectrum, which is caused by this reason (1994). In comparison, investing in a radio station, that is, obtaining radio resources, has a low cost, and holding this resource and not allowing infringement costs more, therefore radio stations infringe each other's frequencies. In the long term, if resources obtained are always infringed, people will have no incentive to obtain those resources. This is one of the reasons why, before the development of laws to protect intellectual property, people had little incentive to develop technology.

Most natural resources have relatively high exclusiveness costs. Today, personal property is universal because people create a lot of technologies and systems that reduce exclusiveness costs. Clearly, houses and yards expand the scope of holding, as walls (fences and barbed wire), doors, and locks are all related technologies. Without these technologies, the scope of personal property would be very limited. We call this **property rights-related technology**. These technologies can even reduce the exclusiveness costs of sights and sounds. Theatres, stages, or cinema (a type of fence) "hold" sights and sounds. Even the natural landscape can be held through fences and generate exclusive "holding." If anyone wants to visit the famous mountain Tai, he must buy tickets at the red entrance door or the entrance in the Out Sky Village. The lock is associated with the door, except that it works when no one watches the door, thus further reducing exclusiveness costs. Today, walls, doors, and locks can be understood in broad terms. Locks can lock not only car doors, but also the engine or the steering wheel to keep others away. Computer or e-mail passwords are also locks—with an electronic key—which can protect electronic documents (particularly finance-related files, such as e-banking account) from being violated at a lower cost.

When the resource has a large amount and a large body, and geographically scattered in different places, it is beyond a person's ability to hold it, despite his use of the property-related technology. For example, one cannot actually "hold" a piece of land. Human beings as a whole of society can reduce exclusiveness costs through the creation of institutions, to make the individual property rights possible. Therefore, in a society, there might be "property rights" before the existence of the government, but the scope of it will be very small. Only when there is a government enacting laws to protect individual property rights and implementing it, the individual property rights become universal, and the rich also appear. When a person's property rights (i.e., the resources he holds in the natural state) were violated, he could request protection to the government in order to retrieve the holding of the resource. We call this **property rights institutions**. At this point, as Commons pointed out, the institutions enlarge the abilities of individuals (1983).

Of course, these technological and institutional efforts to reduce the exclusiveness cost have a limit, that is, it may not be lower than C0 in Fig. 3.4, the scarcity of the resource or the marginal utility at equilibrium. The property rights system formed in this context is called "general property rights system." It was not specially created by the government. If the exclusiveness cost is lower than C0, we know that it is a scarce public resource, and a better choice is a special creation of property rights system or public control specially created by the government. We will discuss this issue in detail in the next section.

3.4 Tragedy of the Commons, Resource Degradation, and Corresponding Institutional Arrangements

When we talk about scarcity, we generally mean that total demand at zero price exceeds total supply from nature. The total supply generally refers to the absolute physical quantity of a natural resource. A resource comes to

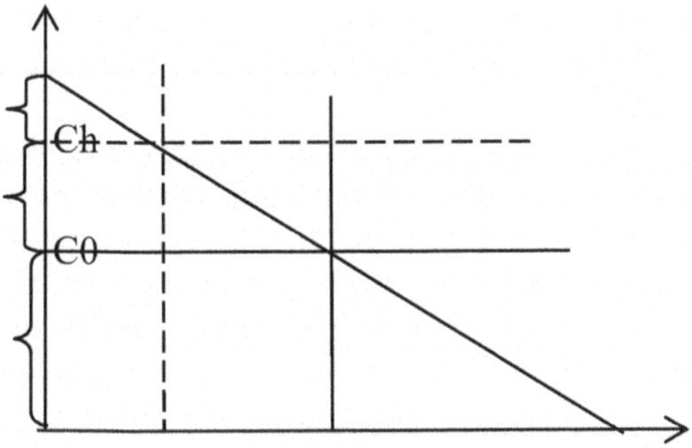

Fig. 3.4 Nature of scarcity and property rights
Note: assume the harvesting cost is 0. The exclusiveness cost curve is a horizontal line because the holding marginal cost remains the same. At C0, the tipping point, the exclusiveness cost is equal to the scarcity (or marginal utility) of the resource. When exclusiveness cost is lower than C0, the nature of the resource is a scarce public resource; when higher than C0, there are two situations: as long as the harvesting cost is lower than C0 (in this figure we assume it is 0), (1) the portion of resources that is lower than the exclusiveness cost Ch will become scarce in the short term, but in the long run, it will be characterized as a non-scarce natural resource, because people cannot effectively hold it and quit, and thus it cannot naturally form individual property rights.(2) The portion of resources that is higher than the exclusiveness cost Ch is a non-scarce natural resource and can form individual property rights naturally. If the harvesting cost is positive and lower than C0, these "exclusiveness cost" should all be reworded as "harvesting costs plus exclusiveness costs"

seem scarce only if we come across this border. For example, when people pluck all fruits on the trees and they still need fruit, they feel scarcity. Many natural resources are non-renewable, or the regeneration time is very long, such as coal and oil, which will disappear when exhausted. For these types of resources, people anticipate scarcity instead of feeling it after using them up, calculating expected mining years on the condition of known reserves and annual production volume. In general, the expected length of time with which people are concerned is not longer than one person's lifetime, for example, 50 years. In any case, this expectation is based on the absolute quantity of the resource. For many renewable resources, the limitation of absolute quantity is even clearer, such as many wild plants: if bamboo is cut up, it will grow out in the next year. Because the labor that processes bamboo products is more expensive than the scarcity of bamboo, bamboo is not used up. Some wild plants, such as some kinds of Chinese herbal medicines, may be exhausted in one year, and grow out normally in the next.

Even if it doesn't affect regeneration capacity, the absolute physical quantity of a resource is a natural constraint which stops the users. Even though there may be congestion in the absence of individual property rights, the cost of congestion is borne solely by the user, without harming the resources themselves. James Buchanan argued in his "Private Ownership and Common Usage" that, in a situation in which there are more than one owner that have multiple, parallel roads, if the road owners can coordinate monopoly pricing, it will achieve an optimal automobile volume; in the case of perfect competition, road owners cannot affect the price, and the competition will bring the price down to the level of zero profit, resulting in congestion. However, congestion costs—that is, waiting time—are borne solely by users (drivers), and road owners suffer no losses (Buchanan 1989). The tragedy of the commons in the story of sheep grazing is similar. The large quantity of sheep will just lead to each sheep eating less grass, and has little impact on the natural resource. According to Buchanan's discussion, as long as there are individual property rights and monopoly pricing, there will be optimal allocation of resources, inhibiting congestion. Individual property rights plus competitive pricing is a second-best choice, because from the perspective of users, congestion (time) and monopoly prices are substitutional, and congestion does not hurt the regeneration ability of the resource. In fact, as long as the congestion cost is higher than the competitive price, the use of resources without individual property rights (i.e., at zero price) and individual property rights plus competitive pricing are similar, because at this point what decides the amount of use is not price but congestion costs (see Fig. 3.5). People will stop spending at the point when the marginal cost of congestion equals the marginal utility of driving. It is even difficult for us to determine if congestion is worse than non-congestion from the perspective of society. Although the passing time for each car increases, the total amount of cars that pass also increases.

However, if the resource is not a highway or something else whose regeneration cannot be damaged, we cannot draw the same conclusions. For example, pulling up some herbs by their roots means the plant will not grow back. This means that the absolute physical quantity of renewable resource will shrink as people harvest the resource. A more typical example of a renewable resource is animals. With improved hunting skills (i.e., per

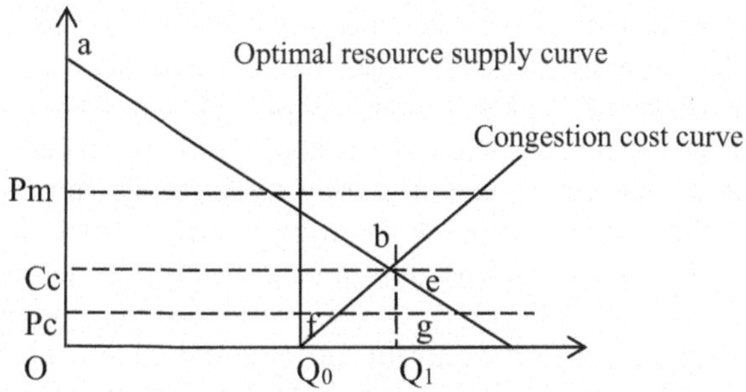

Fig. 3.5 Monopoly pricing and competitive pricing plus congestion cost
Note: When there are individual property rights, the monopoly price (Pm) of owners will curb the overuse of resources while keeping his best interest. But the competitive pricing (Pc) can cause congestion. From the congestion cost curve, the demand at equilibrium is Q1, the total price consumers pay is the competitive price plus congestion cost (Cc). This also means that, even if there is no individual property rights, congestion costs can lead people to automatically adjust their consumption of resources. If the excessive use of resources does not harm the regeneration, the congestion cost is borne solely by consumers, and the situation of non-congestion is not any better than congestion. In the diagram, the area of the sum of producer surplus and consumer surplus at congestion a-Pc-g-e is larger than that of a-Pc-f-b at monopoly pricing

unit cost of hunting is down), the number of animals captured grows and approaches to the absolute physical quantity of the animal. But the regeneration capacity of animals has been injured. For example, when hunting makes the number of adult animals below a certain level, it will reduce the breeding of this animal group, which will lead to its gradual shrinking and eventual extinction if its natural growth rate (birth rate minus death rate) is less than zero; if young animals are still killed after the adult animals are exhausted, there will be no new animals, and the resource will all but disappear. In short, hunting animals beyond a certain threshold will damage the regeneration capacity of the animal group. This threshold is the equilibrium amount that ensures the stable supply of the animal. Therefore, the real effective supply is not the absolute physical quantity of the fauna, but the absolute physical quantity minus the threshold amount ensuring stable supply of the animal population. The so-called scarcity for such resources is such kind of scenario that the real effective supply is less than demand at zero prices. We can call this tipping point a "long-term equilibrium of supply."

In this case, a system with no individual property rights (as we've defined it, the right to possess or use the resource based on labor), or individual property rights plus competitive price, will not allow the market to generate prices that curb excessive demand. Here the so-called excess of demand is that demand exceeds the long-term equilibrium supply. The long-term decline of the resource resulting from excessive demand and excessive use of resources will become apparent only over a long period of time (such as in 10 or 20 years), to which the current market does not react. People only react to the current supply and demand. Therefore, the price will be pushed as lower than would be appropriate considering the long-term costs. This will not only cause congestion, but also will hurt the regeneration capacity and reduce the long-term supply of the resources. Institutional arrangements such as individual property rights plus monopoly pricing or public authority intervention will not create such abuses, and thus are a better choice.

Compared with public authorities, individual property rights clearly have advantages of motivation. For resources that may be divided, exclusive property rights can even push people to protect the regeneration capacity of the resource, whether there is monopoly pricing or competitive pricing. Historically, exclusive property rights are the most common approach to solve problems faced by hunting communities. Exclusiveness costs are greatly reduced after the domestication of wild plants and animals. People can use fences, walls, or specialized guardians to defend their crops and livestock. This is what Douglas North called "exclusive common property rights." At this point, if there are markets for crops and livestock transactions, traders will pay attention to renewable capacity. Any rural person knows that hens that can lay eggs are more valuable, as long as a person can own the hens exclusively. This property rights system can evolve from tribal common property to strictly personal property. Livestock slaughter systems overseen by a public authority have existed, and achieved some success, such as in the Inca Empire, but it appears that they paid high prices, such as government corruption, or efficiency losses from the non-tradable nature of the livestock (Prescott 1996, pp. 59–60). These solutions never become mainstream, beyond a certain scope, suggesting that the individual property rights plus monopoly pricing system is better than the intervention public authority.

The so-called certain scope refers to low exclusiveness costs. When the exclusiveness costs of a renewable resource are high enough that individuals or local forces are insufficient to "hold" it, the public authority intervention system has advantages. A typical example is high seas fish stocks. Overfishing can hurt the regeneration capacity of fish and even result in depletion of fish stocks, while in the high seas it is difficult to hold fish stocks exclusively. In this case, the property rights system does not work. For water resources, overuse interacts with the regeneration capacity of other resources. Through the cycle of rivers flowing into the sea, sea water evaporating, vapor drifting, rainfall, then flowing into the sea again, the water resources regenerate as a system. However, if river water is depleted, it results in vegetation degradation and desertification, eventually reducing the regeneration of water resources.[4] In other words, the threshold amount that ensures normal regeneration or long-term stable supply of water resources is less than the volume of regeneration. However, no individual or group has the capacity to "hold" water resource systems with regeneration mechanisms. As a result, we cannot establish "general property rights" and have to resort to public authority.

Public authority intervention also has several forms, including: (1) controlling channels to obtain resources, or limiting access; (2) creating special property right systems through auction; and (3) establishing total administrative control of the resource. Despite the differences, there are common characteristics in these forms, namely, **the increase of harvesting costs**. The public goods provided by the government are designed to keep resource usage within the appropriate range, or more strictly speaking, within the scope of long-term equilibrium supply. The usage of the resource will not cause degradation of the resource within this scope.

A concrete example of the first form is the control of marine fishing. The methods of control are generally limiting the fishing period, controlling the use of fishing gear, and so on. Fishing bans for certain periods increase the idle time for fishermen and fishing vessels, which naturally increase costs; limits on nets decrease the efficiency of fishing (Clark 1984, p. 40). Despite the reduced economic efficiency, it provides a necessary restraint on overfishing of marine fish (see the following Fig. 3.6).

The second form, which is most widely used, is franchise model that limits the entering quantity—a public authority estimates an appropriate total amount of resource supply. For city traffic, it is a number of cars that do not cause congestion; for fish stocks or water resources, it is the long-term equilibrium of supply. The government sells franchises for the use or

[4] As for this judgment, the author asked Professor Wang Hao, a water resource expert, and received positive reply.

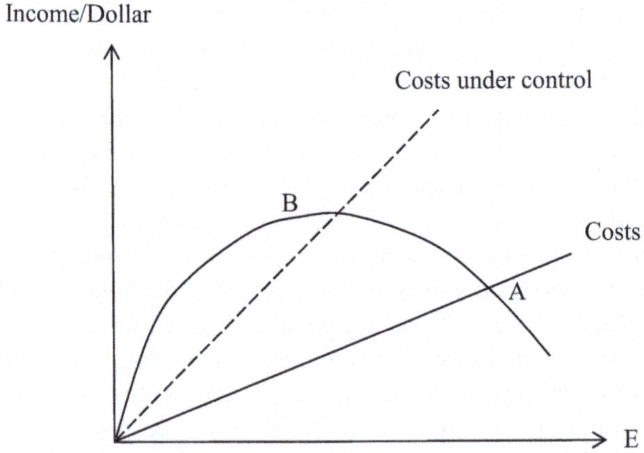

Fig. 3.6 Control of fisheries through increasing costs of fishing
Note: E is the fishing effort; the bending curve is the amount of fishing and the resulting income which varies with the growth of the fishing effort (assuming the price is not changed). Overfishing will reduce fish stocks, thereby reducing catches. The increase of costs because of the regulation makes the intersection of the cost curve and income curve transfer from A to B, the latter being the equilibrium of maintaining the fish scale invariant. This figure is quoted from C.W. Clark, 1984, p. 40, Figure 2.6

development of these supplies through public auction. Under normal circumstances, the franchise price through auctions will make the amount of use or development of franchises equal to the supply quantity limited by the public authority. From a micro view, paying franchises increases costs, which in turn constrains demands on resources; from a macro point of view, such practices stop the overuse of resources and avoid artificially reducing the economic efficiency to increase the cost of obtaining resources. In addition, the income from franchise sales can also be used to provide other public goods. Such franchises, because it prevents the emergence of the tragedy of the commons and resource degradation, according to Sect. 3.2, share the legitimacy of individual property rights (Fig. 3.7).

The third form is that public authority limits the total use of resources through administrative means and assigns the use of resources to individuals and groups. Because of government restrictions, the cost of obtaining resources increases, but the distribution of costs is not fair. Increased costs consist of two parts: the first is the operating costs of government

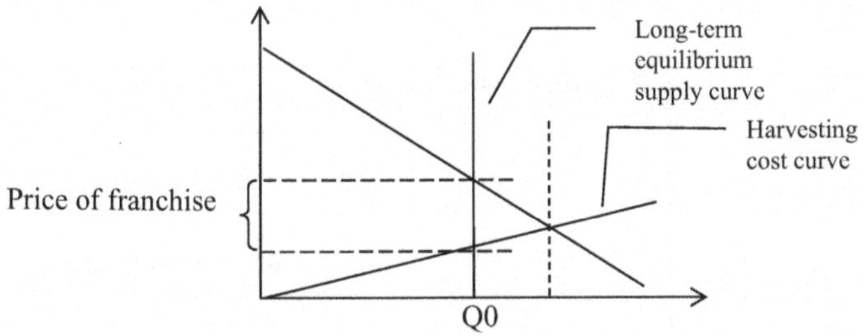

Fig. 3.7 Price of franchise

regulatory bodies. This cost is not shared by the users equally, because this method does not charge the users as directly as auctioning franchises. These costs of the government are paid by taxes, which are theoretically shared by all taxpayers, while taxpayers have different requirements for evaluations of the resource. The other cost is the extent of difficulty for users to obtain resources with the existence of government regulatory bodies. However, without market intervention, administrative allocation of resources can be unfair and leads to corruption such as bribes. Therefore, the difficulties of obtaining resources faced by users are different. As a result, this form is not a good choice, while the first two can be adopted.

Finally, public property rights are meaningful only when the government cannot establish individual property rights; for example, when exclusiveness costs are still too high even with the government's efforts. If air is scarce, the government cannot separate the air that belongs to one person from the air that belongs to another even if it auctioned the right to sue air. Broadly speaking, public goods refer not only to measures of exerting limits, but also to measures of increasing supply, such as increasing green area in order to improve the environment. At this point, since the personal harvesting cost is very low, and the exclusiveness cost is very high, the government could not increase the personal harvesting cost or reduce the personal exclusiveness cost of the fresh air or the beautiful landscape. The only approach is to provide public goods to all. The public goods at this point may be called "pure" public goods. Nevertheless, in theory, this system is not efficient. Although, by definition, all people enjoy equal public goods, their utility evaluation is different. In some cases, they even have negative utility evaluation but still have to pay the same price (assuming the tax is the same to all people for single public goods). This form can be

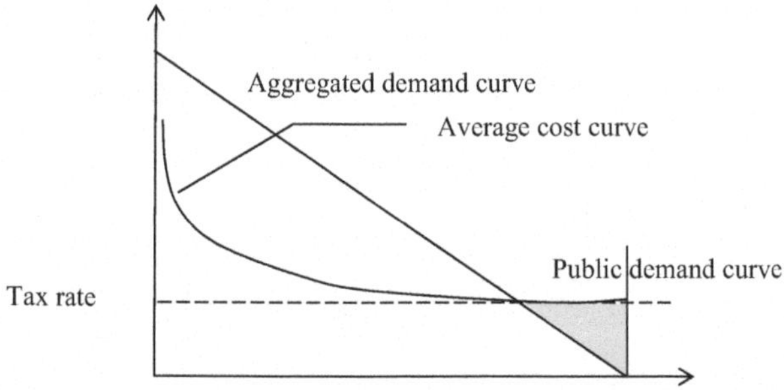

Fig. 3.8 Demand and supply of public goods
Note: The tax rate equals to the intersection point of the cost curve and the demand curve; but the equilibrium supply is not determined by this point as the public goods are not exclusive. The equilibrium supply is at least equal to the demand at zero cost, that is, when the public demand curve is a vertical line. Obviously, the shadow part is the loss of the society, although it is perhaps inevitable

a considered a good choice only in extreme cases, namely when (1) excessive use may lead to resource degradation; (2) the personal harvesting cost is very low while the exclusiveness cost is very high (Fig. 3.8).

3.5 Conclusion

Departing from the long-running economists' argument about the pros and cons of individual property rights and public property rights, this discussion endeavors to discover what property rights system works better under different situations. Factors that make situations different include harvesting costs, exclusiveness costs, and whether the resource can be degraded and depleted due to human behavior. The different property rights systems considered are general individual property rights (at monopoly pricing and competitive pricing), special individual property rights, and public property right. This analysis moves the property rights system further away from ideological debates and places it on a technical footing.

The conclusion of this chapter is as follows:

1. If harvesting costs are higher than the scarcity of the resource, the resource is characterized as a non-scarce natural resource; if lower, the resource is characterized as a scarce public resource. In the for-

mer case, people can establish a general personal property system according to labor without possessing the resource personally; in the latter case, labor has no legal basis for possessing the resource. A special property rights system created by the government or public property rights system may be established depending on other factors.

2. If the harvesting costs plus exclusiveness costs are lower than the scarcity of the resource, this resource can still be a scarce public resource in nature. If the scarcity of the resource is higher than the harvesting costs but lower than the harvesting costs plus exclusiveness costs, this resource is a scarce public resource in the short term, and a non-scarcity natural resource in the long term, without being able to support general individual property rights based on labor. Only when the perceived value of the user is higher than the harvesting costs plus the exclusiveness costs can general individual property rights be established based on labor.
3. When the exclusiveness cost is so high that it exceeds the highest evaluation from the demand side, it is also inefficient to establish individual property rights. Eventually, improvements in technology and systems will likely reduce the exclusiveness costs and broaden the individual property rights.
4. For scarce public resources, if the exclusiveness costs are not too high, general individual property rights plus monopoly pricing are the most efficient system. If the supply of the resource is the absolute amount of the resource, and activities to obtain and use resources do not affect the regeneration capacity, then the congestion costs resulting from excessive acquisition and use of resources are solely borne by users, and general individual property rights plus competitive pricing, as well as no individual property rights, are both second-optimal choices.
5. But when activities to obtain and use resources affect their regeneration capacity, general individual property rights plus competitive pricing and no individual property rights are both inefficient. If the exclusiveness cost is low, it is best to set up the special individual property rights by public authorities through auctioning concessions on the premise of limited supply.
6. Furthermore, public property rights are wise to adopt if the exclusiveness cost is so high that even the public authority is unable to effectively reduce the cost, that is, providing public goods to all members of society through taxation.

It should be emphasized that this chapter proposes an idea rather than provides a detailed analysis of different forms of property rights; it presents an outline for study rather than drawing final conclusions. While this approach has academic interest, it may have an impact on property rights system of the real world.

References

Buchanan, James, "Private Ownership and Common Usage", *Explorations into Constitutional Economics*, Texas A & M University Press, 1989.

罗纳德·科斯, "联邦通讯委员会", 《论生产的制度结构》, 上海三联书店, 1994. (Ronald Harry Coase, "The Federal Communications Commission", Journal of Law and Economics, *the Institutional Structure of Production*, SDX Publishing Company, 1994).

康芒斯, 《制度经济学》, 商务印书馆, 1983. (Translated from: John R. Commons, *Institutional Economics: Its Place in Political Economy*, The MacMillan Company, New York, 1934).

克拉克, 《数学生物经济学》, 农业出版社, 1984. (C.W. Clark, *Mathematical Bio-economics*, Wiley-Interscience; 2 edition (March 15, 1990)).

(Translated from The Review of New Political Economy (《新政治经济学评论》), Volume 1, Zhejiang University Press, 2005).

CHAPTER 4

On the Homogeny, Separation, and Substitution of Rent and Tax

Contents

Steven N.S. Cheung proposes in his article "The Chinese Economic System" that competition among local governments is mainly reflected in the competition on land prices. Such competition can drive land prices to near or even below zero, for local governments can be compensated through collecting taxes (2008, pp. 126–138). This theory in fact views taxes and rents as mutually substitutive and reveals the close linkage between the two. Historically speaking, tax and rent share the same origins.

4.1 The Common Origins of Tax and Rent

The well-field (井田) system is clearly recorded in Chinese ancient literature. It divides a square area of land into nine equal parts, with a communal field in the center, the revenue from which was to be handed to the king. Thus, in early times, the revenues from public land were taken as tax.

Sheng Hong, *Vision and Calculation*,
https://doi.org/10.1007/978-981-15-2898-9_4

This is because in ancient times, land was sufficient for the small population. As long as there were laborers, there would be land for them to claim and cultivate. At that time land could be viewed as an endless resource. Land scarcity, the basis of land rents, did not exist.

However, it takes more than laborers working in the fields to establish an agriculture with predictable and stable income. The growing of crops requires a relatively long period of time and they cannot be harvested right after sowing. If people cannot exclude others from their own fields, then the fruits of their labor may be stolen by intruders. In Douglas North's model of the transition from hunting and gathering to agriculture and animal husbandry, he argues that a crucial factor is the emergence of exclusive communal property rights (1991, pp. 93–98). A tribe had to prevent any outsiders from gathering food in their own fields.

However, these exclusive communal property rights require enforcement. Especially in harvest seasons, people were sent to safeguard the fields from the intrusion of other tribes, a task which frequently requires violence. Societies at that stage began to need organized violence—government. Governments are an institution to provide public goods, particularly those with related to violence. Public goods cannot be provided or traded in the market, so government is there to make up the market's failure to meet demand for public goods. The core basis of government is taxation, which compulsorily requires resources from a population to pay the costs of public goods.

Therefore, the income from the communal fields was indeed taxation. It was because the taxation that the yields on the well-fields had properties of exclusive communal rights and could provide stable economic values to the farmers. The "economic value" refers not only to the agricultural products harvested but also to the stable expectation that these products would not be taken away by others. So, agriculture could develop only after the advent of exclusive communal property rights. Crops were in fact the plants that certainly belonged to their cultivators, and the well-fields were lands on which the products grown would not be infringed. The protection of property rights provided by the government was part of the crops' value. In other words, exclusive communal property rights created part of the value of crops (Fig. 4.1).

In other words, it was the well-field system that created a relatively mature and stable form of government in China. Before the well-field system, governments relied mainly on collecting taxes from hunted or gathered goods, initially in the form of tributes to the gods, which then developed into tributes from local princes to the central government called *ruji* (入积)

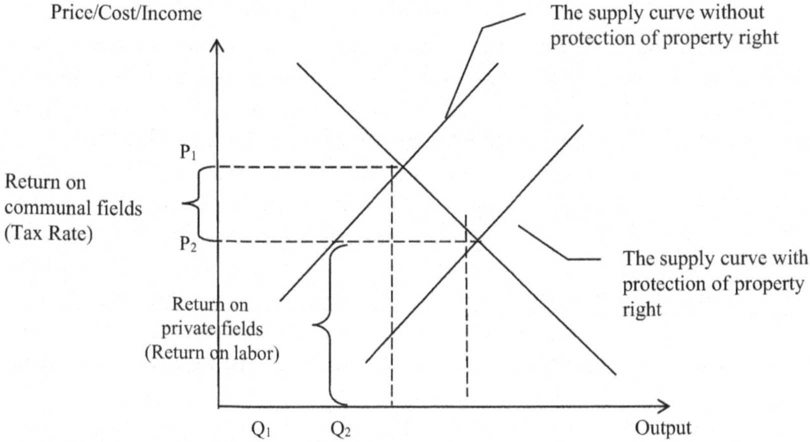

Fig. 4.1 The protection of property right by the well-fields system
Note: For a tribe that does not protect property rights, the total output is Q_1 and the balance cost (price) is P_1, while for one with such protection, the output rises to Q_2 and the balance cost (price) drops to P_2. As long as the unit cost for protecting the rights is lower than P_1–P_2, and it charges protection fees slightly lower than P_1–P_2 to its citizens, then the exclusive communal property right is economically feasible. If we view the government as a natural monopoly, and the absolute value of price elasticity for demand is below 1, then the rate of return for the communal fields or the "tax rate" can be kept at the level of P_1–P_2. In the well-field system, the "fee for protecting property right" is shown as the income from communal fields, and the total income minus income from communal fields is the income from private fields, or the labor income

(Zhang Yan 1999, pp. 238–257) or *jingong* (进贡) (Book of History, "Yugong"). But the yields for hunting or gathering were not stable, and princes often failed to pay their tributes on time. The well-field system provided a stable solution for taxation, guaranteeing the income of the state.

Our previous discussion of property rights relied on the model of the tragedy of the commons, which suggest that the property rights of land are an institutional approach to solve the overuse of land in times of land scarcity. But in this model, the value of the land—grass—is present naturally and only diminished by human activity. In agriculture, crops are produced through human labor and can be stolen unless protected. Therefore, in agriculture, the emergence of exclusive property rights precedes land scarcity. Land scarcity is not the only reason for the creation of property rights to land.

Many people are not surprised when crops are not, just as the land could grow crops. This is in fact a cultural phenomenon arising from thousands of years of exclusive property rights. In talking about a piece of land, people refer to both the land's natural ability to grow corps and the ownership of the yields on it. The first is a natural quality of land, the second institutional. One reflects relations between human and the nature, the other relations among humans. A piece of land without any institutions would only have natural qualities, while the well-field system created exclusive communal property rights to the land, transforming it into "farmland." The well-field system includes both technical and institutional features of the nature.

During the early stages when land was abundant, whoever had the ability to enclose and protect a piece of land could claim its ownership, because they possessed a resource scarcer than land—the ability to provide "exclusive communal property rights." Rather than the protection of property arising from ownership, ownership arose from the ability to protect property. The concept of land property started from the well-field system. Outside the well-fields there existed abundant land, so there was no need to recognize "exclusive rights"; nor was there another exclusive property right system to be implemented at that time. So the government that sponsored this system claimed ownership of land within it.

That well-field system arose in a society without land scarcity demonstrates the importance of one aspect of land property rights—protecting the fruits of labor. Farmers had the alternative of opening virgin land beyond the reach of taxation. People chose to participate not because private fields could grow crops better, but because the crops yielded from these fields would not be taken away by others. So, obtaining land property is inseparable from the owners' actions or commitment to act on tax obligations.

On the other hand, "rent" and "tax" have very similar features. Rent is an economic quantity created by scarcity. It is either the scarcity of a specific asset relative to its demand, or the scarcity of demand (usage) to the asset, the former exemplified as land rent, and the latter the price differences for an asset for its optimal and sub-optimal purposes. If we regard protection of property right as an asset that can only be formed through corresponding institution arrangements, providing protection requires certain resources, and this protection is scarce relative to demand for it. At that time, if the governments providing protection are in a fully competitive market, then their tax rates will be fixed at the point where marginal cost equals marginal revenue. Different efficiency of governments leads to the existence of differential rents, but not the absolute rent. However, the governments are monopolistic in nature, so the tax rate would be higher than the marginal costs, adding the absolute rent into taxation.

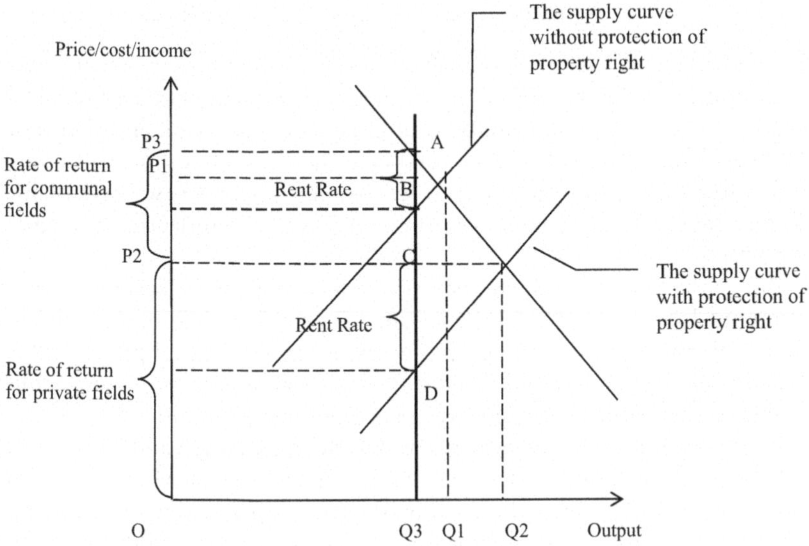

Fig. 4.2 The generation of rent
Note: In the above figure, Q3 represents the limitation of land supply. Because of this limitation, the supply for crops could only reach Q3 at maximum. If the society continues to adopt the well-field system and keep the ratio of communal and private fields unchanged, then the income from both private and communal fields contains the rent for land. In the chart, P2–0 is the rate of return for private fields, and P1–P2 is still the income from communal fields. But as the land becomes scarce, the rate of return for" private fields (P2–0) deducts rate of return for labor (D) becomes the rate of rent (C–D); and the rate of return for communal fields deducts the cost for public goods (tax rate, B–C) also becomes the rate of rent (A–D)

In the well-field system, the income from private fields was the reward for labor while the income from communal fields was the reward to the government. Due to a sufficient supply of land, there was no factor return on land. With the development of agriculture and the growth of population, land became less abundant. But differential rent and absolute rent, while they correspond to land scarcity, were not distinguished. Instead, they were included in the income from the private and communal fields. See the Fig. 4.2 below. During the time of the well-field system, there was no distinction between rents and taxes.

4.2 Separation Between Tax and Rent

Assume that land has variable qualities and is divided into different levels according to its degree of fertility, natural environment, and geographical location. The increase of scarcity would firstly be seen as full cultivation of the finest land. The quality of untilled land then would decline, forming a differential rent. Later on, the land left would only be worse. Eventually, all the land would be claimed, creating a differential rent ladder and absolute rent.

But under the well-field system, the rent would not be seen as a separate item. It was included in the income of private and communal fields. Only with the advent of the crop market, when farmers on private fields (former serfs) were freed, did the well-field system collapse. Land could then be traded freely, then rent was calculated independently.

But this was a very slow process, as described by North and Thomas in "The Rise and Fall of the Manorial System: A Theoretical Model" (North and Thomas 1971). First the crop market developed a system of pricing different products, and farmers were able to accumulate wealth by selling the products of their private fields and use that wealth to free themselves from the obligation of cultivating communal fields. Thus labor taxation was transformed into monetary taxation. The farmers then eventually enjoy freedom except the obligation of paying taxes, communal fields were not distinguished from the private ones, and all land could be traded freely. According to the research of Fu Zhufu, the manorial system in Western Europe and the well-field system were similar in nature (1980, pp. 67–84), so we can take the model of decline and collapse of the manorial system described by North and Thomas as a model of the decline and collapse of the well-field system.

What caused the collapse of the well-field system and the advent of private landownership with taxation? North argues that it is because that the latter one is more efficient. In fact, the well-field system included incomplete private land property rights, in that households owned private fields. The problem of the well-field system was that to achieve exclusive communal property right, it assigned farmers to fixed communal fields, making it impossible for farmers to move freely, hampering efficient resource allocation of land and farmers. On the other hand, "labor taxation" in the communal fields was paid in the form of crops which might not suit the needs of the landlord, while monetary taxation enabled lords to purchase the products they needed on the market (North and Thomas 1971).

On another dimension, the larger the country, the greater the scope of its public violence. The ruling class was divided into different ranks, including the emperor, feudal princes, ministers, and officials, forming a hierarchy from central to local governments. Besides, exclusive communal property rights encouraged a culture of respecting property rights and lowered the costs of protecting land property, even for people outside these social structures. As respect for property grew, the cost of protecting one's own crops fell below the tax rate in the well-fields—that is, 1/9 of the yield. As we know, land was abundant in early stages of the well-field system, and there existed large areas of untilled land. When the cost of claiming and protecting wild land fell below taxation, reclamation expanded rapidly.

However, the two reasons listed above do not fully explain the advent of private land property and land transactions. If the land was still abundant, the improved allocation of labor and land could only be seen in increases in labor incomes and tax revenues. A decrease in losses from stealing was also manifested by increases in labor incomes, but not returns on land. **Only when the land became scarce, at least land of premium quality, could land rent make sense, and did it become significant to own exclusive property rights to a piece of land as an asset**. The selling and buying of land at that time was merely compensation for the costs of reclamation but not the discount value of future rent incomes, so there was no land trading in the sense of land property rights.

In both the cases of ancient China and feudal Europe, there are records of the creation of private land property rights and the collapse of the well-field system or manorial system. In both cases, two groups of people accelerated the creation and development of private land property rights: the first group is the younger sons of royal and aristocratic families, or *yuzi* (余子) (Coulanges, pp. 220, 240; Zhang Shuguo 2008, p. 127). These sons were not entitled to inherit their families' political or tax powers because of primogeniture. They could not enjoy any share of the income from the existing communal fields, so they had to seek their own land outside the well-fields. They gained new land through grants from their fathers or individual reclamation. The land area under the government then expanded to include the newly cultivated fields. These younger sons, already regarded as less fortunate, were generally exempted from tax by their noble parents. Generation after generation, the royal and aristocratic families produced many younger sons who gradually filled up waste land.

Another group was the individuals from foreign or failed families. During the Spring and Autumn period in China, these people were called rustics (野人) to distinguish them from the city men (国人). In western world they were called "common people," in contrast with the "aristocracy" or the "citizens" (Coulanges, pp. 223–227). These rustics or common people were people outside the ruling families. They were mostly conquered or captured in wars or cast out from failed families. They had no ancestors or family gods to worship, and lived in remote suburbs or the countryside, where they enjoyed no protection from the state and possessed no legal land. In the case of China, they were not able to own private fields under the well-field system. But this didn't stop these groups from cultivating new land to make a living, even though they suffered losses from stealing or looting due to a lack of protection from the state. After quite some time, the reality that they had been occupying and cultivating the fields would give them legitimacy in their ownership of the land.

When private land property rights were traded, the rent included in the income of the private fields would be evaluated. Because land was no longer abundant, the price of the land no longer stayed at zero. This trading price of land above zero reflected the land scarcity. In other words, when the rent was evaluated, the value of private land property rights was also quantified, strengthening the existence of private property rights. While the rent was valued, tax was also valued more purely (Fig. 4.3).

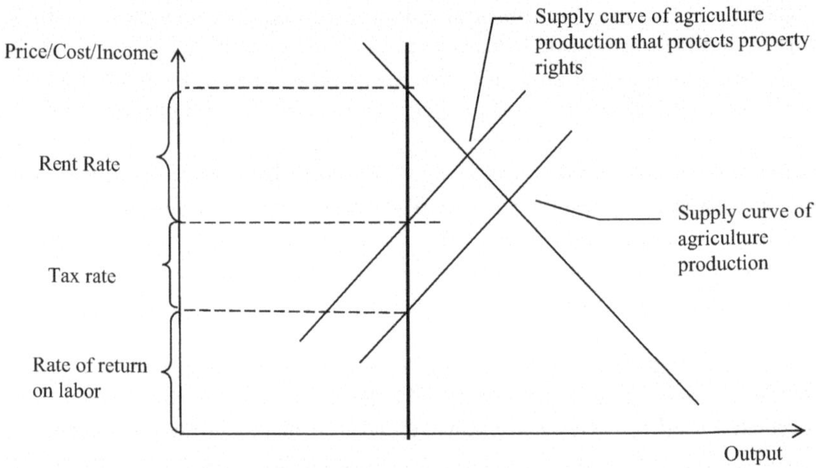

Fig. 4.3 The separation of rent and tax
Note: When the land could be freely traded, and the labor force could move and trade freely, the share of rent and the labor income could be decided by market transactions. And the rate of tax could be decided by product price minus rent and labor income. Thus, rent and tax were separated from each other

At first, traded land might also include the obligation to cultivate communal fields. However, even before the collapse of the well-field or manorial system, people began to pay taxes with money instead of labor (Shen Han 2005, p. 43). Tenant farmers who paid only land rent and were exempt from labor also came into being (pp. 38, 49). This shows that tax rates were evaluated independently even before the collapse of the well-field system or the manorial system. When private ownership of land became more common, the taxation on land developed into a mature form to replace the well-field system. The "Initial Taxation on Farmland" (初税亩) adopted by the State of Lu during the Spring and Autumn Period was a milestone in this sense.

At this time, property rights to land contained both entitlement and obligation. The entitlement was the revenue from rent and the obligation was paying taxes to the government. The revenue produced by the land was equal to the rent minus tax. In a fully competitive land market, rent would be calculated independently; thus the income of labor, rent of land, and taxation would all be separate from each other. However, the money paid by tenant farmers to the landowners included both rent of land and tax, and the money the landowners paid to the government was pure tax. This distribution structure of income was formed not only because the landowners were larger in scale and more stable than the tenants but also because that tax and rent shared similar features.

It should be noted that the "separation of rent and tax" is intended to mean that the rights to collect rents and the power of taxation were assigned to different bodies. The phrase is not intended to suggest that the relationship between the land scarcity corresponding to rent and of the protection of property right corresponding to tax is alienated. After this separation occurred, the right to collect rents, with its function to address land scarcity, and the power of taxation, justified by the protection of the fruits of labor, continued to complement each other through the social division of labor as well as cooperation between the owner of the right to collect rent and the owner of the power to collect tax, so that land property rights can be protected and effectively exercised. In other words, private land property is complete only when there exist services corresponding to taxation and rent collection at the same time.

4.3 The Rights to Tax and to Collect Rent

Following agriculture, other industries developed, including manufacturing, metallurgy, catering, transportation, finance, and commerce. These industries utilized land in different ways, as did the construction of houses.

In this way the concepts of rent and tax were still more generalized. Land was not used only for agriculture, but also for building houses, and for producing and holding other goods. Land scarcity was caused by demand not only for agricultural products but also for other types of products. Due to the concentrating function of commercial activities, demand for relatively small areas of land in trading centers also created localized land scarcity. Although population density was still quite low overall, it was great in cities. The gathering of more people in the city and the growth of commercial interests boosted rents. More generally speaking, land is the place for people to carry out activities. As the population grew, and the types and scope of activities expanded, land only became scarcer in relation to humankind. However, the nature of land rent didn't change. It was still the reward of total output deducting other factor costs. The rent was decided by the degree of land scarcity for a particular usage.

For the government, land property rights were only one form of property rights. Property rights to various commodities, assets, and houses also required protection. After the emergence of private property rights, the government needed to guard against not only exterior enemies but also conflict within the society over human rights and property rights. Besides the direct protection of property rights, the government also needed to protect personal safety, maintain market order, offer impartial jurisdiction, and provide other public goods. Thus, the public services corresponding to taxation grew more comprehensive and more difficult to identify. The forms of tax were also diversified. Besides taxes on land, taxes also began to be levied on trade and property, followed by corporation and individual income taxes. A diverse range of taxes obscured the original emergence of tax from farmland. But fundamentally, the public services funded through taxation still take place in a given place, and the land is a simple manifestation of that complex place. Who could own any space without occupying the land?

Throughout history, many politicians proposed or even implemented tax reforms that attempted to take back taxation to its original form, which is imposing tax only on land. For instance, reformers in the Ming and Qing Dynasties tried to implement "the single whip law" (一条鞭法), which means to integrate several kinds of taxes into one kind of tax, and then "transfer tax from people to land" (摊丁入亩), in an attempt to replace various forms of taxation with a system of pure land tax. The single tax proposed by the French Physiocrat Quesnay was also based solely on land. This idea has legitimacy, for the land is not only a natural resource on which crops can grow, but also a place where the public services are provided. As long as the government taxes land according to area, then almost all public services could be compensated, directly or indirectly. For example, a land-based tax system wouldn't collect much tax directly from an auto manufacturer (except for the minimal amount of land occupied by its facilities), but producing an automobile requires the cooperation of many workers, all of whom have demand for food but almost zero demand elasticity vis-à-vis food prices. The land tax included in the food price would be transferred to the consumer, and the people buying cars would have to pay for this tax indirectly. Of course, the land occupied by the manufacturer will also be taxed.

Furthermore, the original purpose of tax didn't disappear even after the separation of tax and rent. The scarcity of resources needed to protect property rights has value independent of land scarcity. Hence the property rights of land itself still contains property rights protection service. In the ancient times it was said that "Every corner of the land belongs to the king" (普天之下, 莫非王土), and in the modern societies it is embodied as the state ownership of land in a sovereign sense. Certain types of land are not scarce due to lack of economic value or oversupply (such as deserts), and are not capable of supporting private property rights, but the land is still a part of a country's territory. When land is abandoned because of wars or a death without heirs, it will eventually return to the state. This is the most basic meaning of state ownership of the land.

On the other hand, state ownership of land does not exclude or replace the private land property. Private land property is the right to collect rent, defined as income based on land scarcity, while enjoying state protection in return for taxes. The property right here differs from the state landownership in the sovereignty sense in that private land properties can be traded, while state sovereignty cannot. The resources a country uses to protect property rights cannot be acquired from the market. They can only be collected compulsorily by a government empowered to use violence. The use of these resources also contains the nature of violence. If there are several rival groups competing to offer protection, they will inevitably resort to violence, leading to a war among them. At last, the group which utilizes violent resources most efficiently will win the monopoly status of providing the protection of land property, and its relations with the other people who need the resource could have the equality often seen in the market.

The supply of property rights protection was monopolistic, so the tax rate was generally also a monopoly price. Assume that competition among different protection providers is peaceful, just like the competition between different property management companies over market share, and competition would eventually lead to a market balanced price which would be substantially lower than the monopoly tax rate. However, because of the lack of competition and impossibility of trade, state protection services cannot improve resource allocation through market transactions. The degree of land fertility varies due to natural factors, but their allocation to purposes or usages can be improved through trading. The conclusion is that people usually cannot purchase the power to tax,[1] but they can purchase the right to collect rent. There are few measures to improve the resource allocation for property protection services, as the power to tax cannot be freely traded. But the trading of rent-collecting rights can improve the allocation of land use.

Although land and property protection services can be considered as two different assets, and the power to tax and the right to collect rent can be distinguished in their concepts and practices, they can only be effective when working together. Without taxation power or its related property protection services, the right to collect rent and land property would not exist. Without differential rent and free trade in land property, the allocation of land resources could not be upgraded, and the efficiency of land property would never be in full play and could not provide sufficient tax revenue to the taxing power. This is why we say that the rent and the tax are of the same origin.

As more fundamental powers, the power of tax and the protection services of property decide the right to collect rent and the land property. In ancient China, whenever a new dynasty was established, it always started by granting land to its citizens. This power of allocating land resources to the people comes from the state. However, when people purchase land property through trading, the change in the institution won't affect this ownership. A new government can only inherit the power of taxation and the land that was owned by the last institution in a private sense, for instance, royal land, deserted areas from wartime, and territories with no existing private property claims.

[1]A particular case is that under certain circumstances, sovereign states may have the right to purchase territory, that is, the power to levy taxes, for example, the United States bought Alaska from Russia.

The distinction between the power of taxation and right of rent divides control of the land into state sovereignty and private property rights, and it requires a prudential approach to separate the two in practice. This is an efficient power structure for allocating land and public resources. This separation avoids the government's direct intervention in the trading of private land property, thus providing better protection to the property. For the same reason, the subject with both taxation and rent-collecting rights also has the motivation to separate the two.

In practice, this feature was pronounced both in ancient China and in Britain. In China, although there was no strict distinction between tax and rent at early times, since the Initial Tax on Farmland in the State of Lu in the Spring and Autumn Period, tax and rent were gradually detached from each other. There were clear boundaries between agricultural taxes and land rents. The territorial nature in the sense of taxation power is fully manifested in the distribution within the political ruling group. For example, to enfeoff and reward land to royal members, heirs of former emperors, meritorious generals, and statesmen to form so-called fiefdoms or manors (采邑) within the country, the essence of which is to distribute tax power to these people. These were in fact distributing the power of taxation to them. The power was realized by the income from communal fields during the well-field system, and later by taxing the people who lived on the land[2] but not by rent from the land itself.

In Britain, "the king's ownership of the land" is not the same as the private property rights to land. It is said that "During the Norman Conquest, there emerged a concept in England that all public property belongs to the monarch, but the monarch cannot treat these as private property" (Shen Han 2005, p. 2). This idea resembles to a large extent the separation of the power of tax and the right to collect rents. The concept was clearly manifested in modern history by the land systems in the British colonies. For instance, the "Treaty of Waitangi" signed between the British Queen and the New Zealand Maoris clearly stipulates in Article 1 that the Maoris relinquish their sovereignty rights to the British King and in Article 2 that the King promises to protect their land, forests, and fisheries from being infringed upon (Palmer 2008, pp. 367–370). This clearly drew a distinction between land owned in a sovereign sense and land owned

[2] Ma Duanlin said in his General Reference of Literature (《文献通考》): "Although people who are granted a manor may not be able to acquire land entirely in accordance with the system, all taxes are derived from land."

privately, separating the power of taxation and the right to collect rent. This agreement signed in 1840 showed a mature theory on tax and rent developed by the British people and accepted by the Maoris (Palmer 2008, pp. 61–62).

In contrast, the confusion between land owned in a sovereign sense and land owned privately, as well as between the right to collect rents and the power to tax could lead to serious problems. In China after 1949, state ownership of the land was understood as entitling the state to collect both rent and tax. Collecting taxation was natural, so the government focused more on rent. Under the excuse of state landownership, the state and its administrative institutions occupied vast areas of land which originally belonged privately to individuals or institutions. For example, in 1982, the Chinese constitution stipulated that all the urban land belongs to the country; and the *Land Management Law* established that any piece of land that is to be converted into construction land must be owned by the country. These measures made it much easier for the government to requisition land from rural communities. The land was allocated and utilized directly by the government agencies or given to state-owned enterprises, lowering allocation efficiency, breeding serious corruption, and bringing governmental agencies and the state-owned enterprises the power to collect rent. It shows that once a government and its agencies are able to gain and exercise the right to collect rent, they would become traders who could not be limited. Inability to supervise the enforcement of right to rent and the spending of rent money will also harm efficiency and justice.

4.4 The Pricing and Forms of Rent and Tax

Regard the public service of protecting property rights as a factor of production, and it can influence the total output together with other factors like land, labor, and capital. If the supply of these factors is competitive and follows the law of diminishing marginal utility, then at the point when the marginal cost of the factors equals their marginal output, they are considered to achieve the optimal allocation (Samuelson). Shown as:

$$\partial Qt / \partial t = \partial Qr / \partial r = \partial Qk / \partial k = \partial Qw / \partial w = 1$$

∂Qt stands for the marginal output for property protection services;
∂Qr is the marginal output of land;
∂Qk is the marginal output of capital;

∂Qw is the marginal output of labor;
∂t is the marginal input for property protection services;
∂r is the marginal input of land;
∂k is the marginal input of capital;
∂w is the marginal input of labor;
The above outputs and inputs are quantified by currency.

This shows that an optimal allocation will be achieved when the marginal input of different factors equals their marginal output. When the rate of return for all of the owners of the factors can be at the same level of the marginal output, then this optimal allocation can be sustained.

In practice, achieving the above rate of return with optimal resource allocation requires that factor returns be decided by a fully competitive market. Since the property rights of land can be held by and traded among individuals and institutions, many land sellers and buyers have to compete and trade with each other, and the rate of land rent that reflects scarcity is found through market transactions (leasing or selling). Land in different locations and conditions will enjoy different level of scarcity, the differential rents for different land resources established in the transactions forming a relative price system, guiding people in matching other factors properly with land so as to reach optimal resource allocation.

The other major factors for economic activity are labor and capital, which were also scarce and sparsely dispersed. Therefore, they can also reach balanced prices through market competition. Relations among the balanced prices of the factors form a relative price; these factors usually account for a proportion of a product's market price. In particular situations, some factors might be more needed than others, thus taking a larger share of the product price. For example, after the Black Death in the fourteenth century in Western Europe, labor became a relatively scarce factor, so laborers enjoyed an increased share in the product income, and at the same time the differential nature of labors was also more pronounced.

As a factor of production, the service of protecting property rights was bought in the form of taxation. The value of this protection changes with the fluctuation of product prices. For instance, if food prices increase, and the loss rate for services protecting food from being stolen remains unchanged, the value it creates will increase accordingly. So the output of property protection services is dependent on the productivity of the factors and is differential in nature. Therefore, taxation should and has always taken the form of a share ratio. For the Chinese traditional land tax, there were ratios of 1/10, 1/15, 1/30, and so on. But the tax rate is not decided by the market because of the monopolistic nature of the government, so it is not an equilibrium price from a fully competitive market and is to a certain extent monopolistic in nature.

Even monopolies are subject to some restraints. In situations with withdrawal allowed, if the absolute value of demand elasticity for the price is above 1, each percent increase in price will reduce demand by more than 1%, so the monopolist won't elevate prices lightly, out of fear of harming its own interests. When public goods are provided by the government, people will find it difficult to completely quit the service, but they can choose to lower their input, such as reducing inputs of labor, capital, or even land, to reduce their efforts in creating wealth and eventually tax money for the government. This is the meaning illustrated by the Laffer curve. But the government can still choose within the range between a completely monopolistic price and an equilibrium, fully competitive market price. The decision of tax rates for each dynasty and each government depends on the particular situations and the historical understanding of policy makers. In a few words, tax rates are not decided by the market, but by the government based on its previous experience.

A major distinction between the property protection services and other factors is that it has an economy of scale and has increasing returns to scale. The average cost of services will fall as it expands in area (land), but even in a fixed area, the increasing population and companies will also bring down average costs. So, there is a smallest optimal scale for almost every government. In traditional China, this smallest optimal scale for government was county governments. Since governmental services follow the law of increasing returns to scale, the principle of marginal costs being equal to marginal output should not apply in deciding tax rates. Instead, the tax rate should follow Professor Coase's two-part pricing, considering fixed costs and variable costs respectively (Coase 1946). The optimal tax rate should meet the following requirements:

$$\partial Qt / \left(Tf / N + \partial Tv\right) = \partial Qr / \partial r = \partial Qk / \partial k = \partial Qw / \partial w$$

Tf is the fixed cost for property protection services, *Tv* is the variable cost, and *N* is the equilibrium level of supply/demand for property protection services, which could be simply represented by the economic aggregate of the area managed by the government. In many situations, the variable cost is close to zero; for example, one more company moving into a county might not require the government to hire one more police officer. The conditions for optimal tax rate can be expressed as:

$$\partial Qt/(Tf/N) = \partial Qr/\partial r = \partial Qk/\partial k = \partial Qw/\partial w$$

The average fixed cost (*Tf/N*) will fall as the economic aggregate increases. This implies that as the number of companies in a county grows, the optimal tax level will have room to decrease. If the relations between different local governments are competitive, they will lower their tax rates. But within a country, especially one with a single system of taxation, new enterprises will have to pay for taxes at the original level, driving effective tax rates higher than optimal as well as marginal output.

$$\text{If} \quad Ng > N, \quad \text{then} \quad Tf/Ng < Tf/N$$

Ng is the increasing economic aggregate of the area, and when it exceeds the assumed level in formulating tax rates, the optimal tax rate will fall below the effective tax rate.

If we take land as the unit in calculating the marginal input, then *Tf/N* in the above equation can be represented as (*Tf/h*)/(*N/h*), representing the ratio of fixed annual fees for public services on a unit (such as *mu*) of land to the output from the unit of land. Marginal inputs of other factors, including ∂r, ∂k, and ∂w, can all be viewed as the marginal input per unit land per year. When the marginal output of these factors equals the marginal input, and rate of return equals to marginal output, the allocation will be in the optimal condition. Shown as:

$$T = \partial Qt = (Tf/h)/(N/h)$$
$$R = \partial Qr = \partial r$$
$$K = \partial Qk = \partial k$$
$$W = \partial Qw = \partial w$$
$$T = \partial Qt = (Tf/h)/(N/h)$$
$$R = \partial Qr = \partial r$$
$$K = \partial Qk = \partial k$$
$$W = \partial Qw = \partial w$$

T is Tax, R is rent, K is capital gains, and W stands for wages.
Then:

$$Q = T + R + K + W;$$

$$Q = T + R + K + W;$$

Q is the total output per land unit. Divide both sides of the equation by Q, then:

$$1 = T/Q + R/Q + K/Q + W/Q.$$

$$1 = T/Q + R/Q + K/Q + W/Q.$$

T/Q, R/Q, K/Q, and W/Q are ratios of shared total output for different factors. Obviously,

$$\text{When } (Tf/h)/(N/h) > (Tf/h)/(Ng/h)$$

$$T(N) > T(Ng)$$

$$T(N)/Q > T(Ng)/Q$$

The real tax rate will be higher than the optimal rate, and the real share ratio higher than the optimal share ratio. See the Fig. 4.4 below:

In principle, the factors share returns according to certain ratios, but in reality, if owners of some factors do not have easy access to actual output information, or the opportunity costs for getting this information are relatively high, then fixed returns are more preferred for this situation. It is difficult for government to get accurate information from landowners on total yields, so fixed returns are adopted here. But this does not deny that the returns of factors should follow share ratios in principle.

For example, in mainland of traditional China, the rate of rent was usually 50%, while in Taiwan it was 56.8% (Steven N.S. Cheung 2000). In practice there were various forms of fixed or shared rents. It was difficult for government officials to visit the fields and observe the output, so fixed taxes were usually adopted. But this doesn't exclude the differential taxes of land or other factors. In an ancient Chinese literature "Yugong" (禹贡), which described the tribute system in Xia Dynasty (about 2070–1600 BC), the land was divided into different levels, and different type and volume of tributes to the government were required for different levels of land. In

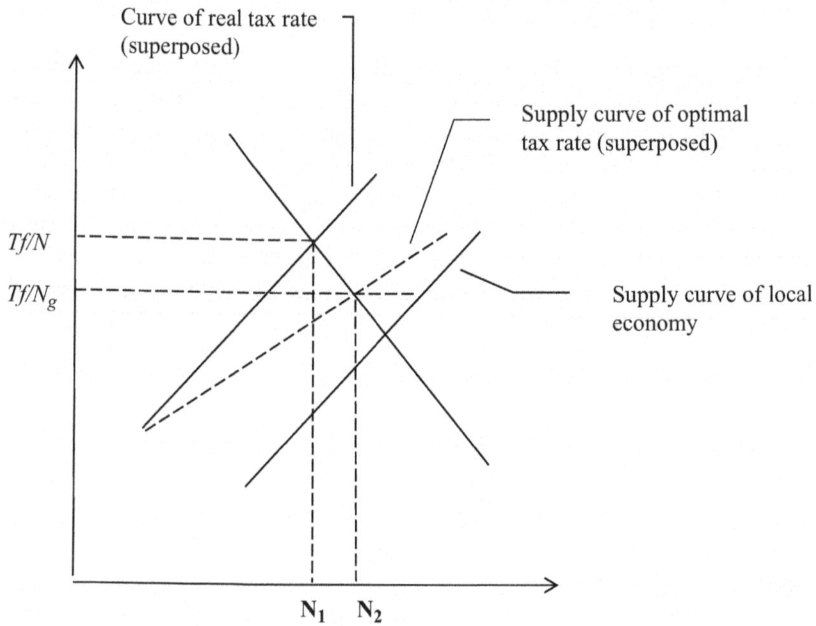

Fig. 4.4 The optimal tax rate and real tax rate
Note: The supply-demand curve of optimal tax rates shows that as the economic aggregate increases, the average fixed cost for supplying public goods declines. The curve of real tax rate shows that the government adjusts the tax rate in proportion to the economic aggregate (such as added value), so it increases in proportion to the regional economy. Apparently there exists a difference between the effective tax rate (Tf/N) and the optimal tax rate (Tf/N_g). We can also conclude that when the tax rate is reduced from real to optimal level, the regional economic aggregate will rise from N_1 to N_2

Qing dynasty land reform known as “Transferring tax from people to land,” the government also divided the land into several levels, charging different amounts of fixed taxes. But the property protection service is monopolistic, so it often takes a larger share compared with other factors like land, labor, and capital.

In specific cases, output fluctuates every year, and the cost for deciding the share through calculating output is high, so a fixed quota is generally adopted such as fixed rent or fixed wage. But in the cases of higher risks (greater fluctuations), share returns are adopted to distribute risks (Steven Cheung 2000, pp. 96–116).

4.5 The Mutual Substitution of Rent and Tax

In land leasing, one only cares about the total cost of leasing a piece of land, regardless of whether it's tax and rent. In ancient China, a tenant paid rent to his landowner, and then the landowner paid tax to the government. The money paid by the tenant included both rent and tax, but he might have never realized that the tax was included in it. In modern China, for a businessman to open a factory, he must rent a piece of land and pay tax to the government. For him the land cost is tax plus rent.

Imagine two regions with identical geographical locations and natural conditions, and they have the same rate of rent and tax rate, which is:

$$T_1 = T_2;$$
$$R_1 = R_2;$$
$$(T_1 + R_1) = (T_2 + R_2)$$

T_i represents the tax rate in area i, and Ri represents the rate of rent in area i. Here $i = 1, 2$.

At this time, what will happen if one of the two areas lowers its tax rate? The rate of rent for this area will rise, until the sum of tax rate and rent rate is equal to that of the other area. Because when the tax rate of an area drops, more companies will rush in, causing a rise in rent. As long as the total sum of tax and rent is lower than that of the other area (assume the tax rate of and the rate of rent of the other area remain unchanged), there will be companies willing to move to the first area until the sum of the two rates goes back to the original level.

$$\left[(T_1 - \Delta T) + (R_1 + \Delta R)\right] = (T_2 + R_2)$$

In this scenario, tradable private land property and the state sovereignty that provide protection of property are two complementary products, with the value of scarce land and the protection of land property being their respective utilities, and rent rates and tax rates their prices. As explained, without state sovereignty to provide protection of property, tradable private land property could not be effectively protected, and the rent might not exist for lack of enforcement; sovereignty without property rights cannot allocate land resources according to their level of scarcity, and the rent return could not be generated. Only through working together can land property be protected, and land resources efficiently allocated, generating revenues for both rent and tax.

With a pair of complementary products, when the price of one product falls, the demand for itself and its complementary product will both increase. Assume the increase in demand for the complementary product is large enough and the resources for its production are limited, and its price will rise. In the case of land, sovereignty and property rights are complementary, when the tax rate decreases; the demand for property protection in that area will increase, thus enhancing land demand. But the land supply is limited, so the rate of rent will rise, until neutralizing the part of tax cut. Similarly, when the rate of rent decreases, the demand for land in the area will rise, boosting the demand for property protection services, and then the tax rate, if adjustable, will go up to offset the decreased rent. See the chart below (Fig. 4.5).

If a subject owns both state sovereignty and land property, then it can capitalize on the complementary natures of the two to protect its overall interests. The subject can only be a sovereign state which also possesses

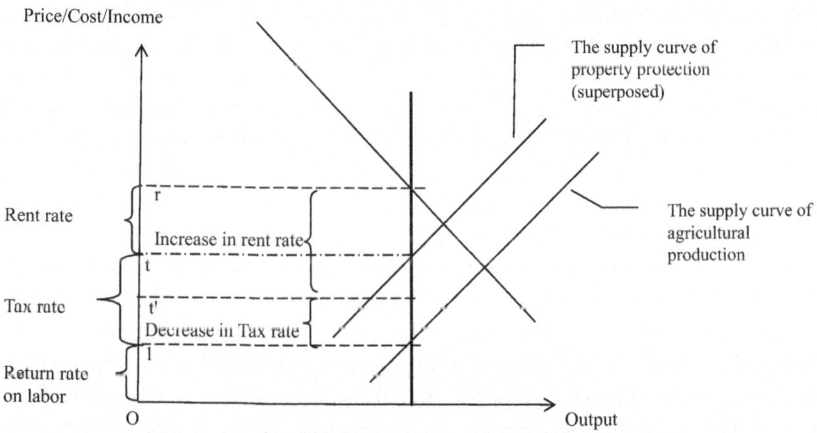

Fig. 4.5 Substitution of rent and tax

Note: In this chart, sovereignty and property rights are complementary, so there are two curves to reflect supply-demand, that is, the output of land composed by both agricultural production and property protection. If we lower the tax rate from t – 1 to t' – 1, the limited supply of land will keep the price of its output at the same level, so the rent will increase until offsetting the part cut by tax rate

land properties in a private sense. If it lowers the tax rate, the rent rate will increase till the sum of the two rates goes up to the original level. For the same reason, it can also lower rent rates while increasing taxes. In doing so the owner won't harm its overall interests, and sometimes can even profit.

From a dynamic perspective, when the tax rate is lowered, the rent will need some time to increase to the new level of balance, and during this process the combined costs of rent and tax will be lower than their original level or that of other areas, thus attracting in more companies before reaching the new balance. But the process itself has already increased investment in the area, and when the balance is restored, the revenues for the owner both of sovereignty and of property rights will even increase due to an expanded scale of economy.

As we discussed, the government or state should not directly own land property. But exceptions do exist in certain circumstances. For example, if among the territory of a country is an area of remote land without any economic value and which is not scarce, property rights will not be established over these pieces of land. The country then will own the initial property right prior to private property rights coming into existence. As the economy expands and the population grows, this remote land will become scarce, and the country can sell the land to whoever willing to buy it out and form new private property rights on it. In this situation, the sovereign body will have both rights at the same time, so it can make adjustments on tax rates of rent rates to achieve the goals of the government.

For example, Hong Kong had a low tax rate when it was under the British colonial rule. The import and export of most goods enjoyed zero tariffs, except tobacco and alcohol, and the jurisdiction was praised as a free port. Other taxes like corporate income tax, individual income tax, and property tax were also lower than those of most of other countries and regions. The low tax rate attracted many companies to invest in Hong Kong, stimulating the development of local businesses together with demand for more land. In this way Hong Kong evolved from a small town to a metropolis. The remote areas that British colonizers occupied started to have urban developing values, which the Hong Kong British Authorities as the sovereign body could sell or lease to individuals or institutions. In this case, the Hong Kong British Authorities had both power to tax and the (initial) right to rent.

The increase in land demand boosted rent rates in Hong Kong. It was reflected in auction land prices, which capitalize the rent rate. According to the statistics, from 1959 to 1979 industrial land surged 132.5 times, non-industrial land 41.5 times, and residential land 86 times (Zheng Deliang 1982, p. 173). Today, Hong Kong remains among the cities with highest land prices. This is to a large extent caused by the low tax rate system in Hong Kong. As the owner of both right to collect rent and power to taxation, the Hong Kong British Authorities was compensated by selling the right to rent in a lower tax rate. Professor Zhou Qiren comments that the Hong Kong government had imposed hidden taxes (2006).

On the other hand, if one subject owns both the sovereignty right and property right of the land, it can also lower the rent rate to gain a higher tax rate. For instance, if a government owns the initial property of a piece of land, and if the current tax policies are not great enough to attract outside capital, then it can consider lowering rent. In doing so the combined costs (tax plus rent) of opening a factory in this county decrease, giving it competitive edge over other areas with better geographic locations.

In lowering rent to raise competitiveness, the government must avoid a mistake: it should not directly operate land properties. The value of land property should be evaluated by the market, and the relative price system of rent in different areas should be decided by their levels of scarcity. As a monopolist, the government takes the rent as a policy variation to attract companies and gives a wrong signal by greatly lowering the rent rate. In the previous case, when the local government lowered its land rent, it distorted the relative price among this county and its competitors, leading to inefficient resource allocation among the competing counties.

Professor Steven Cheung points out in his book *The Theory of Share Tenancy* that after the intentional reduction of rent rate down to 37.5% in Taiwan through rent reform, the return on land fell less than its marginal output, and the return of other factors became unequal to their marginal output,

$$\text{If} \quad R - \Delta R < \partial Q_r, \quad \text{then} \quad W \neq \partial Q_w$$

In such a situation, the allocation efficiency between land and labor will decrease (2000, pp. 156). Furthermore, Professor Cheung argues that intentional rent cuts by the government will harm the land property system. The reduced rent lost by the landowners is not gained by anyone, instead; it is dissipated in competition between tenants (2000, pp. 166–170). This will lead to a net loss for the society as a whole.

4.6 Case Study: Competition Among County Governments

It seems problematic to view from this perspective the "competition among county governments" proposed by Professor Steven Cheung. Professor Cheung points out that when the tax rate and tax share for county governments are at the same level, these governments would compete through lowering their land prices, eventually to near or even below zero. It is worthwhile as long as the return governments get from the companies settling in is no less than the interest rate of land costs. However, this explanation doesn't factor in the opportunity cost of land; that is, the potential revenue land used for other purposes, so we cannot compare the differential revenue of land among different counties, nor their different allocations.

Suppose there are two counties with different levels of differential land revenues due to their different geographic location and natural conditions: county A's fixed land rent is \$10,000 per acre per year, and county B's is \$20,000 per acre per year. For a company, only if it can generate \$20,000 of surplus after deducting its factor costs (including salaries, interest rates, and reasonable profits) and taxation, can it afford to locate in county B, while \$10,000 surplus can justify operating in county A. However, if both county governments cut their land rent lower than the market level because of county competition, they will attract companies that previously couldn't have afforded the rent rate. If county A keeps its rent at the market level while county B intentionally lowers it, then county B will receive businesses that should have been in county A. If both counties cut rent to zero, then all the businesses will swarm into county B. In a word, inefficient allocation of land will occur whenever the rent rate doesn't equal the marginal output of land.

But from a different perspective, if we consider the rent and tax rates as a whole, then a cut in rent can be seen as a cut in tax. Professor Cheung points out that as long as the value added taxes that county governments collect from companies are no less than the interest rate of land costs, the land price can be kept at zero or even negative. According to China's relevant laws, the value added tax rate for companies is 17%, 1/4 of which (4.25% of added value) goes to county governments. So, the formula for pricing land should be:

$$\text{The land cost} = \text{Industrial added value} * 4.25\% / \text{interest rate} \quad (4.1)$$

Here, if we understand the "land cost" that Professor Cheung refers to as the land price decided by the market, the "interest rate of land cost" then can be understood as equal to the rent to price ratio. In general equilibrium situations, the return for investing in bonds should be around the same level as for investing that amount of money in land, which is shown as:

$$\text{Land value} = \text{Industrial added value} * 4.25\% / \text{Rent to price ratio} \tag{4.2}$$

The rent to price ratio and the rent have the following correlation:

$$\text{Land rent} = \text{Land value} * \text{Rent to price ratio} \tag{4.3}$$

The rent to price ratio is the ratio of land rent to its property price. The difference between the total value of output and the added value is whether to include intermediate costs. This is a matter of proportion which only affects the shares of the rent revenue, just as factoring in the costs of seeds and fertilizers in deciding the shares of land revenue for agricultural land. Hence:

$$\text{Share of rent revenue} = \text{Land rent} / \text{Industrial added value} \tag{4.4}$$

Combine (4.4) with (4.3), then we have:

$$\begin{aligned}\text{Share of rent revenue} = {} & \text{Land value} * \text{Rent to price ratio} / \\ & \text{Industrial added value}\end{aligned} \tag{4.5}$$

Combine (4.5) with (4.2), and:

$$\begin{aligned}\text{Share of rent revenue} = {} & \text{Industrial added value} * 4.25\% / \\ & \text{Rent to price ratio} * \text{Rent to price ratio} / \\ & \text{Industrial added value} = 4.25\%\end{aligned} \tag{4.6}$$

This shows that the baseline of the share of rent revenue equals the county governments' share in the value added tax, which also means that the companies have paid the rent by themselves. **Professor Cheung is right to notice that 4.25% of a company's VAT is indeed a "share of rent" but not tax** (2008, pp. 130–131).

However, if the 4.25% of VAT that local governments collect is rent but not tax, then in a zero rent scenario, it's equivalent to zero taxation. This understanding makes sense if we consider that the governments of higher levels have provided the public goods in national and provincial level, that they will also make tax refunds and transfer payments to the county governments,[3] and that the county governments' marginal cost for providing public services to an extra company is near zero, and the fixed costs of providing such services also decline on average as the economy expands. From the perspective of companies, they pay for rent but enjoy a tax cut. Thus, **the competition on land price in fact becomes competition on tax rate**. Shown as:

$$\left[T+(R-\Delta R)\right]=\left[(T+R)-\Delta(T+R)\right]=\left[(T-\Delta T)+R\right]$$

T stands for tax rate and *R* for rate of rent.

As the tax rates are decided by a monopolistic central government, tax rates are like a monopolistic price for public services. Competition among counties can drive the effective tax rate near the balanced level of market competition (the optimal tax rate), as the glide trajectory from *Tf/N* to *Tf/Ng* shows in Fig. 4.4. The range for VAT rate competition is between 12.5% and 17%, and it seems that governments are competing with one another in the market, and on surface they are competing on the range of concession they make to companies in terms of land price.

In such competition that takes the form of rent exemption but in nature tax deduction, it can still be effective as long as the government serves as an equitable market player and evaluates different rates of rent and property prices for different areas through market transaction. Because during this process, the rate of rent equals the marginal output of the land, and the market price of land is the net discount value of its future rent revenue. Land with higher differential rent will have a higher market price and suggests a larger amount of interest. Only companies with relatively greater

[3] For example, according to the data of the National Bureau of Statistics, the transfer payments from the central government to the local government in 2008 reached 2059.8 billion yuan (2009), which is equivalent to 72% of the local government's fiscal revenue (excluding transfer payments). For another example, the transfer payment from the superior government of a county in 1997 was about 101% of the county's fiscal revenue (Zhou Qingzhi 2004, pp. 172, 178).

output can create more industrial added value, compensating the interests of investment in purchasing and developing the land with 4.25% of VAT.

For example, if the land rent is $10,000 per acre for county A and $20,000 for county B, then a company that occupies 10 mu and with an industrial added value of $2.5 million could not locate itself in county B. For the share of 4.25% VAT the county government gets is only $106,250, not enough to compensate the interest rate of land at market price ($200,000 for 10 acres), for as discussed, the creditor's right and the land with the same price should have the same return. But it can locate itself in county A, for the rent there is $100,000. Only for companies with added value of $4,705,882 (4.25% of which is higher than $200,000) should be eligible to enter county B. Therefore, county competition is effective according to Professor Cheung's equation.

The reason that Professor Cheung highly commended county competition is that under uniform national tax rates, through lowering land prices the county government in fact carried out the competition on tax rates, realizing competition among local governments. It's not just a price war, but also a rivalry for the quality of services, or we can put it as the competition among county governments to provide institutional structures to companies.

But such competition in reality is largely different from Professor Cheung's theory. Although the Chinese constitution stipulates that the rural land communally belongs to rural collectives, certain laws such as the Land Management Law have constrained and diminished the communal property rights of land in rural areas, for example, land is restricted to agricultural uses and will be expropriated by the government if changed into construction land, with compensation only 6–10 times of average output. Moreover, the county governments and rural collectives are not equal players in the market, the former often force the latter to accept a price much lower than deserved.[4] Therefore, in most cases, land prices were intentionally repressed, and the relative price system of rent rate in

[4] Steven Cheung said in his article "China's Economic Institutions": "farmers will be compensated if they surrender their farmland. With a 5% discount rate, I estimate that the compensation in 2006 will be a discount of three to five times the rent of farmland. (2008, page 135) If the land rent share is 50% and the discount rate is 5%, the value of farmland should be about 10 times the annual average output value and 20 times the annual rent. In fact, the discount rate should be lower, about 3% at the one-year deposit rate; I estimate that a more reasonable discount rate should be about 2%."

the free market cannot be formed, leading to inefficient allocation of land for failing to give proper signals.

In the above example, if the discount rate and the interest rate are 3%, the land price in B should be around 666,667 yuan per mu. Suppose the average output for agriculture is 3000 yuan per mu, and calculate as the 8 years of annual output as example (assuming the land rent rate for agriculture land is 50%), then government should pay the rural collective altogether 24,000 yuan, lowering the market rent (20,000 yuan per mu) to 720 yuan per mu. Thus, companies with added value of only 170,000 yuan can enter the county. The VAT collected from those companies will be far from the market rent, leading to inefficient allocation of land.

In fact, lowering land prices is basically lowering the rent rate of land. This could be perfectly explained by Professor Cheung's analysis in his book "The Theory of Share Tenancy," except switching labor to capital as the non-land factor. It reduces the rate of returns on land to a level lower than the marginal output of land, and the rate of returns on capital higher than the marginal output. Shown as:

$$\text{If} \quad R - \Delta R \langle \partial Qr, \text{ then } \; K \rangle \partial Qk$$

This will damage efficient allocation between land and capital. More seriously, lowering land prices diminishes or even devastates the land property system; thus the losses suffered by rural communities on land prices are not gained by any individual or group, but are dissipated in the process of capital competition. In this case, the marginal output for capital might even be negative, and the books can be kept balanced only because of a lower spending on land rent or land purchase. This creates a net loss for the whole society.

We can notice that the "county competition" proposed by Professor Steven Cheung requires an effective system for protecting land property, fair trading between owners of land and other market players, and ultimately an efficient system of market land rent. On land issues, the government is suggested to exercise its power only in a sovereign sense—that is, through taxation—and should not interfere in any land property transactions directly except by selling lands which haven't established any property right.

Of course, in doing so, county governments don't have to first acquire land directly from rural communities and then provide it to companies after proper development. If the county governments want to purchase land, they should pay the market price, use the prospective 4.25% value added tax earnings as collateral to get the money from banks, and provide it to businesses at low or zero rates. The county government could also allow rural communities to deal directly with businesses and provide tax cuts or exemptions out of its 4.25% share of value added tax. **Attracting businesses through lowering land prices is hidden and informal tax rate competition, while cutting taxes are open and institutionalized ones**. In fact, as shown in Professor Cheung's "The Chinese Economic System," local governments don't need to intervene in the allocation or trading of land, and all they have to do is implement tax cut or exemption policies, if they want to develop local economies.

Some people will argue that if county competition has made China's land prices lower than other countries, then this can be a competitive edge to bring more capital into the country. And as businesses grow, the land will appreciate and eventually will benefit China's economic development. This question could be developed into another full-length article, but here I will briefly comment on it.

First, China's attractiveness to foreign capital mainly lies in its huge market, instead of its land prices. Second, a lower land price could not distinguish efficient companies from the rest, leading to the entry of many low-efficiency companies. Their presence will hamper the improvement of land allocation in the long term, as demonstrated by the "Upgrading and Switching" issues in many coastal areas. Third, China covers a vast territory, so county level competition in the coastal areas will harm the development of western and central regions. Fourth, underpriced land would create a waste of land resources, and also confuse the urban function zoning, producing outcomes such as the planning of an industrial zone near the city center. Fifth, even if we take dynamic factors into consideration and expect the benefits of rising land prices to arise from attracting more businesses, the governments don't need to drive farmers away. Instead, they can allow farmer collectives to be the main body in the negotiation themselves. Sixth, even when the government feels the necessity to intervene considering limited space, it doesn't have to requisition land directly. Governments can instead use planning, information services, and incentive policies to guide the farmer collectives to join the development in a larger picture. Of course, these judgments still require more proof and further studies.

4.7 Conclusion

A crucial factor for the formation of agriculture is to protect growing or mature crops, so the protection of property rights dates before the emergence of land scarcity. Therefore, in the well-field or other similar systems, income from the communal fields in nature was taxation instead of rent.

With population growth and economic development, land became increasingly scarce. So, the income from both private and communal fields in the protected well-field system began to include the rent of land.

The collapse of the well-field system and the emergence of private land property occurred not because the yeoman system or the tenancy system is more efficient. The real cause was increasing land scarcity.

Since the scarcity of land can be evaluated only through free trade, producing proper price signals to guide the efficient land allocation, and the tax rate on land was uniformly priced by the monopolistic government and cannot be traded in the market, so the taxation for property protection services and the rent for land scarcity were separated. The rights to collect rent and the power of taxation were also detached from each other.

The government is not suitable to be a market entity because of its monopolistic and compulsory nature. It should only have the power of taxation, but not directly process and exercise land ownership. In principle, states and governments should only own taxation power but not the right to collect rent.

The factor returns for optimal tax rates, like other factors, should be equal to its marginal output. However, the protection of property is a monopolistic service with economies of scale, with its input being large amounts of early-stage fixed investments and low or even zero variable costs. The optimal tax rate will drop as the scale of the protection services expands, so the effective tax rate is often higher than its optimal level.

Scarce land and property protection are usually viewed as complementary products, and tax rate and rate of rent are their prices. When the tax rate is lowered, the demand for property protection will increase, and then the demand for land property will follow, eventually driving up the rate of rent until the sum of the two rates goes back to its original level.

A subject with both powers to tax and to collect rent can use the above characteristic of tax and rent to attract companies and people through lowering taxes; it will then be compensated by a higher rent rate. During this process, the local economic scale will also expand and will altogether generate more revenue.

However, a subject with both powers to tax and to collect rent should not attract capital through underpricing land rent. An artificially lowered rent rate can send a distorted signal to the market, leading to inefficient allocation of land resources.

In the case of "county competition" described by Professor Steven N.S. Cheung, it seems that governments compete with one another through cutting land prices (or the discount value of rent rate). However, as their marginal tax rate approaches zero, competition is in fact conducted through lowering tax rates. Real tax rates are generally monopolistic prices and tend to increasingly exceed the optimal rate as the economy expands, so competition involving tax rate drives tax rates toward their optimal level and is thus efficient competition.

However, in China land property is not well-protected, and local governments sometimes force the farmers to give up their land at a price lower than a market rent or market price. Such a distorted land rent will lead to the inefficient allocation of land resources.

Instead of requisitioning land, county governments can take their taxation as collateral and purchase land at market price with the money they loan from banks. Then the governments can provide the land to companies for free or grant them a cut of value added tax up to 4.25%, in doing so rendering hidden tax rate competition open and transparent.

References

Coase, Ronald, The Marginal Cost Controversy, *Economica, New Series*, Vol. 13, No. 51 (August 1946).

North, Douglass and Thomas, Robert, "The Rise and Fall of the Manorial System: A Theoretical Model", *Journal of Economic History*, 31 (December), 1971.

傅筑夫, 《中国经济史论丛》上卷, 生活.读书. 新知三联书店, 1980; (Fu Zhufu, Studies on Economic History of China, 1980).

库朗热, 《古代城邦》, 华东师范大学出版社, 2006; (Translated from: Fustel de Coulanges, La cité antique: étude sur le culte, le droit, les institutions de la Grèce et de Rome, Paris: Durand, 1864).

诺思, 道格拉斯, 《经济史中的结构与变迁》, 上海三联出版社, 1991; (Translated from: North, Douglass, *Structure and Change in Economic History*, W. W. Norton & Company, 1981).

Palmer, Matthews, *The Treaty of Waitangi in New Zealand's Law and Constitution*, Victoria University Press, 2008.

沈汉, 《英国土地制度史》, 学林出版社, 2005; (Shen Han, A History on the British Land System, Xuelin Publishing House, 2005).

徐喜辰，《井田制度研究》，吉林人民出版社，1982; (Xu Xichen, *A Study on the Well-field System*, Jilin People's Publishing House, 1982).
张五常，《佃农理论》，商务印书馆，2000; (Cheung, Steven, *The Theory of Share Tenancy*, Commercial Press, 2000).
张五常，《中国经济制度》，花千树出版有限公司，2008; (Cheung, Steven, *The Chinese Economic System*, Huaqianshu Press, 2008).
张树国，《春秋贵族社会衰亡期的历史叙事》，中国社会科学出版社，2008; (Zhang Shuguo, *A Historical Narration of Aristocracy's Decline in the Spring and Autumn Period*, China Academy of Social Science Press, 2008).
张岩，《「山海经」与古代社会》，文化艺术出版社，1999; (Zhang Yan, *Shanhaijing and Ancient Society*, Culture and Art Press House, 1999).
郑德良，《现代香港经济》中国财政科学出版社，1982; (Zheng Deliang, *Modern Hong Kong Economy*, China Financial Science Press, 1982).
周庆智，《中国县级行政结构及其运行》，贵州人民出版社，2004; (ZHOU Qingzhi, *Chinese Administration Structure at County Level and its Operation*, Guizhou People's Publishing House, 2004).
周其仁，《收入是一连串事件》，北京大学出版社，2006; (Zhou Qiren, *Income is a Series of Incidence*, Peking University Press, 2006).

Classical Literature

《尚书》(The Book of History).
马端临编，《文献通考》; (Ma Duanlin, Edited, General Reference of Literature).
(Translated from Research of Institutional Economics (《制度经济学研究》), Volume 38, Issue 2, 2012).

CHAPTER 5

The Economic Nature of the Permanent Tenancy

Contents

In China and even worldwide, permanent tenancy seems peculiar. In fact, this peculiarity is human-made because no insightful understanding exists toward this economic institution, and a description of a simple theory in a textbook was taken as the institutional arrangement in reality, which then is estranged.

Acknowledgment to Gao Wangling, Zheng Zhenyuan, Tan Shuhao, Yang Xiaowei, and Liu Yejin for their constructive comments on the draft version at the Unirule Academic Bi-weekly Forum.

Translated from *Research of Institutional Economics* (《制度经济学研究》), Volume 46, Issue 4, 2014.

Sheng Hong, *Vision and Calculation*,
https://doi.org/10.1007/978-981-15-2898-9_5

Through profound exploration, we discover previously ignored institutional features of permanent tenancy, thus deepening our interpretation of institutions.

5.1 Permanent Tenancy Rights, a Result of Property Rights Separation

As the term permanent tenancy rights implies, tenants under permanent tenancy are entitled to lease land permanently. Zhao Gang comments that such an institutional arrangement indicates not only lasting rights to tenancy but also independence—the rights can be transferred freely without the consent of landowners. Once in the market, permanent tenancy rights are valued independently, known in China as "permanent tenancy rights" or "surface land rights." Landownership apart from those is referred to as "land-bone rights" or "undersurface land rights." Prices of undersurface land rights and surface land rights are formed in land markets. In general, no fixed proportion exists between the prices of both such rights, and the price of undersurface land rights is not necessarily higher than that of the surface land rights. Sometimes the permanent tenancy price is even higher than the land price (Table 5.1).

Property rights prices are noted as bearing no fixed proportion to tenancy rights prices. Does this relationship indicate that permanent tenancy rights are ambiguously defined and unstable? The rent rate of property rights is not stable with the rent rate of tenancy rights as well.

Table 5.1 Property rights price and permanent tenancy rights price in Tunxi region during the Qing Dynasty

Time	*Property rights price* (tael)	*Tenancy right price* (tael)
1707	6.50	2.91
1727–1752	7.62	7.38
1782–1800	10.79	8.49
1802–1807	11.48	9.71
1814–1817	18.01	37.04
1821–1850	17.75	14.27
1851–1861	9.29	10.39

Note: This table was compiled by Zhang Youyi based on files of the Tunxi region during the Qing Dynasty from the Institute of Economics, Chinese Academy of Social Sciences. Cited from Zhao Gang 2005, p. 49

For instance, according to Zhang Ming, during the Republican era, the big rent rate (that of land-bone) was generally approximately 17.5%, accounting for half of the land rent rate of 35%. However, big rent rates obviously deviated, for example, 14.4%, 8.2%, 7.3%, 16.6%, 10.7%, 12%, 10.1%, 12.1%, and 5.5% (2012, pp. 311–322). In turn, tenancy rights rent rates varied as well, implying that neither the rent rate of undersurface land rights nor the rent rate of surface land rights represented the price of "pure" permanent tenancy rights.

The literal value of permanent tenancy rights lies in the expenses saved by permanent tenancy relative to impermanent tenancy, including occupational stability and the reduced time and cost of identifying a new tenant. How does this phenomenon influence the pricing of permanent tenancy rights? Generally, tenancy and leasing rights are treated equally, and transaction fees are shared by both parties. When the rights are equal and the bargaining space is narrow, the fees shared do not differ significantly. Therefore, the rights to permanent tenancy bear no definitely advantageous value; neither do permanent leasing rights.

In that sense, permanent tenancy rights are more than just leasing that lasts, which could be detected from several hypotheses on the origins of permanent tenancy rights. According to Zhao Gang, permanent tenancy has three origins: rent deposit, opening up wasteland, and pawn (2005, pp. 16–24).

A closer look reveals that all of the origins involve tenants' input into land as property. Under the so-called rent deposit institution, tenants are expected to pay a deposit to landowners. The amount of the deposit varies. If it is too high, landowners may fail to refund it all immediately when tenants withdraw, which in turn hinders the surrender of tenancy. In that case, tenants are allowed to continue the tenancy. If such continuity keeps happening, the tenancy becomes permanent. During the tenancy, interest on the deposit, which is more than the amount covering the risk of rent default, is in fact tenants' input into the land.

The so-called contribution to cultivating virgin land is the assistance that tenants provide to landowners during the cultivation of land, construction of irrigation, and water conservancy, and it is paid back with permanent tenancy rights. This situation involves the input of labor.

Third, through pawn, landowners sell land for financing purposes but maintain the rights to redemption and tillage. To keep their tillage rights, the pawn prices offered are typically lower than market value. This situation is equivalent to landowners preserving part of the land property rights with a certain amount of capital. Therefore, they pay for cheaper rent. Similarly, some landowners sell outright their land and only preserve the tenancy rights.

These three origins indicate that the acquisition of permanent tenancy rights is attributed to tenants' extra inputs, particularly from the perspective of the third origin, which is more akin to a thought experiment. We can imagine that, when pawning or selling the land, a landowner could reduce the price at will to within the range of 100% of the market value to zero. Accordingly, the rent he pays as a tenant to the lienee or buyer varies within the range of 100% of the market rent rate to zero. Assuming that the percentage of the real pawning price (or land price) that accounts for the market pawning price (or land price) is a, and 0>a>1, the lienee or buyer then acquires a% of the property rights. The land rental rate that he receives is a∗100% of the market rate as well, which could help answer why the property rights price (rental rate) of undersurface land is not a fixed proportion to the property rights price (rental rate) of surface land: prices or rental rates of different property-tenancy relationships would vary remarkably.

Such a thought experiment demonstrates that permanent tenancy rights are actually a combination of the right to permanent tenancy and a part of the property rights, the percentage of which is determined by its contribution to input. The difference between the rent paid by a permanent tenant and the market rate is in fact the result of the tenant's part of the property rights. We could simply divide property rights into n shares and buy one share at a price of 1/n of the property's market value or buy k shares at a price of k/n of the property's market value. We are aware that, in the real world, forms that reflect property rights divisions exist, such as stocks.

Therefore, in reality, permanent tenancy rights represent a division of property rights combined with rights to permanent tenancy. However, a more attractive pattern leads to the misunderstanding that such an institutional arrangement only represents "permanent tenancy."

5.2 Separation of Permanent Tenancy Rights and Property Rights Is a Division of Comparative Advantages

The separation of permanent tenancy rights and of undersurface land property rights is not identical to the division of capital by stocks, after which the rights and obligations represented by each share are identical.

The separation of permanent tenancy rights and undersurface land property rights is not an equal division of rights, which means that their respective rights and obligations are different. We could refer to the separation of the former as horizontal and that of the latter as vertical or, more simply, a division into layers and blocks. Using a building as a comparison: several apartments exist vertically, and floors are horizontal.

The two types of rights divided from land property differ most in that an owner of undersurface land property rights is obliged to tax, whereas the owner of permanent tenancy rights is not. Other differences are that tenancy right owners take more care of the land and, for example, decide what to grow. In that sense, the separation could be described as a division of several activities contained within the performance of property rights.

For instance, some are good at dealing with the government, whereas others are better at agricultural decision making. Those who are good at dealing with the government are more familiar with taxation than those who are not, and those agricultural decision makers cost less during the process than the non-professional. In agreement with this argument, when the full property rights of land are divided into undersurface land rights and surface land rights, transaction and production costs are reduced if the person who is good at dealing with the government holds the undersurface land rights and the person who is good at making agricultural decisions holds the surface land rights, allowing both to give play to their strengths. Therefore, people can better exercise their land rights and operate property, which in turn promotes efficiency (Fig. 5.1).

In fact, such a scenario is quite common in other areas. Take house leasing, for instance. A landowner leases a house to a principal tenant, who then leases the house to a tenant. The landowner is likely good at fundraising, insightful about the real estate market, and pays taxes, whereas the principal tenant is better at the maintenance and decoration of the property and dealing with tenants. Two layers of rents are in place: one charged by the landowner to the principal tenant and the other charged by the principal tenant to the tenant.

In general, as long as economic players agree, complete ownership could be divided into multiple property rights shares—a portfolio that could be referred to as a bundle of property rights. Such a division scales down the unit of property rights, requiring less financing for buyers with smaller wealth. In addition, the division is based on people's comparative advantages during the different stages of operation, facilitating its efficiency. The property rights of UN's Millennium Hotel in New York are

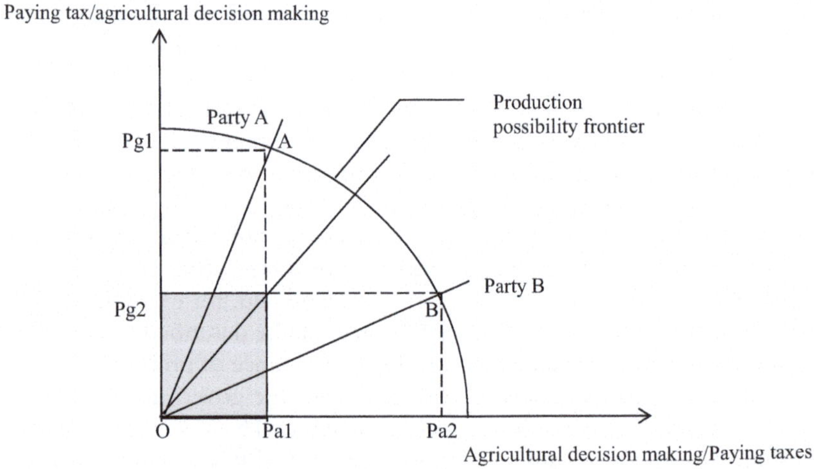

Fig. 5.1 Comparative advantages of property rights exercise and separation of land rights

Note: Party A is good at agricultural decision making but bad at dealing with the government (represented in the figure by paying taxes), and Party B is the opposite. Both are crucial elements to the determination of the production possibility frontier, that is, the elements of property rights exercise. In the figure, the production possibility frontier of farmland is the indifferent curve of taxation and agricultural decision making, representing the results generated by the different portfolios of these two property right operations. The horizontal axis is the input to agricultural decision making, and the vertical axis is the input to dealing with the government—both are the prices of one another. Therefore, the cost of agricultural decision making is measured during the time consumed dealing with the government and vice versa. The cost of paying taxes and the agricultural decision-making cost of Party A are Pg1 and Pa1, respectively, and those of Party B are Pg2 and Pa2, respectively.

Party A is good at agricultural decision making and bad at paying taxes, and Party B is the opposite. Should A hold the property rights, his operating cost is represented by the rectangle Pg1A Pa1O, and is rectangle Pg2B Pa2O for Party B. After the separation of property rights, Party A holds permanent tenancy rights and focuses merely on agricultural decision making, whereas Party B holds property rights and exclusively pays taxes. Assuming that the production possibility frontier maintains the same, the cost incurred by their collaborative operation is reduced substantially—only in the gray area.

divided into nine shares of independent property rights, including one share of land property rights, two shares of air property rights, one share of renting mortgage rights, and four shares of property mortgage rights. In fact, each apartment building has in place multiple independent property rights: the property rights of the apartments include simultaneous partial rights to the land on which it stands.

5.3 Combination of Permanent Tenancy and Fixed Rent Changes the Property Rights Boundary

Under a leasing contract, parties A and B are commonly viewed as holders of property rights and users of leased property. However, in reality, they are not as clearly defined.

Zhao Gang commented that permanent tenancy more often occurred under a fixed rent (2005, p. 2). That situation leads to the significant result that permanent tenants are motivated to invest in the land because the benefit generated could be acquired entirely by themselves. For instance, the current output of a plot is 100 jin (about a half kg) of rice, and the fixed rent is 100 jin per mu (about 0.165 acre). After investing to improve the land's fertility or irrigation, the output is increased to 300 jin. Considering that the rental of 100 jin is fixed, the tenant receives the newly increased output that, in turn, drives him to invest in this manner.

Once investments of this type are made, the boundary of land property rights changes. In that scenario, the increased 100 jin of rice represents the incremental land rent. The land price, which is determined by its yield rate, increases accordingly. If the land price is 25 times the rent, rice increases from 2500 jin to 5000 jin. If the permanent tenant is entitled to acquire a rental of the increased 100 jin of rice, he is then entitled to a land price corresponding to this part of the rent from the land transaction. In this case, the amount is 2500 jin of rice. At this moment, he apparently owns a portion of the property rights.

As time passes, permanent tenants constantly invest in land based on their needs and resources, causing the boundary between them and property rights holders to change. Therefore, as previously mentioned, the price of undersurface land/surface land and the rent of undersurface land/surface land have no stable proportion.

However, in the long term, because permanent tenants have access to all of the proceeds from increased investments, their investments in land

Table 5.2 Rent rate adjustment before 1887

Farmland No.	*Original rate (grain*, jin)	*Adjusted rate (grain*, jin)	*Adjusted/original (%)*	*Note*
1	198.8	125	62.9	First round of adjustment
2	125	110	80	Second round of adjustment
3	120	85	70.8	
4	80	30	37.5	
5	280	175	62.5	
7	200	150	75	
8	120	56.3	46.9	
9	87	42.5	48.9	
10	160	80	50	
11	160	70	43.8	
12	160	70	43.8	
14	130	50	38.5	
16	320	187	58.4	
17	240	216	90	
Total	2380.8	1446.8	60.8	

Source: Zhang Youyi 1988, p. 206

continue to accumulate, giving them more land property rights and lowering their rent to landowners. The history since the Ming and Qing Dynasties suggests the same. According to Gao Wangling, since the late Ming Dynasty, China's land rent has been declining (2005, p. 29). Zhang Youyi's studies on Huizhou indicated that, during the late Qing Dynasty and early Republican era, rent in Huizhou plunged. Table 5.2 indicates that, in the 14 rounds of rent adjustments in 13 localities up to 1887, the land rent declined by 39.2% on average.

In the 12 rounds of rental rate adjustments in 10 localities from 1890 to 1922, land rent declined by an average of 3.6% each time. See Table 5.3.

The constant decline in land rent was partly attributed to tenants' increased share of property rights given their sustained investments. According to Zhang Youyi, before the Opium War, fixed rent dominated in Huizhou and share tenancy disappearing (Youyi 1988, p. 325). Zhang Youyi commented that landowners' investments in agriculture facilities were very limited: among the 335 cases of facility reparations in the east and west village of the Qimen area from 1833 to 1857, landowners directly paid with money or grain for 33 cases, accounting for less than 10% of the

Table 5.3 Rental rate adjustment 1888–1924

Farmland No.	*Adjustment time*	*Original rate (grain, jin)*	*Adjusted rate (grain, jin)*	*Adjusted/ original (%)*	*Note*
1	1921	110	180	163.6	
6	1890	130	70	53.8	First round of adjustment
	1902	70	105	150	Second round of adjustment
7	1897	150	137.5	91.7	
10	1916	80	120	150	First round of adjustment
	1922	120	112.5	93.8	Second round of adjustment
13	1897	63	20	31.7	
14	1915	50	60	120	
18	1914	100	75	75	
27	1910	150	140	93.3	
28	Before 1902	80	71.4	89.3	
31	Before 1902	190	160	84.3	
Total		1923	1251.4	96.8	

Source: Zhang Youyi 1988, p. 207

total, and the rest was covered by tenants' handing over less rent to landowners (p. 332). Therefore, tenants' investments in farmland offset part of the rent.[1]

This situation suggests that "permanent tenancy rights" contain in part the rights to land property.

5.4 Influence Exerted on Property Rights by Permanent Tenants' Direct Deployment of Land

The real value of property rights lies in the exercise on the practical occupation, utilization, and control of the rights' subject matter—in this case, land. Compared with property rights owners, permanent tenants actually

[1] Such a phenomenon is ambiguously defined. If landowners charge less once to offset tenants' investments, it could be viewed as the landowners' investment; however, if the investment is refunded through a lower annual rental, then this refund indicates that landowners recognized tenants' investments and their increased share of property rights.

control the land. Legally, the property rights that they shared are equal; however, tenants are able to take actions to protect their property rights once they are violated. Property rights holders of undersurface land are entitled to take action as well. However, they are physically disadvantaged, given that tenants have a labor advantage that effectively gives them permanent tenancy. In addition, property rights holders lease in large quantities, indicating that they are less populated (Gao Wangling 2005, p. 82, p. 119). Second, landowners fail to be closely tied to the land.

If property rights holders resort to government protection, the aid may be too slow to be helpful. Villages are far from counties, making government protection costly and tardy. Furthermore, application for such protection involves complicated procedures, let alone the possibility that the government may not judge in favor of property rights holders.

Therefore, if conflicts emerge between a property rights holder and a permanent tenant, the one who better performs the land rights dominates—in reality, this is usually the tenant. Such a situation influences the negotiation between the two and their strategies to deal with property disputes.

For example, considering tenants' actual control of the land and their mastery of harvest information, landowners may compromise on the rental rate or the real rent. In fact, the more unreasonable that tenants feel is the negotiated rental rate, more likely for them to harness their information asymmetry advantage.

Furthermore, land rent is submitted by tenants who have actual control over the agricultural products. A frequent strategy is delay. Landowners who cannot afford the delay compromise on the rental rate, which is why defaults occur after the tenancy contract is signed. Instead of the occasional behavior, the habit is actually a long term one that tenants take for granted (Gao Wangling 2005, pp. 79–90). This is a state of equilibrium achieved by property owners and tenants.

Would the default behaviors end if the landowner withdraws from the tenancy, that is, terminates the contract? Doing so does not work well given its lack of feasibility. If landowners cannot make tenants contribute the rent on time, how can they force them to surrender the tenancy? If landowners cannot rely on administrative forces to prohibit tenants from defaulting, how can they expect to force the surrender of tenancy with government support? When tenants refuse to terminate their tenancy, the situation is the same as what happens with a default. Although cases exist in which landowners terminated tenancy through the government's

Table 5.4 Real paid-in rent during Ming and Qing Dynasties

Period	*Real paid-in rent ratio*
1550–1650	80%–90%
1651–1750	70%–80%
1751–1790	60%–70%
1791–1850	70%–80%
1851–1890	69%–70%
1891–1900	50%–60%

Source: Gao Wangling 2005, p. 29. Ambiguous wordings such as century, the first half of, or several tenth were replaced with specific figures

support, the proportion was too small to be a credible threat (Gao Wangling 2005, pp. 107–118).

Therefore, such an imbalanced performance of property rights develops into habits or even legal institutions after perennial transitions. In rural areas, only tenants' voluntary surrender of tenancy is legitimate (Gao Wangling 2005, p. 112). The regulation for permanent tenancy established during the Qing Dynasty provided that a landowner was entitled to terminate the tenancy only when the tenant failed to pay rent for more than three years (Gang 2005, p. 37).

This relationship does not stabilize at an equilibrium level. Because facts prove the existence of such an impact, it works slowly and imperceptibly. The transformation most likely occurs after generational change. The son of permanent tenants already regards the paid-in rent as the contracted rental rate. After taking tenancy, he is likely to make use of his actual utilization and control of the land in exchange for a lower real rent. Generations after generations, the real paid-in rent obviously declines. Gao Wangling pointed out that during the four centuries of the Ming and Qing Dynasties, the real paid-in rent ratio decreased gradually, as indicated in Table 5.4.

The advantages and disadvantages of landowners and permanent tenants in exercising their property rights may also be reasons for the long-term decline in nominal rental rates, which works in conjunction with the increased share of property rights attributable to the increased investments in farmland mentioned in the previous section. Zhang Youyi's research found that landowners agreed to lower the rent because, relative to an unrealistically high rental rate, a slightly reduced one would be more effective in attracting tenants to fully pay-in (Table 5.5).

Table 5.5 Comparison of average paid-in rental three years before and after adjustment

Farmland No.	*Period of adjustment*	*Three years before*		*Three years after*		*Adjusted paid-in (%)/original paid-in*
		Average paid-in (grain, jin)	*Paid-in ratio (%)*	*Average paid-in (grain, jin)*	*Paid-in ratio (%)*	
6	1890	64	49.2	70	100	109.4
7	1897	131.3	87.5	134.6	97.9	102.5
13	1897	14.8*	23.5	19.4	97	131.1
27	1910	135.9	90.6	139.6	99.7	102.7
18	1914	89.1	89.4	75	100	83.9
10	1922	111.3	92.8	107.5	95.6	96.6

No record of collection in 1893; therefore, no listing.

Source: Zhang Youyi 1988, p. 208.

Such a phenomenon indicates that, as time passes, permanent tenants and their descendants constantly make use of the advantages of their actual performance of land rights to force landowners to lower both the nominal rental rate and the paid-in rent ratio. If this argument stands true, it justifies the significant fact that property rights might be transferred to non-property rights owners if they have been long utilized and controlled the subject matter. This statement also explains the following event. In the United Kingdom, land is nominally held by the King. However, since the Norman Conquest and the establishment of feoffment in the eleventh century (Xian Hongchang 2009, pp. 25–29), tenants have ultimately become the actual landowners, and the King's claim on land remains merely nominal.

5.5 Efficiency of Permanent Tenancy

In Sect. 5.2, we prove that the separation and independence of undersurface land property rights and surface land property rights (permanent tenancy rights) give play to comparative advantages, thus lowering the cost of exercising a right. That constitutes the core of institutional transition and determines whether or not the institution is better.

To have permanent tenancy is better than not to have it. Then, from the perspective of function, where are the merits of this institutional arrangement?

First, permanent tenancy is a lasting contract, indicating a sustainable time horizon. In Economics, a longer time horizon results in more efficient resource allocation. Resource allocation bears implications on the future; allocation institutions conducive to the current are not necessarily favorable in the future. Therefore, only visionary individuals are able to allocate resources and take into account future perspectives. A future-friendly resource allocation is about investments. Whether it is the old Chinese saying that grinding a chopper will not delay cutting firewood or the economic doctrine of roundabout production, that investment is superior to merely production is telling.

Second, the merit of permanent tenancy is about its flexibility of property rights reallocation while preserving their permanence. Economics suggests that, given the constant evolution of the environment, resources, institutions, technologies, and supply-demand, previously efficient allocation might not be so, thus requiring reallocation. The transfer of resources' property rights is achieved through interpersonal transactions. The independence from each other and the free trade of undersurface and surface land property rights create an ideal space for the free transfer of land rights.

Third, the lasting feature and fixed rent of permanent tenancy have inspired tenants to, first, resolve the problem of preserving the subject matter of property rights, that is, land, and further motivate them to cross the boundary of property rights and invest in the land. Without harming the interests of property rights owners, it benefits tenants to turn seemingly conflicting parties into win-win collaborators.

Fourth, permanent tenancy decreases the scale of property rights and reduces financing costs.

Therefore, permanent tenancy turns out an efficient land institutional arrangement.

5.6 Contemporary Implications of Permanent Tenancy

Given the perception of permanent tenancy, we could better explain the ongoing land institutions in China and even provide solutions to existing issues within the institution.

Under ongoing land institutions, especially those in rural China, land contracted to households is collectively owned. The title indicates it has nothing to do with permanent tenancy. However, seeing through, the ongoing rural land institution is in fact a variation of permanent tenancy.

The so-called rural collective is a community-based collective unit that can be compared with landowners or property rights holders. By contracting farmland, rural households establish a contract with the collective unit, thus acquiring the tenancy. In that case, rural households have permanent tenancy for the following reasons:

(1) Their rights to cultivate on collective land are permanent, which is expressly provided in legal documents. The Land Contract Law provides that the contract period of arable land is 30 years, within which the contract-issuing party will not withdraw the contracted land. The Property Law provides that, at the expiration of the contract period, individuals who enjoy the contractual right to the land are entitled to continue the contract in accordance with relevant regulations. Such permanent rights are community members' implied rights that are recognized by farmers.
(2) Rural households (permanent tenants) pay a fixed rent to the rural collective unit (landowners). During the long period after the launch of the contracting system, principle was that farmers paid the government a fixed amount as taxes, paid a fixed rent to landowners, and maintained the rest. The institutional arrangement changed after the central government canceled agricultural taxation. Both taxes to the government and rent to landowners were abolished—tenants are entitled to their entire output, which could be viewed as zero tax rate. Rural households offset the rent that they are supposed to pay with their share of the rent of a member of the rural community, leaving the essence of fixed rent untouched. Households who have immigrated are supposed to pay rent.
(3) Rural households (permanent tenants) subcontract (lease) or transfer (sale) their contracted land to others, identical to when property rights owners of surface land lease out or sell their permanent tenancy rights. The Land Contract Law provides that land contractual rights will be circulated in accordance with the law through subcontracting, leasing, exchanging, transferring, and others. Those pursuing subcontracting, leasing, exchanging, or others are required to inform the contract-issuing party only for the record. This process indicates that the contractual right is an independent permanent tenancy right.

The ongoing household contract system fits the criteria of permanent tenancy and is in fact a variation of permanent tenancy.

More than that, rural households with permanent tenancy rights are motivated to invest in land after paying a fixed rental. Since its adoption, the household contact system has existed for three decades. Rural households have already invested heavily in their contacted land, suggesting that the share of land rights by their permanent tenancy rights has increased. In fact, ongoing laws recognize investments in land by rural households. The Land Contract Law provides that, within the contract period, contractors are entitled to compensation for their investment to improve the productivity of the land when they give back land or contract-issuing parties withdraw land.

Rural households' permanent tenancy rights are assumed to account for none of the land property rights when the land contract system was introduced. After 30 years of fertility increases and other facility inputs, an annual investment worth 200 Yuan per mu at a compound interest of 3% is worth approximately 9546 Yuan. If the current rent is 800 Yuan per mu, the market value of agricultural land is approximately 20,000 Yuan per mu, resulting in rural households' tenancy rights accounting for 48% of all land property rights.

Predictably, in the long term and not considering the limits of economic technology, the share of surface land property rights approaches 100%, squeezing out undersurface land property rights. By then, the identity of the rural collective unit as landowners disappears spontaneously.

The ongoing institutions are, of course, not the same as permanent tenancy, which has three deficiencies. First, the subcontract (sale) of contractual rights (permanent tenancy rights) requires the consent of the contract-issuing part, making surface land rights not independent.

Second, rural collective units' identity as the contract issuing parties (owners of undersurface land rights) is prescribed rigidly by ongoing laws. Their undersurface land rights are forbidden from transactions. During the Ming and Qing Dynasties, when permanent tenancy was prevalent, undersurface land rights were open to transactions. In this sense, the current institutional arrangement is not a complete permanent tenancy.

Third, land property rights of rural collective units are weakened by ongoing legal institutions. Suppose they are allowed only for agricultural purposes. For construction use, land is to be transferred first as state-owned land, which in fact makes it easier for governments to acquire land for non-public use. The Land Management Law provides that compensation for acquired land is six to ten times the average three-year production value, or only 24–40% of the market value of land used for agriculture.

Just because the current contract system has features of permanent tenancy and flaws to be solved at the same time, our institutional transition is able to approach an ideal state based on the status quo. We aim to develop the current land contract system into a complete permanent tenancy. To that end, the following steps need to be completed:

(1) Cancel or reinterpret the terms in the Land Contract Law that state that the contractual rights to the transfer of land require the consent of contract-issuing parties. What matters is allowing rural collective units to choose on their own whether or not the consent of issuing parties is necessary.
(2) In the legal framework, the rural collective unit is regarded as a legal person whose members (rural households or individuals) determine through legitimate procedures its founding, expansion, downsizing, and termination. Through this principle, rural collective units as land underneath right holders (or landowners) are allowed to determine through legitimate procedures whether to sell their underneath rights.
(3) The land rights held by the nation need to be explicitly defined as rights in a sovereign sense, represented by taxation on the land or on their output, which does not conflict with land property rights.

In general, such reform objectives and ways are feasible or even conservative in some respects as they achieve more efficient institutional arrangements. They deliver reform goals without major modifications to ongoing land institutions, even without any amendments to legal texts and are, thus, a low-cost and effective reform solution.

References

高王凌, 《租佃关系新论——地主、农民和地租》,上海书店出版社, 2005. (Gao Wangling, *New Tenancy: Landowners, Peasants and Rent*, Shanghai Bookstore Publishing House, 2005.)

咸鸿昌, 《英国土地法律史》, 北京大学出版社, 2009. Xian Hongchang, *History of British Land Law*, Peking University Press, 2009.

张明, 《民国时期皖南永佃制实证研究》, 人民出版社, 2012. (Zhang Ming, *Empirical Study on Permanent Tenancy in Southern Anhui Province During the Republican Era*, People's Publishing House, 2012.

章有义,《近代徽州租佃关系案例研究》, 中国社会科学出版社, 1988 年 6 月第 1 版。(Zhang Youyi, Case Study on Tenancy Relationship in Modern Huizhou, Press of the Academy of Social Science of China, 1st edition, June 1988.)

赵冈, 《永佃制研究》, 中国农业出版社, 2005. (Zhao Gang, *Research on Permanent Tenancy*, China Agriculture Press, 2005.)

CHAPTER 6

Transactions and Cities

Contents

The research on spatial economics led by Krugman primarily names economies of scale in production as the reason for spatial agglomeration (Fujita et al. 1999). However, some gaps exist between this statement and the facts. In fact, most of today's cities are mainly finance-, trade-, commerce-,

---

This chapter reflects the author when taking charge of an urban planning project under the auspices of the Unirule Institute.

Translated from *Research of Institutional Economics* (《制度经济学研究》), Volume 41, Issue 3, 2013

Sheng Hong, *Vision and Calculation*,
https://doi.org/10.1007/978-981-15-2898-9_6

education-, and entertainment-oriented, and they house government agencies. These functions can be summed up in one word, "transaction." Industrial production is generally located in suburbs not far from the city. Explaining the origination of cities with economies of scale in production may apply to the industrial period of the eighteenth century but not to today.

The purpose of this chapter is simple: to explain the origination, development, and spatial layout of cities with "transactions." The "transactions" to which this chapter refers is a broad term in institutional economics that means the interactions between people, including transactions in the market, management and collaboration within enterprises, and interactions between the government and citizens, the government and businesses, such as taxation and paying taxes, public goods provided by the government, and enjoyment by citizens and businesses.[1]

In particular, transactions include remote transactions, often called "trade." However, the "trade" referred to includes only local activities and impact; that is, regardless of where goods are bought and sold by a trader, we only count his results in local transactions—we only assume that all or part of the transaction benefits fall to local places. This understanding even includes offshore trading and online transactions; that is, both producers and consumers of that product are not local. This is similar to our understanding of the fact that trade creates wealth. The purpose is only to consider the impact of trade locally to simplify the problem.

We will find that once we make "transactions" the basic unit of the research on spatial economics, we associate this theory with institutional economics because "transactions" is also the basic unit of institutional analysis (Commons 1983, p. 73). When we use "transactions" as the "common unit" for spatial and institutional economics, we can both spatialize the institutions and add institutional and policy variables into spatial economics, which significantly expands the dimensions of the analysis.

6.1 The Spatial Nature of Transactions

Economists believe that transactions create value, which refers to not only the dynamic results—the transaction price may guide the effective allocation of resources and promote the deepening of the division of labor and

[1] Basically, it corresponds to Commons' "Bargaining transaction," "Managerial transaction," and "Rationing transaction" (1983).

specialization—but also to a static value—the increase in the present welfare attributable to different resource endowments and comparative advantages. In this chapter, we discuss only the static value of transactions and assume that each transaction has benefits, as indicated in Fig. 6.1.

Because achieving a deal creates a benefit of transaction, people have an incentive for more transactions. To achieve this goal, they must overcome the obstacles posed by transaction costs. In the broadest sense, transaction costs contain much content, one of which is distance costs. A significant change is traders moving their place of residence closer to other traders, which significantly reduces the distance costs, even approaching zero.

The phenomenon of traders coming close to each other can be described as "space congregation," and its popular name is "city." Compared with "fragmentation," "congregation" creates a permanent asset. If the distance costs for A's round trip from his residence to B's residence is a, and the benefits that he gains from transactions with B is greater than a, this is equivalent to permanently reducing the cost of a if A moves to B's residence, and the value of the assets is as follows:

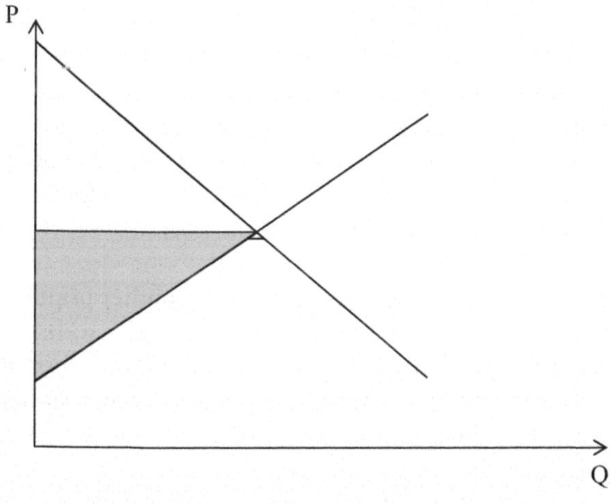

Fig. 6.1 Transaction benefits. Note: The triangle represents transaction benefits and consists of two parts: consumer surplus (the white part) and producer surplus (the gray part). The benefit of consumer surplus is expressed as lower prices, and producer surplus can be expressed as money or, approximately, as value added or GDP

$$V = A / r$$

where V is the value of congregation assets, A is the total distance costs for one year, and r is the discount rate.

In addition to significantly reducing traders' distance costs, congregation also brings about the unexpected benefit that the transactions achieved are disproportionately higher than the number of traders gathered. This benefit is also referred to as the "network externalities of the market." This term borrows from the concept of "network externality": as the number of nodes increases, the number of relationships between the nodes increases at a faster rate. The reason for "externality" is because the benefit from the increase in the number of transactions brought by congregation is not the result of traders' efforts but of other traders' congregation, whereas the latter is the external factor for this trader. If we use ME to represent the network externality of the market, it can be expressed as follows:

$$\text{ME} = n(n-1)/2$$

where n is the population density or the number of people per unit area. This formula represents in certain areas the combinations of the one-to-one relationships among n people and represents the potential market transaction volume. In practice, within a certain period, not every person can engage in one-to-one transactions, but a certain percentage of people will. Therefore, the formula can be multiplied by a coefficient of less than 1 (such as 1/100), but the trend that the formula represents remains unchanged. See Fig. 6.2.

If congregation only has such features, then a higher population density and larger city are preferred. However, congregation also brings opposing forces that prevent cities from expanding indefinitely. For example, as more people congregate in a city, the economy becomes similar to a large economy from which the marginal utility of a product or service decreases and its marginal costs increase as the population density increases. That is, the marginal transaction benefits decrease with an increase in population density, as shown in Fig. 6.3.

Considering this factor as within the network externalities of the market, the formula can be revised as follows.

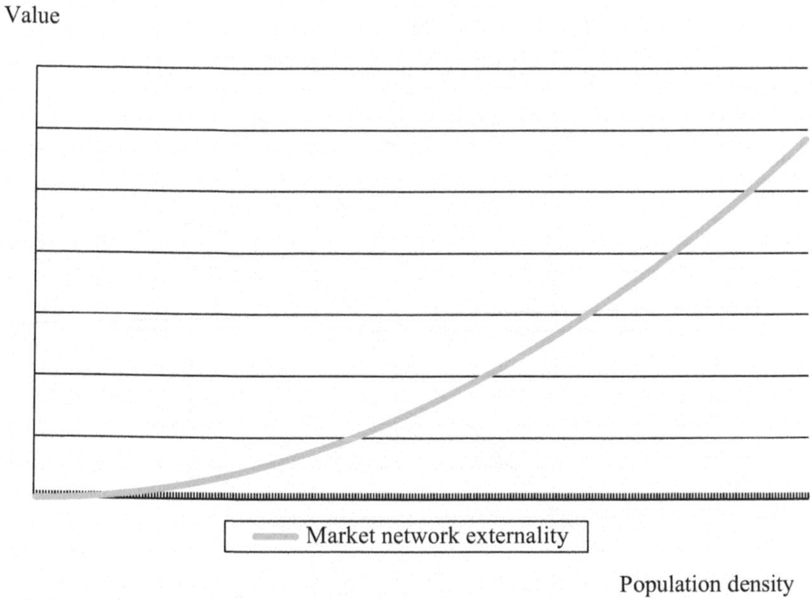

Fig. 6.2 Population density and market network externality. Note: The horizontal axis is population density (100 persons per square kilometer), and the vertical axis is market network externalities (number of transactions)

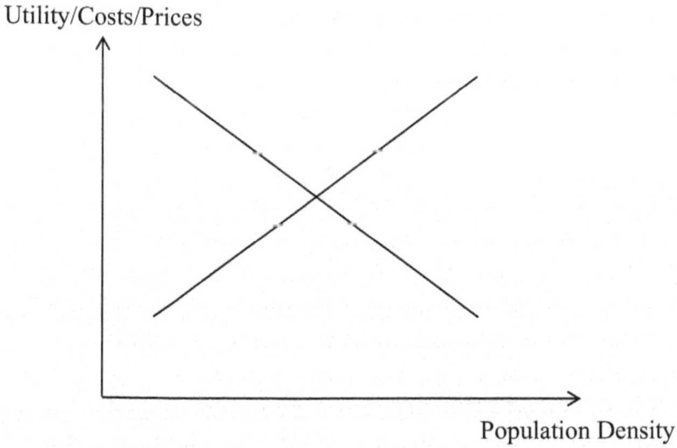

Fig. 6.3 Marginal transaction benefit

$$CE \approx \sum(a-c)n-(b+d)*n^2)$$
(for a detailed derivative process please see Annex 1)

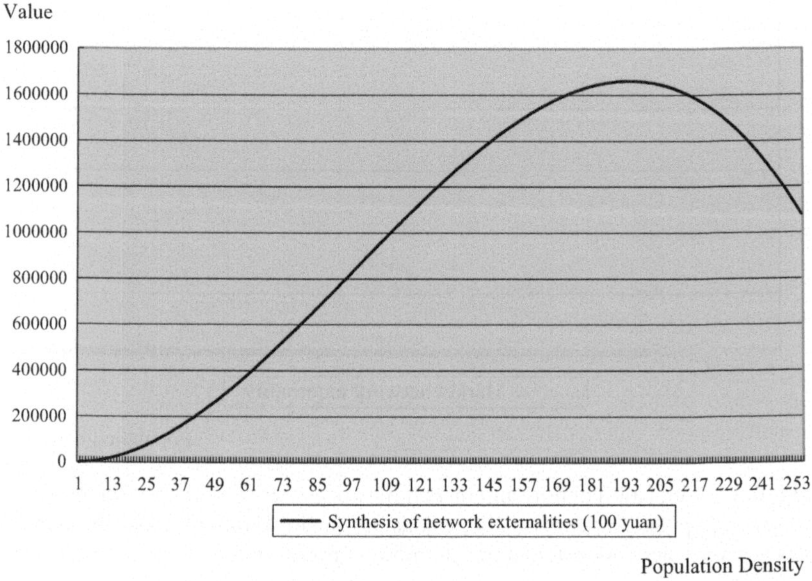

Fig. 6.4 Population density and network externality of marginal transaction benefit. Note: The horizontal axis is population density (100 persons per square kilometer), and the vertical axis is the network externalities of marginal transaction benefits (100 yuan per square kilometer)

where CE is the network externalities of marginal transaction benefits; a and b are the intercept and slope of the marginal utility function, respectively; and *c* and *d* are the intercept and slope of the marginal cost function, respectively. We draw the following trend, as illustrated in Fig. 6.4.

In contrast, an increase in the population density also leads to pure cost increases, such as an increase in the costs of congestion externalities. Assume that the city is in the shape of a circle and that the commuting population lives outside the city and only enters the city when going to work or shopping. If we calculate according to the city's highest population density within one square kilometer and consider the proportion of people living inside and outside the city, we can assume that there are N_{in} people (100 people) entering the city center. If the transport resource is the land that is covered by roads, we assume that the circumference of any radius of the circle from the center of the city is transport resources. When people move toward the city center, the radius distance from the city center decreases, and the circumference—the transport resources—also lessens, but the number of people has not decreased, which leads to congestion. The costs of congestion cannot be attributed to a single person but, rather, to the congregation of all traders who gather. Therefore, negative "externalities" exist that can be expressed as follows:

$$JE = N_{in} / \left[2(N\pi / n)^{0.5} \right] * n^{h}$$

(for a detailed derivative process please see Annex 2)

where JE is congestion externality, N_{in} is the number of people entering the city center daily (per square kilometer) and includes not only the employed but also external consumers; and H is the congestion coefficient, a number greater than 1. Congestion externalities change as the population density changes, as shown in Fig. 6.5.

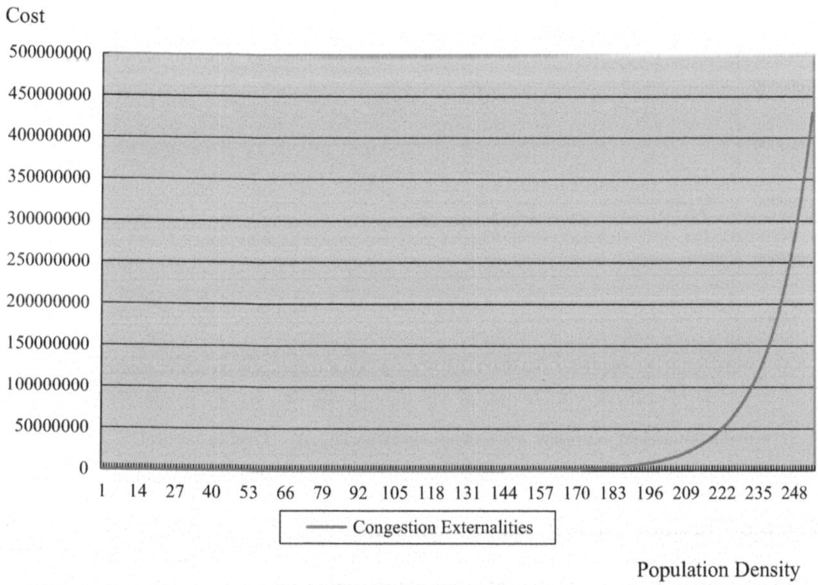

Fig. 6.5 Population density and congestion externality. Note: The horizontal axis is population density (100 persons per square kilometer), and the vertical axis is congestion externalities (100 yuan per square kilometer)

6.2 Equilibrium Scale and Population Density Distribution of Cities

Clearly, the equilibrium level of the population density brought by congregation, or the equilibrium level of a city's population density, is determined by both market-network externalities of marginal transaction benefits and the costs of congestion externalities. That is, at different population density levels, market-network externalities (congregation benefits) minus congestion externalities (congregation costs) are what we call "congregation rent" (see Appendix 3 for the formulas), as shown in Fig. 6.6.

Figure 6.6 shows that congestion rent increases with an increase in population density and begins to decline when reaching the maximum point. This relationship indicates that this maximum point is the optimum scale of urban population density.

"Optimal population density" is emphasized as not referring to the overall size of the city or the population density in all areas of the city.

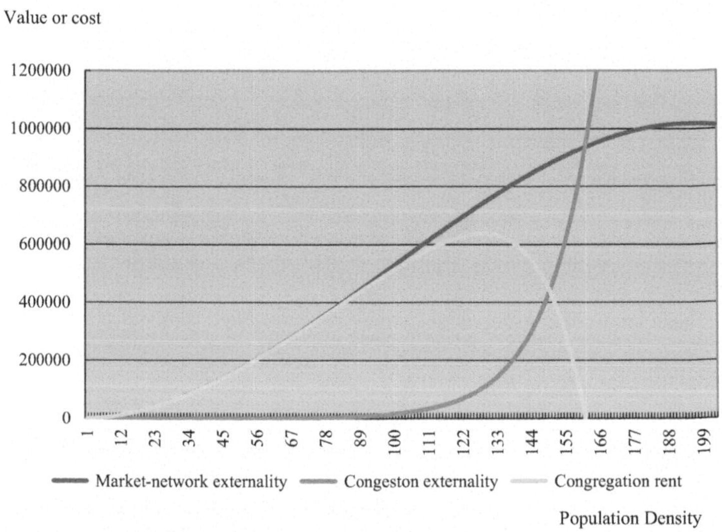

Fig. 6.6 Relationship between population density and economic benefits, as well as optimal population density. Note: The horizontal axis is population density (100 persons per square kilometer), and the vertical axis unit is 100 Yuan/square kilometers. The light blue line is the congestion rent curve

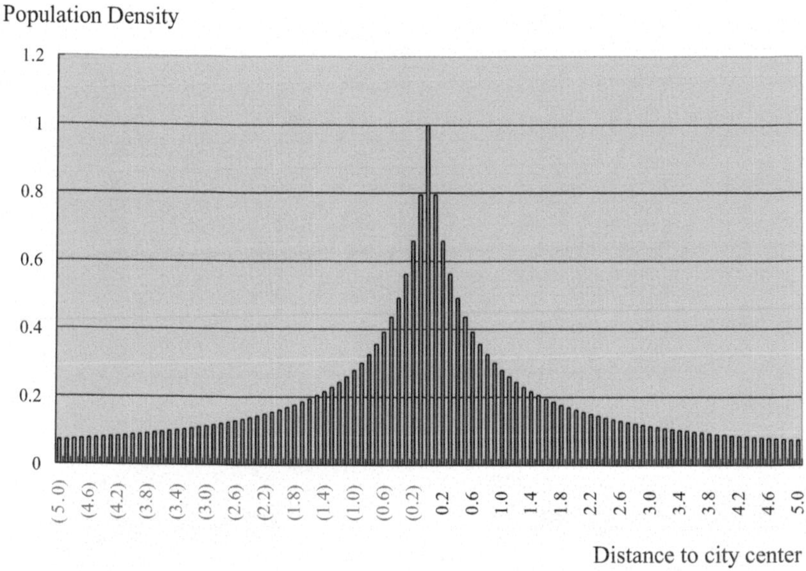

Fig. 6.7 Population density and distance to city center. Note: The horizontal axis is the distance to the city center, and the vertical axis is population density. Figures in brackets are negative values

Instead, optimal population density refers to the population density of the city center. This model can provide both the population density in the city center but also the urban population density in any area of the city. In reality, the population density varies in different parts of the city. Generally, in a single-centered city, the population density is higher in areas closer to the city center and lower in areas closer to the edge of the city. Transforming these coordinates, with the horizontal axis as distance to the city center and the vertical axis as population density, the specific circumstance is shown in Fig. 6.7.

The three-dimensional figure is shown in Fig. 6.8.

Practically, we use a city's geographic data and our model to simulate a population density map. See Fig. 6.9.

Given that the distribution of the population density is related to the economic variables, such as transaction benefits or congregation rent, the density distribution of these economic variables is quite similar. See Fig. 6.10.

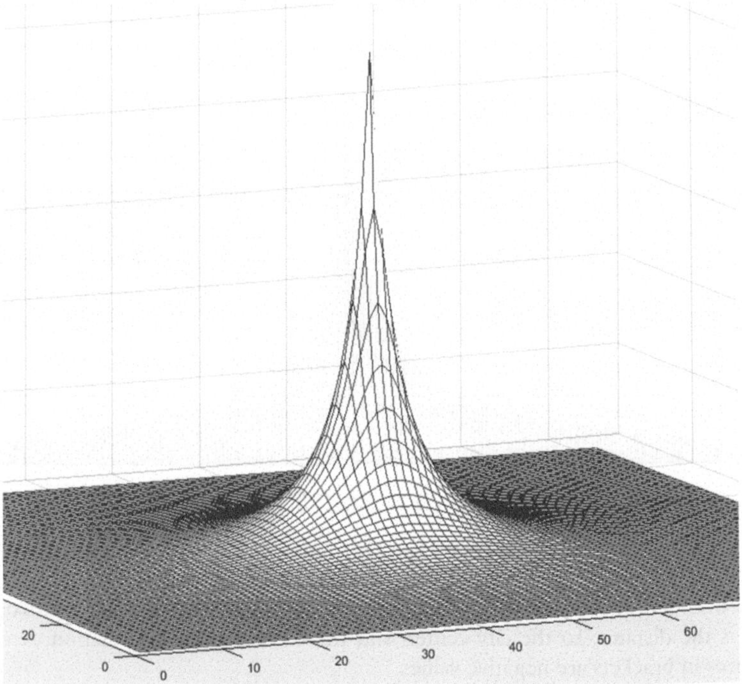

Fig. 6.8 Population density and distance to city center (three-dimensional)

The distribution of population density and other economic densities presents the equilibrium density of various parts of the city and provides a possible forecast for urban planning. Meanwhile, by integrating the population density or other economic densities in various parts of the city, we obtain the aggregate data, that is, total population, total congregation rent, or total GDP. We also obtain the per capita or per area economic magnitude by dividing these total data.

In the previous analysis, we assume that a sufficient number of people exist around the city, and the supply of resources such as water is also abundant. However, in reality, this is not always the case, and we have found that some cities are large and some are very small, implying that different needs and resource constraints exist on premises with the same theoretical scale.

The so-called demand constraint for urban development refers to the demand of the population congregation for urban space. This constraint

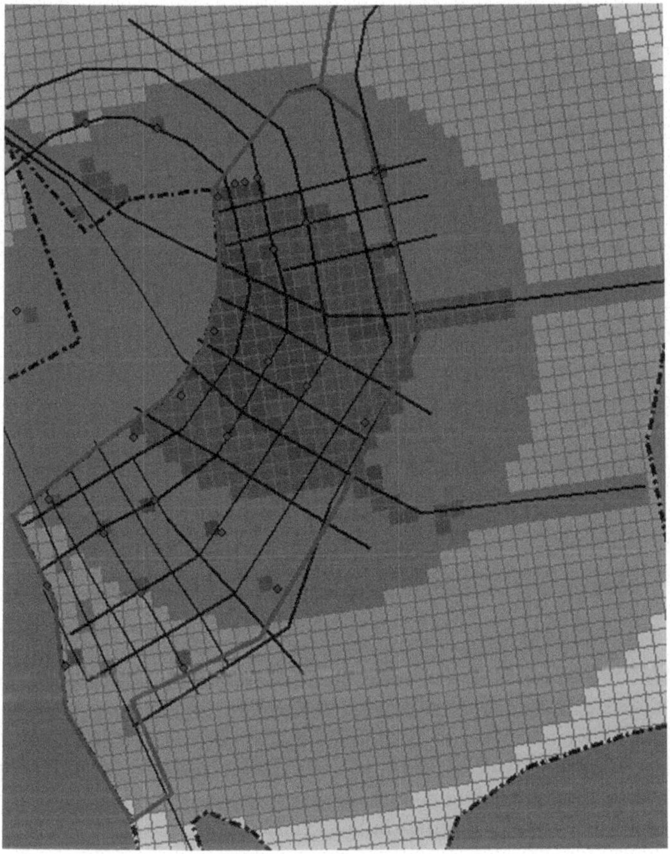

Fig. 6.9 Single center city area diagram. Note: This diagram is generated using ARCGIS software with data from EXCEL. Each small square represents a space of 100 meters × 100 meters. Different colors represent different population densities, with darker colors indicating higher population densities

depends on the amount of peri-urban population as well as the city's geographical location. In a sparsely populated area, even if urban space can be formed theoretically, it is impossible to form large cities. The scale of the city simulated by the previous analysis can be compared to a bottle, and the demand for urban space is water. The real scale of the city is determined by the water inside the bottle. Of course, if the water is beyond the space of the bottle, it will flow out to another bottle—another city.

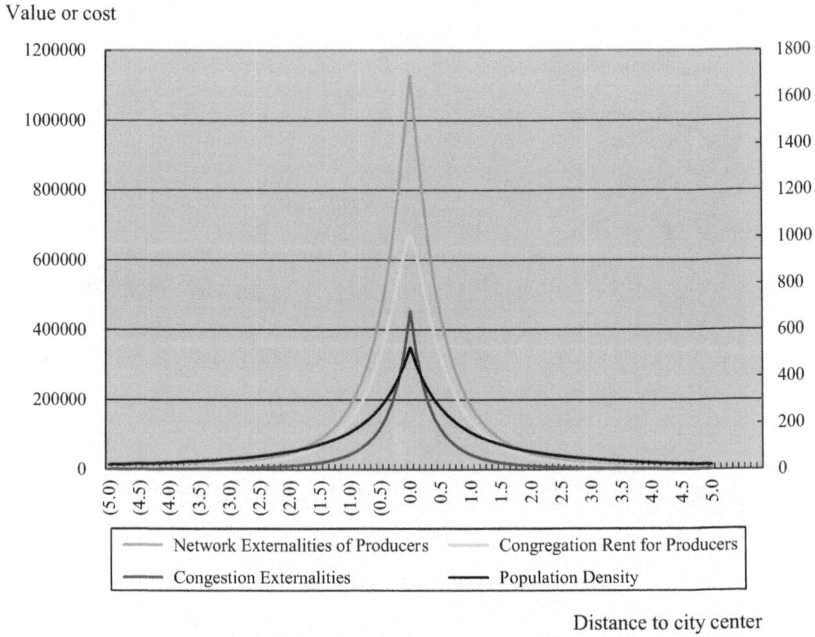

Fig. 6.10 Economic density and distance to city center. Note: The horizontal axis is the distance from the city center (km), and the vertical axis is economic densities (100 persons per square kilometer, yuan per square kilometer). Among them, producers' network externalities and congregation rent and congestion externalities are set according to the left axis, whereas population density is set according to the right axis. Figures in brackets are negative values

Similarly, the resource constraint compares the city's maximum scale at which resources around the city would be able to sustain with its theoretical scale, and selects the smaller of the two as the real "space supply."

Therefore, if we want to determine the scale of a city in reality, we need to compare its theoretical scale subject to resource constraints, that is, the actual "space supply," and its actual "space demand" and choose the smaller one as the actual scale.

6.3 Formation of the City

The power of the formation of urban congregation comes from the agents of the market economy, that is, individuals and institutions as economic agents. Figure 6.11 illustrates that the maximum value of per capita

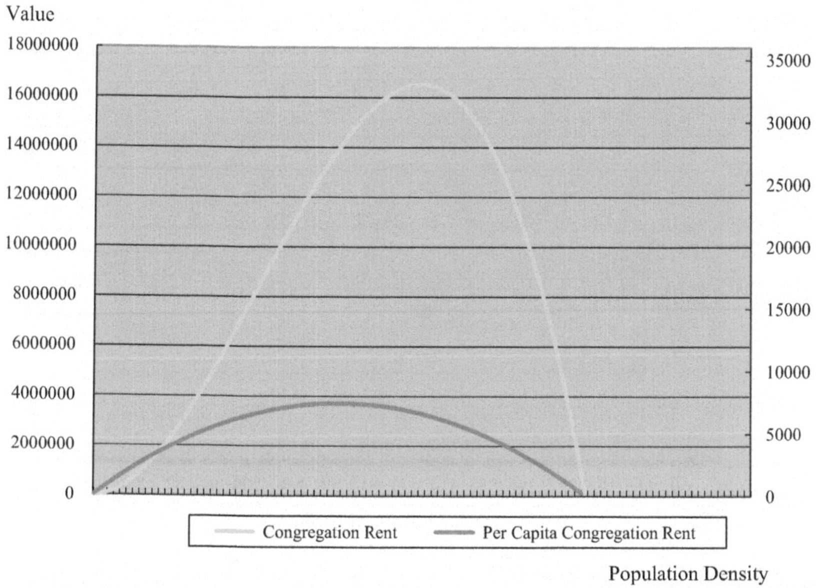

Fig. 6.11 Diagram of congregation rent and per capita congregation rent. Note: The horizontal axis is population density, and the vertical axis is congregation rent. The congregation rent is set according to the left axis, and the per capita congregation rent is set according to the right axis

congregation rent is to the left of the maximum value of congregation rent as a whole. This comparison indicates that economic individuals have more motivation to gather in urban areas and, thus, become the main driving force for the development of a city congregation. In turn, the population density increases, especially before the maximum point, further encouraging people to gather in urban centers. This process is said to be of congregation and density increase as reciprocal causation.

This diagram also shows that (1) when the per capita congregation rent passes the maximum value point, people still have the incentive to enter the city center because it is more competitive than other places despite the diminishing returns; and (2) when the per capita congregation rent is reduced to a certain level that is not enough to compete with other places, people lack the motivation to enter the city center and stop entering. At this time, the population density reached its maximum equilibrium levels.

From the derivative of congregation rent, we see more clearly that the increasing "speed" of the economic benefits is different as the population

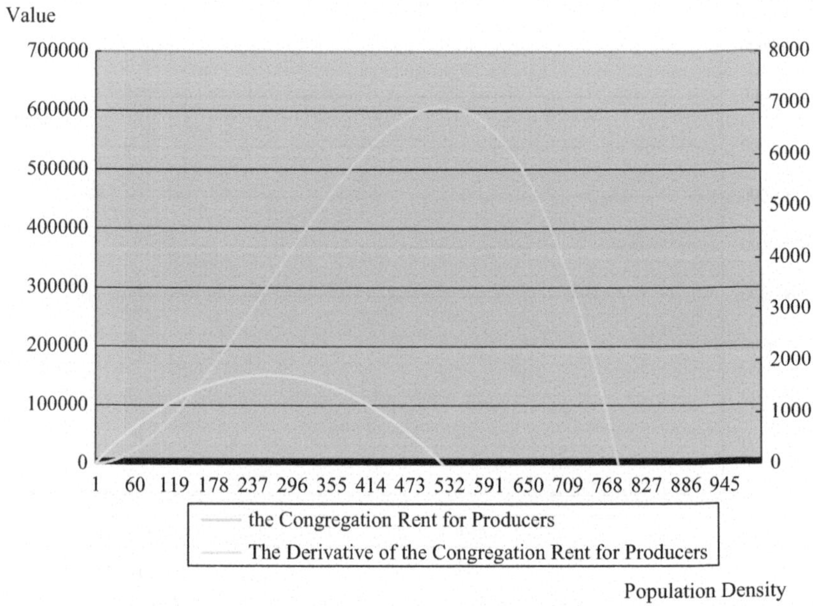

Fig. 6.12 Congregation rent and derivative of congregation rent. Note: The horizontal axis represents population density, and the vertical axis represents congregation rent and its derivative. The congregation rent for producers is set according to the left axis, and the derivative of the congregation rent for producers is set according to the right axis

density increases. It starts slowly, then speeds up, and finally slows down. See Fig. 6.12.

If the amount of revenue directly corresponds to the intensity of the motives, this derivative curve for congregation rent is the time distribution of motives.

In general, the greater benefit an economic activity, the greater motives people have and the faster they move. We use this relationship to derive the speed of urban congregation—the development speed—to estimate the time distribution of urban development.

Assume that di/dn is the differential of economic benefits to population density and dn/dt is the differential of population density relative to time. Generally, the growth speed of population density and the change in economic benefits relative to population density are similar in terms of direction and speed. Therefore:

$$dn / dt = f(di / dn)$$

Simply put:

$$dn / dt = di / dn$$

We directly switch the coordinates of population density (n) with coordinates of time (t) as follows:

$$dn / dt = di / dt$$

The derivative of the congregation rent reflects changes in the population density relative to the changes in the congregation rent. Therefore, this derivative directly describes the density changes per unit time.

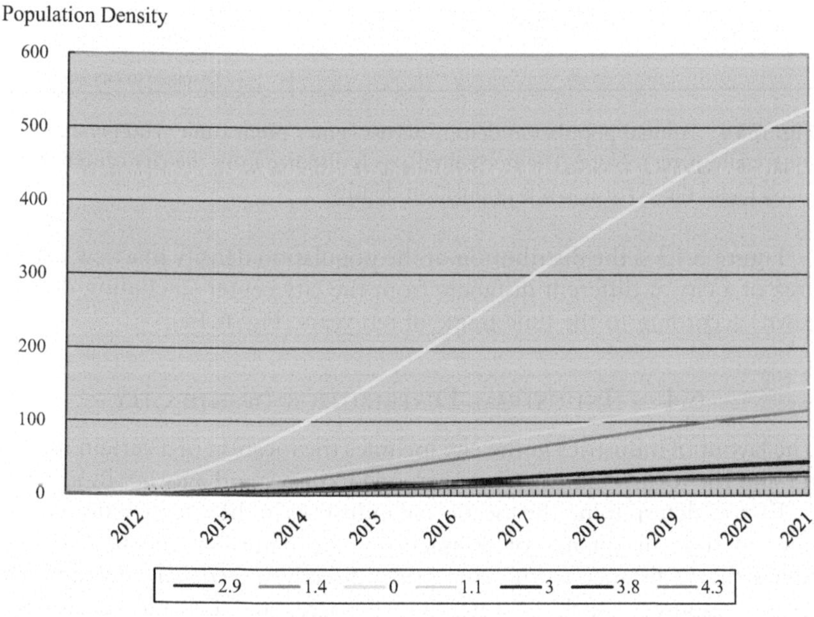

Fig. 6.13 Changes in population density in different locations over time (unit: 100 persons per square kilometer). Note: The vertical axis represents economic density, and the horizontal axis represents time. Curves of different colors represent different locations from the city center in kilometers

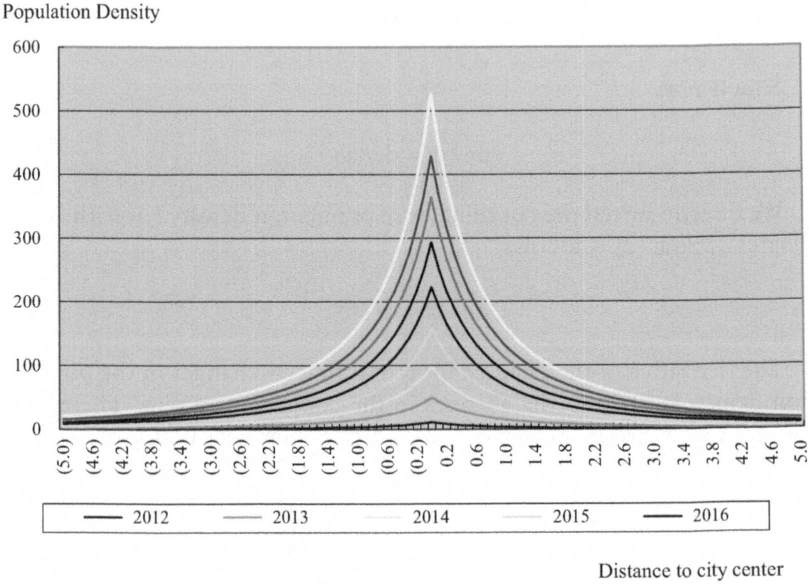

Fig. 6.14 Annual population density across center point (unit: 100 persons per square kilometer). Note: The horizontal axis is distance from the city center (kilometer), and the vertical axis is population density

Figure 6.13 is the distribution of the population density in a new urban area of a city at different distances from the city center (including downtown) according to the time frame of ten years (Fig. 6.14).

6.4 Industrial Distribution of the City

The layout of industries in the city includes the location of a certain industry and the relative position between one industry and another industry.

Factors determining the location of industries in the city include economies of scale, frequency of transactions, the nature of the face-to-face transactions, distance to the enterprises directly served, and demand for special resources (such as water, green space, and cultural resources). Among them, one of the important factors is the industry's economies of scale. Masahisa Fujita and Krugman pointed out that people are less sensitive to economies with increasing returns of scale because its advantages mainly manifest as congregation (1999, p. 70); they also indicated that when the industry's "fixed cost increases, the distance between cities will also increase; this indirectly reflects the amount of the fixed costs, which can be used to roughly measure the importance of economies of scale" (1999, p. 150). In other words, higher industry economies of scale result in a higher the degree of congregation and the closer the industry should be to the city center. It should be pointed out that Masahisa Fujita and Krugman and others mainly refer to economies of scale of industrial establishments, whereas we discuss economies of scale of the transaction industry.

Specifically, the larger the average size of the enterprises in an industry, the more people it will provide services for—theoretically—and the closer it should be to the center of town. This theory is generally reflected in the bidding of the rent; that is, enterprises with greater economies of scale generate higher revenue in the city center (given the high population density); however, with the increasing distance from the city center, their revenues decline rapidly.

Economic descriptions of different industries mainly reflect the differences in the scales of their economies, demand and supply functions, market structure, and market scale.

Because demand and supply functions are difficult to obtain, this chapter only does a rough estimate of these functions mainly to describe different industries with different scales of economies. The market structure is used to adjust the transaction costs; that is, the monopoly market structure has higher transaction costs than the competitive market structure. Scale is used to estimate the total size of the market.

Because the object of our study is the service industry, the supply function mainly reflects transaction costs.

The cost function for a general industry is as follows:

$$C(q) - F + vq$$

where F is fixed costs, v is variable expenses, and q is output. We can also use n to replace p, which is the number of people being served. That is:

$$C(n) = F + vn$$

More simply, we only consider the fixed costs as follows:

$$C(n) \approx F$$

Large-scale industries have a greater F value, and the corresponding maximum number (n) of people served is also greater. Conversely, smaller-scale industries have smaller F values, and the maximum number (n) of people served that corresponds is also smaller. Specifically:

$$C(n) \approx n / \tilde{n} * F$$

That is, when the amount of people in need of services exceeds the technical limits that a fixed asset is able to offer regarding those services, we need to invest in more of the same fixed asset.

According to Krugman and Masahisa Fujita, industries with greater economies of scale will be much more congregated. Thus, we obtain the spatial locations of different industries.

Assume that three industries exist, and their costs functions are as follows:

$$C_1(n) \approx n / \tilde{n}_1 * F_1$$
$$C_2(n) \approx n / \tilde{n}_2 * F_2$$
$$C_3(n) \approx n / \tilde{n}_3 * F_3$$
$$F_1 > F_2 > F_3, \tilde{n}_1 > \tilde{n}_2 > \tilde{n}_3$$

The congregation rent (CR) corresponding to each population density or spatial location (in this case, we assume that congregation rent and fixed costs are measured with the same time unit) separately divides the fixed costs of the three industries representing the asset scale (depreciation plus the return on the opportunity assets). We can obtain the unit asset's return per unit area, which we refer to as return on assets or, in short:

$$\text{Return on Industrial Assets}(\mathrm{I}_i) = \mathrm{CR} / (n / \tilde{n}_i * F_i)$$

where i = 1, 2, 3, ... represents industries. The unit is unit currency per unit asset per kilosquare meter.

This determines their degree of congregation and location in the city, that is, at any point where the industry with the highest return on assets should be distributed. At a certain place:

$$MAX\left(I_1, I_2, I_3, \ldots, I_i, \ldots\right) = I_j, \text{then Industry } j \text{ should be located at this place.}$$

See Fig. 6.15.

In contrast, the relative position between industries is determined by the supply and demand relationship and the degree between them. We use the logistics, information, finance, trade, and technology services industries as examples. These industries are both suppliers and markets to each other; they are mutual penetrating, complementing, and reinforcing. According to the 2007 Chinese input-output table (National Accounts Division of the National Statistics Bureau 2009), adjusting with the added value of 1 results in the input-output relations of five industries (the "Direct Consumption Coefficient"), as shown in Table 6.1.

The input-output relation in Table 6.1 is better reflected using the diagram in Fig. 6.16.

In the diagram, the larger the ring with colored lines, the higher degree of interdependence this industry has with other industries. The diagram also indicates the following points:

1. Each industry has a high input-output relation with itself; for example, the input-output ratio of the finance industry with itself is up to 12.3%, that of the information industry is 10.2%, and that of the logistics industry is 6.6%. These percents describe the high input-output relationships with segments within industries. For example, in the finance sector, the securities industry and the banking industry have a close relationship, and information providers have more business relationships with the software industry.
2. Relative to other industries, the finance industry has a higher input-output relationship with the other industries category. In addition to its high input-output ratio with itself, the input-output ratio of the finance industry to the trade industry is 8.4%, to the information industry is 4.2%, and to logistics industry is 4.1%. Although the technology services industry does not need many financial services, its major clients—science and technology enterprises—have a very high demand for finance industry services, such as venture capital, bank loans, and issuing stocks and bonds in the securities market. Therefore, the finance industry should be in the central position according to either the economic logic or the space.

3. In second place is the information industry.
4. In contrast, the trade industry's output has a relatively lower dependence on other industries, indicating that it has the characteristics of initial incentives and sources.

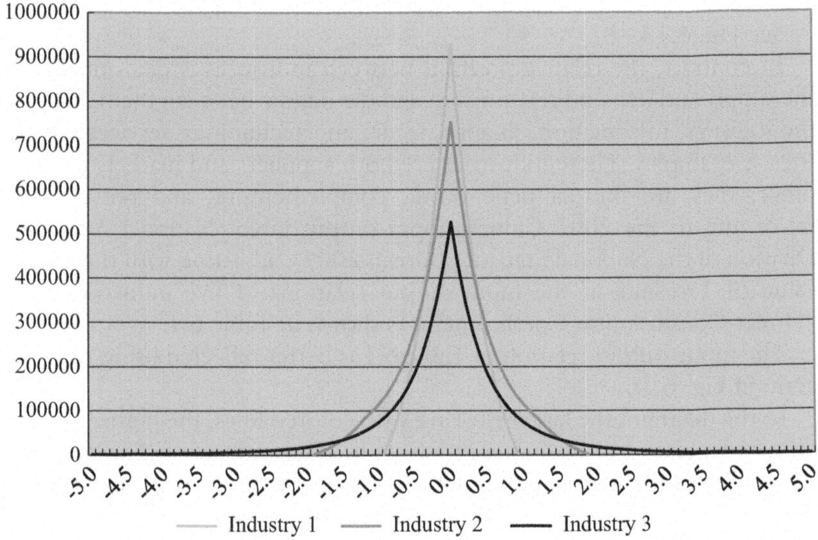

Fig. 6.15 Economies of scale, degree of congregation, and positioning of three industries. Note: The horizontal axis is the distance from the city center (kilometer), and the vertical axis is the return on assets of the industries. Different colors represent three different industries. At any point, industries with a higher yield (monetary unit/per unit asset/per square kilometer) should be distributed at this place

Table 6.1 Direct consumption coefficient between five industries (with added value of 1)

	Logistics	*Information*	*Finance*	*Trade*	*Technology serves*
Logistics	0.065645	0.005121	0.009932	0.010061	0.008007
Information	0.020272	0.101682	0.07027	0.008091	0.008375
Finance	0.042536	0.041444	0.122872	0.083761	0.023816
Trade	0.006417	0.034878	0.041919	0.031653	0.00617
Technology services	0.001296	0.011529	0.001703	0.001585	0.049698

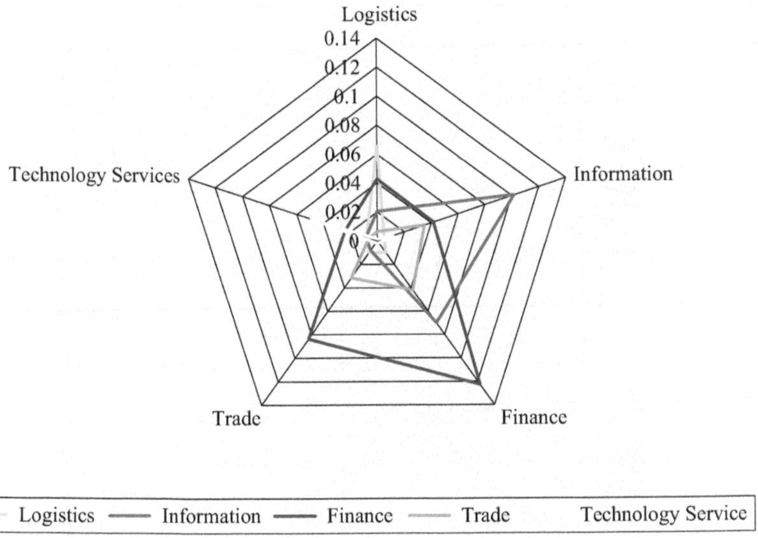

Fig. 6.16 Supply and demand relationship between five industries

These analyses further strengthen the previous judgments made on economies of scale. We can use the actual data of a certain place as an example and draw up the spatial distribution of these industries, as indicated in Fig. 6.17.

Given the diversification of the economic and technological characteristics of enterprises within an industry, that we can only use the average date to estimate the reasonable layout of the industry should be stressed. This statement precisely proves that this layout structure has no rigid boundaries. In practice, the business space in which most enterprises engage is in the form of an office building, which is universal and interchangeable. Therefore, overemphasizing borders between industries is not needed. Instead, enterprises should be encouraged to find their own locations based on market signals, which is more efficient.

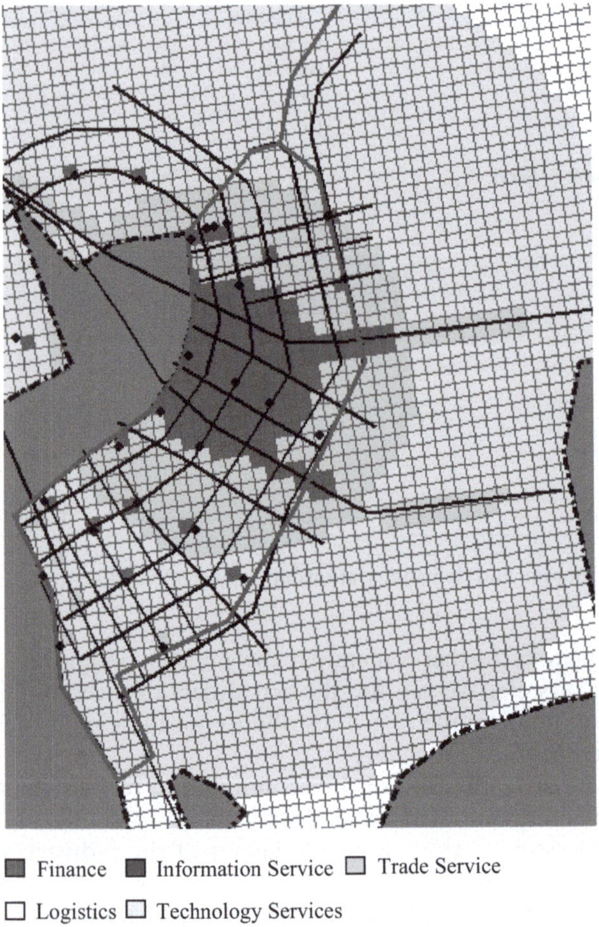

Fig. 6.17 Industrial distribution of an urban area

6.5 Institutions and Policies That Promote Urban Development

Because cities form and develop through transactions, and the transaction is the basic unit of institutions (Commons 1983, p. 73), institutions themselves determine the efficiency of transactions and, thus, affect the density and scale of a city. A combination point of institutional economics and spatial economics exists. In general, we can use transaction costs—strictly, unit transaction costs—to evaluate institutions. Under the same transaction utility, institutions with lower unit transaction costs have higher efficiency and vice versa (Hong 1992, p. 152). Conversely, institutional innovation and technological innovation will, in turn, reduce transaction costs, which will also promote transactions and contribute to the formation and development of the city.

In this chapter, we discuss institutional innovation. Institutional change or innovation includes many aspects, the most important of which is the protection of property rights, the safeguarding market order, and fair adjudication of disputes. Normal market order includes the freedom to access the market, fair competition, and the elimination of monopolies. Here, the market includes both the product market and the factor market.

From a market perspective, we can divide transaction costs into two types. One is transaction costs that are market-oriented, can be measured and traded by currency, and are managed by professionals or businesses; these are expressed as the incomes of those professionals and enterprises' revenues, including also government taxes. The other type of transaction costs is the non-market costs that, at least for the time being, cannot be measured in monetary terms, and no professionals or businesses exist to manage these costs. The main reflection is the time and trouble of dealing, which reduces transaction volume and, thereby, reduces the economic density and scale of the city. See Fig. 6.18.

Market-oriented transaction services can replace the time loss and trouble of non-market services, the unit transaction costs of which are significantly lower than those of non-market transaction services. Moreover, only completed transactions are charged, such as commissions. If not completed, fees are not charged. In addition, ad valorem taxes or fees are only charged after the transaction is completed in proportion to their income, such as sales tax and income tax, and the income of services personnel can also form market demand without reducing average transaction volumes. Non-market transaction activities have the characteristics of time and trouble, which potentially affect the realization of the transaction, thereby reducing transaction volumes. An increase in aggregate market-oriented transaction costs indicates that market-oriented transaction services replace non-market transactions, increasing efficiency and transaction volumes. See Fig. 6.18.

Overall, with the development of the market system, the ratio of aggregate market-oriented transaction costs to GDP probably increases and

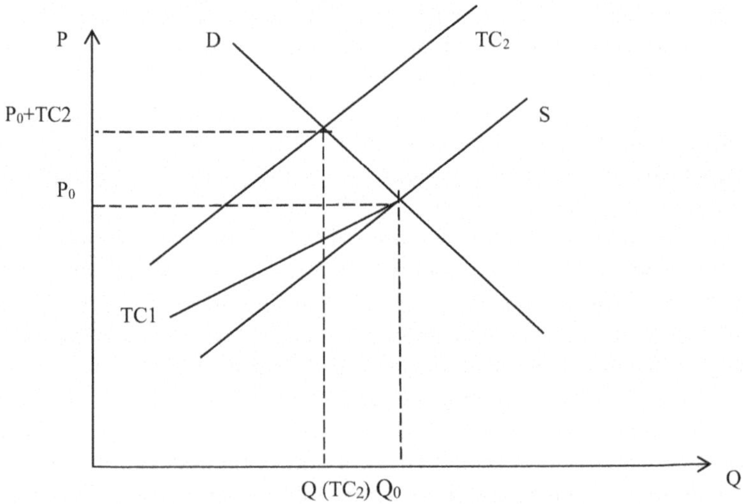

Fig. 6.18 Two types of transaction costs. Note: In the diagram, S is the supply curve excluding transaction costs, and TC2 is the supply curve of non-market transaction costs added to the supply curve. When counting non-market transaction costs, the price increases from P0 to P0+TC2, and transaction volumes are reduced from Q0 to Q (TC2). The TC1 curve is the curve of market transaction costs, which decrease as producer surplus decreases and, eventually, confluences with supply curve S at the equilibrium point. No negative impact occurs on the price and trading volumes. When non-market transaction costs (TC2) are replaced by market transaction costs, transaction volumes increase from Q (TC2) to Q0

non-market transaction costs decline. See Fig. 6.19. According to the estimate from North et al., total transaction costs in the United States are increasing in the long run (Wallis and North 1986, pp. 95–162). This increase is occurring probably because, first, institutional and technological changes in modern times reduce unit transaction costs and increase the transaction volumes. Second, more non-market transaction activities are improved into services provided by the market and, thus, can be incorporated into the currency calculation. The estimate of North et al. in fact refers to market-oriented transaction costs. This estimate also indicates that the market system can promote the monetization and professionalization of transactions and, meanwhile, save time and reduce problems in transactions.

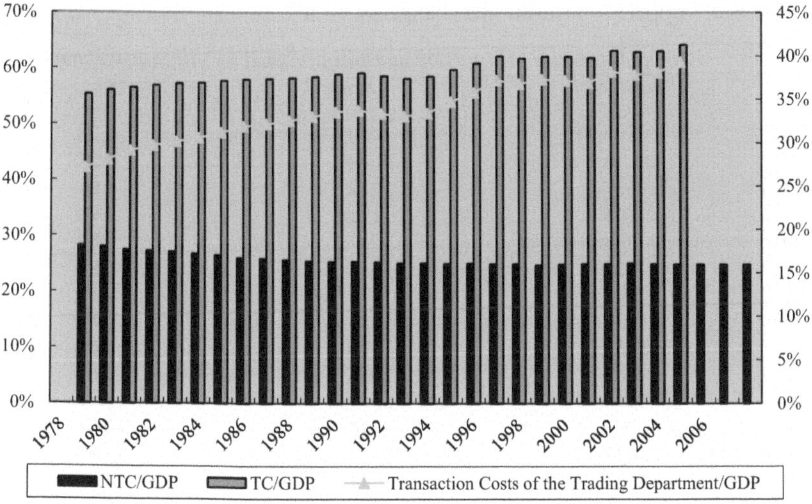

Fig. 6.19 Aggregate transaction costs of China, non-market transaction costs, and transaction costs of transaction sector. Source: Jin Yuguo, Dec 2006; Da Fengyuan, Zhang Weidong, 2009. Note: TC is the aggregate amount of transaction costs, and NTC is non-market transaction costs

Conversely, we can determine whether institutional efficiency has been improved simply by examining non-market transaction costs, which should decline if institutional reform was conducted. This relationship has been proven by numerous facts. Since the reform and opening up of China, the ratio of non-market transaction costs to GDP has been declining (Da Fengyuan and Zhang Weidong 2009). Intuitively, large non-market transaction costs affect the amount of transaction benefits and further exert a stronger impact on transaction volume similar to a lever, which will ultimately hinder the increase in urban economic density and equilibrium scale. Therefore, the decline in non-market transaction costs indicates that market-oriented services and transaction volumes increase. As a result, urban density and scale will be increased.

In particular, when calculating the balanced urban economic density and scale, the congregation rent per unit of time minus the non-market transaction costs is used. Changes in the latter lead to changes in the urban equilibrium economic density and scale and eventually lead to changes in the aggregate economy. In our model, we could simply simulate the results of changes to the aggregate GDP by adjusting non-market transaction costs.

Table 6.2 Impact of institutional change on GDP

	GDP under current institution	*GDP under institutional change*	*Institutional impact (%)*
2012	0.44	0.45	2.2%
2013	8	8	3.2%
2014	37	38	4.0%
2015	106	111	4.9%
2016	233	247	5.8%
2017	429	458	6.8%
2018	698	753	7.8%
2019	1037	1128	8.8%
2020	1432	1572	9.8%
2021	1865	2066	10.8%
2022	2298	2569	11.8%
2023	2701	3046	12.8%
2024	3035	3453	13.8%
2025	3261	3744	14.8%
2026	3345	3875	15.9%

In 2007, China's non-market (non-monetary) transaction costs accounted for 24.8% of the GDP (Fengyuan and Weidong 2009), or approximately 22% of the GDP after deducting the transaction costs associated with transportation. Taking these data into account, we use the estimated development of a specific urban area as an example. Assume that under the existing system, non-commercial transaction costs are approximately 22% of the GDP. If we continue to promote market-oriented reforms and reduce the institutional barriers for factors flow, the non-monetary transaction costs are reduced by 8% in 15 years, reaching 14% (of the GDP). In addition, the speed of institutional change in 15 years has been even. The impact on GDP simulated by our model is shown in Table 6.2.

Figure 6.20 illustrates that institutional changes can result in irreversible and sustained economic growth. Compared with policies, the impact of institutional change is longer term and more stable, and accumulates. The longer it takes, the more significant the impact of institutional change will be.

Under the premise that the market system is the basic system for urban development, market failures occur in urbanization and industrial development, including the following:

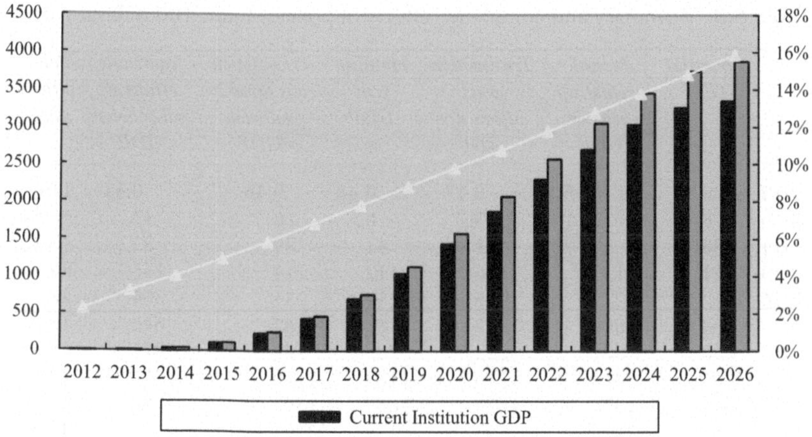

Fig. 6.20 Impact of institutional change on GDP

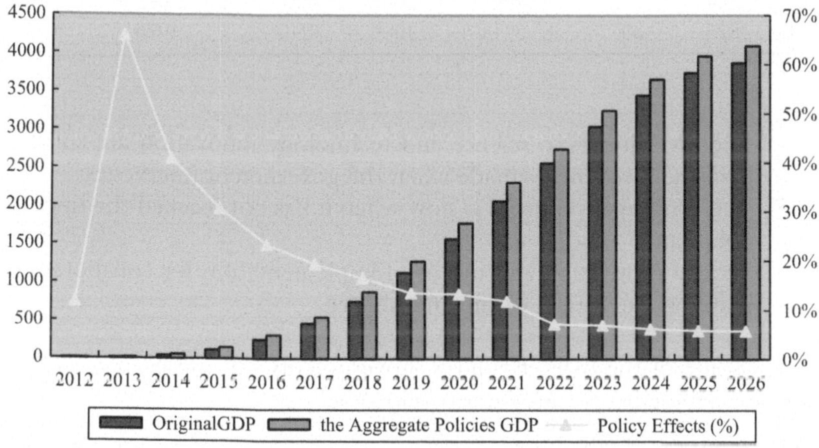

Fig. 6.21 Overall effects of policies (unit: 100 million yuan)

1. Lack of forecast for the vision of urban development and the final equilibrium scale;
2. Difficulty bearing the advanced financial costs of large-scale urban infrastructure investments;
3. Unable to generate valid intellectual property rights and protect and enforce them effectively;

Table 6.3 Summary and cumulative effects of policies (unit: 100 million yuan)

	Original GDP	*Initial promoting policies GDP*	*Transaction costs allowance GDP*	*Housing rent GDP*	*Transaction costs saved by coalition GDP*	*Aggregate effects of all policies GDP*	*Policy impact (%)*
2012	0.45	0.45	0.47	0.48	0.46	0.51	11.6%
2013	8	12	13	8	8	13	65.8%
2014	38	50	51	41	39	54	40.7%
2015	111	133	136	117	114	145	30.5%
2016	247	279	285	259	251	304	23.3%
2017	458	500	513	481	467	546	19.3%
2018	753	801	824	788	767	877	16.5%
2019	1128	1212	1215	1183	1150	1280	13.5%
2020	1572	1626	1672	1649	1602	1780	13.2%
2021	2066	2110	2173	2158	2101	2309	11.8%
2022	2569	2604	2622	2684	2613	2750	7.1%
2023	3046	3083	3105	3183	3099	3255	6.9%
2024	3453	3469	3496	3604	3513	3664	6.1%
2025	3744	3750	3784	3907	3808	3962	5.8%
2026	3875	3877	3914	4040	3940	4096	5.7%

4. The investments in science and technology innovation are smaller than the investments made when the government intervenes;
5. The congregation speed is slow when it has not reached the tipping point; and
6. Lack of motivation and means of implementation for collaboration between enterprises within an industry.

For some of the market failures, governments can use corresponding policies as remedies, including the following:

1. The favored policy at start-up;
2. The house rent allowance policy;
3. Policies on transaction cost allowances; and
4. Policies promoting industrial alliances and association development.

For the content and analysis of the impact of these policies, please see Annex 4.

These policies can be implemented simultaneously and have cumulative or even integrated effects. Table 6.3 presents our summary and cumulative effects of various policies.

Overall, compared with the urban development mechanism and institutional change, the role of policy is smaller. Policy has a larger role only in the early stage of development, which has gradually declined over time. Therefore, prudent and appropriate implementation of policies and putting more effort into improving the market system and promoting businesses and residents to participate in the market is the best way for the government to promote urbanization.

6.6 Conclusion

Transactions can form cities, and an analysis of transactions can help improve urban economics and spatial economics theory. On the basis of the transaction analysis, we found that constructing a theory of cities is not difficult and can better explain their formation and development.

This finding is because the economic variables and their characteristics involved in transactions, such as market-net externalities, have a more congregation nature than economies of scale in production. Put another way, these variables lead to more pronounced congregating results.

The analyses of transactions (omitting the analysis of production costs) focus only on transaction costs. The basic methods of analysis compare transaction costs and transaction utility (or transaction benefits) and identify the dynamic characteristics of which transaction utility is higher than transaction costs, thus further identifying the dynamic characteristics of urban spatial congregation.

Analyzing only transaction costs is within the field of institutional economics because institutional economics believes that the transaction is the basic unit of an institution, and transaction costs and transaction utility are important concepts in the analysis of institutions. Here, spatial economics and institutional economics overlap and generate organic links.

The conclusions of this chapter are as follows:

1. The underlying cause of urban congregation is the growth in market network externality benefits, which is caused by the growth in population density but is faster than the latter.
2. Two main factors counteract congregation. One is the diminishing marginal utility and increasing marginal costs resulting from the increase in the scale of the market, and the other is the increase in congestion externalities costs.

3. Congregation rent is the difference in (by diminishing marginal transaction benefits) the market's corrected network externalities and congestion externalities costs. When the congregation rent reaches the maximum point given an increase in population density, in theory, the city's population density reaches its maximum balance.
4. Other constraints on the scale of the city are the demand for urban space and resources.
5. The subjects of urban congregation are individuals or enterprises; because the per capita congregation rent has a variation feature that it arrives sooner than the aggregate congregation rent to the maximum points, first, economic individuals have at least an early motivation to promote congregation, namely, to promote urbanization; second, the congregation rent of individuals declines after the maximum point, indicating that economic subjects represent the major force that brings the city automatically to the stable equilibrium points.
6. Because the individual's motivation is proportional to how much he earns, the speed of action is also proportional to the motivation. We can simply use a derivative of congregation rent to approximately estimate the congregation process and the economic density distribution.
7. Industries with larger economies of scale have higher degrees of congregation; therefore, by comparing the return on assets of different industries at the same place, we will be able to identify the most suitable industry for the location.
8. Urban development has a close relationship with transactions and transaction costs and a very close relationship with institutional innovation. Therefore, to promote institutional change, particularly centrally planned economies promoting market-oriented reform, market-oriented reform should be further promoted. Institutional change has an increasingly significant impact on urban development.
9. Because market failures occur during the process of urbanization, policies implemented by the government to address these market failures will also promote urbanization. However, on the one hand, the influence is notable in the early stages but decrease later. On the other hand, compared with institutional change, the impact of policy is not very significant.

Appendix 1: Derivation of Market-Network Externalities Considering Diminishing Marginal Transaction Benefits

$$\text{The aggregate demand function of the entire society relative to the population density : Marginal Utility} = a - b * n$$

$$\text{The aggregate supply function of the entire society relative to the population density : Marginal Costs} = c + d * n$$

$$\begin{aligned}\text{Marginal Transaction Dividends} &= \text{Marginal Utility} - \text{Marginal Costs}\\ &= (a - b*n) - (c + d*n) = (a-c) - (b+d)*n\end{aligned}$$

$$\begin{aligned}&\text{Network Externalities of Marginal Transaction Benefits(CE)}\\ &= \Sigma \text{Marginal Transaction Benefits} * (\text{ME}(n) - \text{ME}(n-1))\\ &= \Sigma((a-c)-(b+d)*n)*[n(n-1)/2-(n-1)(n-2)/2]\\ &= \Sigma((a-c)-(b+d)*n)*(n-1) \approx \Sigma((a-c)-(b+d)*n)*n\\ &= \Sigma((a-c)n-(b+d)*n^2)n = 1,2,3,\ldots\end{aligned}$$

Appendix 2: Derivation of Congestion Externalities Formula

Assume that the city is a circle, and the commuting population lives outside the city and enters the city when going to work or shopping. According to the city's highest population density per square kilometer and considering the proportion of people living in and outside the city, we assume that N_{in} (100 people) enter the city center from outside. The transport resources are the areas covered by roads, and transport resources are assumed to be the circumference of the circle of any radius from the center of the city. When people move from outside to the city center, the radius to the center is smaller, and the circumference (transport resources) is decreasing, but the number of people is not reduced, which leads to congestion. See the following figure.

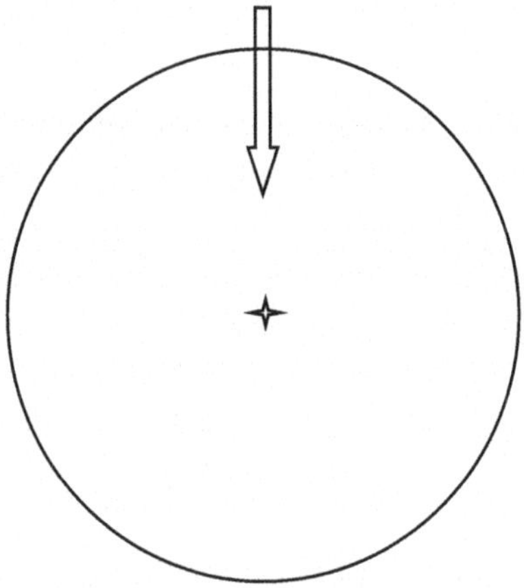

Assume that the number of people entering the city to the total number of people in a square kilometer of the city center is a ratio (N_t); then, the number of commuting people entering the city is as follows:

$$N_{in} = N_t * N(\text{per square kilometer})$$

$$\text{Unit Transport Resources Capacity} = N_{in} / \left[2\pi (N / \pi n)^{0.5}\right] = N_{in} / \left[2(N\pi / n)^{0.5}\right]$$

In fact, obtaining the population per square meter in a downtown area is very difficult because, in the absence of data for congestion externalities, we cannot determine the city center at equilibrium and its population density. Nonetheless, in the end, multiple iterations can achieve this information.

However, the congestion has not only linear proportional relations to the reduction in the number of transport resources per capita but also non-linear reduction relations. Therefore, we need to add an index associated with population density, which we call the congestion coefficient, and it is represented by *h*:

$$\text{Congestion Externalities} = \text{N}_{\text{in}} / \left[2\left(\text{N}\pi / n\right)^{0.5}\right] * \text{n}^{h}$$

Appendix 3: Formula for Congregation Rent

$$\text{Congregation Rent}\left(\text{CR}\right) = \text{CE} - \text{JE}$$
$$= \left[\left(a-c\right)-\left(b+d\right)*n/2\right]\left(n*\left(n-1\right)/2\right)-\text{N}_{\text{in}}/\left[2\left(\text{N}\pi/n\right)^{0.5}\right]*n^{h}$$

Appendix 4: Analyses of Policy Effects

Policy Promotion at Startup

As previously mentioned, when the economic density is low, the market-led congregation speed is slow; only when the density reaches a certain point will the effects of the market increase. Therefore, if during the startup stage the government promotes urban districts to cross the tipping point earlier through policy and other operations, such as utilizing its influence to attract direct investments and to move in public institutions, doing so would also develop the city. However, this governmental role should not be overestimated. Table 6.4 assumes that, through government policies and operations, an urban district reaches 3000 people per square kilometer at the outset of economic development, and the contrast situation is one without these promotional procedures (Fig. 6.22).

This chart shows that the government's initial push has an obvious impact in the first years, reaching up to a maximum of 55% of the GDP (2013). However, it decreases later and has almost no effect after ten years. Additionally, in this model, we do not count the cost of government promotion in industrial congregation policy.

Housing Rent Subsidy Policy

To facilitate the industrial congregation planned, the government can adopt policies to subsidize housing rents or prices. Beijing Financial Street subsidizes 1000 yuan/square meter to attract financial firms.

Table 6.4 Policy effects by the government's initial promotion (unit: 100 million yuan)

	Original GDP	*Initial promoting policies GDP*	*Policy impact (%)*
2012	0.45	0.45	0.0%
2013	8	12	54.6%
2014	39	50	27.4%
2015	111	133	20.0%
2016	247	279	12.9%
2017	458	500	9.1%
2018	753	801	6.5%
2019	1130	1212	7.3%
2020	1572	1626	3.5%
2021	2066	2110	2.2%
2022	2569	2604	1.4%
2023	3046	3083	1.2%
2024	3453	3469	0.5%
2025	3744	3750	0.2%
2026	3875	3877	0.0%

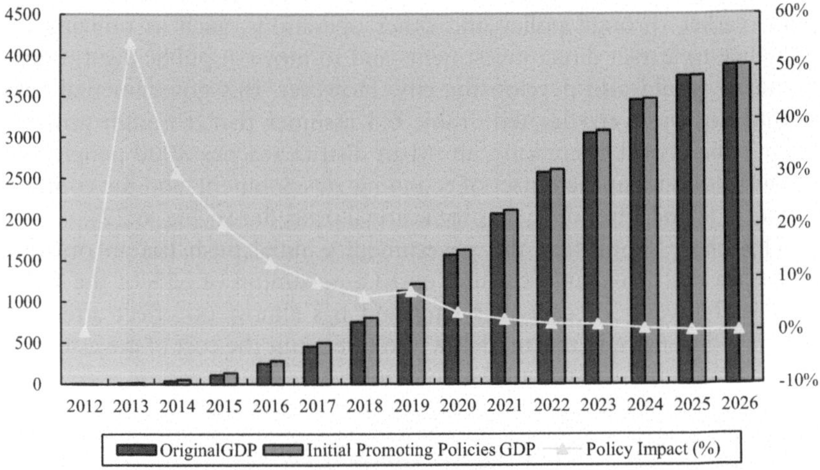

Fig. 6.22 Policy effects by the government's initial promotion (unit: 100 million yuan)

We will consider a 10% subsidy of the housing rates, which is also equivalent to a permanent 10% rental subsidy. Table 6.5 and Fig. 6.23 represent the effect of the housing rent subsidy policy.

Table 6.5 Effects of housing rent subsidy policy (unit: 100 million yuan)

	Original GDP	*Housing rent subsidy GDP*	*Policy impact (%)*
2012	0.45	0.48	5.5%
2013	8	8	5.7%
2014	38	41	6.0%
2015	111	117	5.3%
2016	247	259	4.8%
2017	458	481	5.0%
2018	753	788	4.7%
2019	1128	1183	4.8%
2020	1572	1649	4.9%
2021	2066	2158	4.5%
2022	2569	2684	4.5%
2023	3046	3183	4.5%
2024	3453	3604	4.4%
2025	3744	3907	4.3%
2026	3875	4040	4.3%

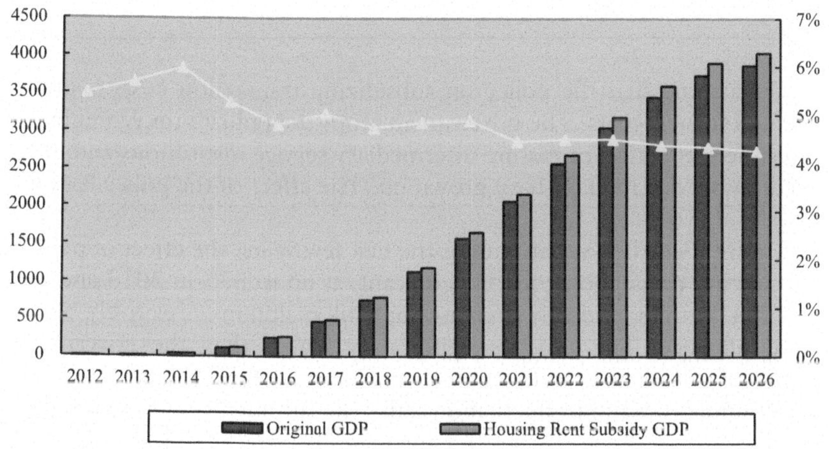

Fig. 6.23 Effects of housing rent subsidy policy (unit: 100 million yuan)

Figure 6.23 shows that, although the impact of subsidizing rent is not very significant—usually at approximately 4%–5%—its effects last long and eventually bring a certain increase in total GDP.

Policies Subsidizing Transaction Costs

Administrative departments may establish related funds to subsidize transaction costs, namely, by providing subsidies to each transaction procedures, including the following:

Applications for intellectual property rights;
Technical standards;
Venture capital investment;
Open of the laboratory;
Incubation;
Credit rating;
Loan;
Mediation services;
Public offerings;
Purchasing information products;
Bringing up intellectual property litigation;
Establishment of information system; and
Others.

We assume that the policy on subsidizing transaction costs is implemented for ten years. The government stops the policy's implementation after the incubation of mature intermediary service institutions and intermediary service markets have grown up. The effect of the policy is as follows (Table 6.6).

Figure 6.24 shows that, during the first few years, the effect of policies subsidizing transaction costs is significant, at up to 57% in 2013 and 30% in 2014. It then gradually decreases but still maintains a relatively significant influence. The effect is significantly higher than the government inputs of subsidies for transaction costs (2% of the GDP). Until 2021, the effect undergoes minor fluctuations after the subsidy policy is stopped.

Policies Promoting Industrial Alliance and Association Development

The administrative departments may lead or support enterprises or civil organizations to establish industrial alliances or associations or to support these industries by purchasing their products. The supporting policy can be implemented for ten years. After that, industry alliances and associations develop and operate by themselves. The assumption is that the results of this policy reduce transaction costs (1% of total value added).

Table 6.6 Effects of policy subsidizing transaction costs (unit: 100 million yuan)

	Original GDP	*Subsidizing transaction costs GDP*	*Policy impact (%)*
2012	0.45	0.47	2.6%
2013	8	13	56.7%
2014	39	51	30.1%
2015	111	136	22.1%
2016	247	285	15.5%
2017	458	513	11.9%
2018	753	824	9.4%
2019	1130	1215	7.5%
2020	1572	1672	6.4%
2021	2066	2173	5.2%
2022	2569	2622	2.1%
2023	3046	3105	1.9%
2024	3453	3496	1.3%
2025	3744	3784	1.1%
2026	3875	3914	1.0%

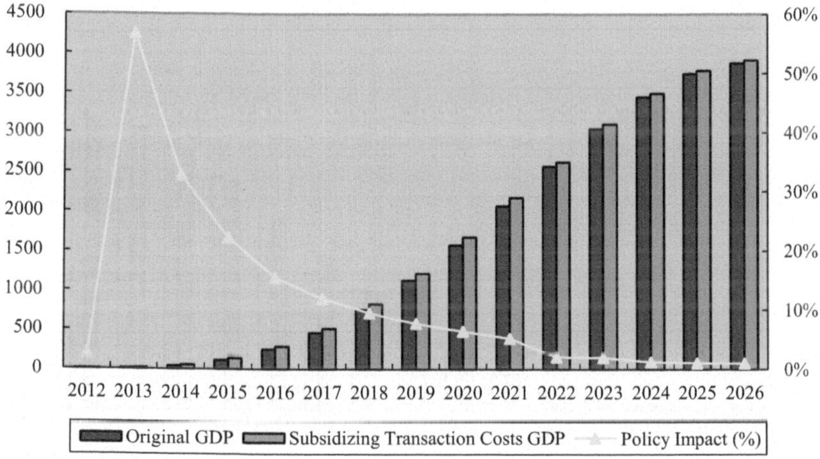

Fig. 6.24 Effects of policy subsidizing transaction costs (unit: 100 million yuan)

The effects of policies are as follows (Table 6.7).

Figure 6.25 shows that this policy has played a role; however, relative to other policies, the effect is not significant but is very efficient compared with the input. Furthermore, this result is only a static analysis. From a dynamic perspective, if this policy develops relatively mature industry associations and industry alliances, it will bring long-term benefits.

Table 6.7 Effects of policies promoting industrial alliances (unit: 100 million yuan)

	Original GDP	*Transaction costs saved by industrial alliances GDP*	*Policy impact (%)*
2012	0.45	0.46	2.0%
2013	8	8	2.6%
2014	38	39	2.5%
2015	111	114	2.5%
2016	247	251	1.8%
2017	458	467	1.9%
2018	753	767	1.9%
2019	1128	1150	1.9%
2020	1572	1602	1.9%
2021	2066	2101	1.7%
2022	2569	2613	1.7%
2023	3046	3099	1.7%
2024	3453	3513	1.7%
2025	3744	3808	1.7%
2026	3875	3940	1.7%

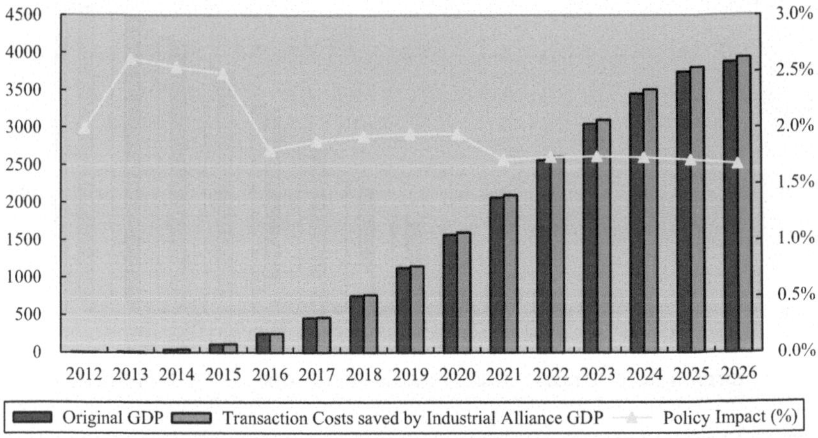

Fig. 6.25 Effects of policies promoting industrial alliances (unit: 100 million)

References

笪凤媛和张卫东, "我国 1978–2007 年间非市场交易费用的变化及其估算", 《数量经济技术经济研究》2009 年第 8 期 (Da Fengyuan and Zhang Weidong, Changes of Non-market Transaction Costs and its Estimation in China from 1978 to 2007, *the Journal of Quantitative and Technical Economics*, 2009 (8)).

国家统计局国民经济核算司, 《中国投入产出表(2007年)》, 中国统计出版社, 2009. (Department of National Accounts of the National Bureau of Statistics, China Input-Output Table (2007), China Statistics Press, 2009).

金玉国, "中国交易费用变动的动态机制和传导路径——一个基于VAR方法的实证研究", 《财经研究》, 2006 年第12期。(Jin Yuguo, Dynamic Mechanism and Pathway of Change of Transaction Costs in China--an Empirical study based on VAR method, *Journal of Finance and Economics*, 2006(12)).

康芒斯, 《制度经济学》, 商务印书馆, 1983. (Translated from: Commons, Institutional Economics: Its Place in Political Economy, Macmillan Company, 1934).

盛洪, 《分工与交易》, 上海三联书店, 1992. (Sheng Hong, Division of Labor and Transactions, Shanghai Sanlian Publishing Company, 1992).

藤田昌久, 克鲁格曼和维纳布尔斯, 《空间经济学——城市、区域与国际贸易》, 中国人民大学出版社, 2005. (Translated from: Masahisa Fujita, Krugman, Paul and Venables, Anthony J., The Spatial Economy—Cities, Regions and International Trade, The MIT Press, 1999).

Wallis, John and North, Douglass, Measuring the Transaction Sector in the American Economy, Chapter 3 in *Long-Term Factors in American Economic Growth,* edited by Stanley L. Engerman and Robert E. Gallman, University of Chicago Press, 1986.

CHAPTER 7

How Should the Institutions Change?

A Comparison Between Institutional Transitions of Chinese and British Land Institutions

Contents

7.1 Britain: Change Without Reform

I was surprised to learn, when reading Xian Hongchang's history of British land law, that British legal institutions for land haven't changed much since the eleventh century—the era of William the Conqueror—except that feudal land tenure was abolished in 1925. Later I met the author, who explained that British land institutions continue to use nominal tenure even today. I was surprised because the United Kingdom was the first to enter industrialization as well as modern urbanization. According to both Marx's five stages of human development and the institutional economics view of human history, it seems that such a land system cannot provide the corresponding institutional conditions for industrialization and urbanization, so that land can be more effectively redistributed to the uses needed for industrialization and urbanization. How to explain this paradox?

Translated from ***Academics*** (《学术界》), Issue 12, 2014.

Sheng Hong, *Vision and Calculation*,
https://doi.org/10.1007/978-981-15-2898-9_7

This paradox in fact exists only in the minds of theorists, who tend to project their pet issues onto the whole of history. For instance, seeing class struggle as driving force of history, Marxism naturally holds that feudal landowners must fight for feudal land tenure, thus having nothing to do with industrialization or urbanization. To deliver modernization and industrialization, feudal land institutions must be reformed. Feudal lords, the theory goes, benefit from feudal institutions, they are reluctant to change, and violence is therefore required.

Free from theories and assumptions, we can find that the truth is nothing like that. In that case of Britain, without feudal land institutions changing, the Industrial Revolution happened. Why? First of all, feudal lords, like any reasonable economic people, didn't reject new ways of profiting. They therefore not only kept tenants working on their land but also invested in industry and mining, or even operated such businesses on their own lands. As ***A History of British Land Institutions*** noted, "In 1750, the Lauser family spent 500,000 pounds on developing their coal mines in West Cubran." "From 1819 to 1854, the Marquis of Delhi from London invested 1000,000 pounds to develop coal mines and build West Ham Port. Count Durham's mine was valued at 540,000 pounds in 1835" (Shen Han 2005, p. 282). Lords can also benefit from renting their mines. For example, "Cornwall landlords get their benefit almost entirely in the form of rent from mines." Generally, rent rates are between 1/15 and 1/20 (Shen Han 2005, p. 283). This shows that the Lords are not confined to agriculture.

In addition to mining, feudal lords also invested in steel, railways, shipbuilding, and even finance. For instance, in the southern Yorkshire in the eighteenth century, Marquis Rockingham of the second generation established coal mines, iron mines, quarries, and blast cupola furnaces near his mansion, Wentworth Woodhouse. Between 1833 and 1845, a handful of aristocrats, landlords, and squires invested in railway corporations, whose shares of the Great Joint Railway in 1833, the London and Birmingham Railway in 1837, and Great Joint Railway in 1845 accounted for 20%, 31%, and 34%, respectively. From 1830 to 1887 the Biaothou family invested a sum of capital in the Cardiff Docks. Sykes opened on January 1, 1790, a local bank, three branches of which possessed currency worth £1500 and promissory notes worth £27,000 (Shen Han 2005, p. 285).

Feudal lords were not stubborn old fogeys living in castles as we imagine, but often science-loving and well-educated individuals who were exposed to the ideas prevalent in Britain and the rest of Europe. John

Napier, the discoverer of logarithms, was the lord of Merchiston Castle in Scotland. Born in 1550, Napier was devoted to religion in his early years and later became so obsessed with mathematics that he spent 20 years calculating the world's first logarithmic table, creating a very efficient instrument for scientific calculation (Eli Maor 2010, pp. 1–7).

Feudal lords engaged in economic activity directly, and through property rights transactions they transferred land to others involved in industrialization and urbanization, especially the bourgeoisie. Such transactions of property right were, however, hindered by feudal land institutions. Under this institutional arrangement, each piece of land, instead of being an independent asset, is linked to a certain chain. Land, in theory, is ultimately held of the king, who enfeoffs major lords as vassals. Vassals subenfeoff the lands of their fiefs to lesser lords, whose lands are subinfeudated to tenants. Such tenure imposes various duties upon landholders, especially military service. Landholders are required to provide superior lords with soldiers and military supplies. Other duties include religious services and miscellaneous affairs.

Vassals and tenants are not authorized to sell their lands directly. They have to resort to "replacement" and "sub-infeudation" for transactions. In "replacement," the holder transfers land together with tenancy to other individuals, and in "sub-infeudation," the tenant adds another person to the bottom of the chain, becoming a "secondary lord" (Xian Hongchang 2009, p. 72). Not only the lands, but also the obligations to the original feudal lord were transferred to the new tenants. Though these approaches make it possible to transfer land, they are inefficient.

As time passed, the transfer and leasing of lands became more frequent. People integrated elements of free trade into the feudal tenure. For instance, after signing a leasing contract, a tenant was supposed to hold the lands according to the requirement by form of "transferred tenure" under free tenure (Xian Hongchang 2009, p. 267). That meant the lessee was the nominal tenant, and the leaser is the nominal landlord. The tenant was allowed to further lease or sublease the lands to others, becoming a landlord in theory. Lessees, who theoretically didn't enjoy the rights of tenure, were treated as tenants for certain purposes (Xian Hongchang 2009, p. 268), overriding the opposition between contents and format and making free leasing of lands possible under the framework of feudal tenure.

Despite that, land transfer under feudal tenure was heavily restricted. Taking advantage of the land leasing system, Francis Moore, a lawyer, invented the format of "lease and release," dividing the legal process of land transfer into two parts. In a so-called release, the common law required landowners in written form to relinquish their interests in the property to lessees. Both leasing procedures and release of land were simple, endorsing the transferees with rights of renting and leasing. "Lease and release" combined the rights of renting and leasing into free tenure, while avoiding the complicated procedures of tenure transfer (Xian Hongchang 2009, p. 274). It is believed that "lease and release" emerged as the prevailing form of land transfer in the seventeenth century (Xian Hongchang 2009, p. 274). Again, under the framework of feudal tenure, people through innovative contracting approaches successfully bypassed institutional obstacles, lowering transaction costs and making land transfer possible.

The above-mentioned changes in British land institutions are what Douglass North called secondary institutional changes. North divided institutional changes into primary and secondary, the latter being the reform of contracting approach. Compared to primary institutional change, secondary institutional change is more flexible and easier to accomplish. When the reform of contracting develops to a certain point, it leads to the change of fundamental institutions: that is, new legislation. Contracting change differs from legislation change most significantly in that the former happens at the will of the parties, while the latter is compulsory.

The fact that lands can be leased and transferred freely under the framework of tenure allowed British land law to be revised while maintaining the features of tenure. Xian Hongchang pointed out that the unique historical origin of British Land Lease Law possessed elements of land tenure and contract law (2009, p. 271), thus making it a legal form with British features different from civil contract laws. The difference is that when the lessee does not pay the rent, under Continental contract law, the lessor has creditor's rights to the lessee, while under the tenure system, the lessor has the right to seize the property. This distinction remained in the Property Law of 1925 (2009, p. 272). Furthermore, just as lease and release overtook transfer of tenure, it was overtaken two centuries later in 1845, the law replaced lease and release with "grants" (2009, p. 274).

In fact, British land institutions had been changing since the era of William the Conqueror, but most of the changes happened to secondary institutions, leaving primary ones untouched. The institutions of property rights remained unchanged, but the contracting forms beneath underwent profound transitions. More importantly, such transitions contributed to the evolution of legislation and institutions of property rights. Prof. Steven Cheung argued in his Theory of Share Tenancy that efficiency varies with different contracting forms (2000). Previous theories on new institutional economics mainly focused on the institutions of property rights, while neglecting the potential for institutional evolution under the same nominal institutions. With the contractual theory we can better understand the transitions of British land institutions.

Contracting fundamentally changed British land institutions, enhancing the rights of tenants and facilitating the transfer of tenure (Xian Hongchang 2009, p. 273), and therefore providing the industrialization and urbanization with institutional possibilities for property rights transactions. There emerged a large volume of property right transactions. For instance, from 1561 to 1640, royal land reduced by three quarters and the land of the great feudal aristocracy reduced by half, while that of the new aristocracy increased by one fifth. From 1551 to 1600, 2500 manors in 7 counties transferred 1/3 of their lands. The transfer of lands between 1601 and 1640 was more massive–comparable only to the Norman Conquest (Chen Zihua 1992, pp. 2–3). In general, 1/6 of British lands have been transferred since the sixteenth century (Chen Zihua 1992, p. 5).

Admittedly, British land transactions after the sixteenth century were driven by religious and political factors, such as the confiscation of church lands by the crown during the Reformation. It is believed that Catholic convents once held almost 1/3 of British land (Chen Zihua 1992, p. 1). The confiscated lands were transferred to the King's courtiers or sold to others. Similarly, the lands of the King and royalists were confiscated and auctioned after they were defeated in the Civil War (Chen Zihua 1992, pp. 2–4). Those were one-off transfers. Only sustained reallocation could guarantee an efficient disposition of land resources, which requires an institutional environment favorable to property right transactions. The above-mentioned reform of contracting facilitates the transfer and leasing of lands, which is key to industrialization and urbanization.

On the other hand, despite of the evolution of contracting forms, land transfer, compared with land leasing, remained difficult. Transfers had to "go through at least 20 departments and procedures, each of which was risky, time-consuming, and expensive." In 1846, "the cost of land transfer equaled three years of land proceeds," or "even five years of proceeds," some believe (Xian Hongchang 2009, p. 346). To reallocate land, people naturally chose leasing. They learned to take advantage of this system: during litigation over tenure, they adopted roundabout of "writ of encroachment on the leased

Table 7.1 Increase of England's urban population (1520–1750), unit: thousand people

Year	*1520*	*1600*		*1700*		*1750*	
Region	*Total*	*Total*	*Comparison to 1520(%)*	*Total*	*Comparison to 1600(%)*	*Total*	*Comparison to 1700(%)*
England	2400	4100	71	5060	23	5770	14
London	55	200	264	575	188	675	17

Source: Lihua 2002, p. 130

land": that is, through legal techniques, turning the disputes between tenants into disputes between lessees. This was the major litigation procedure over land tenure disputes for nearly 300 years after the sixteenth century (Xian Hongchang 2009, pp. 276–277).

People preferred reallocating land through leasing, especially in agriculture, allowing a number of commercial farms to emerge. In 1887, leased commercial lands accounted for 35.6% of the total, and as high as 82.2% in 1922 (calculated with the figures provided by Shen Han, pp. 296–297). Similarly, feudal lords leased out their lands to miners. Miners were risk-taking when leasing diggings. A proportion of their proceeds was paid to landlords, generally 1/15–1/20 (Shen Han 2005, p. 283).

Though British land institutions maintained the features of feudal tenure during its lasting period of modernization and actually had many regulations obstructing land transfer, they did not prevent industrialization and urbanization. We lack literature about how lands were transferred from rural areas to cities during the period. Data, however, indicate that, under such circumstances, the United Kingdom began urbanization fast, ahead of other countries. The population of urban residents in 1750 increased 140% compared to that in 1520 (see Table 7.1 below). British urban population accounted for 65% of the total in 1811, and reached as high as 86% in 1871 (quoted from Liu Shulan 1982, p. 97).

We assume that this is partly the result of being flexible under ongoing land institutions. The flexibility is achieved by two adaptations: One is to maintain the form required by feudal tenure during land transfers, such as replacement and subinfeudation. Another is to, among alternative institutional arrangements, choose less expensive institutions, say, lease and release, by which land transfer is replaced by nominal land leasing. We have reason to believe that the land transfers which drove British urbanization were conducted through land leasing.

7.2 China: Revolution Without Evolution

In China, the case is opposite. Chinese feudal land institutions ceased to exist after the Spring and Autumn and Warring States Period. Till the Han Dynasty, a unitary land-contracting institution had been set up. After State of Lu launched its "initial tax on land per-mu," well-field system was disappearing, as the obligations of tenants could be replaced by goods or currency. After the Qin and Han Dynasties, the central and local governments were structured through a system of prefectures and counties, weakening the connection between the emperor and feudal lords.

With more than 2000 years of development, such land institutions have become more mature in the Ming and Qing Dynasties, making land transactions more convenient. The relationship between leasers and lessees, as influenced by many interpersonal factors, is hard to change. The free transfer of property rights however turns out to be a solution. During the Qing Dynasty and the Republican era, it even developed into a permanent tenancy. For the landowner, his land rights are generally referred to as "undersurface land rights"; for the permanent tenant, his land rights are generally referred to as "surface land rights." Under this permanent leasing institution, both landowners and tenant farmers are authorized to transfer the lands to others freely, without the consent of one another. Separating the integrated property right to lands for the purpose of transaction indicates that the institution has extends to its extremes.

Theoretically, such a free land transaction institution was conducive to the society's industrialization and urbanization, as the cost of land reallocation was rather low. Surprisingly however this land institution was viewed as an obstacle to modernization. Since modern times, people advocating social revolution, like the KMT led by Sun Yat-sen and the later CPC, had held the equalization of landownership as their objective. The CPC even referred its campaign as Land Revolution. People appealing for land reform went with drastically different theories; they however had one thing in common: disapproval of ongoing land institutions. Their reasons could be listed as follows. First, it's about unfairness. The unequal distribution of property rights led to excessively high renting rates and harsh exploitation on tenants. The second was inefficiency: exploitation caused low efficiency and poverty. Third, the feudal land institutions represented an underdeveloped production relationship, hindering Chinese capitalism and urbanization.

Table 7.2 Farmland distribution before the land reform

	Household %	*Population %*	*Land %*
Poor peasants and farm laborers	57.44	52.37	14.28
Average peasants	29.2	33.1	30.94
Rich peasants	3.08	4.66	13.66
Landlords	3.79	4.75	38.26
Other	6.49	5.09	2.88

Source: National Bureau of Statistics 1980, p. 19. Quoted form Dehong 2010

However, there are opposite evidences to all of these three points. As for the unfair distribution of land property rights, according to Zhao Gang's research, during the end of Qing Dynasty the Gini Coefficient of land distribution among tenants went around 0.2–0.4, during the Republican era around 0.3–0.5, and in certain area, the range extended to 0.03–0.7 (2006, pp. 64–70), indicating a rather fair distribution. Put it simply, this Gini Coefficient represented the proportion of lands held by landowners and rich peasants. Based on some research conducted in 1930s, the proportion stood around 40–65%, far less than the so-called 70–80% (Mao Zedong 1993, pp. 118–245). During the early 1950s, Du Runsheng questioned in front of Mao Zedong the percentage mentioned above and said that the lands held by landowners in Central South area only accounted for 40% (Du Runsheng 2005, p. 9). Later research found out the Mao Zedong included public farmlands as landlords' property, and leasers of small plots as landlords, which caused the evaluation to be exaggerated (Guo Dehong 1989).

After the CPC took office, National Bureau of Statistics issued comparatively authoritative figures in this regard. The Table 7.2 below demonstrates that lands held by landlords and rich peasants account for 51.92%.

There are two points that could be revised, although the data is like this. Large proportion of landlords' and rich peasants' lands was public farmlands. Mao Zedong claimed in his Xunwu Investigation that public farmlands accounted for 40% of the total. Investigation on land distribution before the Land Reform in the East and Central South pointed that public lands and other accounted for some 14.48% of the total. The item "other" in Table 7.2 apparently didn't include public farmlands, which were highly possible to be counted as lands held by landlords and rich peasants.

Table 7.3 Prices of undersurface land rights and surface land rights (unit: liang/mu)

Period	*Price of undersurface rights*	*Price of surface rights*
1763–1707	6.5	2.91
1727–1756	7.62	7.38
1782–1800	10.79	8.49
1802–1807	11.48	9.71
1810–1817	18.01	37.04

Source: Gang 2006, p. 76
Note: **Liang** is a weigh unit to indicate the value of silver, while **mu** is a space unit. A liang is about 50 gs while a mu is about 0.165 acre

Another issue was the existence of permanent tenancy. Permanent tenants were nominal tenants who in fact owned land rights partially, that was surface land rights. Such rights could be performed independently, without landowner's restriction. The price of surface land rights sometimes even exceeded that of undersurface land rights (see Table 7.3 below). According to Zhao Gang's calculation, taking into account surface land rights, the Gini Coefficient of Suzhou, which is once regarded as high as 0.784, would drop to 0.398 (2006, p. 83).

In areas where land distribution was relatively fair, relationship between landowners and tenants was not as fierce as claimed by revolutionists. According to Gao Wangling's studies, both nominal and real renting rates had been declining. Zhang Youyi's research indicated that Huizhou down regulated its renting rates 14 times before 1887, with an average decline of 39%; and 12 times between 1890 and 1922, with an average decline of 3.6%. Moreover, renting had long been under claimed, while the real collection rates kept dropping. See Table 7.4 below.

Till the Republican era, land rent rates were fairly low. Gao Wangling estimated that the average was about 40% of the production, and even 30% if real collection ratio was considered (70–80%) (Gao Wangling 2005, p. 177). The so-called default rather than temporary was a long-term phenomenon, lasting for several decades (Gao Wangling 2005, pp. 79–90). Whenever a dispute emerged between landowners and tenants, since the Ming and Qing Dynasties, landowners could hardly resort to the government. Even a lawsuit being proceeded, the judge may not necessarily side with landowners (Gao Wangling 2005, pp. 149–169). The assumption

Table 7.4 Ratio of real collecting rent

Period	*Ratio of real collection*
1550–1650	80%–90%
1651–1750	70%–80%
1751–1790	60%–70%
1791–1850	70%–80%
1851–1890	69%–70%
1891–1900	50%–60%

Source: Wangling 2005, p. 29. Terms such as "century," "the first half," and "several tenths" are replaced with specific figures in this table

that peasants were harshly exploited by landowners seemed indefensible. Zhao Gang held that tenants in Southern Jiangsu were richer than landholding farmers, and even than some landlords (2006, p. 81).

There existed some arguments over the effectiveness of land institutions during the Ming, Qing, and Republican eras. Franklin King, who visited China, Japan, and Korean in the early twentieth century, wrote a book after back home called *Farmers of Forty Centuries.* He spoke highly of Chinese agriculture, seeing it as the optimal allocation under such geological climate and population density. He claimed that he had learnt from Chinese preservation and exploitation of natural resource over thousand years and was impressed by their high productivity (2011, p. 2). Some compared China's agriculture with those of the United States and Russia, accusing of Chinese agriculture to be underdeveloped due to lack of scale and mechanization. Compared to this point of view, King's comment proved more professional.

That was because King recognized that China varied from the United States and Russia. Despite their differences, one thing in common for the United States and Russia was that they both possessed abundant land resources through military expansion, and meanwhile were less populated. In contrast, after thousand years of evolution, China was densely populated with limited land resources. U.S. and Russian patterns therefore could not be applied to China. Back then there were few however recognizing this difference, rather they rushed to deny Chinese land institution. The events happened later could prove the functionality of land institutions during the Ming, Qing, and Republican era. According to Cao Guanyi's estimation, in 1887 a single labor force could produce crop of 2000 jin (1989, p. 852), a level never to be achieved during 1948–1978. We'll discuss that later.

Considering of British then land institutions, we could not come to the conclusion that Chinese land institutions back then was underdeveloped. As discussed before, British land institutions, at least on the surface, remained feudal tenure. British however flexibly chose under this feudal framework another more efficient institutional arrangement, leaving industrialization not influenced by tenure system. That actually indicated that for higher efficiency, no institution has to be abolished with violence. On the opposite, just because that violence was involved, the institutions established were doomed inefficient.

Anyway, be it the KMT led by Sun Yat-sen or the CPC who revised the appeal of "equalization of landownership," scholars and mainstream views during the Republican era intended to change ongoing land institutions. The CPC referred to their first warfare against the KMT as the War of Land Revolution. During its second warfare with the KMT and immediately after its victory, the CPC launched Land Reform campaign, which cost the lives of 2–3 million people (Daniel Chirot 1996, p. 187). Whether or not this campaign brought about more just, efficient, and industrialization-friendly results?

The answer was negative. First, depriving millions of people's lives just because they acquired more lands by equal and willing transactions under the market system was the biggest injustice. The deprivation of their lives failed to go through legal process, and some of them were even abused to death. Zhao Lin, who later doubted the wisdom of violent revolution, was involved in the abuse of landowners in her early years. The land reform workgroup she was in put landowners in water vat in the winter (Jiang Fei 2004). If acquiring lands through fair transaction was unjust, seizing lands by violence was far worse. Let alone that the so-called equal distribution of lands actually marked the beginning of land transfer on larger scale. The distributed lands were no longer governed by their nominal owners soon after and finally not belonged to them even nominally.

Then what about efficiency? In traditional Chinese society, the occupation of lands was associated with individual's ability of plantation and of operation. The equal distribution of lands actually transferred lands from the productive to the less productive, inevitably leading to the decrease of production efficiency. Besides, with violent exploitation of rich peasants' property being an unspoken rule, farms ceased to work hard for better income, in case they would be the target of exploitation. The land reform at the same time undermined rural commercial network, disabling effective circulation of goods and of production factors, which in turn lowered the efficiency of rural areas in general. Shandong Province, thanks to the land reform in 1947, registered a record low harvest in 1948—provincial average production dropped from 180 jin/mu to 85 jin/mu, causing famine in some areas. By the March of 1948, over 2 million people suffered food shortage (Wang Youming 2006, p. 172).

What about its contribution to industrialization? Suppression upon landowners directly impacted local industry and commerce. Jünan (莒南) County, Shandong Province, dramatically impaired industry and commerce operated by landowners. Property gained by commercial exploitation was confiscated and some handicraftsmen took a heavy blow (Wang Youming 2006, Page 168). Infringement of industry and commerce in Village 25, Sangzhuang District, Jünan County, was listed as follows.

After the land reform, households performing industry and commerce in Jünan County declined from 1520 in 1936 to 235 in 1946 (Youming 2006, p. 169)—only 15.4% of the original.

In the wake of the land reform, people no longer conducted wealth accumulation, thus having no capital for commercial investment. A large share of British industrial investment, during its early stage, came from landowners. Compared to that, China's industrialization was short of capital. Since modern times, some Chinese landowners had invested in industry and commerce. For example, Mao Zedong's father, a rich peasant, was once involved in commerce (Gao Jucun et al. 1999, pp. 108–112), which contributed to industrialization. The exploitation of their property and physical injury hindered this process.

That was not the end of the story. Soon after the land reform was complete, the governing party moved on to collectivization. From the perspective of institutional arrangements, land institutions formed under the influence of collectivization were nothing but backward, making efficient land transactions impossible. First, rural collectivization was a mandatory process—rural households were forced to participate by the political leadership. Once farmers submitted their lands to cooperatives, free contracting became impossible. Furthermore, farmers lost their personal freedom. Evolving from elementary rural cooperatives to higher ones and ultimately people's communes, land was integrated into larger collective units. They were not under the control of farmers, but rather administrated directly by the government, who through administrative mechanisms distributed land and other production materials and subsistence. That pattern was described as "equalitarianism and redistributing properties arbitrarily,"

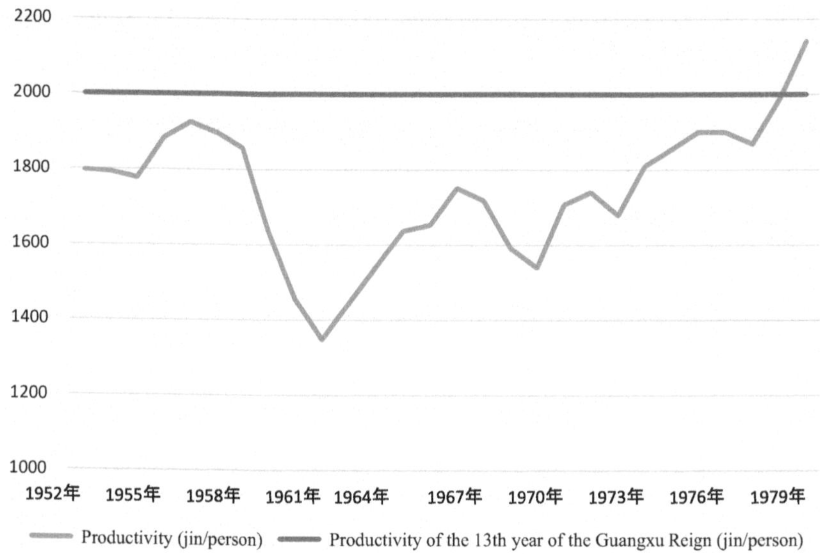

Fig. 7.1 Agricultural productivity (1952–1979), unit: jin/person. Source: productivity is calculated based on "output of major crops" http://data.stats.gov.cn/workspace/index?m=hgnd and "number of urban and rural employee" http://data.stats.gov.cn/workspace/index?m=hgnd published on NBS website. Productivity of 1887 from Cao Guanyi 1989, p. 852. Note: **Jin** is a weight unit, about 500 gs

while "large scale and public ownership." Market-oriented land allocation was completely abolished.

There is no market signal telling people how to arrange the structure of agricultural products, or even assessment of total amount. Administrative orders replaced agricultural skills, while public cafeterias and indiscriminate distribution regardless of workload hurt farmers' enthusiasm, all of which caused production efficiency to plunge, as did total output. Taking the productivity in the 13th year (1887) of the Guangxu (光绪) as 100, according to official statistics, it dropped to 90 in 1952, bouncing back a little in subsequent years. Since 1956 however, the productivity had begun to decline, standing at merely 73 in 1960 and 67 in 1961 (see Fig. 7.1 below). The downward trend coincides with evolution of rural collectives, especially with the period of people's communes.

Table 7.5 Infringement of industry and commerce in Village 25, Sangzhuang District, Jünan County

Infringed household	*Cotton fluffer*	*Embossing machine*	*Loom*	*Phar*	*Dye house*	*Oil pressing*	*Cloth*	*Other*
81	1	4	14	6	2	1	2	18

Source: Youming 2006, p. 169

Table 7.6 Chinese cash crop output, unit: thousand dan

	1931–1937	*1957*
Rapeseed	5080	1775
Sesame	1810	625
Tobacco	1830	1220
Tea	399	223
Cocoons	419	225

Source: Agriculture Development in China, 1368–1968, Perkins, D.H., Shanghai Translation Publishing House, 1984, p. 377–382. Gao Wangling 2013, p. 14

It should be noted that, thanks to collectivization, crop portfolios became oriented toward food cultivation, while cash crops experienced a pronounced decline (see Table 7.6 below). Food output therefore was higher.

The government levied taxes on peasants' income in the form of grain, a counterpart of taxes on land. In 1950–1953, the ratio was about 10%, 150%–400% higher than the tax ratio of the later Qing Dynasty, which was about 2–4% (Wang Yejian 2008, p. 165). The government conducted acquisition as well. The acquisition, performed through market, was not counted as a part of the land tax. The tax ratio in general was acceptable. After 1954, however, the government launched a state monopoly on the purchase and marketing of grain, which in fact replaced the market. The state price was dramatically lower than the former market price; therefore, it could be viewed as a part of land tax. It became worse after 1958. The government suspected that peasants were "concealing output" and used the government's power to "oppose concealing output," which showed that the so-called acquisition was also mandatory and could be merged into land tax. According to then statistics, after 1954 the real land tax ratio, that is the requisition ratio, increased remarkably, reaching nearly 40% in 1959 and even 50% in 1960 (Table 7.7).

At the same time, agricultural production was allocated and governed by administrative forces, with authorities of all levels put in actual control of production. Dominated by internal administrative mechanisms, under

Table 7.7 Real land tax ratio (grain forced procurement ratio), unit: %

1950	*1951*	*1952*	*1953*	*1954*	*1955*	*1956*	*1957*	*1958*	*1959*	*1960*	*1961*
10.1	10.4	8.62	9.52	30.1	31.8	28.3	25.8	26.6	39.6	49.0	37.4

Source: the data of the amount of grain acquisition and procurement is from the National Bureau of Statistics, "New China Statistical Data Compilation in the Past 50 Years," "The Anthology of Chen Yun (1949–1956)," "the Important Compendium of Rural Collectivization"; Quoted from NetEase. Food production data is from the National Bureau of Statistics website, "National data." "major crop production," http://data.stats.gov.cn/workspace/index?m=hgnd

This was calculated with officially published figures. Some believed the real ratio would be higher. Gao Wangling for instance commented that though immediately after the founding of PRC agricultural tax rate decreased from 20% to 15%, it remained as high as 19.5% if taking into account local taxation (2013, p. 15)

which the income of local authorities was dependent on their supervisors' will, officials exaggerated production figures to cater to their supervisors. The estimated output of 1958 was 425 billion kg, 112.5% higher than the actual output of 200 billion kg (Yang Jisheng 2008, pp. 722–723). Thanks to such exaggeration, the government requisitioned grain based on reported output, causing the real land tax ratio to reach 40% within 3 years after 1959.

In short, the compulsory land institutions launched by the government led to stark declines of grain. To make it worse, the government took an even larger share. That resulted in the Great Famine, which cost the lives of 30 million farmers or more.[1] According to Deng Zihui, some 20 million agricultural labor forces were starved to death (editorial committee of ***Biography of Deng Zihui***, 1996, p. 558; Gao Wangling 2013, p. 151).

The painful tragedy demonstrated that the land institution established under the framework of land revolution was in essence backward. Rather than creating the paradise for farmers it claimed, it sent them to hell. The core of this institution was to deprive farmers of their right to land, and to other subsistence materials like houses and kitchenware. Public canteens deprived farmers of their right to meals. Leaders of production units could arbitrarily withhold farmers' provisions. Many people starved to death because they were administratively deprived of food (Yang Jisheng 2008, pp. 347–349). The rights deprived were concentrated in the government. Even in the most favorable scenario, the unitary allocation of lands by government proved a least desired land institution.

First, with the market replaced by administration, there existed no pricing system reflecting land production, and therefore no pricing signals for

[1] Gao Wangling: it was noted that the death toll reported to Shaoqi Liu was 45 million, possibly an underestimation. It could be as high as 55 million, or even more than 60 million, which was supported by documents (2013, p. 151).

farmers, nor even for the authorities responsible for land allocation. So poorly did information travel in 1958, Mao Zedong was even concerned about how to deal with the oversupplied grain after he visited the fake demonstration site in Xushui County, Hebei Province (Yang Jisheng 2008, pp. 239–244). The entire country was two years into the famine when it came to 1960, with tens of million starved to death. Mao Zedong condemned Xiannian Li for exaggeration when the latter reported the food emergency to Mao (Jiang Guanzhuang and Gao Jingzeng 2008).

Second, without a pricing system and farmers' responses to that system, the state was not able to make informed decisions on what, when, and how much crops to plant, thus lowering allocation efficiency. In addition, administrative officials liked to make great achievements and commanded blindly for the achievement projects, and efficiency was further undermined (Yang Jisheng 2008, pp. 145, 160–161, 172, 195, 225).

Third, under such institutions, a large proportion of farmers' output was forcibly procured by the state. What was left was not enough to eat. Since hard work did not pay off, farmers were not motivated to work hard on collective lands. After the Great Famine, under the institutions of tertiary ownership based on production teams combined with reserved private plot (自留地), farmers tended to devote more labor to their reserved private plots. Evidence suggests that average output of reserved private plots was 4–5 times of that of public ones (Gao Wangling 2013, p. 226). Du Runsheng commented several times that after introducing the contracting system, it took farmers only 24 days to finish their original share of annual workload (cited from Wangling 2013, p. 177). We can infer from this figure that the efficiency generated by land institutions from 1962 to 1977 was 1/15 of the normal, and that of the institutions during the Great Famine period could be worse.

Fourth, land institutions that deprived farmers of their land rights at the same time deprived them of political and basic personal rights. As mentioned before, the land tax was as high as 40–50%, which was rare in Chinese history. During the rule of Emperor Wen and Emperor Jing during the Western Han Dynasty (180–141 BC), the tax ratio was 3.3%, and 5% during the rule of Emperor Kangxi (1661–1722). Even back to the Qin Dynasty (221–207 BC), the ratio was about 33%.[2] Never had we ever heard of any government who assigned officials to visit peasants' homes

[2]The compilation group of ***Chinese Financial History***: *"The tax burden was heavy during the Qin dynasty, which imposed loads up to two-thirds according to history"* (1986, *p. 77*). *In*

and use violence to search for hidden grain. Under most circumstances, peasants didn't have grains and were beaten to death—assailants were legally exempt (Yang Jisheng 2008, pp. 20–24, 66, 93, 106, 132, 139).

Fifth, such institutions reinforced the state's privilege, leaving its power unchecked. When evidence suggested that China was undergoing a large-scale famine, the government denied it and suppressed the spread of relevant information (Gao Wangling 2013, p. 150). People were even forbidden to flee from famine-stricken areas. Local authorities were afraid to tell the truth, fearing that they could be accused right-leaning (Yang Jisheng 2008, pp. 16, 31–32, 35, 39, 67, 105, 119, 134, 141, 149). Such doings delayed disaster-relief, the situation got worse, and death toll increased.

Apparently, far from the expectations of land revolution advocates, such institutions were not able to facilitate China's industrialization and urbanization. China's per capita GDP dropped from the 40th in the world in 1948 to the last but one in 1978 (Zhou Tianyong 2008). The country's industrialization rate reached 44.1%; however, this was the result of a higher pricing of industrial products under planned economy, and at the cost of underdeveloped agriculture and tertiary industry. Steel output stood around 30 million tons, and industrial technology lagged far behind that of world leading countries, even 20 years behind that of the four Asian Tigers, Brazil, and other developing countries (Zhou Tianyong 2008). As for urbanization, the ratio increased from 10.6% in 1949 to 13.7% in 1954, and to 19.7% due to the reduction of the rural population in 1960. By 1978, however, the ratio was only 17.9%. Under so-called advanced land institutions, both industrialization and urbanization were suppressed.

Such land institutions, which cost millions of lives during the Land Revolution, millions of lives during land reform, and tens of millions of lives during collectivization, proved to be a form of remarkable institutional backwardness. Wan Li used to comment that in people's communes farmers were actually treated as "slaves" (Wan Li 1988; Gao Wangling 2013, p. 3). Dong Furen commented as well that the people's commune was in essence about slavery (quoted in Xu Jin 2008). Such arguments are borne out by many historical documents. Gao Wangling said that the "industrial army for agriculture" made by the people's commune waged a thorough war against farmers (2013, p. 149). This is illustrated by a neat historical parallel: When the United States drafted its constitution,

general, this land tax was imposed on the landlord. The rate of rented land is in general 50% in the Qin dynasty (see Table 7.5), *so the land tax rate was about 33%.*

delegates from the south denied citizenship to slaves in the hope of preserving slavery, while at the same time counting slaves for purposes of representation to get quantitative superiority. The constitution counted slaves as 3/5 of a person when apportioning representatives (Term 2, Article 1). During the era of Mao, China's Election Law provided that in terms of voting rights, a rural resident shall be counted as 1/4 of urban resident (Article 14, Chap. 2).

Facing this backward and rights-violating institution, farmers fought back, most often in non-violent, passive, and subtle ways (Gao Wangling 2013). Reserved private plots emerged as a compromise, at the cost of tens of millions of lives. After that, farmers fought to preserve and extend their private plots. Since the purpose of collectivization was to complete the targeted procurement of the government, and after the Great Famine, the government realized that it would be impossible to procure an excessive share of grain, the total amount of duty grain and forced procurement from farmers was actually fixed. Expanding the space of reserved private plot did not threaten the demands of government as long as their target was met. Farmers invented a new "well-field system," surrounding public land with private plots (Gao Wangling 2013, p. 201–212). As in a poem of ***The Book of Songs***, "it rains the public land meanwhile benefits my private plot" (雨我公田, 遂及我私). It's like a time machine, taking us back to the Shang and Zhou Dynasties 3000 years ago, at which time the well-field system was an institutional innovation.

The high efficiency of private plots caused government to consider levying taxes on them as well. According to Gao Wangling, the Hunan provincial CPC committee determined in 1957 that private plots were not exempt from taxation. Later, under the system of contracting collective land, farmers were required to submit a fixed amount of agricultural output or cash (Gao Wangling 2013, p. 212). Again, history repeated itself—the initial tax-levy on farmland, a land institution established in the State of Lu during the Spring and Autumn period, and which finally led to the collapse of the well-field system. The taxation on private plots in turn sealed the legitimacy of such plots. For output of collective lands, after submitting a fixed amount of taxation, farmers were allowed to preserve the rest output—a situation that in fact recognized farmers' rights to lands. After Reform and Opening, China's land institutions evolved from fixed duty for each household to a household contract system—similar to the evolution of the initial tax on farmland in the Spring and Autumn period to private property rights on lands after the Qin and Han Dynasties.

7.3 Comparing and Rethinking

Looking back, we are astonished that this costly evolution of land institutions in modern China is just a repeat of what our ancestors did thousands of years ago. It brought nothing but harm to the country. Should we not learn a lesson from that bitterness? Most effective, lasting, and stable institutions in human history are time-proven and costly. If we turn a blind eye to that, we'll pay the price repeatedly.

First of all, we should reflect on the inferiority of Chinese intellectuals toward China's institutions since modern times. Military failure caused them to think less of China in all perspectives. Without a thorough analysis, they denied entire economic institutions. As discussed above, in terms of markets, China had established since the Qin and Han Dynasties a set of institutions under which property rights were clearly defined, and land was open for transactions without feudal restrictions. When it came to the Ming and Qing Dynasties and Republic era, these institutions had developed into a purely free contracting pattern. Permanent tenure was the effective result of such institutions. In contrast, British land institutions remained nominally feudal. Ironically, the United Kingdom realized its modernization without eradicating this seemingly backward institutional arrangement, while China abolished institutions conducive to modernization, which in turn retarded the country's development.

The second lesson is about the fundamentalist understanding and implementation of a certain theory. Marxist class struggle and views of human development were oversimplified explanations of human history. Despite their academic value, these theories, once adopted as a political belief and rigidly applied in practice, produced procrustean conformity. The theory of class struggle divides people into good and bad, identified with the advanced and the backward respectively. To deliver institutional reform, good ones are encouraged to resort to violence to wipe out or even torture the bad. This theory and its attendant practices totally ignored the diversity of human beings, who not only play certain roles in production, but also belong to different communities based on different criteria. For example, in the United Kingdom, landlords could be scientists or industrialists—they are not limited to one fixed position. That's exactly why the evolution of society is so complicated and unpredictable.

The third lesson is about rigid perceptions and simplified thinking about institutional development. People divide institutions only into good ones and bad ones. In this view, anything is worth sacrificing to set up good institutions. But this view fails to recognize that an institution is an organism which is generated internally from a society, as is its evolution. A new institution derives from an old one. Successful and low-costing institutional development is achieved by the interaction of emerged and past institutions. New institutions emerge naturally as solutions to problems that couldn't be solved by the old ones, which in turn complement the new ones, which are often too radical and lack tradition. Such interactions prevent traumatic discontinuities. That was exactly what happened in the United Kingdom: its institutional evolution was not that radical. Alongside inevitable industrialization there was traditional culture of gentry to be against it (Wiener 2013). However in the 1950s, slogans were everywhere in China, claiming "people's communes as the bridge to the communist heaven," and crude and foolish behaviors of "forcing peasants to take the path of communism with proletariat weapon" (Gao Wangling 2013, p. 182).

The fourth lesson is about the constructivist view of institutions, which leads to the belief that with political forces, the government is able to deliver an effective institutional evolution within a short timeframe. The evolution of land institutions is a prolonged and natural process—for instance, traditional Chinese land institutions based on the market developed following a spontaneous course. Constructivism, however, holds that human beings are capable of designing optimal institutions, including land institutions, which is impracticable and sometimes counterproductive. In the United Kingdom, people respected natural courses and refrained from rushing into institutional changes with political force. Under the existing legal framework, they respected peoples' choices of legislation and contracting, which in turn facilitated the institutional change, and ultimately resulted in the evolution of legal systems. However, in China during collectivization, we witnessed a fatal conceit—existing institutions were denied at all respects, and so-called new institutions were blindly worshiped without trial and error or experience.

The fifth lesson: an institutional change based on political forces definitely integrates political considerations into the set-up and design of the institutions. In China, judgments on land issues were distorted by political interests. The top leaders of the ruling party insisted that the concentration rate of land reached 70–80%, while many experts believed it was only 40–60%. The land reform had been a battlefield for different political forces. To distinguish itself from its competitors, the CPC closely associated the land reform policy with its own legitimacy, anxious to bring about a miracle immediately. Later, when running into problems, the leader of the Party refused to take responsibility. Instead, the leader was busy covering the truth, only to miss the best chance for disaster relief, causing a catastrophe unprecedented in human history. Despite the disputes over the Grain Law and land tax, never had land institutions ever been such a political issue in the United Kingdom.

The sixth lesson is that since modern times, Chinese intellectuals have also deviated from their understanding of social problems. Admittedly, there existed wealth disparity in rural China. Such a disparity, however, was exaggerated to an unreasonable extent. Although peasants under permanent tenure might even be richer than landowners, scholars still upheld the equalization of lands as a major social mission. No matter whether we look at the era of people's communes or now, a review of the situation back then would reveal that the elite class made major mistakes which contributed to later disasters. The intellectual elite, instead of solving current problems, attempted to establish an ideal world once and for all. In the United Kingdom, despite being influenced by socialist philosophy as well, British dominated by the tradition of experientialism never thought of setting up an ideal society instantly.

The final lesson, and the most important, is to understand how institutions should evolve. The direction could be rather different, but what really matters is whether institutions are changed in a violent or non-violent way. First, such a difference determines if institutions can work. As James M. Buchanan pointed out, the optimal institutional change is Pareto Improvement, under which at least one individual is better off without making any other individual worse off. He held that the correspondent political arrangement to Pareto Improvement is unanimous consent, which is illustrative of people's attitude toward institutional changes: they won't disagree if they are not worse off, and they agree if they are better off. A reform that harms no one and brings benefit produces gains for the entire society. A voluntarily accepted and commonly supported reform, therefore, will actually promote efficiency. In contrast, without the consent and support of the public, an allegedly advanced institution implemented by violence is bound to harm the majority, thus undermining social prosperity.

Second, institutional changes implemented by violence will definitely lead to allocation disparity. It requires violence to maintain such institutions, under which the allocation is decided by and favors those who possess the resources of violence—that is, the government. In that sense, a violently implemented institution brings about government-favored allocation institutions. This implicates a lasting issue of human society—conflict between officials and civilians. Violently implemented institutions only reinforce such conflict.

Third, institutions established by violence, such as the land institutions, are naturally those the government dominates to allocate resources. We are aware that only under certain circumstances that government functions more effectively than the market, say in the area of public supply. If the government allocates resources in all respects, efficiency will be lowered remarkably. No wonder, then, that violently implemented institutions are ineffective.

Reviewing the institutional changes in land institutions of China and the United Kingdom, the above arguments are valid. Though many people sought to cover up the death toll during the land reform, they couldn't deny the violation against landowners' and rich peasants' property and lives. Despite their tiny share of the population, such violations are morally intolerant. In terms of social utilitarianism, these groups turn out to be a crucial component of society. Violations against them wipe out the most enterprising, and destroy the free contracting system, which inevitably cause productivity to decline. During the collectivization era, tens of millions of famers are forced to join cooperatives and people's communes. They paid heavy cost of their lives later during Anti-Concealing of Outputs Movement and withholding of provisions in the Public Canteens (Yang Jisheng 2008, pp. 67, 70, 103–107, 124, 127–129, 133, 140). Productivity dropped to a record low accordingly.

The household contracting institution, though referred to as a "reform" like the land reform, was not compulsorily implemented by the government. Before its official implementation, tens of millions of farmers in rural areas got involved on their own. CPC members in Xiaogang Village, Fengyang County, under risk of being imprisoned, implemented the Fixed Duty for Each Household. This institutional arrangement was accepted by the leadership not because they recognized its advantages of it, but because they recognized that the public had the right of free choice (Du Runsheng 2005, p. 119). Once free choice was allowed, the Fixed Duty for Each Household became widespread nationwide within a few years, barely encountering resistance. Agriculture then saw remarkable growth. Accordingly, from the figures of the National Bureau of Statistics, the total value of agricultural output registered an average annual growth of 3% in

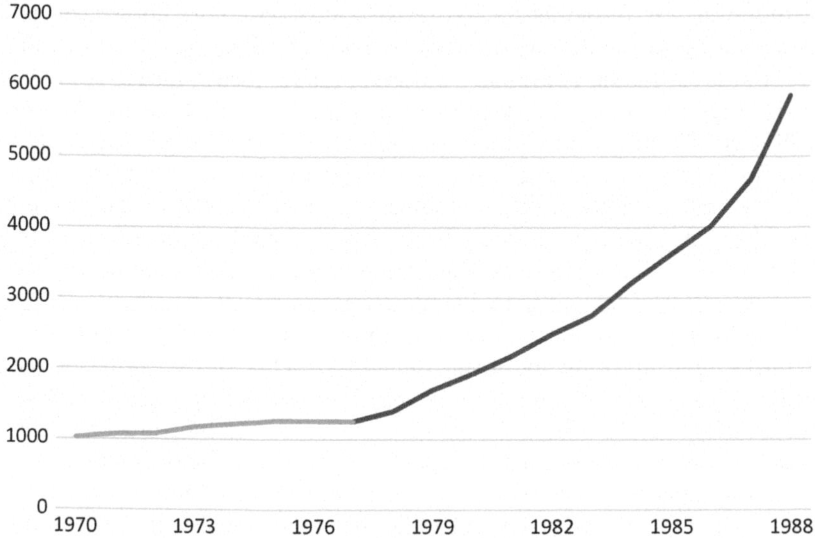

Fig. 7.2 China's total value of agricultural output (1970–1988), unit: hundred million Yuan. Source: National Bureau of Statistics

1970–1977, but 15% in 1978–1988.[3] In micro perspective, Gao Wangling recorded that in a village of Zhangqiu County, Shandong Province, the output of cotton per *mu* was 17 *jin* one year before, and 130 *jin* one year after the reform. In another village, the output per mu one year before was 10 *jin* and 7 *liang* and grew to 81 *jin* after the reform of Fixed Duty for Each Labor. One production team delivered bumper harvests for consecutive years, with its total grain output increasing from 200,000 *jin* to 1.1 million *jin* (2013, p. 186) (Fig. 7.2).

Therefore, whether an institutional change is willing or enforced, and peacefully or violently implemented, rather than other indicators, determines if it is a "good" one—that is a change to make institutions more efficient. Justin Yifu Lin pointed that instead of collectivization, it was coerced collectivization that caused the Great Famine from 1959 to 1961. This means that joining people's communes was compulsory, while

[3] Calculated according to "gross output value of agriculture, forestry, animal husbandry and fishery and its index" in the "national data," "agriculture" section of the website of the National Statistical Bureau.

withdrawal was forbidden. There existed no constraints upon laziness, contributing to the decline of productivity (Lin 1990). Israeli kibbutzim are a kind of public commune; however, unlike their Chinese counterparts, they are set up by their own members voluntarily (Yang Mansu 1992, pp. 79–83). Had Chinese farmers been allowed to participate and exit the people's communes freely, the Great Famine wouldn't have happened, while land institutions recognizing farmers' landownership would have been maintained. Should China's land reform have been peacefully implemented, it would have facilitated industry and commerce like Taiwan's reform did and spared landowners this brutal tragedy.

Would it be possible for an institutional change, existing only in a genius's mind, to bring about the immense benefits for the entire society, while at this moment undermining the interests of the majority? Does such a genius really exist? The answer is negative. An individual's intelligence has its boundaries, hardly capable of predicting the future of a society as a complicated system or designing its institutions. Only based on the voluntary interactions of tens of millions of individuals can institutions develop forward spontaneously. Such interaction is a process of evolution that is complicated and cannot be understood by rationality. Therefore, the claims of those who say they have mastered laws of human historical development can only be seen as rationalistic arrogance in their attempt to bring human beings to the paradise of the world through the compulsory means of the government.

Throughout history, transactions among individuals have turned out to be the most effective catalyst for institutional changes. Interestingly, a transaction can simply be done by two individuals, but its implications are far beyond that. People could transact products, components, or even contracts. Contracting is what Douglass North calls secondary institutional arrangements. As long as a kind of contractual form is convenient, it will soon be widespread, such as the institution of currency. Even slaves can accumulate currency by market transactions and ultimately redeem their freedom, which collapses the brutality of slavery. As transactions are simple and flexible, people are willing to bypass the legal process with alternative dealing patterns. For instance, British employed replacement, subinfeudation, leases, and releases to transfer land, replacing complicated transfer formalities with leasing contracts and ultimately reallocating land resources within the framework of feudal tenure.

Is there any institutional change that must rely on violence? Generally speaking there is none. There is an exception only when the original institutions are compulsory and violently maintained. As for American slavery, Robert Fogel once commented that most countries wiped out slavery peacefully, but the United States is an exception (Fogel and Engerman 1974, pp. 32–37). That's because in the US slavery plantations enjoyed higher efficiency than free ones.[4] Slaves were forced by their owners to work intensively within unit intervals. Fighting against such institutions could be compared to Chinese classical revolutions—the Revolutions of King Tang (汤) and King Wu (武). Back to the tyrannical reigns of the Xia King Jie (桀) and the Shang' King Zhou (纣), national institutions were preserved merely by violence, only when they completely lost the support of the public, King Tang of the Shang Dynasty and King Wu of the Zhou Dynasty could prudently resort to arms. Despite that, Confucius viewed King Wu's conquest over Shang as imperfect. Though it is reasonable to facilitate institutional changes through violence, it must be done cautiously.

Another field that involves compulsion is public affairs. Public facilities, though necessary, do not necessarily make everyone happy. Under democratic institutions, decisions are made by vote. The majority principle, however, can be unfair to the minority. Once a public policy is formed, it will be enforced. Therefore, even legal institutions which are made by democratic procedures can undermine the interests of some and feature compulsion. That is a problem that remains to be solved. Democracy may minimize the violation against minorities by adjusting certain principles regarding policy making, like changing ratios of majority and increasing the weight of the minority. The problem is insoluble, and the optimal scenario is to avoid institutional changes based on public choice. That's the reason why British laws changed at such a slow pace—they only changed when a contracting approach was profoundly evolved and proved well functioning. That's exactly what happened to land institutions.

In short, the history of land institutional changes in China and the United Kingdom for centuries tells us that a simple way to determine whether an institutional change is effective or "good" is whether the economic parties involved accept it voluntarily; rather than anything else, such as how logically rigorous and eloquent its background theory is, how noble the moral standards of the demands, even how active the majority mobilized, or what kind of doctrine it is. As long as we stick to this point,

[4] Efficiency in southern slavery plantations was 28% higher than that in free farms. (Fogel and Engerman 1974, p. 192).

we can avoid the huge cost of ill-advised institutional changes and reduce the missteps that have been rife in the modern history of China's land institutional change, but always move toward the same direction with real impetus to promote institutional change.

References

《邓子恢传》编辑委员会, 《邓子恢传》, 人民出版社, 1996. (Editorial Board of The Autobiography of Deng Zihui, The Autobiography of Deng Zihui, People's Publishing House, 1996.)

曹贯一, 《中国农业经济史》, 中国社会科学出版社, 1989. (Cao Guanyi, History of China's Agricultural Economy, China Social Sciences Press, 1989.)

陈紫华, 《一个岛国的崛起 英国产业革命》, 西南师范大学出版社, 1992. (Chen Zihua, The Rise of an Island Country: British Industrial Revolution, Southwest Normal University Press, 1992.)

Daniel Chirot, *Modern Tyrants: The Power and Prevalence of Evil in Our Age*. Princeton University Press. 1996.

杜润生, 《杜润生自述:中国农村体制变革重大决策纪实》, 人民出版社, 2005. (Du Runsheng, Du Runsheng's Narration: Documentary of Major Policies in the Institutional Reform in Rural China, People's Publishing House, 2005.

Eli Maor, 《e的故事》, 人民邮电出版社, 2010. (Eli Maor, The Story of E, People's Post and Telecommunication Press, 2010.)

Fogel, R.W. and Engerman, S.L., Time on Cross, W.W. Norton & Company, 1974.

高菊村, 龙剑宇, 陈高举, 刘建国, 蒲苇, 《毛泽东故土家族》, 西苑出版社, 1999. (Gao Jucun, Long Jianyu, Chen Gaoju, Liu Jianguo, Pu Wei, Mao's Family, Xiyuan Publishing House, 1999.)

高王凌, 《租佃关系新论: 地主、农民和地租》, 上海书店出版社, 2005. (Gao Wangling, New Tenancy: Landowners, Peasants and Rent, Shanghai Bookstore Publishing House, 2005.

高王凌, 《中国农民反行为研究》, 中文大学出版社, 2013. (Gao Wangling, Research on Chinese Peasants' Anti-action, Chinese University Press, 2013.)

郭德宏, "旧中国土地占有状况及发展趋势", 《中国社会科学》1989 年第 4 期. (Guo Dehong, Land Tenure and Development Tendency in China Before 1949, Journal of Chinese Social Science, 4th Edition, 1989.)

郭德宏, "对毛泽东二三十年代农村各阶级土地占有状况的调查分析的重新研究", 《党的文献》, 1989 年第5期; 又载于《探寻历史的真相》, 中共党史出版社, 2010. (Guo Dehong, Re-examination on Mao's Research and Analysis on Land Tenure of Various classes in Rural China from 1920s to 1930s, The CPC Literature, 5th Edition, 1989 5; contained as well in Exploration of Historical Facts, Chinese Communist Party History Publishing House, 2010.)

国家统计局,《建国三十年全国农业统计资料》,中国统计出版社,1980. (National Bureau of Statistics, National Agricultural Statistics 30 Years after the Founding of PRC, China Statistics Press, 1980.)

江菲,"寻找林昭",《中国青年报》,2004年8月11日。(Jiang Fei, Looking for LIN Zhao, China Youth Daily, August 11, 2004.

江立华,《英国人口迁移与城市发展:1500–1750》,中国人口出版社,2002. (Jiang Lihua, British Migration and Urban Development: 1500–1750, China Population Press, 2002.

蒋冠庄和高敬增, "李先念呕心赈粮荒", 《百年潮》2008年第1期。(Jiang Guanzhuang, Gao Jingzeng, LI Xiannian Spared no Efforts to Relieve Food Emergency, Hundred Year Tide, 1st Edition, 2008.

金,富兰克林,《四千年农夫》,东方出版社,2011. (Translated from: Franklin King, Farmers of Forty Centuries, Dover Publications; Dover Ed edition (March 19, 2004)).

Lin, Justin Yifu, Collectivization and China's Agricultural Crisis in 1959–1961, The Journal of Political Economy, Vol. 98, No. 6 (Dec. 1990)

刘淑兰,《英国产业革命史》,吉林人民出版社,1982. (Liu Shulan, History of British Industrial Revolution, Jilin People's Publishing House, 1982.)

毛泽东,《毛泽东文集》第一卷,人民出版社,1993. (Mao Zedong, Mao Zedong Collection, Volume I, People's Publishing House, 1993.)

沈汉,《英国土地制度史》,学林出版社,2005. (Shen Han, History of British Land Institutions, Academia Press, 2005.)

万里,"农村改革是怎么搞起来的",《中国经济时报》。(Wan Li, How did Rural Reform Start, China Economic Times.)

万里,"农村改革是怎么搞起来的",《中国经济时报》,1988. (Wan Li, "How did Rural Reform Come About", China Economic Times, 1988.)

王业健,《清代田赋刍论 (1750–1911)》,人民出版社,2008. (Wang Yejian, On Farmland Tax in Qing Dynasty (1750–1911), People's Publishing House, 2008.)

王友明,《革命与乡村,解放区土地改革研究: 1941–1948》,上海社会科学院出版社,2006. (Wang Youming, Revolution and Rural areas – Research on Land Reform in Liberated Areas: 1941–1948, Shanghai Academy of Social Sciences Publishing House, 2006.)

威纳,马丁,《英国文化与工业精神的衰落: 1850—1980》,北京大学出版社,2013. (Translated from: Wiener, Martin, English Culture and the Decline of Industrial Spirit: 1850–1980, Cambridge University Press; 2 edition (September 13, 2004))

Wikipedia, land reform campaign, http://zh.wikipedia.org/wiki/%E5%9C%9F%E6%94%B9

咸鸿昌,《英国土地法律史:以保有权为视角的考察》,北京大学出版社,2009. (Xian Hongchang, History of British Land Law: In the Perspective of Tenure, Peking University Press, 2009.)

徐堇, "文贯中:中国还需要一场土改", 《中国经营报》, 2008 年 7 月 6 日。(Xu Jin, Wen Guanzhong: China Needs Another Land Reform, China Business News, 2008, July 6.

杨继绳, 《墓碑》, 香港天地图书, 2008. (Yang Jisheng, Gravestone, Hong Kong Cosmos Books, 2008.)

杨曼苏, 《以色列:谜一样的国家》, 世界知识出版社, 1992. (Yang Mansu, Israel: A Mysterious Nation, World Knowledge Publishing House, 1992.)

张五常, 《佃农理论》, 商务印书馆, 2000. (Steven Cheung, Theory of Share Tenancy, Commercial Press, 2000.)

赵冈, 《中国传统农村的土地分配》, 新星出版社, 2006. (Zhao Gang, Traditional Land Allocation in Rural China, New Star Press, 2006.)

中国财政史编写组, 《中国财政史》, 中国财政经济出版社, 1986. (Compiling Group of Chinese Financial History, Chinese Financial History, China Financial and Economic Publishing House, 1986.)

周天勇, "三十年前我们为什么要选择改革开放", 《学习时报》, 2008 年9 月。(Zhou Tianyong, Why Chose the Reform and Opening-up 30 Years Ago, Study Times, September 2008.

CHAPTER 8

Contracts Matter: Toward a More Developed Explanation of History

Contents

8.1 Contracts Are Also a Kind of Institution

Professor Douglas North summarizes the essence of institutional economics with the phrase "institutions matter." As institutions are comprised of various institutional arrangements, the dictum "institutions matter" further implies that "property rights matter," "laws matter," "organizations matter," and "morality matters." Because of the crucial role of the concept

Originally published in *Man and the Economy*, Volume 3, Issue 1, June 2016, with the title, "Contract Matters: An Explanation of China's Recent Economic History")

Sheng Hong, *Vision and Calculation*,
https://doi.org/10.1007/978-981-15-2898-9_8

of transaction costs in institutional analysis, it can be taken that transaction costs also matter. Hence, institutional economics can be divided into the economics of property rights and the economics of transaction costs. The main contributors to the former include Alchian and Demsetz, while Williamson represents contributors to the latter.

Professor Steven N.S. Cheung focused on contracts. Among his contributions to economics, Cheung's research on contracts stands out, such as *The Theory of Share Tenancy.* The book focuses on different types of tenancy contracts, such as fixed rent agreement, rent share contract, or wage contract. Cheung found that where transaction costs are zero, all contracts are equally efficient (Cheung 2000, p. 159). When transaction costs are positive, the real choice of contract form is actually the best one possible in the specific condition. Therefore, different contract forms under the same property rights arrangement are all efficient (Cheung 2000, p. 85). On the other hand, as institutions matter, when transaction costs are positive, as an institutional arrangement, contracts also matter. In other words, under the same circumstances, different forms of contract vary in terms of efficiency.

Another classic of the field is *The Contractual Nature of the Firm.* In this paper, Professor Cheung illustrates that the scope of different types of contract is much larger than previously imagined. Professor Cheung argues that firms, normally considered different from the market, also arise from a series of contracts. It is form that distinguishes the contracts of firms from those in the market. Within firms, contracts of products are usually substituted by contracts involving factors of production. Applying this view to firms, we can see that firms are permeated by contracts and finally disappear; or to put it in another way, the boundary of the firm is impossible to find. Contracts are all that is left (Cheung 1983). The broad application of contracts illustrates the importance of contract theory.

8.2 Contracts and Property Rights

How important are contracts? Many institutional economists have emphasized the importance of property rights, including Alchian (1977) and Demsetz (1964, 1967). The importance and the unique features of contracts can be seen by comparing them with property rights.

Property rights are exclusive rights to property, whereas contracts are unanimous agreements between all contracting parties. Property rights and contracts have some overlap but differ in certain aspects. Property rights describe relationships between people. Exclusivity implies that all other people are "excluded"; property rights describe a relationship between one person and all others. In the process of property right formation, there is an implicit reaching of contract. This process involves other people agreeing to the ownership of a certain property by a certain person, and that this certain person will also have to respect others' rights to property. Hence, a mutual agreement about property rights is also a contract. Under this contract, property owners have property rights which other relevant parties are obliged to respect. Naturally, as the institution of property rights expands, the consent of immediate "neighbors" alone is not sufficient to guarantee the respect for and protection of a certain property right.

This is because truly effective property rights require the respect not only of immediate neighbors, but of all people. Getting everybody in a society to consent to the property rights of a property owner is not practical and those who have not consented may infringe the property right for their own benefit. Beyond contracts, there must be a principle of legal property rights, which means that if immediate neighbors recognize a certain property right, then this property right should be recognized by all others. To uphold this principle and protect property rights, coercive power through laws enforced by the government is required.

Contracts differ from property rights in that a contract is the result of a unanimous agreement normally entered into by two contracting parties. Therefore, contracts are usually implemented voluntarily, though there may be infringement. Sometimes, though not often, there may be a need for coercive intervention under the law due to infringement. By contrast, legal force is needed more often to enforce property rights as they are rights excluding all other people.

There has been much debate on how the reform of property rights can increase efficiency. One argument stipulates that establishing exclusive property rights allows for long time horizons and long-term arrangement of resource allocation, which is more efficient than short-term arrangements. For example, Professor Douglas North gives the example of publicly owned property rights. Publicly owned property rights can allow a society of hunter-gatherers become one of herders because such a society can make long-term arrangements for livestock under which people do not necessarily kill livestock immediately as they did with animals in the wild (North 1982, Chap. 7).

Another argument is that clearly defined property rights help to reduce property right-related conflict and resulting non-productive investment. Property rights that belong to smaller groups, even households or individuals, provide more incentives. As small groups or individuals are more aware that they will bear the result of how a resource is utilized, they will be keener to utilize it wisely (Alchian 1977, Chap. 5). At the same time, the scope and form of property rights become much easier for transaction purposes. For instance, when a large asset is divided into smaller portions, such as under the shareholding system, it becomes easier to trade as financing demands decrease. Thus, the securitization of assets makes transactions easier.

The main outcome of contract reform is a decrease of transaction costs. Transactions for which costs were previously prohibitively expensive become possible due to reduced transaction costs. For example, money was introduced as a new form of contract compared to barter, greatly lowering transaction costs. In a money-based economy, transactions of greater value and variety are conducted compared to a barter-based system. Typically, the more general the contract, the greater the potential benefits of changing the form of the contract, and the bigger the impact on society.

From the perspective of institutional evolution, the reform of property rights differs from that of contracts. North's work introduced the concept of fundamental institutions and secondary institutions. Fundamental institutions refer to legal institutions and secondary institutions refer to contracts. North argues that the evolution of contracts is easier than that of legal institutions, and that in history, changes to legal institutions only take place when changes to contracts accumulate to an extent that causes major shifts in society or politics (North and Thomas 1971).

According to Professor Steven Cheung's contract theory, we can thus deduce that when transaction costs are positive, different forms of contract will result in different levels of efficiency and that changing the contract form can improve efficiency. If we accept that institutional change is very important to human society, we should also recognize the significant role that changing forms of contract (contract reforms) play in institutional change. The significance of contract reform lies not only in efficiency gains but also in that the associated transactions costs are lower, making such change more likely than change of legal institutions. This makes contract evolution a dominant force in the history of institutional change.

Generally speaking, contracts are enforced voluntarily and laws are enforced coercively. In predemocratic times, the law was mostly converged by the judicial precedents of the judge system, and also infiltrated by the private opinion of the ruler, so some people or even most people felt infringed. Under democracy, laws are shaped by the votes of an elected legislature. However, laws are enacted according to majority rule, which is to say that laws are passed against the will of a certain minority. Therefore, once a law is passed, a minority of people are forced to accept it and it is very difficult for that minority to change the law without resorting to violence. In comparison, as contracts are entered into voluntarily, they can also be changed voluntarily without violence. As mentioned above, the allocation and institution of property rights is mostly guaranteed by law. Therefore, it often takes political action backed by violence to change the allocation of property rights or the institution of property rights. Unsurprisingly, voluntary institutional change with its low costs dominates over this coercive form of institutional change.

8.3 Extending the Coase Theorem

To further the argument, the evolution of contracts is not parallel to that of legal institutions. The recurring problem is that, for various reasons, legal institutions may not act efficiently or follow the principles of justice. In this case, the evolution of contracts may play a supplementary role.

Indeed, this issue was touched upon when Coase illustrated what later became known as the "Coase Theorem." The theorem stipulates that if transaction costs are zero, no matter how property rights are initially allocated, mistakes in the original allocation can be corrected to reach the optimal efficient outcome as long as there is free transaction (Coase 1960). A related proposition is that even if transaction costs are positive, as long as they are sufficiently low, an initial misallocation of property rights can be fully or at least partially corrected.

Regarding the Coase Theorem, many hypotheses have been proposed. For example, if we change the assumption of zero transaction costs to positive transaction costs, we arrive at the conclusion that "allocation of property rights matters." This issue is directly discussed in Coase's *The Problem of Social Cost*. Coase states that if transaction costs are high, the original misallocation of property rights cannot be corrected by free transactions. Therefore, it becomes more important to allocate property rights to those who will fully utilize them at the beginning (Coase 1960). We can call this **Deduction One**. Another proposition is that clearly defining property rights will aid transactions and help correct the original misallocation of property rights. Hence, having clearly defined property rights is important. Since the assumption of "zero transaction costs" implies "clearly defined property rights," we cannot regard Deduction One as independent.

Normally, the implications described above are considered to capture the whole significance of the Coase Theorem. However, this neglects two other apparent deductions.

Deduction Two: If free transaction leads to optimal resource allocation, then coercive intervention in allocation will decrease resource allocation efficiency.

Deduction Three: If the government or law incorrectly assigns property rights to a certain party or stipulates a certain suboptimal institution of property rights, this can be corrected by free transactions.

On closer look, the situations described in deductions one and two are not just theoretical postulations but are ubiquitous in the real world.

Steven Cheung is familiar with both phenomena through his research on contracts. In *The Theory of Share Tenancy*, Cheung discusses the "375 rent reduction" land reform in Taiwan.[1] This was a typical government/legal intervention in free contracts and fits with the situation described in Deduction Two. Cheung argues that the difference between the higher market rent and the lower set rate cannot be captured by tenants because the appeal of lower land rents will increase either competition for land tenure or labor investment by the original tenants to harvest more output from the land. As the marginal productivity of land increases, the marginal productivity of labor decreases and may even become negative. When the two are offset with each other, the overall efficiency decreases (Cheung 2000, Chaps. 5, 6, and 7). This so-called rent dissipation phenomenon that Cheung showed in Taiwan supports one deduction from the Coase Theorem, namely that government intervention in free contracts results in a loss of efficiency.

In Hong Kong, Cheung found evidence for Deduction Three. He originally believed that government intervention in housing rental, such as stipulating that rent should be one-tenth of the market level, should lead to obvious rent dissipation. However, no such phenomenon was found.

[1] Under this reform, by law, rents were reduced from an average of 56.8–37.5% of annual harvest (Cheung 2000, p. 88).

Rather, Cheung found many shared rental houses and wooden terraced houses. Such houses can be seen as efforts to avoid rent dissipation under price regulation. The method of rent retention is by contract. Professor Cheung observed that only a quarter of rent dissipated due to the use of shared rent and wooden terrace houses (Cheung 2000, F25–F28). This follows Coase Theorem logic because the contracting cost is positive. The quarter of rent dissipated is due to transaction costs. Is this therefore a classic case of where legal misallocation of property rights is corrected by free contracting?

Cheung observed that cases such as shared tenancy and wooden terrace houses are not particular to Hong Kong. He extended the observation to all price-regulated situations. As long as the regulated price is lower than the market price, and the difference between the two is not assigned exclusively to a designated person, as if in the case of terra nullius, then the difference may become dissipated rent. However, people don't want to see their interests diminished and will try to retain economic rents in various ways, such as contractual arrangements (Cheung 1974). For example, price controls are ubiquitous in a planned economy but people can still retain rent through black market trading to partially correct the misallocation of resources due to coercive intervention by the government. Hence, it is common to correct suboptimal outcomes caused by law by using contracts.

Also worth noting is that in saying that contracts can correct or partially correct mistakes of the government/law, we imply that the mistakes of government or law may remain temporarily uncorrected. Or, to put it in a more practical way, these mistakes cannot be corrected easily. This leads to:

Deduction 3.1 Even if a mistaken intervention by the government/law cannot be corrected momentarily, contracts offer a way to correct this mistake and so mitigate the difficulty or cost of the intervention.

Later on we will come to see how important this deduction is in the institutional change of human society.

8.4 Contract Reform Has the Same Effect as Property Right Reform but with Much Lower Costs

Professor Cheung's contract theory is important not only for its beauty and logical coherence but also for its empirical grounding. When Albert Einstein published his theory of general relativity, the British scientist Sir

Arthur Stanley Eddington undertook an expedition to the southern hemisphere to observe a solar eclipse that provided one of the earliest confirmations of general relativity. This real-world observation was one of the reasons that general relativity began to gain acceptance by the scientific community. Who, then, is Professor Cheung's Sir Eddington?

The extent of China's great famine between 1959 and 1961 shocked the world. Misguided property rights institutions established by the government contributed to the tragedy. These included the main feature of people's communes, "large in size and collective in nature" (一大二公), and the regulated price of agricultural products lower than market levels. This in turn led to a severe decrease of efficiency, that is, rent dissipation. In 1961, agricultural productivity was only 61% of what it was in 1887, the 13th year of the Guangxu Emperor's reign. However, at the time, there was almost no feasible way to correct for this misguided institution of property rights. Behind the arrangement of property rights lay the coercive power of the government and ideological beliefs of political leaders at that time.

However, even when there seemed to be no alternatives to the current institution of property rights, there was still space for changes to contractual arrangements. At that time, Deng Zihui was one of the most prestigious agricultural experts within the Communist Party of China.[2] In 1961, Deng Zihui was inspired by the practice of the "household responsibility system" (包产到户) and "contracted farmland" (责任田) in Anhui and Hunan provinces. He thought they provided a good way to increase productivity without changing the institution of property rights set by the government. In essence, the household responsibility system changes the form of contract under existing collective property rights. In the early period of people's communes, land and other production inputs belonged to people's commune. A member's contract with the people's commune was a kind of employment contract. No matter how much a peasant worked, they earned a fixed amount. Under the household responsibility system, a household could keep any surplus once they had handed over a fixed quantity of their output to the government and a fixed quantity to the collective. This shift was equivalent to changing from an employment contract to a fixed land rent contract.

[2] Deng Zihui was Minister of Rural Work of the CPC Central Committee from 1953, Vice Premier of the State Council, and Vice Chairman of the Fourth National Committee of the CPPCC. He died in 1972.

Even minor changes of contract form can lead to significant increase of efficiency. For instance, when Fuli region in Anhui Province trialed the "contracted farmland" policy in 1961, crop yield increased by 18% (Chen et al. 1996, p. 557). This increase happened while there was heated debate among the senior leaders of the CPC on the household responsibility system and despite Mao Zedong's explicit objection to this practice. Household-reserved plots achieved a yield per *mu* four to five times that of collective land (Gao Wangling 2013, p. 207). If we compare the legally protected household-reserved plots before and after Reform and Opening-up, we find examples such as a village in Zhangqiu County, Shandong Province, where cotton yield per *acre* rose from 51.6 kg to 394.6 kg. In another village, the increase was from 32.5 kg to 246 kg. In one production team, every year after Reform and Opening-up was launched saw bumper harvests with total crop yield increasing from 100,000 to 550,000 kg (Gao Wangling 2013, p. 186). These yields are five to eight times that typical for collective land. The gap between the two is due to rent dissipated under the inefficient institution of collective landownership.

Deng Zihui was not fixated on public landownership. He presumed that Mao Zedong would not compromise on the institution of collective property rights. This led him to propose the household responsibility system, which implied a contract reform without altering the underlying institution of property rights. In his own words, "contracting farmland did not change the nature of ownership" (Chen et al. 1996, p. 564). Under the household responsibility system, "responsibility" refers to the fixed quota of crops handed over to the government and the collective (Deng Zihui 2007, p. 386). This practice brought about a large increase in agricultural productivity. This persuasive and plausible reform plan was supported by most senior CPC leaders, but when Deng Zihui visited Mao twice in 1961 he rejected it both times (Chen et al. 1996, pp. 564–566). In other words, Mao not only rejected any change to property rights institution but also contract reform. He ordered that people's communes shift from being "large in size and collective in nature" to "three level ownership based on a production team" (三级所有, 队为基础).[3] Mao's argument was that the polarization of incomes should be avoided. He realized that once Deng Zihui's proposal was adopted, those good at growing crops would soon see their incomes increase.

[3] It is equivalent to reducing economic accounting units from township to natural village.

Despite Mao's rejection of contract reform, it was impossible to constrain people's demands to be fed and to increase their incomes. Even where constrained by the government, farmers made efforts to retain the economic rents that would otherwise dissipate. For example, in some regions, the government stipulated that the proportion of household-reserved plots should not exceed 5% of total land, but people still secretly expanded their household plots. In many regions, the proportion of household-reserved plots reached 40–50% of the total, even reaching 72% or 86% if newly cultivated land is included (Gao Wangling 2013, pp. 201–210).

The household responsibility system was often practiced in secret. While Mao Zedong opposed the practice and the CPC Central Committee issued multiple documents to suppress it, use of the system remained widespread in rural areas. In 1960, for villages in Anhui Province, land under the household responsibility system accounted for 40–74%, reaching as high as 80% in some areas (Gao Wangling 2013, p. 220). Even in the 1970s, when the household responsibility system was suppressed most severely, 10–50% of production teams in two districts of Luxian County, Sichuan Province, secretly continued the practice (Gao Wangling 2013, p. 223).

Other variants of the practice of household responsibility included farmers "borrowing land" from the collectives, cultivating virgin land, and "fixing responsibility for the production group." In effect, these practices served a similar function to terrace houses in Hong Kong—reducing rent dissipation—albeit on a larger scale (Gao Wangling 2013, pp. 228–234). Such practices were of critical significance. These contract reforms, while not sanctioned by the government, reduced rent dissipation and helped to prevent another tragedy like the Great Famine of 1959 to 1961.

After Mao, and in particular under Deng Xiaoping's rule, Deng Zihui's suggestion of the household responsibility system was proposed again. At that time, Deng Zihui's associate Du Runsheng was a representative of this proposal.[4] Despite intense objections, the proposal also won the favor of some senior political leaders, especially Deng Xiaoping. In a seminar on agricultural issues in early 1979, when debate on the household responsibility system had become stagnated, a compromise was reached to

[4] Du Runsheng is known as the "father of China's rural reform." He served as Vice-Chairman of China's National Agricultural Commission from 1979, Director of the Rural Policy Research Office of the Central Committee of the Communist Party of China, and Director of the Rural Development Research Centre of the State Council.

"neither forcefully correct, nor criticize and prosecute" farmers who adopted the household responsibility system (Du Runsheng 2005, p. 106). In practical terms, this meant not using coercion to stop farmers implementing contract reform, or in other words adopting the household responsibility system. In 1980, a notice on "Issues about Enhancing and Completing the Agricultural Responsibility System" (Document No. 75) stipulated that "the right to free choice by the people should be recognized" (Du Runsheng 2005, p. 119). This document noted that in remote and poor areas, "people have lost faith in collectives and asked to adopt the household responsibility system. Such demands should be supported so the household responsibility system can be adopted." It also emphasized that "the collective economy remains the unshakable basis of the modernization of China's agriculture."

It can be said that the contract of household responsibility is not a free contract between people as it involves interests between citizens and the government. What eventually made high-level political leaders accept the change is that the original collective contract, namely the contract that effectively turned farmers into government workers, failed to bring more revenue for the government. As Gao Wangling pointed out,

> Ever since the adoption of the state monopoly of purchase and marketing, the amount of 'mission yield' from farmers on a yearly basis, including all 'duty yields' and 'leftover yields', did not grow much but stayed at around 80 to 90 billion *jin*.[5] That is to say, farmers succeeded in sabotaging the government's original intention of expropriating the 'left-over yield' and kept what they produced. The government did not obtain the anticipated increase in crop yield, but instead got 'fixed rents.' Besides [...] after the Great Famine, the proportion of the total crop yields purchased by the government decreased from 25% to 20%, until the Reform and Opening-up era. (Gao Wangling 2013, p. 160)

Now that the grain to be handed over to the government is a certain even declining amount, there would be benefit rather than loss for the government if it imposed such an amount on farmers.

As the new contract form of household responsibility under collective landownership gained support at high levels of the CPC, legal protection followed and enhanced the potential of this practice to correct the misallocation of property rights and reduce rent dissipation. In turn, this

[5] Here Gao omits the extreme situation during the Great Famine.

facilitated the promotion of this practice nationwide. In 1982, the No. 1 Document of the Central Committee of the CPC formally recognized the household responsibility system and promulgated it as a typical contract form for China's rural areas, later known as the household-contracted farmland system. The basics of this contract form are that, while maintaining the premise of collective landownership, farmers can obtain the rights to crop and harvest the land through a contract with the collective. There may also be conditional transfer of these rights. The obligation of the farmers included handing over a fixed amount of duty yield to the government and to the collective. In the words of farmers, "whatever is left after that handed over to the state and the collective is my own." In effect, this is a fixed-rent permanent tenancy contract. From this point, China's rural areas were changed forever.

In his 1974 paper, "A Theory of Price Control," Cheung wrote that as long as one have the right to use, the right to enjoy income, and the right to transfer, he or she in fact has private property rights (Cheung 1974). That is to say, if via contract one gets the right to use, harvest, and transfer a certain piece of land, then one does not have to have ownership of that land to have the same effect. While the theoretical difference is negligible, in practice, the difference between contracting and ownership allows us to substitute the reform of property rights with the reform of contracts. This can mitigate the difficulty of reforms to a large extent and allow reforms to be carried out. Apparently, Professor Cheung was aware of the key difference between these kinds of reforms. In "Will China Go Capitalist?" Cheung writes "China will never officially denote its economic system as 'capitalism', or even adopt the term 'private property'. The prediction is simply that China will eventually adopt a structure of rights which is resembles, or functions in the manner of, a private-property economy" (Cheung 1986, p. 23).[6]

[6]Steven Cheung later mentioned in Economic Interpretation, "As early as 1968, in Chicago, I saw a book on Contract Law in Communist China. It is strange that countries without private property rights have contract law. It was mentioned to Stiegler and Demsetz at the time and they thought it might be empty talk, useless. I see that the book is very thick and useless and won't spend so much ink on it. The information provided by Cai Junhua confirms that the contract existed as early as in Communist China. The implication is important. China's reform of its rights structure can go through the channel of contract revision, which is excellent, because it cannot only avoid another bloody revolution, but also bring about stable effects" (2014, p. 297).

Perhaps Chinese policymakers did not get a chance to read such words. Indeed, it doesn't matter and in some ways illustrates even more if they did not. The situation and the strategic space they were faced with were very relevant to Professor Cheung's theory of contracts and its analytical framework. The macro-institutional environment was a coercive property rights institution that came out of various errors made in history, which was very difficult to alter for political and ideological reasons. These errors led to apparent rent dissipation. However, contract reform presented an alternative reform strategy that mitigated the dissipation of rent to a large extent without changing the underlying institution of property rights. Policymakers decided that it was right to shift the goal from income equality to economic growth. Besides, they had seen that the voluntary practice of the household responsibility system and household-reserved plots had increased productivity.[7] Furthermore, this contract reform is less costly than reforming property rights. It is worth considering, what other choices wise policymakers would have made?

8.5 The Role of Contract Reform in China's Market-Oriented Reform

To further this logic, it can be observed that contract reform was applicable not only for China's rural areas, because public ownership and the planned economy applied all over China. Due to the mismatch of property rights and the distortion of the planned economy, rent dissipation was ubiquitous. Therefore, in all places, contract reform had the effect of reducing rent dissipation.

As illustrated before, the institution of property rights suffered from two problems. One is the mismatch of property rights and the other is price regulation. The latter means that the person holding the property rights is not able to obtain the whole market value of his or her property or asset. The household responsibility system was a way to correct this mismatch of property rights by applying fixed rent contracts, a reform which also achieved progress in urban and industrial regions. It does not seem easy to correct a misallocation of resources simply by adopting a

[7] Du Runsheng, in Chapter IV of Records of Major Decision-Making in the Reform of Rural System in China, "The Great Change of Family Contracting System for Public Land," describes many of the high-level decision-makers' understanding of the economic effects of contracting production to households in the late 1970s and early 1980s (2005, pp. 96–138).

fixed rent contract. This is because the fixed rent contract only determines the distribution between the owner and the user of the resources on a micro level, that is, households and firms, instead of directly altering the price system. In agriculture, there were relatively few kinds of products and a few grains were favored by the government. This made it easier for the government to bear potential losses due to the adjustment of the grain prices.

In addition, the planned price system is a regulated price system for all products. Modifying one price will change relative prices for all other products, thus redistributing income and making it an issue of political economy. Therefore, correcting the error of price regulation encountered not only political and ideological objections but also caused social discontent due to the redistribution of income effect. That is to say, it is very difficult to eliminate price regulation and contract reforms on the micro level are not able to significantly correct the misallocation of resources that results from price regulation. In the case of Hong Kong observed by Professor Cheung, subtenancy and terrace houses can escape price regulation by using contracts, helping to correct the misallocation of resources. Subtenants are beyond the "depth" of price regulation, while terrace houses lie beyond the "scope" of price regulation. In addition, it should be recognized that price regulation for apartments was just one control in a market price system, while price regulations under the planned economy in mainland China were ubiquitous.

What followed was contract reform beyond the "depth" and "scope" of the planned price system. That is, market prices emerging from transactions under market rules for products produced by township and village enterprises, urban collective enterprises, and self-employed entrepreneurs. A dual-track price system came into being in which the two tracks were the parallel planned price system and the market price system. However, the two tracks did interact. Without legal backing, the planned price system would have been devoured by the market price system. However, politically, while the planned price system lacked ideological support of the sort public ownership enjoyed, the massive income redistributions arising from altering price systems entailed high risks. Hence, when policymakers realized that abolishing price controls would greatly reduce rent dissipation and decided to conduct price reforms, they encountered by panic buying and social unrest.[8]

[8] In 1988, when China's policymakers decided to abolish the planned price system, there was a serious rush to buy products. Policymakers were forced to abolish this price reform. In 1989, corruption caused by the dual-track price system made people dissatisfied and political unrest caused by the death of Hu Yaobang led to the "June Fourth Incident."

After the panic buying of 1988 and the social unrest of 1989, a total abolition of the planned price system seemed unacceptable. However, on a field investigation to Shanghai in 1990, I observed that only 10–20% of products on the market were subject to planned production quotas. That means about 80% of the products were exchanged through the market. Surprised and inspired, I later wrote a paper entitled "Seeking a Stable Way for Reform" (Sheng Hong 1991). The paper proposed that every enterprise and local government had planned rights and obligations under the planned economy, or "planned rights" and "planned obligations" as I called them. Illuminated by the market price system, the real value or cost of such rights and obligations became apparent. If enterprises and local governments were allowed to exchange their planned rights and obligations, then the misallocation of resources brought by the planned price system could be corrected. Eventually, the planned price system itself would be abolished without any political action.

One example of trading planned rights is foreign exchange quotas. Indeed, this may be the only legitimate trading of planned rights. Under this practice, every enterprise entitled to export was rewarded extra foreign exchange when it exceeded planned output. This came in the form of a "foreign exchange quota," that is, the right to buy foreign exchange at the official rate up to a certain quota. Quotas could be sold if not utilized. The price of the foreign exchange quota was the difference between the market foreign exchange rate and the official exchange rate. This practice would correct the misallocation of foreign exchange resources. This is described in the paper "Transaction of Foreign Exchange Quota: A Case of Planned Rights Transaction" (Sheng Hong 1995). However, this case does not explain why most products entered the market quietly and unnoticed.

In fact, the widespread practice of "planned rights trading" became a form of hedging. A local government or firm would hedge its planned rights against its planned obligations, or hedge its planned obligations against the planned obligations of a relevant organization. To quote an official from the Shanghai Industrial Bureau, "if we don't get steel from the state at the regulated price, we don't provide cars to the state at the regulated price." As we know, in a planned economy, planned rights usually go together with equivalent planned obligations. Therefore, hedging does not require extra compensation. In specific operations, hedging is the simplest choice as actual agreements are not needed with other institutions. Although Unit A may harm Unit B's interests if it reneges on its planned obligations to Unit B, Unit B may also renege on its planned obligations to Unit A, they are balanced. In reality, hedging usually comes from higher-level governments. Firstly, the central government is unable to fulfill its planned obligations, and therefore, local governments renege on their planned obligations in return. Interestingly, it is hedging that eventually dissolved the planned price system itself (Sheng Hong 2003).

I provide more general discussion of this point in the paper "Condition, Limitation, and Forms of Marketization" (Sheng Hong 1992). The paper proposed two reforms to implement the shift from a planned economy to a market economy through changing laws and contracts. These reforms have varying costs and should be selected accordingly. In general, if the transaction cost associated with the new institution is lower than losses due to resource misallocation under the old system, reforms can be implemented until the point where the transaction cost equals the loss due to resource misallocation (i.e., rent dissipation). However, the feasibility of the reform also depends on the cost of the reform. Comparatively speaking, even when democratic public choice shapes governmental or legal reforms, relatively high reform costs may arise as minority interests are infringed, leading to active or passive opposition from the minority group and the subsequent failure of the reform. However, market or contract reforms do not impinge on anyone's interest as they occur by mutual consent.

8.6 The Role of Contract Reform in World History

More generally speaking, the evolution of contracts has played a major role in institutional change throughout world history. Two examples discussed below are the evolution of the British land institution and the disintegration of serfdom in Western Europe.

In the eleventh century, William the Conqueror invaded England and established the unjust system of feudal landownership or land tenure. Under this institution, the king enfeoffed land to suzerains, suzerains enfeoffed land to vassals, and vassals enfeoffed land to tenants. Under this series of relations, the latter pledged service to the former, normally in the form of military, religious, or other service. The UK's land institution did not go through radical changes in legal texts since it was established under William the Conqueror. Transfer of landownership occurred after the wars between the Crown and Parliament, as the Parliament mainly consisted of landlords whose real desire was to change land property rights rather than the institution of land property itself. It can be deduced that the original allocation of land property rights was inefficient. Not only was land not allocated to those who could best use it, but it was also very difficult to correct this misallocation by contract. Under land tenure, parties were related to landownership not as free and equal economic agents, but as people subjugated to an appendage status. The procedures for land transfer were highly complex and transaction costs could be as high as three to five years' yields (Xian Hongchang 2009, p. 346).

However, with the passage of time, the actual practice of British land tenure evolved. Today, even though land in the UK belongs to the Queen in name, in reality, this is true only in the sense of land sovereignty—"feudal land tenure does not hold any actual meaning today" (Lawson and Rudden 2009, pp. 85–86). Tenants were the real owner of land property rights and transaction of land property rights was easier. British law did not formally abolish land tenure until 1925. The land tenure system remains influential—"a number of concepts and technical terms are still common in the common law world, even in the United States, which has long resisted the monarchy" (Lawson and Rudden 2009, p. 86). British history has not seen the kind of intense political or legal reform of land witnessed in China, such as the initial tax on land per-*mu* or "the abolishment of fiefs and establishment of counties" that occurred through war. This implies that the change of the actual practice of land tenure was achieved not by legal reforms, but more often by contract reform.

There were several forms of contract under land tenure, such as free tenure, copyhold, leasehold, and villeinage. These can all be regarded as different contract forms. What differed between these forms is the distribution of rights and obligations between the landlord and tenant. Free tenure entailed more rights for tenants compared to their obligations to landlords; leasehold was similar to market contractual relations; the villeinage is a status close to that of a serf; and copyhold is subject to the local rules of the Lord of the Manor rather than the king's common court rule. Between the fourteenth century and sixteenth century, villein tenants decreased in number because "the majority of villein tenants paid a ransom for their freedom," which "in some areas reached ten pounds" (Shen Han 2002, p. 30). Only later did the British parliament discuss an act that ushered in general emancipation (Shen Han 2002, p. 31).

On the other hand, as time passed, leasehold developed rapidly. By the sixteenth century, according to Tony's investigation of 16 manors, the land under leasehold accounted for 40–90% of manor land. "Farmland under leasehold has become a major form of operation in English manors" (Shen Han 2002, p. 80). Free tenure also flourished. According to the British Council for Agriculture, by the turn of the nineteenth century, free tenure was the most common form of tenancy in the majority of the UK (Shen Han 2002, pp. 198–211). Free tenure is a form of tenure applicable to common law, while rental tenure is a form of free contract applicable to the market. Therefore, these two forms both imply more actual rights for the peasant holder. Therefore, the increasing proportion of land under free tenure and rental tenure increases the rights of peasant holders under the framework of established property rights. The only change this depends on is one of contract.

Furthermore, free tenants handed over fixed rent to their landlords, but their period of rights was very long. Normally, it lasted for one's lifetime and could be unconditionally inherited. Leasing tenants also turned over fixed rent to their landlords. The period of tenancy typically lasted 50 to 60 years, sometimes even 90 years (Shen Han 2002, p. 70). This is similar to permanent tenancy. Under fixed-rent contract, tenants are encouraged to invest in the land as they could retain any increased yield. Therefore, as time went by, due to the increased unit yields of the land and inflation, "the fixed rent of a small amount disappeared over time [...] in the 16th and 17th century, the feudal burden of freehold tenants was negligible. After the Restoration, free tenants were exempt from all feudal burdens" (Shen Han 2002, p. 212). A similar situation applied to leasing tenants.

If kings and lords did not collect land rent in practice, they could not be regarded as the true owner of land property. Labor services linked to the land were replaced by taxes. As for how taxes were distributed among the king and the Parliament, this was determined by the competition of political forces and belongs to the realm of national fiscal issues, something that does not affect the nature of land property rights. On the contrary, any land property right of a natural person or a legal representative is a property right under a certain land sovereignty that entails tax obligations. Therefore, land directly belonging to the king eventually became the tenant's land without any bloodshed. Ultimately, the phrase "crown land" came simply to mean sovereign territory.

With regard to slavery, the institution was clearly unjust and inefficient. It is self-evident that slavery is a most inefficient mode of resource allocation as it devalues a human being with unlimited creative potential to nothing more than a tool. Slavery was established and maintained through violence. However, the emancipation of slaves did not have to be violent. Fogel pointed out that except the United States and Haiti, most countries ended slavery peacefully. To quote at length:

> *Many, perhaps most, of the slaves outside of the southern United States were freed under programs of gradual emancipation. These schemes usually involved the freeing, not of adults, but of children born on some date after the emancipation law was enacted. Moreover, the freeing of slave children was delayed until their eighteenth, twenty-first, or in some cases, twenty-eighth birthday. Under such arrangements, slaveholders suffered no losses on existing male staves or on female slaves who were already past their childbearing years. Having control over the services of a newly born child until his or her twenty-first or twenty-eighth birthday meant that most, if not all, of the costs of rearing such slaves would be covered by the income they earned between the onset of their productive years and the date of their emancipation.* (Fogel and Engerman 1989, p. 35)

From a contract perspective, the practice described above is similar to an asset purchase contract. The slave emancipation plan cannot purely be considered a change of contract because the state also issued multiple emancipation laws. However, as legal reform usually lags behind real practice, one may guess that these legal changes came as a result of contract reform. Most of the slave emancipation acts were passed in eighteenth to nineteenth centuries (Fogel and Engerman 1989, pp. 33–34).

In the fifteenth century, serfdom started to disintegrate in Western Europe. *The Rise and Fall of the Manorial System: A Theoretical Model* by Douglass North and Robert Paul Thomas provides a helpful discussion of this process. Firstly, labor became scarcer than land after the Black Death of the thirteenth century. Serfs got better treatment after they escaped their homeland, while landlords competed to provide better terms for serfs in order to get more laborers. As population began to recover, the market beyond manors developed. The market offered a price reference for manor products, which encouraged landlords to exchange their products into currency and use that money to procure their favored product combinations instead of ordering their tenants to grow the products directly. Serfs were also allowed to sell their products in the market.

Against this backdrop, a critical change of contract form took place. Firstly, rent in the form of labor services could be transformed into taxes. In the beginning, these may have been equivalent in value, but it reduced transaction costs as it enabled serfs to liberate themselves from manor labor, thus constituting a foundation for full liberty. As serfs accumulated a certain amount of money through market transactions, they were able to pay a ransom for their freedom. In regard to landlords, the treatment of serfs was determined by labor-land relations after the Black Death. Once the price of labor determined by the market was exceeded, they became willing to accept the ransom and grant serfs freedom. Therefore, by changing the contract form, through the contract that bought one's freedom, serfs were emancipated. Similar events happened continuously, eventually leading to the disintegration of the manor system in Western Europe.

In one paper, Professor North and his associate adopted Professor Cheung's logic from *The Theory of Share Tenancy* and pointed out that "different contracts require varying efforts in enforcement and negotiation" (North and Thomas 1971, p. 784). The cost of reforming a contract, a secondary institutional arrangement, is lower than that associated with changing a fundamental institutional arrangement. Therefore, institutional change usually takes the form of contract change at first. There are two types of contract revision. The first type is the renegotiation of the property price of a certain asset, such as a renegotiation of the price of land or labor, resulting in a change of relative prices; or a change of boundaries of other rights and obligations, such as the increase of free tenants. The second type of contract revision is a change of the contract form, such as the shift from labor rent or tax to monetary rent or tax. Both changes reduce rent dissipation. At the same time, like the elimination of planned prices, the original legal relationship is overhauled, namely, the attachment of the serf to the land.

Taking one step further, Professor North and Thomas also took into account the influence of contract changes on fundamental institutions: "The cumulative forces of such changes which violate, modify, or otherwise bypass existing fundamental institutional arrangements will induce growing pressure for more basic- and more costly-modification in primary institutional arrangements" (1971, p. 786). Later on, the king's court overruled the court of the manor and common law overtook customary law. Finally in 1925, the British Law of Property Act ended the feudal land institution.

8.7 Contract Reform and Its Need for Legal Protection

Professor Cheung called contract theory the "missing link" of economics. Yet, while contract theory has been proposed, it has not yet been sufficiently acknowledged in the field of economics, leading to an imbalance in our understanding of institutions. Today, when we talk about institutions, what comes to mind first is property rights; when we talk about institutional reform, we mainly refer to the reform of property rights. By contrast, contract reform is rarely discussed. This gap has led us to misunderstand history. Since property rights are associated with law, and law with coercive power, hence, reform of property rights is associated with critical political events, even bloodshed and war. People tend to pay more attention to tension and conflict and believe such events are what really shape history. However, this may not be the case. Just like the story of looking for one's keys under the light, in reality, often the key is actually in a dark place that light does not reach.

By contrast, the reason contract reform has been neglected is that the process is too peaceful or commonplace. Commonplace does not mean that there is no tension or conflict, but that the cost of reform cost is low, and so therefore the reform is relatively smooth and successful. This absence of friction stems from the fact that, by nature, contracts are formed via the mutual consent of negotiating parties. No one is harmed, so no one objects. This process of achieving unanimous consent, or what Professor Buchanan called "the political counterpart of the Pareto optimal," can be regarded as efficient. Therefore, the contract reform itself achieves efficient outcomes at low cost.

Unlike legal reforms that drive a larger reform process, contract reform has another important advantage, namely that is it is conducted at the level of the smallest unit—the transaction. As long as a mutual agreement can be reached, contract reform may commence. From a macro perspective, this kind of institutional reform is decentralized and incremental. This process is less intense, allowing people and society to adapt to and avoid the cultural shocks and historic fractures caused by radical revolutions. When the potential benefits to be gained by changing contracts are exhausted, the reform will come to a halt rather than being overdone. Another advantage is, unlike legal reforms, contract reform does not force people to take identical actions. This allows those who are against the reform to keep their own form of contract. Hence, contract reform is able to preserve a diversity of institutions.

Reviewing legal system reform, it is not necessary to say that law must be "coercive" under autocracy or even democracy. As unanimous consent among multiple parties is rarely possible, in general, majority rule is adopted. This inevitably means harming the interests of certain parties, which makes it impossible to achieve Pareto efficiency. Indeed, some laws that appear to hurt interests of the minority may, in the long run, harm the interests of the majority or even everyone. Therefore, successful legal reform is relatively less probable.

When legal reforms involve changes to property rights and ownership, intense social conflict may occur as such reforms go against some people's interests. Besides, legal reforms usually go hand in hand with political shifts, when different social groups tend to overdo legal reforms and push property rights institutions to extremes. For example, the political group that considers private property rights problematic tends to establish public ownership, which is less efficient. Such reforms that initiate massive wealth redistribution may incite violent conflict or even war. This kind of change can cost lives and is unacceptable in any case, as the bitter lessons of the French Revolution, the Russian Revolution, and the Chinese Revolution tell us.

Even at the cost of blood and lives, it is doubtful whether the political shift associated with legal reform will create more efficient institutions. To put it in another way, there is no proven positive correlation between the price paid and the quality of the institution formed. In extreme cases, there may even be a negative correlation. The more opposition and bloodshed there is, the more unfair the eventual arrangement of winners and losers and the more unbalanced interests will be. This will lead to poorer outcomes in terms of justice and efficiency. For example, the land system established after China's land reform was a system that had regressed by thousands of years, directly leading to the starvation of tens of millions of people.

In a narrower sense, Professor Steven Cheung's contract theory can be used in a specific situation, that is, where a system of property rights is known to be wrong but cannot be corrected by legal means due to political or other reasons. In this case, adopting the approach of contract reform, on the premise that the mistaken property right system continues to exist, we can significantly reduce rent dissipation caused by misallocation of property rights at a lower cost. This contractual change will help to correct the initial misallocation of property rights and achieve visible gains, providing a reference for subsequent legal reform while minimizing resistance to the change.

This insight may be applied to policy making. When a political group realizes that the existing property right system has problems but the political conditions for immediate reform are lacking, an important decision is to allow people to continue contract reform and safeguard reform outcomes on the premise of maintaining the existing system of property rights. This is what the ruling party of China did for 15–20 years after 1979, for example in implementing the household responsibility system and the trading of planned rights.

Previous analyses of China's economic reforms have usually failed to take the perspective of contract theory, leaving observers confused as to how China achieved its economic miracle without apparent property right reforms. Many observers declare that property rights theory fails to explain the situation, or apply property rights theory in a complicated way or attribute the Chinese miracle to previous property rights institutions. Some even claim that China's success is due to multiple interventions by the government and the massive development of state-owned enterprises. However, applying contract theory to our analysis sheds light on what led to the Chinese miracle; essentially, that "contracts matter." It is contract reform that helped reduce rent dissipation and increase efficiency.

Contract theory also suggests an explanation for why China's reform process may have seen a sudden reversal around 2000. Above, it was argued that the political group should respect the current property rights institution and reduce rent dissipation by contract reform. We should also add the condition that **no new inefficient property rights institutions should be set up**. If inefficient property right systems are continuously re-established, this will start new rounds of rent dissipation. A further condition is **that the outcome of the contract reform, that is, the property rights that emerge, should be respected.** Otherwise, the stimulus and benefit from the reform will dissolve and the saved rent will dissipate. Around 2000, policymakers exempted state-owned enterprises from the obligation to surrender profits to the state and gave them control of their own profits. In addition, a series of monopolies were set up and the legitimate land rights of village collectives were weakened. In effect, this set up new inefficient property rights institutions and resulted in new rent dissipation. Meanwhile, the legitimate property rights of village collectives and privately owned enterprises were infringed, such as the seizure of famers' land and mining rights to natural resources purchased by private owned enterprises.[9] These actions resulted in the deterioration of China's economic environment.

[9] The seizure of farmers' land refers to a practice from the 1990s until the present where the local government expropriates land from farmers by force at a below-market price. Seizure of property rights of private owned enterprises refers to the forceful acquisition of coal mining rights previously sold by the provincial government of Shanxi to Zhejiang private enterprises.

In short, the explanatory power of economics for historical and institutional changes can be significantly enhanced by further developing and applying contract theory. In this respect, Professor Steven Cheung, as the pioneer of contract theory, has made significant contributions to the field.

References

Alchian, Armen, *Economic Forces at Work*, Liberty Fund Inc. 1977.

陈丕显等, 《邓子恢传》, 人民出版社, 1996. (Chen, Pixian, et al., *Deng Zihui: A Biography,* People's Publishing House, 1996.)

Cheung, Steven, "A Theory of Price Control", *The Journal of law and Economics,* Vol. 17, No.1 (Apr., 1974), pp. 53–71.

Cheung, Steven, "The Contractual Nature of the Firm", *The Journal of Law and Economics,* Vol. 26, No.1 (Apr., 1983), pp. 1–21.

Cheung, Steven, *Will China Go Capitalist?* (Hobart Papers) Institute of Economic Affairs; 2nd Revised edition (August 19, 1986).

张五常, 《制度的选择》(《经济解释》卷四), 中信出版社, 2014. (Cheung, Steven, *Choice of Institution*, *Economic Explanation (Volume 4)*, Citic Press, 2014.)

Coase, Ronald, "The Problem of Social Cost", *The Journal of Law and Economics,* Vol. 3 (Oct., 1960), pp. 1–44.

Demsetz, Harold, "The Exchange and Enforcement of Property Rights", *The Journal of Law and Economics,* 11–25 (October, 1964).

Demsetz, Harold, "Toward a Theory of Property Rights", *American Economic Review*, May 1967.

邓子恢, 《邓子恢自述》, 人民出版社, 2007. (Deng Zihui, *DENG Zihui: A Self Account*, People's Publishing House, 2007.)

杜润生, 《中国农村体制变革重大决策纪实》, 人民出版社, 2005. (Du Runsheng, *Du Runsheng Talks about Significant Policy-making in China's Rural Reform*, People's Publishing House, 2005.)

Fogel, Robert, and Engerman, Stanley, *Time on the Cross*, W.W. Norton Company, 1989.

高王凌, 《中国农民反行为研究(1950~1980)》, 香港中文大学出版社, 2013. (Gao Wangling, *A Research of Anti-Behavior of Chinese Farmers (1950–1980)*, The Chinese University Press, 1989–2013.)

劳森和冉得, 《英国财产法导论》, 法律出版社, 2009。(Translated from: Lawson, F.H., and Rudden, Bernard, *The Law of Property*, Oxford University Press, 2002.)

North, Douglass and Thomas, Robert, "The Rise and Fall of the Manorial System: A Theoretical Model", *Journal of Economic History*, 31 (December), 1971.

诺思,《经济史中的结构与变迁》,上海三联书店出版社, 1991. (Translated from: North, Douglass, *Structure and Change in Economic History*, W. W. Norton & Company, 1982.)

沈汉,《英国土地制度史》, 2002, 学林出版社。(Shen Han, *History of British Land Institution*, Academia Press, 2002.)

盛洪,"一个价格改革的故事及其引出的过渡经济学的一般理论",《管理世界》, 2003年第5期。(Sheng Hong, "A Story about Price Reform and a General Transitional Economic Theory Inspired by it". *Management World*, Issue 5, 2003.)

盛洪,"寻求改革的稳定形式",《经济研究》, 1990年第11期。(Sheng Hong, "Seeking for a Stable Way of Reform", *Economic Research*, Issue 11, 1991.)

盛洪,"外汇额度的交易:一个计划权利交易的案例",《中国社会科学季刊》,总第十三期(1995年11月)。(Sheng Hong, "Transaction of Foreign Exchange Quota: A Case of Planned Rights Transaction", *Quarterly Journal of Social Science of China*, Issue 13, 1995.)

咸鸿昌,《英国土地法律史》,北京大学出版社, 2009. (Xian Hongchang, *History of British Land Laws*, Peking University Press, 2009.)

张五常,《佃农理论》,商务印书馆, 2000. (Cheung, Steven, The Theory of Share Tenancy, The Commercial Press, 2000.)

盛洪,"市场化的条件,限度与形式",《经济研究》, 1992 年第11期。(Sheng Hong, "Condition, Limitation, and Forms of Marketization", Economic Research, 11th issue, 1992.

CHAPTER 9

Hedge Funds, Financial Markets, and Nation-States

Contents

Various explanations for the East Asian financial crisis have emerged since 1997, some of which are fraught with sentimentality, such as accusations of "conspiracy theory" or the rendering of "globalization." This chapter takes a classical economics approach to the crisis and reaches the following conclusions. First, it finds that all agents in the crisis were acting to serve their self-interests; second, the results of these actions could have been different. At one extreme, an action could have been taken at the direct expense of others, creating negative externalities in economic terms; at the other, it could have reached a so-called win-win position, and generated an optimal solution.

Translated from ***Economic Research*** (《经济研究》), Issue 12, 1999.

Sheng Hong, *Vision and Calculation*,
https://doi.org/10.1007/978-981-15-2898-9_9

As this chapter is not only concerned with national situations but interaction between countries, it is necessary to distinguish these two situations. The first is that within a nation-state, there exists a society and a national government, whereas in the international sphere, nations in the world are in a situation not far from anarchy. The second is that within a country, people have the freedom to move from one place to another, but they do not have the same freedom to move from one country to another. That said, the same action or policy leads to different outcomes at the national level and international level.

Economic freedom, as emphasized by liberal economics, operates under certain rules, such as exclusion of any action that might hurt others. The pursuit of self-interest will therefore simultaneously enhance social welfare. Heretofore, these rules can only be approximately realized when there is a government. In discussing international affairs, therefore, we should pay attention to the change of meaning of freedom. Our aim is to find a way to form rules so that economic actions between countries can achieve mutually beneficial results. Otherwise, actions harmful to others' interests will not only lead to unfair distribution of wealth, but also, together with victim's revenge, reduce people's welfare across the whole world, including that of "beggar-thy-neighbor" people.

This chapter focuses on hedge funds, financial markets, and nation-states. These are not only different institutions but also represent three groups of people. We will thus search for the possible explanations for the financial crisis amidst the interaction between institutions and these groups of people.

9.1 A Nation-State and a Monetary System

A monetary system is an institution, which a nation-state provides as a public good. A nation-state is no more than the specific embodiment of a government, a kind of institutional arrangement, which in today's world offers protections to peoples differentiated from each other by historical, cultural, or other factors. Intriguing issues raised so far include: why is a monetary system a public good that corresponds to the domain of a nation-state and what factors prevent it from becoming universal? What kind of role does a government play in the operation of a monetary system?

People have realized the benefit of a currency with insufficient value in circumventing situations where economic growth is depressed by a short supply of precious metals. Once a currency of insufficient value comes into being, especially when there are many of them, a tendency of "adverse selection" in which bad money drives out good ensues, which invariably creates instability in the monetary system.[1] As the functions of a currency entail, among other things, stabilization of its value, a government backed by force has no choice but to monopolize its issuance to guarantee it keeps its value. With the lengthy evolution of currency that for now has settled upon paper money, government action that enforces the credit of the money in circulation is required even more.

Once people accept usage of a currency, the issuer of the currency can earn seigniorage—the difference between the face value of the currency and its production costs. As the government of a nation usually enjoys seigniorage, the nation's people should own the wealth generated. If the government abandons currency issuance and uses the currency issued by another country, it is tantamount to preventing its people enjoying what is theirs. This is an important reason for nation-states to issue their own currency.

Another is the impossibility of free flow of population between countries. Suppose there were only one unified currency in circulation in the world with free flow of commodities and capital, the money supply of one country would as a result be determined by its trade balance, surplus, or deficit (Lindert and Kindleberger 1985, p. 360), which, in turn, would rely primarily upon the productivity of the tradable goods' sector. Countries running trade surpluses would have more currency in circulation, whereas those running trade deficits would end up with less money supply. If imbalance in the productivity of trading nations persisted, situations with money supply would be likely to remain for a long period, enough to check the growth of those economies with short supply of the currency. The free flow of money and capital would enlarge the difference of money supplies between nation-states, for the nature of capital makes it seeking for the profits in the flourishing regions or industries (Haberler 1963, pp. 434–481). But in today's world, people cannot migrate freely among countries, and the differences in economic development caused by variations in money supply among countries cannot be adjusted through

[1] In the long history of China, from the Spring and Autumn Period to the Warring States Period to the Republic of China, we can from time to time see the coexistence of multiple currencies, the proliferation of privately minted coins, the situation of ""bad coins drive out good coins"," and the resulting currency system chaos and social and economic turmoil. See Yufu 1984.

population flow. Therefore, a nation-state has sufficient reasons to control the initiative of money supply in its own hands by issuing its own currency.

In abstract terms, the target of money supply is to materialize all the transactions that would lead to full employment of resources available, including labor, mediated by the currency in circulation. Achieving such a target does not necessarily require a central government to issue the base money. Rather, it relies upon the financial markets that can be generally divided into two main categories: the equity market and the debt market (Fabozzi and Modigliani 1998, p. 11). The financial markets as a whole will push the money supply to its limit in an economy, namely, to the last transaction that depends on the intermediary of money, and the productive activity related to that transaction.

As market participants realize that the debt instruments based on currency issued by government have their credits as high that they themselves can be used as means of payment, these instruments thus possess the functions of money as they continuously change hands in money and/or capital markets. In particular, the existence of banking system can expand the money supply by a multiple of the injection of base money, as the system can repeatedly create deposits by making loans which then become new deposits except a portion of reserve (Commons 1983, Volume II, pp. 1–86).

In addition, the financial markets, through the exchange of financial instruments, constantly search for and probe the boundaries of money supply. Under ideal circumstances, an economic activity accomplished with an arrangement of the market for debt will be deemed efficient so long as the rate of return of an economic activity is not lower than the market interest rate which is at the level of so-called natural interest rate. When the market rate is equal to the marginal productivity, an equilibrium between money supply and money demand that represents the economic activities in a society would be reached (Commons 1983, pp. 248–58).

In reality, however, economic activities are not as simple as they look, since modern circuitous production mode prolongs the cycle and increases risks. If risks are too high, the debt market cannot play its normal function, as unredeemable debts could not only destroy the market credit but also lead to a contraction of money supply. In consequence, the market demands collateral to reduce risk. On the other hand, it pushes those financial transactions with too high risks involving economic activities to the equity market, which, unlike the debt market, would not cause a contraction of money supply once an incident of loss occurred.

In brief, if there is no equity market, either some risky economic activities cannot be financed, or debt transactions contain too much risk, resulting in the instability of the money supply itself. If there is no debt market, the cost of financing will be too high, owing to insufficient money supply. An equity market is such an institutional arrangement that avoids the instability in the monetary system because of high risks, while financing those economic activities with high risks. The scales of the two markets, furthermore, are interrelated at a certain proper ratio that is determined by their relative prices. Therefore, there is a sensitive relation between the prices of the two markets.

From the perspective of international economy, the monetary system of one nation cannot be in a state of complete independence. The flow of commodities and capitals will invariably have impacts on the money supply of a nation. When a country's monetary policy is fixed, the balance of trade will increase or decrease the money supply; a foreign loan will also produce a monetary multiplier (such as the effect of a U.S. dollar loan in Europe, see Lindert and Kindleberger 1985, pp. 443–8). Such a phenomenon will naturally tie a currency of one nation to those of others. The relative prices (i.e., the exchange rates) of currencies will fluctuate just like those of common commodities do. The level of exchange rate is related with the trade balance as well as with the level of the domestic money supply that can be judged by the real interest rate (i.e., the difference between nominal interest rate and inflation rate) of an economy. Hence, rates of interest and of exchange are sensitively related to each other if currencies may be convertible.

As for the government of a nation-state, one of the public goods that it should provide is an effective and stable monetary system. Since financial markets have the function of creating money and of probing the boundary of money supply, the government should promote the development of the financial markets and make use of their strength. To do so will lead to a higher efficiency of the monetary system; thus every one unit of currency may work with a larger multiplier. Insofar as international effects are concerned, moreover, uncertainty has been and will remain the dominant feature in the global economy. External factors can sometimes propel the development of an economy (e.g., via trade surplus), and sometimes restrict it (e.g., via capital flight), or even threaten stability in the monetary system of a nation-state (e.g., via shocks of international hot money). When deliberating monetary policy, a government, therefore, must take into account policies regarding the trade and exchange rate while keeping external factors in mind.

The paradox a government faces is that if the economy is left wide open, it is subject to all sorts of external shocks that will not only induce instability in internal markets but also offset the effectiveness of domestic economic policies. However, if the government regulates its international economic affairs, for instance, by imposing a fixed rate on foreign exchange, its domestic macro-policy might confront a dilemma. For example, a government may usually raise the interest rate of the domestic currency when a trade deficit occurs, but the result is to reduce a money supply that has already been tight. Therefore, there is no certain conclusion in the modern international economics about what kind of exchange rate policy should be adopted by a government (Lindert and Kindleberger 1985, pp. 406–431).Nevertheless, it is clear that the monetary system of a country is not only founded on fiat currency, but also needs fine-tuning and protection through various policy mixes.

9.2 Financial Markets and Hedge Funds

Financial markets are institutions within which are groups of people whose pursuance of maximizing self-interest engenders the function of the market in allocation of resources in society, and bestow upon it an indispensable status in the monetary system. In the modern period, the financial markets, through innovations of financial instruments and organizations, such as financial securitization and the emergence of the stock exchange, continually lower transaction costs that in turn enhance the efficiency of the monetary system. The benefits brought about by these innovations have been shared by market participants and society broadly.

Driven by interests, the markets have been vigorous in continuous innovation. Such interests, however, do not always run in the same direction as that of society. The benefit of a stock exchange, for example, is closely related to the volume of trade. In other words, the larger the volume, the higher the commission obtained. As a result, there is enough incentive for innovation to increase the trading volume. Insofar as society is concerned, it is not always the case that benefits increase alongside volume. Exuberant growth of credit, or excess investments, for example, may disturb a delicate balance in an economy. From an economic viewpoint, only transactions proven to improve market efficiency are acceptable, or they would not differ substantially from the Las Vegas' zero-sum game:

while they may be similar to a transaction, they serve no function in increasing efficiency.

A competent government, therefore, should exercise great caution in regulating innovation in financial markets. Ever since the 1970s, when the first financial futures contract came into being in Chicago Board of Trade, innovations in financial markets have been centered around the financial instrument of futures and options, called "financial derivatives." Nevertheless, these innovations were only legalized after intense investigation (i.e., public hearings and inquiries) conducted by the American Securities Commission (Fabozzi and Modigliani 1998, p. 306). One of the principal reasons for their legalization is that these financial derivatives can serve a function in hedging exposure risks contained in financial transactions, and can be regarded as an improvement in efficiency from an economic point of view.

However, things started to take an about-turn when these financial derivatives intertwined with another kind of innovation in financial organizations—the rise of the hedge fund. The original purpose of such funds was to hedge exposure risks in financial transactions; once in operation, some of them (represented by George Soros' Quantum Fund) gradually found that certain attributes of derivatives facilitate their use for profit-making.[2] The first attribute (taking the option as an example) is that it can be used to leverage a larger transaction with a certain quantity of capital to influence market prices, provided the transaction is large enough (see Fig. 9.1).[3] The second one is that as a buyer of an option contract has the right, but does not have the obligation, the buyer of the contract does not have to actually exercise it if the strike price on the date of delivery is not favorable (see Galitz 1998, pp. 193–8). This kind of arrangement lowers the buyer's risk while encouraging people to invest more riskily (i.e., speculation). The third feature is that the more the executive price of the

[2] There are lots of types of hedge funds, most of them are still "traditional" (see Gang et al. 1999; Van hedge fund advisors international 1999a). What are discussed here are those represented by George Soros' Quantum Fund.

[3] Along with the repetition of operations and accumulation of experience, people gradually realized that the financial derivatives could bring a new force for a trader. For instance, Nick Leeson, the famous rogue trader who was responsible for the bankruptcy of Barings Bank, acknowledges that he intended to make the price moving toward the direction which he desired by trading a large quantity of futures (1996, pp. 144, 198). Afterward, people clearly realized the impact of transactions of financial derivatives, and used the transactions as a one-off means to make profit in the financial markets.

Fig. 9.1 Increasing supply by hedge funds

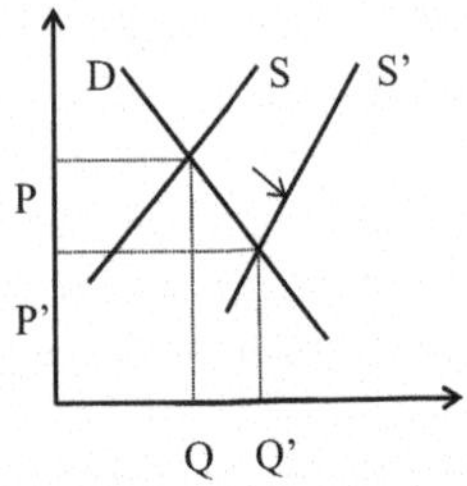

option deviates from the spot price of the asset underlying the option, the lower the price of the option itself (Hull 1997, p. 161), which facilitates speculation by hedge funds.

When a hedge fund has a firm grip of the attributes of the derivatives, its investment strategy will start to change. The original hedging portfolio begins to evolve toward a strategy that obtains profits by manipulating prices of related financial markets through large transactions. In the previous section, we have pointed out that there exists a sensitive relationship between prices of different financial markets, which can also be expressed through mathematical formulas. The relationship between the price of the stock market and that of the money market, for example, is as follows:

$$S_m = (p/i)S_b$$

Where: S_m = market price of a stock;
p = rate of profits;
i = interest rate;
S_b = book value of a stock (see David W. Pearce ed., 1983, pp. 545–6)

Similarly, the relationship between interest rates and exchange rates of the two currencies can be expressed as follows:

$$e_f(1+i_a) = e_s(1+i_b)$$

Where: e_f = forward exchange rate;
e_s = spot exchange rate;
i_a = domestic interest rate;
i_b = foreign interest rate (quoted from Rao Yuqing 1983, p. 325)[4]

[4]About the relationship between interest rate and exchange rate, Paul Krugman and Maurice Obstfeld have discussed in detail in their work, ***International Economics: Theory and Policy*** (1998, pp. 352–5).

Many textbooks on economics or finance have written about these relationships. However writers have viewed these relationships solely as the results of interactions between markets. The central bank of a country may use these kinds of relationships, for instance, to influence prices in its stock markets, currency markets, and others by adjusting the rediscount rate. Hedge funds of the type represented by Soros, assume that if prices in one market (e.g., the currency market) are sharply changed for a short period, prices in other markets may see corresponding changes. Equipped with a sufficient investment portfolio, hedge funds can squeeze profits out of various markets in which favorable price movements take place. Of course, the so-called beauty contest effect after social panic buttons have been pressed can also be included in their strategy, as it induces further instability to the market prices.

Financial derivatives have indeed been a centerpiece of attempts to manipulate the markets. The kind of strategy, though not yet expressed openly, is visible through certain cases. For example, in May 1997 hedge funds began an attack on Thailand by aiming to depress the Thai baht by selling spot and options, while at the same time, buying U.S. dollar options at the undiminished exchange rate of the Thai baht. In another case, hedge funds depressed the exchange rate of the Hong Kong dollar while also buying Hong Kong stock options. Their aim was to change interest rates by changing the exchange rate of the Hong Kong dollar. Hong Kong's stock market plunged after the Hong Kong monetary authorities raised interest rates to maintain the linked exchange rate.

As the investment strategy of hedge funds changes, so does the role of the institution. It is about time that hedge funds, in the aftermath of the financial "mayhem" caused by their activities, should be put under close scrutiny to ask whether their practices are in line with the interests of society and global welfare. From an economic perspective, price manipulation brings about inefficiency, since firstly, it distorts market signal for the allocation of resources. Secondly, a large amplitude of price fluctuation in the financial market within a short period induces instability to the monetary system, and could even lead to its total collapse. One economic theory points out that a stable pricing system is more efficient than an unstable one (Lindert and Kindleberger 1985, pp. 554–8). Furthermore, the collapse of the monetary system may damage the real economy.

Such manipulation can be compared to creating monopolies, since the core rule of monopoly is to rig market prices through sheer quantity to attain profits. The difference, however, is that as financial institutions, hedge funds cannot match the scale of those monopolistic monsters in the goods market, and the duration of manipulating transactions is far shorter. This may be the reason that hedge funds remain at large, receive less condemnation and have no restrictions imposed upon them.[5] Nevertheless, monopolistic behavior, be it in financial markets or in general, runs counter to the rules of the market.

In a sense, manipulation is very similar to monopoly. The core content of monopoly is to change the price by manipulating the number of transactions and to profit from the changed price (i.e., monopoly price). Therefore, we can approximate the manipulation of hedge funds on financial markets to having a financial monopoly. In fact, financial monopoly, like general monopoly, is against market rules. One of the reasons why it has not been widely condemned and forbidden by law is that it differs from classic monopoly on the surface: (1) hedge funds, as a kind of enterprise, are intuitively small in scale, while classic monopoly enterprises are usually huge; and (2) it manipulates the market by controlling the volume of transactions for a relatively short time, while the classic monopoly enterprises occupy the field for a long time.

9.3 Mercantilism and International Currency

As discussed, the balance of trade can have an impact on the money supply of a country. Hence, trade policy, to a certain extent, also has the function of monetary policy. When there is only one currency in the world, trade policy is the only monetary policy. In fact, we can from this perspective get hold of the long lasting mercantilism that has existed ever since the outset of the modern era.

In the early modern world, the current account of trade between countries was settled by a precious metal, such as silver. Thus, it would not be wrong to consider the world as having had only one currency. Under such

[5] In fact, there are a few economists, such as Paul Krugman, to have pointed the nature of market manipulation of the hedge funds, and to claim regulating it (1998).

circumstances, the regular trade surplus would be entailed if the money supply for sustaining the speed of the growth in a nation was maintained. This has in one way explained why the countries with rapid economic growth are those who have successfully exercised the notion of mercantilism.

The trade policy of mercantilism, to a certain extent, can be regarded as the expansionary monetary policy. As being long before pointed out by Keynes, mercantilism goes a long way toward the economic growth of a nation as trade surplus not only leads to an increase in overseas investment but also increases domestic investment by reducing interest rate (1977, pp. 285–6). Modern international economics also attests that under the fixed exchange rate, a trade surplus is tantamount to a direct increase in money supply (Lindert and Kindleberger 1985, pp. 360–1).

Yet, sustaining the money supply is not the sole objective for adopting a mercantilist policy. In a world with many different and vying nation-states, a free trade policy will bring about an enhancement of the national welfare that mainly is reflected from consumers' surplus via lowering prices of commodities. Such welfare cannot be gathered together in a way that would form a so-called state capacity. In a world where many nations exist and confront each other, mercantilism could nonetheless do the job through the wealth in form of currency (i.e., precious metals or foreign currencies) that can be controlled and mobilized by a central management, and thus has a strong implication in international political economy. In other words, such a wealth will affect in the power struggle among various vying nation-states.[6]

In return, the state capacity is not only able to "promote" trade and maintain the firmness of a currency but also capable of protecting domestic industry and impairing that of rival countries, and thus elevate nations to more advantageous positions. Among the nations that have made their rises in succession from the early modern age onward, be it Spain, England, France, or the United States, Japan, and the so-called four tigers of East Asia, there are no exceptions to adopting mercantilism.[7]

[6] So Keynes pointedly argued out that mercantilists "pursue the interests of the country, as well as the relative growth of national power" (1977, p. 295).

[7] About the history of the mercantilism in these countries, especially in Britain, see Chen Xiwen's work, ***A Research on Britain's Economic Reform and Policies in Sixteenth Century*** (1995, pp. 156–83), Joseph A. Schumpeter's work, ***History of Economic Analysis*** (1996, pp. 500–52), W.W. Rostow, ***How It All Began: Origins of the Modern Economy*** (1997,

Suppose, however, that all nations in the world adopted mercantilism. No sustained trade surplus would be available. This kind of policy can exist because some countries do not adopt it, as they can, in one way or another, maintain their trade deficits for a long period. Such kinds of countries are either those made to unilaterally carry out free trade policy due to defeat or occupation, such as China, India; or a country with "monetary hegemony," which uses its own currency as the world currency to pay the trade balance, the recipient countries either reserve it or use it as a means of payment for trade with other countries.[8]

With the shift in the form of money, there has been an evolution in the form of international currency. In the early stage, the role of the international currency was assumed by a certain precious metal found by some countries like Spain. As time went by, the role had increasingly been interwoven with a nation's economic and military power. By the time of the rise of the British Empire, the international currency in circulation had started to shake off the precious metal contained, as the British realized that the currency supply backed by the government decree could be multiplied so long as a certain proportion of precious metals was kept as reserves. Hence, for the first time in the evolvement of the international currency, the seigniorage was collected by British Sterling.

Since the end of the Second World War, when the United States became dominant in the economic, political, and military spheres, the U.S. dollar has taken the role of the international currency. After the collapse of the Bretton Woods system in the 1970s, when the dollar was disconnected from the gold standard, and finally was supported only by the economic, political, and military power of the country, thus more seigniorage was collected for every dollar. Because of seigniorage, the currency hegemony could tolerate the trade deficit. In fact, it is the trade deficit that is the main way for the currency hegemony to issue the dollar to the world. A kind of equilibrium between mercantile countries and the "currency hegemony" has as a result been temporarily reached.

In the long run perspective, however, such equilibrium would hardly be sustained. On the one hand, the mercantilist policy cannot be implemented for a long run, since it would finally result in inflation, increment

pp. 31–86), and L. S. Stavrianos' work, ***Global Rift: The Third World Comes of Age*** (1997, First Volume, pp. 178–83), and so on.

[8] For example, during 1864–1948, China had only 8 years' trade surplus in the 85 years (Chuanding, 1985, table 4–14, table 5–1, table 6–1, table 7–10, table 7–11).

of the cost of labor, and low interest rate (i.e., excess of capital).[9] At this time, export competitiveness declined and economic growth stagnated.

On the other hand, the indefinite tolerance of mercantile behavior will create an uneven playing field that would in the long run weaken or even destroy the domestic industries of the "currency hegemony" country, and might make it decline even if it once had relatively strong economic strength. In modern history, there are some countries that successfully carried out the policy of mercantilism, and achieve the position of superpower, including currency hegemony, such as Britain and the United States, and there also are some countries that paid the costs of mercantilism, and fell down, such as Spain.

As for those countries who still keep a firm hold on the policy of mercantilism, therefore, it would be better off for them to opt to gradually change their protectionist policy and make efforts to shift their currencies to be international currencies. On the other hand, regarding those so called "currency hegemonies," what they should do is to reduce the long-term trade deficits and find other way to issue their currencies to the world.

After the Second World War, the United States can be regarded as a country with "currency hegemony," while Japan and other Asian states can be seen as newly established mercantilist countries whose rapid growth was heavily assisted by the U.S. economy, that is, the United States endured constant trade deficits. The background of the Cold War strengthened this pattern as the United States made greater concessions to emerging mercantilist countries for the sake of international political strategy. However, the United States was worried by the speed at which these countries developed, which it considered too rapid. In order to avoid the situation where its domestic industries are sacrificed for the mercantile behavior, the United States has since pressed hard for the adoption of free trade policy. Not only would such a policy benefit consumers of all nations, but it would also benefit the United States itself. On the other hand, the United States may not desire the reduction in the seigniorage because of that in trade deficit. Another way of issuing U.S. dollars is to provide U.S.-dollar loan to foreign countries. Therefore, the argument of "free flow of capital" implies the interest of the United States.

[9] Keynes has said, it would have negative effects, decreasing of cost and increasing of interest rate in foreign countries, as well as increasing of cost and decreasing of interest rate in the home country, if the mercantilist policy would be carried out excessively (1963, p. 286).

In addition, from a pure currency point of view, there is an existence of the implicit imbalance within the balance between mercantilism and "currency hegemony." The currency with the international status has unmatchable higher generality than others in the global transaction. Such a difference can be shown with an analogy in that a domestic currency possesses higher generality than a commodity, even though currency itself is a kind of commodity. As we can manipulate the prices of commodities with a kind of domestic currency, people can also rig the prices (e.g., exchange rate) of the national currencies by exploiting this property of an international currency to the full in their interests. Therefore, it is easy for us to find that it is the U.S. dollar that is the materials used by the managers of hedge funds, such as Soros, to attack the monetary systems in Asian countries.

9.4 Attacks Upon Nation-State by Hedge Funds

To maximize their own interests, hedge funds' managers would choose nation-states with the most vulnerable monetary system as prime targets. Such nation-states possess particular features.

The first feature is being small-scale. If the trading scale of a financial market is small, hedge funds can have a greater impact on price. Achieving a certain degree of price manipulation in a smaller monetary system requires investing less money, thereby reducing the cost of financing. Secondly, problems with macro-fundamentals as well as balance of payments, such as inflation and trade deficits, exist. In other words, a strategic timing of an attack on a financial market should be chosen in this kind of period. Thirdly, fiscal problems in both governments and enterprises are prevailing in these economies, which are reflected on, for example, a diminishing return to the capital invested, too high the ratio of leverage, and their debts to be exposed to the risk of insolvency, and so forth. Finally, at tactics' level, the time of day to launch an attack is when the debts would be matured.

Insofar as the Asian financial turmoil is concerned, the countries under attack, in general, shared similar characteristics. Their economies and their money supplies were much smaller compared with that of the United States (see Fig. 9.2). As these nations (except Singapore) had reached the final stage of mercantilism, their domestic prices were rising, labor costs creeping up, and trade deficits emerging. In 1996, the proportion of trade deficits in the GDPs of Thailand, Hong Kong, Malaysia, Philippines,

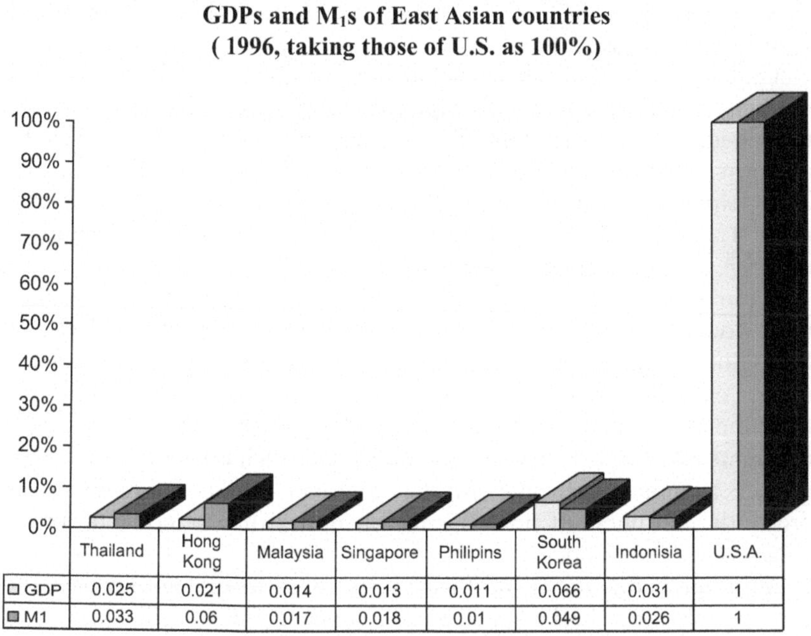

	Thailand	Hong Kong	Malaysia	Singapore	Philipins	South Korea	Indonisia	U.S.A.
GDP	0.025	0.021	0.014	0.013	0.011	0.066	0.031	1
M1	0.033	0.06	0.017	0.018	0.01	0.049	0.026	1

Fig. 9.2 GDPs and M_1s of East Asian countries (1996, taking those of the United States as 100%)

South Korea, and Indonesia stood at 7.9%, 11.6%, 4.8%, 2.4%, 7.4%, and 3.1%, respectively.[10] However, under the long-term mercantilist policy, enterprises mainly engaged in export business to economically developed countries. As more and more countries joined the ranks, competition was fierce, and as the United States tightened trade concessions to these former allies after the end of the Cold War, profit margins generally declined. Due to adopting a strategy of imitation and learning, these enterprises had less market risk and mostly adopted debt financing, which led to higher asset-liability ratio. Moreover, because the government mostly adopted the linked exchange rate or fixed exchange rate policy, most enterprises

[10] Hong Kong is a very special region, because until 1997, Hong Kong had been ruled by the United Kingdom, so it cannot adopt mercantilist policy as an independent political entity; on the surface it has been a free port. But the pattern of its rise is similar to that of other countries in East Asia. So by 1996, Hong Kong could also be seen as a "late mercantilist" region: rising labor costs and a growing trade deficit.

were not aware of the risks in foreign exchange, so they did not hedge their foreign exchange debts.

Under pressure for "liberalization of capital," these countries opened up their capital markets in an abrupt and disorderly manner. The inflow of foreign loans meant that domestic monetary policy lost efficacy and led to inflation and resulted in a large quantity of reckless short-term debts (such as the situation in Thailand, see Kirida Bhaopichitr 1999).These factors made Thailand and other southeast Asian countries, from the beginning of 1997, a prime target for hedge funds.

It can be argued that the massive problems associated with these economies would have been dealt with by their governments, the markets, or both. Soft-handed approaches, for example, could take the form of fiscal, trade, exchange rate, or tariff adjustments, to rebalance macro-fundamentals and trade balance. Nonetheless, on the one hand, the governments have lost their measures of policies for their opening the financial markets at an improper time. On the other hand, the hedge funds would prefer the sharpness of price-fluctuation rather than a moderate price-adjustment. They launched attacks.

Although hedge funds and their "allies" need to strategically pave the way for a clear attack, the key step is to influence prices in a financial market (mostly the foreign exchange market) through a large number of sell-offs, dramatically changing them toward the direction expected by investment strategies. At this time, either the government will defend the existing foreign exchange system, intervene by raising local currency interest rates and operating in market (as the Hong Kong and Thai governments initially did), or abandon the fixed exchange rate system (as the governments of Taiwan and Brazil did). In the former case, an increase in interest rates will lead to a decline in the stock market; in the latter case, the local currency will depreciate substantially. No matter what happens, as long as the hedge fund's strategy is foreseen, gains can be made.

However, both outcomes will damage the real economies of the countries under attack. Firstly, the victory of the hedge funds is based on the cost of loss of firms and even governmental agencies. They would go bankrupt in terms of finance because of the losses. Secondly, the prices of the financial markets (exchange rate, interest rate, and prices of stocks) are important parameters for the businesses of the firms and other economic organizations. Once these parameters are sharply changed and the structures of assets and liabilities of economic organizations thrown into confusion, some of them may not survive in financial terms even if they were healthy in terms of technology. For instance, a large depreciation of domestic currency equals a sharp increment of foreign debt, which would result in insolvency; the rise of interest rate would cause the financial cost of a firm to go up; and a fall in stock prices may shrink the assets of the firm which hold stocks to be its assets.

Once some firms and financial organizations cannot repay their debts at term, other debts at once become matured debts. They must plead bankruptcy. A bankruptcy means the default of debts and leads to bankruptcies of the creditors in poor financial condition. Chain reactions occur. A large number of bankruptcies worsen the crisis in two respects. For the real economy, the bankruptcy of firms means disintegration of the production factors that have once been put together, discontinuity of the process of the production or service, and the reduction of social output. In monetary terms, the bankruptcies of firms, especially of financial institutions, discharge of liability, and the destruction of credit by default of debts may lead to deflation in the whole society, for most of the money is constituted of debts. On the other hand, a great deal of capital flight under the condition of the depreciation of the domestic currency furthers the deflation, since foreign currency has been a part of money supply under the condition of free flow of capital.

Damage to the real economy may in return affect the deteriorated financial markets. The accretion of losses and bankruptcies of firms may directly lead to the fall of stock prices; the weakening of domestic economy may further the depreciation of the domestic currency. Further deterioration of financial market price parameters will make enterprises worse. The deflation reduces the total demand of the country, thus striking the real economy again. Along the process of a positive feedback of worse and worse, an economy rapidly sinks to the bottom. At an extreme, the collapse of the monetary system and real economy may result in political and social crises, even lead to the government of a country (even a big country such as Russia) to go bankrupt.[11]

[11] Keynes said, "To destroy its monetary system is the most excellent and most efficient way, if one want to overthrow a current social fundamental. This process can stimulate all potentialities of destroying economic orders, and to do so in a way that no one can diagnose it." This economist who knows the secret of a monetary system very well had revealed the whole process discussed above.

It is obvious for us that the prices of the financial markets would continuously change toward the direction the hedge funds expect only when the disturbance of those prices causes the damage to the real economy and the monetary system. Therefore, the more grievous the destruction of the economy of the country under attack, the more advantage gained by the hedge funds launching the attack. As a result, there would be redistribution between the hedge funds and the state-nations. In terms of fairness, what the hedge funds gain is close to monopolistic profit if we regard their behavior as similar to that of a monopoly. As what the circle of economics acknowledges, the monopolistic profit is made as an unfair redistribution. The reason that mainstream economics has less condemnation for this kind of profit-making is that not only that the monopolistic feature of the manipulation by the hedge funds can be difficult to ascertain but that their transactions seem to be in accord with market conventions. In a market, prices either rise or fall; economic agents either win or lose. People are willing to tolerate loss as they deem that a market not only provides equal opportunities to all agents, but is also an efficient mechanism for allocating resources, as long as there is no price manipulation. However, once someone manipulates prices, not only does the chances of winning or losing become unequal but it also causes damage to the market itself, including the monetary system, and does not improve market efficiency. From the perspective of economic values, since there is no efficiency, there is also a lack of moral basis. Because of the redistribution of wealth caused by this kind of behavior, the winner's income is made at not only greater loss to the loser, but even the collapse and failure of the monetary system and economic mechanisms; from a global perspective, it is a net loss of welfare.

Following the analysis above, we may deduce that some monetary transactions may lead to a consequence of hurting fairness as well as damaging efficiency, although those transactions seem to be fair on the surface. Fernand Braudel once pointed out that "the money is a measure of exploiting others both in home and abroad" (1992, p. 522). We may discover that transactions of money can become a means of plunder, if we notice that the significant difference between currencies and different ways to trade currencies. As discussed above, U.S. dollar as an international currency may be the means of manipulating the prices of other currencies. Recurring to financial derivatives, advanced information technology, and modern credit system, the hedge funds may obtain money at much cheaper cost. With such a cheaper currency, one may rob the higher-cost currency from general residents and firms just like making staggering profits by manipulating in a particular commodity with a general currency.[12]

9.5 Several Possible Consequences and International Political Economics

Now, we start to base our thinking on the larger picture, that is, the global community with different nation-states as individual units of this enlarged society. Our first set of questions asked thus is, what consequences will there be for the community if the hedge funds are on the loose, continuing their manipulation and speculation in financial markets? Under such circumstances, how many options are there for the global community, or a nation-state for that matter? And what impact will each of the options result in? The second set of questions is what the total global welfare and what kind of redistribution among different nation-states will eventuate under the different options? The last is, whether or not it is likely under the present international political setting for the world community to agree upon a scenario as to maximize the global welfare?

Including laissez-faire, there are four possible approaches for different nation-states and the international community: (1) adopting a hands-off approach; (2) setting up rigorous regulations, such as returning to fixed exchange institution with a strict restriction on capital or even currency flow for transnational financial activities, and banning all transactions with derivatives; (3) opting for tit-for-tat strategies, namely a government intervention in the currency market by counter-buying or selling domestic currency; and (4) applying a targeted approach with policy instruments, that is, restricting the behavior of price rigging in financial markets while ensuring the normal flow of currencies and capitals.

The first approach would spell the eventual collapse of global financial markets and lead to great economic depression. It would result in more and more resources being the subject of financial speculation, given the

[12] A story that Fernand Braudel tells may help us to understand the kind of practice of making money with money: In the seventeenth century, the Portuguese discovered a kind of money called "cinbo" made of shells, "Portuguese considered thoughtfully: they controlled the "field of manufacturing money," that is the fishing ground of producing cinbo around Loanda in 1650. This kind of money was devalued 90% from 1575 to 1650 (translated from Chinese version, 1992, p. 525).

success of hedge funds.[13] However, this tendency may reduce the possibility of success in manipulating prices of markets, since it may lower the degree of certainty of investment strategies. The main reason why hedge funds succeed is that its expectations have a high degree of certainty, as the number of them involved in actual price rigging is small. The players, therefore, are more capable of "foreseeing" a subsequent price movement. If their numbers increase, the degree of certainty would decrease as the strategies applied by various hedge funds can exert offsetting or reinforcing effects in the same market. Even if they operate in different markets, a successful operation in one market by one hedge fund could possibly create an uncertain outcome for another since prices of different markets are inextricably related. This may make it harder for hedge funds to stay profitable[14] as they face greater risks, and may even lead to the collapse of hedge funds that engage in manipulation (e.g., the failure of Long Term Capital Management in the United States).

If some hedge funds go bankrupt as a result, commercial banks, as their creditors, may also go into free fall. Financial market crisis combined with "credit crunch" will in turn eat into the real economies, especially that of the United States, where most hedge funds have originated and developed. Together with the crises in East Asia, Russia, and the Latin Americas, the collapse of the American economy may lead to another worldwide great depression.

The second and third approaches are types of reactions to hedge fund behavior. The main difference between them is that the former is more passive than the latter. The second approach, though greatly insulating an economy from possible external shocks and enhancing the effectiveness of domestic policy instruments, will cut off the normal flow of capital that will in turn reduce the degree of efficiency in allocation of international financial resources. Furthermore, the global financial system and international specialization would disintegrate if more and more countries adopt such a policy. As for the third approach, it could immediately leave a

[13] Data support this judgment. Statistic by Van Hedge Fund Advisors International (Nashville) in the United States shows that from the fourth Quarter of 1993 to the third Quarter of 1998, the returns of the top ten of hedge funds in the United States are higher by 14.4% than those of mutual funds, and those of top 10% of hedge funds are higher by 38% than those of mutual funds (Van Hedge Fund Advisors International 1999a).

[14] Also data and information show that the performance of the hedge funds has been getting worse and worse since 1998. See Van Hedge Fund Advisors International 1999b; CCTV 1999.

government, or financial institutions for that matter, exposed to a higher degree of risk, and even aggravate the financial and economic crisis caused by the manipulation of hedge funds.

In comparison to the first three approaches, the last approach is far more positive, as it regulates certain financial activities to restrain or eliminate market manipulation and thus prevents the global financial system from moving toward systemic breakdown. It also ensures a healthy flow of global capital and currencies that in turn enhances the efficiency of allocation of global financial resources.

Moving to the second set of questions, in terms of total global welfare, the first and the third approach would lead to the worst result to the world community, since systemic breakdown so induced in both financial and real economy will directly forgo part of the global output, thus constituting a net loss to the welfare. The second approach, which by and large blocks the free flow of global capital and thus checks the enhancement of allocating efficiency, is anything but ideal. The fourth approach, dealing with the disadvantageous fallout of the free flow of the global capital, stands out as the only contributor to global welfare.

From the point of view of redistribution of wealth among countries, the first choice is beneficial to the western countries with relatively developed financial sectors, especially to the United States, given its monetary hegemony, but not to emerging countries and regions with competitive manufacturing industries. Firstly, the active speculation of hedge funds and the increasing trading volume of financial derivatives will bring huge profits to the financial sector (including stock exchanges, banks, etc.).

Second, the profits obtained by the hedge funds' manipulation in external financial markets will ultimately end up in their native countries.

Third, in the structure of mercantilist countries and monetary hegemonic countries, the currencies the hedge funds plunder from other countries will mean that foreign exchange reserves accumulated by mercantilist countries through trade surpluses are transferred back to the monetary hegemonic countries through currency speculation, thus alleviating the competitive pressure of mercantilist countries on their industries.

Fourth, with the monetary system of many countries destroyed, more and more people will turn to using the dollar outside the United States, and more and more countries will consider replacing their own currency with the dollar, that is, a trend of dollarization will result.[15] This trend will increase the demand for dollars around the world, thus increasing the seigniorage tax paid to the United States by people in other countries.

Although the second and the third options lessen the benefits accrued to the countries with the status of "currency hegemony" while reducing the damage to other countries, they would lead to greater inefficiency of capital allocation and increment of financial risks. Hence, the fourth option is much fairer in terms of redistribution, especially in the long run, even though it is not as immediately favorable compared to the first option to those financially developed countries. To say so reflects the truth that by restraining the price rigging activities in financial markets, it will bring stability into the international monetary system, which will no doubt benefit all.

However, from the perspective of international political economy, it is more than difficult to have the fourth option implemented, even though it is the best choice on hand. Because of the competition between financial centers and nations for financial transactions and capital, any measure to control the flow of money and capital will reduce the "competitiveness" of capital financial centers and nations.[16] Even countries or regions that have implemented certain controls will be deregulated again because of competition between them (e.g., competition between Hong Kong and

[15] About Dollarization, see Stephen Fedora's article, *To lose or to dollarize,* (January 19, 1999); Reuters, *Dollarization splits Latin Americans,* (January 31, 1999); Discussion and Research on it, see Steve H. Hanke and Kurt Schuler, *A Dollarization Blueprint for Argentina,* (March 11, 1999); Zhang Yuyan, *Dollarization: reality, theories and implications of policies* (1999).

[16] In fact, from the very beginning, there is restriction on the quantities of the transaction of financial derivatives. In the United States, the Exchanges regulate the largest quantities of option contracts one investor holds. For instance, the quota of Digital Equipment Co.'s quota is 8000 contracts when contracting (Hull 1997, p. 149). Once crisis comes, many of the Exchanges impose automatically regulations on the derivatives transactions. For example, after the failure of Long Term Management, some countries and some financial institutions put some restrictions on derivatives transactions one after another. London Metal Exchange declared new order of transaction, preventing hedge funds and other speculators from manipulating the markets by selling short. Japan revised its Security Transaction Law, forbidding beating down the prices of stocks by selling short. Before then, Hong Kong announced a series of regulations on short sale of stocks and holding quantities of futures, for purpose of guaranteeing fair play of transactions and restricting manipulations. The regulations also include the demand of disclosure of information to big traders, and the ceiling of loans provided by the commercial banks to hedge funds, and so on (Shuchun 1998). However, once the crisis is over, those regulations may loosen gradually.

Singapore, which led to the deregulation of Hong Kong's financial authorities, see Chen Dingyuan 1998).

Second, in an international society without a world government, a unanimous action of the global community entails vigorous participation of heavy weights—large countries with economic as well as political power. It is a bit unfortunate, however, that most of these countries are likely to be direct or indirect beneficiaries of manipulating activities of hedge funds. Hence, we cannot expect, at least in the short run, that there is any incentive for them to carry out such a heavy duty of implementing the Option 4, that is to be united together for regulating financial manipulation.

9.6 Conclusions

(1) Up to the present day, almost all so-called economic freedom can only be approximately realized when there is a government. Therefore, in the international area we cannot guarantee economic activity, even if dubbed "freedom," truly results in both efficiency and fairness, which is the true meaning of freedom, since there is no world government.

(2) An efficient and stable monetary system is a public good, for which the government of any nation-state has responsibility to provide and protect through institutional arrangements and policies.

(3) Without a world government, the dream of free trade has not yet been realized. The balance of international trade is not one of free trade but one between the mercantile countries and "currency hegemony."

(4) The core strategy of hedge funds is to manipulate prices in financial markets, a behavior similar to that of monopoly. Therefore, managers of hedge funds represented by Soros are not heroes of the free market but its destroyers.

(5) Gains of hedge funds made through financial speculation cause more loss to the people in the countries attacked, and may even include collapse of the monetary system and the real economy. This results in net loss of world welfare, including damage to the global financial system and real economy. Therefore, their manipulation can be viewed as a crime committed on those countries attacked and the world, and can be viewed in the same way as killing elephants for ivory.

(6) Two factors facilitate hedge fund manipulation. One is the introduction of financial derivatives, which enables large quantities of transactions; the other is the status of the U.S. dollar's "currency hegemony" which enables its use as a weapon to attack nation-states with weaker currencies.

(7) To avoid further great depressions, international organizations should regulate manipulation, which requires unanimous agreement between most countries, especially those that are dominant. However, those countries reap short-term benefits from financial speculation, so we cannot expect this to be carried out soon.

(8) For East Asian countries including China, this financial crisis tells us that, (a) the "East Asian miracle" post-WWII is just a particular case in the history of modern economic development; (b) the situation of monetary system and of financial institutions may in return affect the real economy heavily; (c) due to the absence of world government, there is neither free trade nor free flow of capital that results in fairness. The precondition for achieving economic freedom at the global level is fair order in the international economy. Forming this order requires participation from all countries including East Asian countries.

References

陈定远, "两虎相争 必有一伤? —— 论新加坡和香港的期指大战", 《言论》, 1998年12月1日; 再印于《香港传真》,1998 年 12 月 28 日.(Chen Dingyuan, *Two tigers strive with, one would be hurt: on fighting of futures indexes between Singapore and Hong Kong*, Saying, Dec. 1, 1998; reprinted in Hong Kong Fax, Dec. 28, 1998.)

陈曦文, 《英国 16 世纪经济变革与政策研究》, 首都师范大学出版社, 1995; (Chen Xiwen, *Britain's Economic Reform and Policies in Sixteenth Century*, Press of Capital's Normal University, 1995.)

David W. Pearce ed., *The Dictionary of Modern Economics*, Macmillan Press, London, Revised version, 1983;

弗兰克. J. 法博齐和弗朗哥. 莫迪利亚尼, 《资本市场:机构与工具》经济科学出版社, 1998. (Translated from: Frank J. Fabozzi and Franco Modigliani, *Capital Markets, Institutions, and Instruments*, Prentice Hall Inc., 1996.)

布罗代尔, 《15 至 18 世纪的物质文明、经济和资本主义》, 生活. 读书. 新知. 三联书店, 1992. (Translated from: Fernand Braudel, *Civilisation Materielle*

Économie et Capitalisme, XVE- XVIIIESIECLE TOME1, Les Structures Du Quotidien: Le Possible Et L Impossible, Librairie Armand Colin, Paris, 1979.)
哈伯勒，《繁荣与萧条》，商务印书馆，1988. (Gottfried Haberler, *Prosperity and Depression: A theoretical Analysis of Cyclical Movements*, New revised and enlarged edition, Ruskin House, George Allen & Unwin Ltd., Museum Street, London, 1963.)
约翰.赫尔，《期权、期货和衍生证券》，华夏出版社，1997. (John C. Hull, *Options, Futures, and Other Derivative Securities*, Prentice-Hall, Inc., 1993, 1989.)
康芒斯，《制度经济学》，商务印书馆，1983. (Translated from: John R. Commons, *Institutional Economics: Its Place in Political Economy*, The MacMillan Company, New York, 1934.)
凯恩斯，《就业利息和货币通论》，商务印书馆，1977. (Translated from: John Maynard Keynes, *The General Theory of Employment Interest and Money*, Macmillan and Co., Limited, London, 1936.)
约瑟夫.熊比特，《经济分析史》，商务印书馆，1996. (Joseph A. Schumpeter, *History of Economic Analysis*, eleventh printing, Oxford University Press, 1980)
Kirida Bhaopichitr, *Thailand's Road to Economic Crisis: A Brief Overview*, Internet, March 17, 1999.
洛伦兹.格利茨，《金融工程学》，经济科学出版社，1998. (Translated from: Lawrence Galitz, *Financial Engineering: Tools and Techniques to Manage Financial Risk*, revised edition, original English language edition published by Pitman Publishing, a division of Pearson Professional Ltd., 1994, revised 1995.)
斯塔夫里亚诺斯，《全球分裂》，商务印书馆，1997. (Translated from: L. S. Stavrianos, *Global Rift, The Third World Comes of Age*, William Morrow and Company, INC. New York, 1981.)
鲁传鼎，《中国贸易史》，中央文物供应社，1985. (Lu Chuanding, *The History of China's Trade*, Press of Central Cultural Relic Supplying, 1985.)
尼克.李森，《我如何弄垮巴林银行》，中国经济出版社，1996. (Translated from: Nick Leeson, *Rogue Trader*, Little, Brown (February 19, 1996); (Paul Krugman, The return of Dr. Mabuse, 1998;
保罗.克鲁格曼和茅瑞斯.奥伯斯法尔德，《国际经济学》，中国人民大学出版社，1998. (Translated from: Paul Krugman and Maurice Obstfeld, *International Economics: Theory and Policy*, fourth edition, 1997. Chinese Version, People's University of China Press, 1998.
彼得.林德特和查尔斯.金德尔伯格，《国际经济学》，上海译文出版社，1985. (Translated from: Peter Lindert and Charles Kindleberger, *International Economics*, Richard D. Irwin Ltd., 1982)
饶余庆，《现代货币银行学》，中国社会科学出版社，1983. (Rao Yuqing, *Modern Theory on Money and Banking System*, Press for Social Sciences of China, 1983.)
路透社，"'美元化'使拉美分裂"，达沃斯，《参考消息》，1999 年 2 月 2 日. (Translated from: Reuters, *Dollarization splits Latin Americans*, Davos, January 31, 1999.)

石毓符,《中国货币金融史略》,天津人民出版社, 1984. (Shi Yufu, *A Brief History of China's Money and Finance,* People's Press of Tianjin, 1984.)

Steve H. Hanke and Kurt Schuler, A Dollarization Blueprint for Argentina, Cato Foreign Policy Briefing, March 11, 1999;

Stephen Fedora, To lose or to dollarize, Financial Times, January 19, 1999.

Van Hedge Fund Advisors International, Strategy and Sector Definitions, Inc., Nashville, TN, USA, Internet, www.vanhedge.com.definit.htm, 1999a.

Van Hedge Fund Advisors International, Current Hedge Fund Index Returns, Inc., Nashville, TN, USA, Internet, www.vanhedge.com.current.htm, 1999b.

罗斯托, 《这一切是怎样开始的——现代经济的起源》, 商务印书馆, 1997. (Translated from: W.W. Rostow, *How It All Began: Origins of the Modern Economy*, McGraw-Hill Book Company, 1975.)

易纲、赵晓和江慧琴, "对冲基金.金融风险.金融监管", 《国际经济评论》, 1999年1-2月(总第19期). (Yi Gang, Zhao Xiao and Jiang Huiqin, *Hedge funds, financial risk and financial regulation,* International Economic Review, Jan.-Fec., 1999.)

张宇燕的"美元化:现实、理论及政策含义", 天则所内部文稿系列, No. 4, 1999. (Zhang Yuyan, Dollarization: reality, theories and implications of policies, Unirule Working Paper, No. 4, 1999).

中央电视台, "美国对冲基金仍萎靡", Internet, http://www.cctv.com.cn/economic/main/xinwen/985.html, 1999 年7 月 13 日 0:15; (CCTV, American hedge funds still being listless, Internet, http://www.cctv.com.cn/economic/main/xinwen/985.html, July 13, 1999).

周树春, "国际投机者日益受到限制", (新华社伦敦 10 月 18 日 电) 经济日报 1998 年10 月 20 日. (Zhou Shuchun, International speculators being restricted increasingly; Xinhua News Agency, Oct. 18, 1998, Economic Daily, Oct. 20, 1998.)

CHAPTER 10

The Institutional Factors of the Financial Crisis in the United States

Contents

The financial crisis in the United States appears to be the accumulated outcome of a series of errors that could have been avoided according to the current understandings of the market system and the U.S. political structure. However, the financial crisis happened, giving us reasons to reflect on the following questions.

Translated from *Research of Institutional Economics* (《制度经济学研究》), Volume 32, Issue 2, 2011

Sheng Hong, *Vision and Calculation*,
https://doi.org/10.1007/978-981-15-2898-9_10

1. Why is a rational economic person willing to purchase financial products with obviously high risks?
2. Why are financial institutions driven to develop and sell financial products with increasing risks if they understand the prospects of losses and even bankruptcy?
3. Why are financial products developed faster than physical products, and why is the growth of financial assets much faster than that of physical assets?
4. Why do a few financial institutions obtain greater market power?
5. Why do a few fund managers and traders receive more favorable conditions in their contracts?
6. Why are financial exchanges unmotivated to restrain the trading of excessively risky financial products?
7. Why has the U.S. government failed to effectively regulate trading of high-risk financial products?

This chapter attempts to provide some perspective on these questions through an institutional analysis.

10.1 Risk-Associated Market Failure

For a better understanding of the risks behind financial products, I would like to introduce a more typical model for risk-associated behavior—gambling. The commonality of gambling and investments is in their uncertainties. Gambling requires making a choice without knowing the results and then accepting the results of randomness as "destiny." The price of financial products fluctuates because of various factors. It is possible to predict only the long-term trend of economic and industrial development but not short-term price fluctuations because of their complexity. The Efficient Markets Hypothesis even suggests that this unpredictable fluctuation is an important symbol of market effectiveness; that is, market prices absorb a variety of factors related to supply and demand changes, and no one can know all of the information. Thus, when purchasing a financial product, the buyer has no idea how the product's price will change. In fact, the buyer is "betting on the price," which is no different from playing the lottery.

Another feature shared by investments and gambling is that their uncertainties are of the same nature, that is, so-called risk. Frank Knight defines "risk" as the uncertainties that people can use to predict their probability distribution and as not knowing the uncertainty of a probability distribution as "real uncertainties" (2006, p. 233). Therefore, the so-called risk level is not the amount of information about uncertainty but the degree of risk probability predicted by individuals.

In this sense, traditional investments, venture capital, and high-risk financial products are no different from gambling. They all include a type of risk that reflects the uncertainty of known probability distribution. Gambling takes the form of standard risks. When betting during dice-rolling, the player has a winning rate of 1/6. However, investment risks are much more complex than one-dimensional risks in rolling dices; hence, predicting their probability distribution of investments is more difficult. For an asset investment, the risk probability is generally estimated according to market prices and past success rates of similar assets. The main role of financial engineering is to price financial derivatives based on historical data and the current market price, and the pricing will reflect the risk probability of that financial derivative. The only difference among different types of investments and gambling is the different probability distributions of uncertainties or, in other words, the different degrees of risk. A higher risk results in a lower success rate.

A general rule about investments or gambling is that, regardless of the risk, people's expected return is at least greater than the investment or at least the rate of expected return (expected return/investment) is greater than 1 regardless of the time factor. Expected returns are equal to the success rate multiplied by the return on success. In most cases, the expected rate of return in the form of stable investments or gambling is close to 1 because it is impossible for people to choose an expected rate of return less than 1. When the expected rate of return is greater than 1, more people are attracted to invest. Because the number of projects for a certain form of investment is limited, people must pay the "rent" formed by the scarcity of opportunities, which eventually reduces the expected rate of return to 1. This reduction indicates that, regardless of how risky people invest in projects, their behavior is rational and not surprising.

According to financial theories, we can quantitatively describe an investment's risk by measuring the standard deviation of its returns. This measurement can be directly related to the winning rate (or risk probability) in gambling. The lower the winning rate (or the higher the risk probability) of gambling, the more likely the player suffers losses—often in high numbers. A general conclusion of financial theories is that among several financial products with similar expected returns, the most valuable one is that with the smallest standard deviation (Levy and Sarnat 1984, pp. 243–273) (Fig. 10.1).

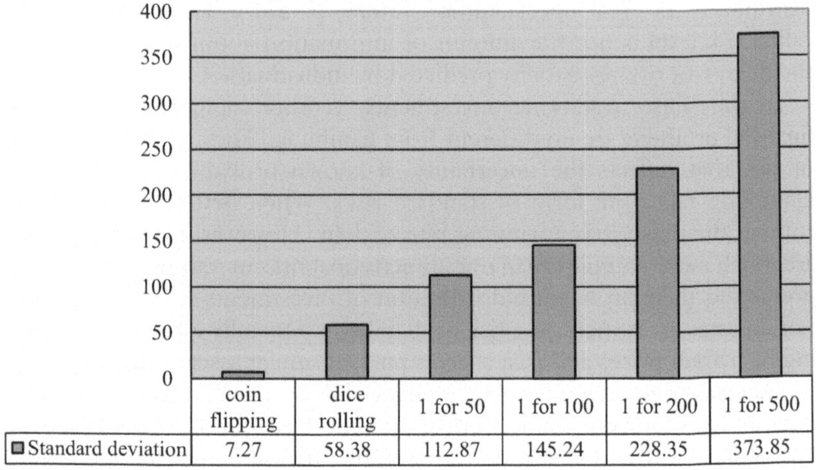

Fig. 10.1 Standard deviation of several gambling games. Note: The rule of this game is for each player to put in 1 yuan in each round, and there are N players. Here, N equals 2, 6, 100, 200, and 500. The winning rate is 1/N, the return of each win is N yuan, and the expected return is 0. This experiment simulates the situation 254 times for coin-tossing, dice-rolling, and gambling with other success rates using an Excel program. The results shown in the figure are from a throw of these games

Therefore, why are people willing to make risky investments or even gamble? Once successful, the returns are high enough to compensate for low success rates, enabling the player to at least recover the amount invested. For instance, for a game with a success rate of 1/6, if only its potential return is six times the input, then it is attractive enough for the players. In fact, most investments and gambling are of this nature. Assuming that the success rate for investing in a high-tech company is 20%, people are willing to invest as long as it offers the potential return of more than five times. A highly risky financial product—an option—is also designed to address such logic. Options are priced based on the accumulated probability of the price being higher or lower than the strike price according to the historical price of underlying instruments. Generally, the less possible it is for the price to be higher than the strike price, the cheaper the option price (Hull 1996, pp. 221–260). Gambling is designed by strictly following this rule. From two people tossing coins to millions of people playing the lottery, as long as the number of players increases, the return from winning definitely increases, and the success rate decreases accordingly.

When the risk is relatively lower, the actual outcomes of investments or gambling tend to draw near the expected return. As in the case of coin-tossing, the two players are most likely to be neck and neck with each other, as are long-term investments in the stock of traditional enterprises. The real income is close to the expected return or the risk-free interest rate of the investment.

However, as risk increases, the actual returns are often lower than the expected returns for both individuals and institutions, which is how loss occurs. First, people's lifespan is limited. When the risk is extremely high or, in other words, when the success rate is extremely low, a person cannot live long enough to succeed. Suppose that the probability of winning the lottery is one in a million, and a person can live infinitely and play the lottery constantly. One day, he will win the top prize. However, if he only lives for 90 years and starts playing the lottery every day from the age of 20, he can play 25,550 times. In this scenario, the probability of him winning is only 2.5%. Hence, in reality, the vast majority of people playing the lottery never win.

Second, people are also subject to the limitations of the wealth available for investment. Once the money is drained, one has to withdraw from the investments or the games. Many people leave casinos because they have emptied their pockets. Once they leave, the originally estimated risk probability (1 – winning rate) changes accordingly. If the probability for a big win is 1/100, but the player has lost all of his money in the 50th round, then his actual winning rate declines to 1/200. If the expected return of the big win is 100 times the input, the actual expected rate of return at this time becomes 0.5 (less than 1), imposing a loss on the player.

Most people are aware that higher risk probability implies a greater chance of losing. People also factor in the limitation of one's lifetime and wealth when making decisions. Generally, only wealthy people invest in ventures because their huge wealth enables them to afford possible multiple failures. Traditionally, in China, sophisticated and stable families forbade gambling because they understood that the real returns were often much lower than expected. Most people draw a strict distinction between gambling and investing, spend a small amount of money on a lottery, and put larger sums into the stock market. People also consider the "risk premium" in the market; that is, they expect higher returns as compensation for higher risks.

However, at a given point, the expected return is not limited by life expectancy or wealth. Each time one gambles, the risk probability or winning rate is real because gambling exists as a complete system of facts, and the players are rational when calculating the expected return at the moment. Their participation can be viewed as spending money to buy the possibility to get rich overnight. However, given the limitations in one's life and wealth, a gap exists between the expected and the actual returns. When people choose to invest in high-risk instruments with higher expected returns that are adjusted by the risk premium, they face the possibility of having lower returns than the risk-free expected returns if they do not have infinite life and wealth.

Generally, the assumption is made that a rational economic person would not tolerate losses. This assumption is not always true. The assumption in textbooks of this rational economic person leads us to think that he or she would never decide to harm his or her interests. When we think out of the box, we find that this is not always the case, as previously discussed. An economic person makes his or her decisions rationally according to his or her judgment of expected returns. However, these decisions sometimes bring losses because the actual returns can be lower than expected with the increase in risk probability—a result that most people can accept. Most people playing the lottery never win, but they do not regret the decision. **In economic terms, a rational economic person sometimes accepts behavior that leads to losses, which is called the "loss equilibrium."**

This finding—that a rational economic man would not automatically reject behaviors that could bring losses to him—is significant. Viewing society as a whole leads to inefficient outcomes. Although almost all of the investments and games are transactions between people, the results of these transactions are a zero-sum game when the time factor is excluded. However, for society, extremely high risks could lead to a negative sum game because higher risks create a greater disparity in wealth distribution. For example, games with 1/100 success rates cause greater disparity than those with 1/50 success rates. As the return increases, its marginal utility for the winner decreases.

As mentioned, in a given period, a higher risk makes it more likely for a player to suffer losses or even lose everything and, from the perspective of all of society, a larger proportion of people lose money or even lose it all. In particular, the proportion of people who have lost all of their money increases significantly as risk increases. It can also be said that, given the increase in risk probability, the proportion of people who lose money

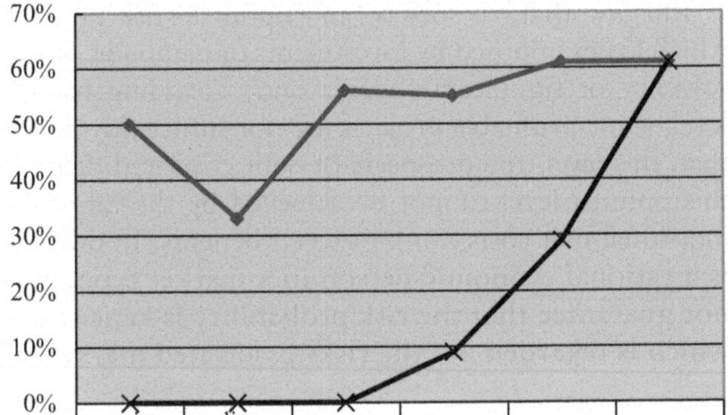

	coin flipping	dice rolling	1 for 50	1 for 100	1 for 200	1 for 500
percentage for loss	50%	33%	56%	55%	61%	61%
percentage for complete loss	0	0	0	9%	29%	61%

Fig. 10.2 Percentage of people losing some or all of their money in different games. Note: The rule of this game is identical to the previous one. "Loss" is defined as the total income of a player being lower than the average (0). One suffers a complete loss when he put 1 yuan into each round without winning once. In this case, a complete loss is losing 254 yuan

gradually increases, but the proportion of people who lose all of their money rapidly increases; that is, the loss degree of each person who loses money increases. See Fig. 10.2.

In America, the trend in financial innovations for the past several decades has been to invent new products with higher risks. Take the two financial derivatives of futures and options as an example. Given the nature of futures and options, one only needs to pay part of the price for a financial product's futures or options and, at maturity, may lose all of his or her advance payment. This possibility makes the fluctuations of futures and options greater than their underlying instruments. Obviously, because futures and options are riskier, an increase in these types of transactions brings about social changes led by higher risk probabilities, that is, an increase in the number of people affected and the severity of their losses.

When losses occur at such an extensive scope and serious degree that they affect people's spending habits and even result in an inability to pay off debts, then society witnesses a series of breaks in the debt chain, creating a currency contraction equivalent to the money multiplier of society.

Imagine that, in society, an "optimal" risk probability level exists at which losses imposed by investments or gambling could not damage one's solvency or significantly affect one's spending habits. Lower than this level, some profitable projects are not sufficiently funded, whereas higher than this level, the prospects of debt crisis and deflation exist. However, this optimal level cannot be achieved by the rational judgment of each individual that costs cannot exceed benefits. In other words, **if everyone is a rational economic person in a market economy, society still cannot guarantee that the risk probability is kept at the "optimal" level, which is regarded as "the risks-associated market failure."**

10.2 Financial Innovations with Few Cost Constraints

In a competitive market economy, when pursuing profits, companies must continuously develop new products and services to meet people's new demands for utility and to increase their income. This continual development slows down the depreciation of physical assets caused by the diminishing marginal utility for the entire society.

However, the production and consumption of new products and services are still limited by both demand and costs. On the one hand, people with limited income may not be able to afford the new product or service. On the other hand, the production and development of material goods are subject to the constraints of material resources and technologies or, in general, cost constraints. Costs are incurred when developing or manufacturing new products. Using the cost of developing new products as fixed costs and the cost of producing as variable or marginal costs, if the total cost is higher than the total benefit at the point at which marginal costs equal marginal utility, then the patent income is insufficient to compensate for the cost of research and development and the new product is not feasible.

To increase the demand for new products, the financial sector has invented house mortgage loans, auto credits, and other consumer credit products. These products increase the total demand in society. The reasons behind the increasing demand are (1) consuming in advance; (2) consuming new physical products; and (3) indirectly, growth in income as a result. This situation also creates a market for companies producing the products, thus elevating their market values. Given their huge scope, these industries cannot solely depend on internal funding, meaning that financial institutions invented stocks and corporate bonds as a way to raise money.

However, the development and production of new physical goods and services still cannot bypass the cost constraint. New demand for physical goods created by financial innovations is ultimately limited by incomes and costs—a limitation on the development of new goods and services. The growth in investment demand for physical products is also subject to the demand for consumer goods.

In contrast, when a financial institution provides financing for consumption and physical investments, it also creates a financial product with independent investment value. In addition to direct and indirect financing in the real economy, other financial products include refinancings and derivatives. A source of revenue for financial institutions is the sale of financial products. When the traditional financial products market is saturated, revenue growth depends on the introduction of new financial products. Similar to physical products, a new financial product creates new market demand; thus, constantly introducing new products means continuously expanding the market and, in this way, a business can continue to grow.

Developing new financial products is much easier than developing physical products. Although research and designs exist for economic rationality and contract terms, the costs for developing and producing financial products are quite low without the limits of technical and material resources. Theoretically, financial products could be infinite. In particular, financial derivatives depend not on real assets or businesses but on existing financial products; therefore, the cost for their development and production is even lower. Some economists have proposed a formula for pricing financial derivatives, which is in fact pricing by calculating the risk probability of a product based on historical data. This formula significantly reduces the transaction cost for pricing and strongly promotes the trading of financial derivatives.

More importantly, the expected return of financial products is not limited by any physical, psychological, or technical constraints. As was discussed in the previous section, financial products' expected return can remain unchanged when their risk increases because an increased risk probability or a reduced success rate can be compensated for by higher potential returns. Therefore, financial institutions can always increase the risk probability of their products and invent new products if they maintain the expected rate of return at higher than 1. When the market for financial

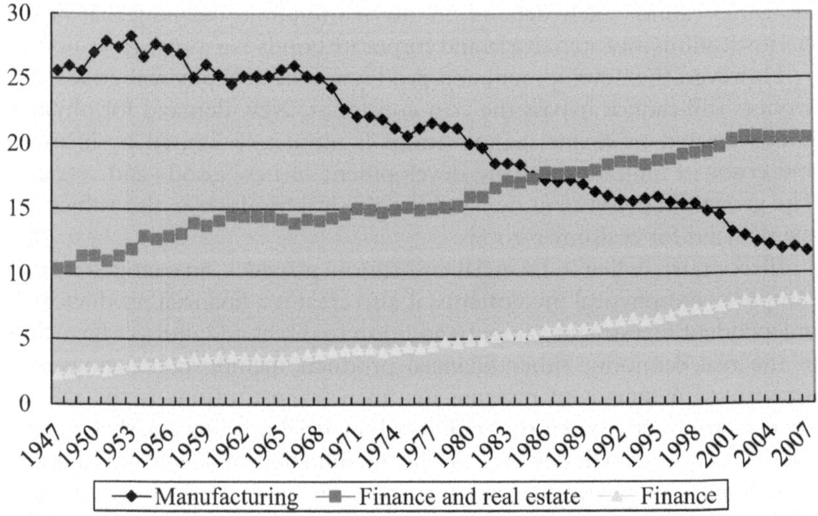

Fig. 10.3 Changes in the share of GDP of financial sector and manufacturing in the United States (1947–2007). Source of data: Bureau of Economic Analysis, U.S. Department of Commerce. Website: http://www.bea.gov/

products with a 50% risk probability is saturated, they can simply unveil a new product with a 51% risk probability, such as increasing the interest rate for bonds with higher risks.

We have also demonstrated that people can rationally accept high-risk financial products that can result in losses. Therefore, for society as a whole, the risk level of financial innovations increases. When the expected rate of return for physical investments continues to decline because of consumers' diminishing utility, the expected rate of return for financial products remains stable. This pattern has led to an increasing proportion of financial investments and a shrinking proportion of physical investments in the economy. For example, in the United States, manufacturing's share of GDP declined from 25.6% in 1947 to 11.7% in 2007, whereas the financial sector's share of GDP increased from 2.3% in 1947 to 7.9% in 2007. See Fig. 10.3.

Because financial products are monetary in nature, the development of the financial industry and the increase in financial assets suggest an increase in the money supply for the entire society. Although the costs of developing and producing financial products are low, the rights and obligations and the right to future earnings contained in the products are opportunity costs, which can also restrict people's demand for financial products. However, given the low cost of financial innovations, we have seen a greater variety of financial products, reduced transaction costs, and increased liquidity, attracting more people to spend more on financial products. Meanwhile, financial innovations also accelerate the circulation of money, increasing the money multiplier and, consequentially, the total money supply in a given monetary base, leading to greater inputs in financial products.

According to theories of finance, risk is quantified as the standard deviation of the price volatility for a financial product. When the expected returns are the same, a higher standard deviation implies greater price volatility and, hence, higher risk. This condition also holds true for society as a whole. For societies of similar expected returns, the one with more financial products and higher risks for these products tends to witness a greater range of price volatility for financial products and higher risks for the entire society. When the risk for a society reaches a certain level, the entire society could be in crisis, depression, instability, or even total collapse. Common businesses or individuals can afford small-range price fluctuations, and the small losses during a price fall could be recovered by the surplus created during a price rise without any threat of bankruptcy. In terms of greater price fluctuations, especially when the rate of decline is too fast, enterprises or individuals may suffer significant losses, making them unable to pay their debts and, eventually, go bankrupt. In a society, bankruptcy of many businesses and individuals could lead to depression throughout society (Fig. 10.4).

Judging from the Dow Jones Average Index, from 1929 to 2008, the average range (annual standard deviation/annual average, calculated monthly) of the price volatility has been widening. See Fig. 10.5. In the 1930s, the largest fluctuation was 27.55%, 43.63% in the 1940s, 45.68% in the 1950s, 48.50% in the 1960s, 56.79% in the 1970s, 58.35% in the 1990s, and 60.56% in the first decade of the twenty-first century. These fluctuations reflect, to some extent, the trend of rising risks in U.S. society. If we consider the large number of financial derivatives developed in recent years, their income fluctuations are likely to be greater, further increasing risk in U.S. society.

When human rationality fails to constrain an individual from investments with a higher risk probability and fails to prevent the entire society from declining efficiency or even falling into depression, human rationality

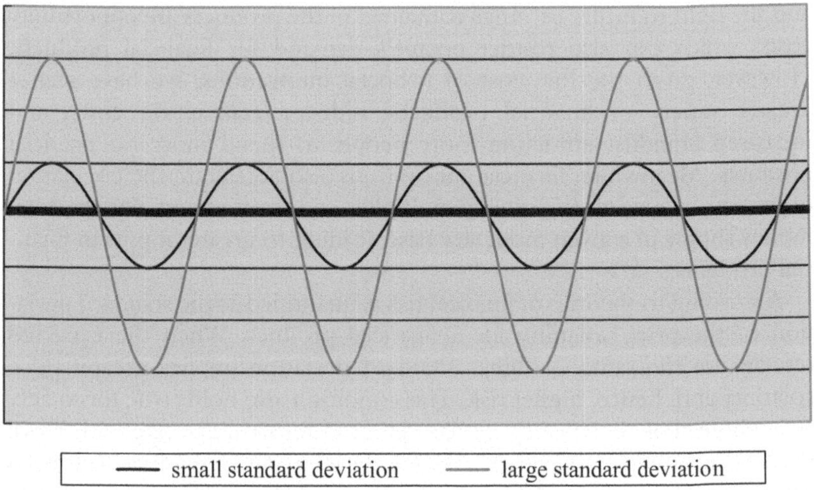

Fig. 10.4 Different standard deviations of price volatility

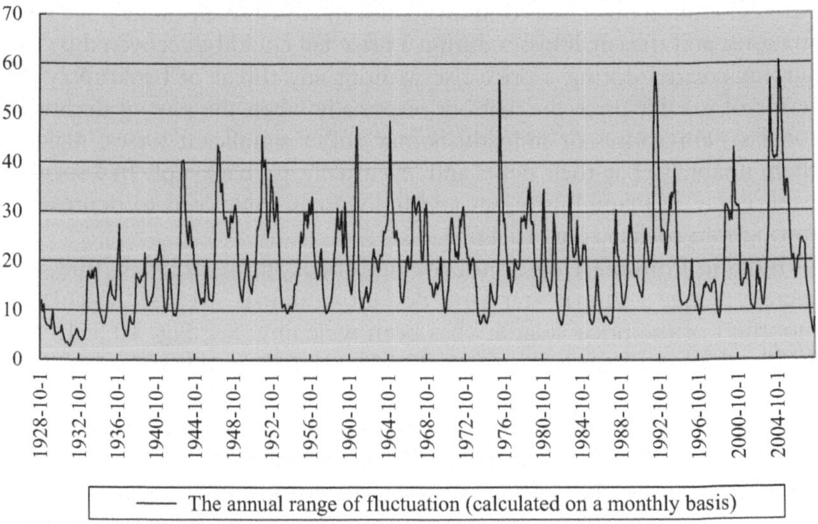

Fig. 10.5 Range of volatility of Dow Jones Average (annual standard deviation/annual average, calculated on a monthly basis, %, 1929–2008)

also cannot stop financial institutions from providing these high-risk products. Therefore, **whether from the demand side or the supply side, a risk-associated market failure exists that indicates that the market system cannot stop society from high-risk investments surpassing the "optimal" level.**

10.3 Risk Probability for Bankruptcy: Single Risk Probability, Amount Available for Investment, and Betting Ratio

Although people do not mind losing money to buy the possibility of obtaining a large fortune, not all of these risks lead to a sharp decline in personal income that significantly affects his or her consumption or inability to pay debts. For example, buying lottery tickets is a highly risky act, but few people go bankrupt. Ordinary people buy lottery tickets because the proportion of money invested in them relative to their income is quite low. Losses on lottery tickets are insufficient to cause a sharp decline in purchasers' income or insolvency.

The main reason for the significant decline in income or insolvency is for an individual or institution to lose all of his or her money available for investment and be unable to enjoy the probability of winning. Three factors are linked to reason. The first factor is the risk probability or winning rate of an investment project—referred to as a "single risk probability." The second factor is "money available for investment," and the third factor is the ratio of the amount in a single bet to the money available for all investments or the "betting ratio." All other conditions being equal, the higher the single risk probability, the less the money available for investment; alternatively, the higher the betting ratio, the more likely that the player suffers fatal losses and bankruptcy (see Figs. 10.6, 10.7, and 10.8). The money available for investment is that within one's financial ability or is from loans obtained using future income and assets as collateral. Losing this money does not affect the investor's normal life.

To briefly prove this statement, we again resort to the coin-flipping and dice-rolling model. Assuming that one person makes the same investment 254 times, excluding the time factor, the expected rate of return is 1 and a certain risk level exists, indicating that the person sometimes could not receive any return from the investment. Assume that the initial amount available for the player is 30 yuan and the betting rate is 1/30 (1 yuan each

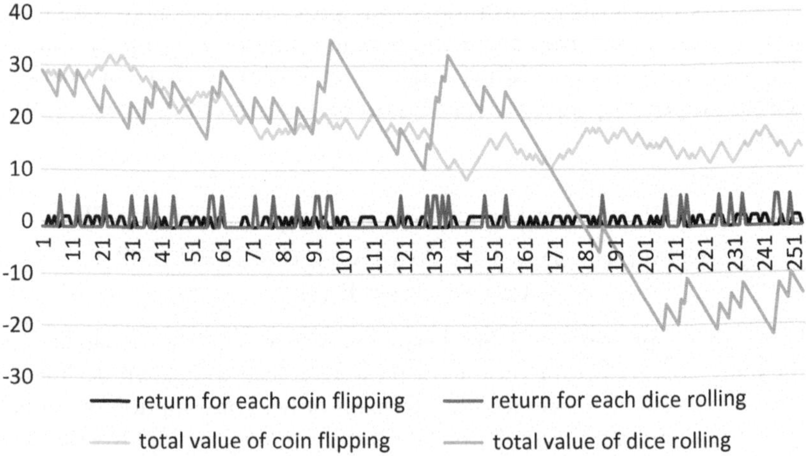

Fig. 10.6 Changes in total for different single risk probabilities

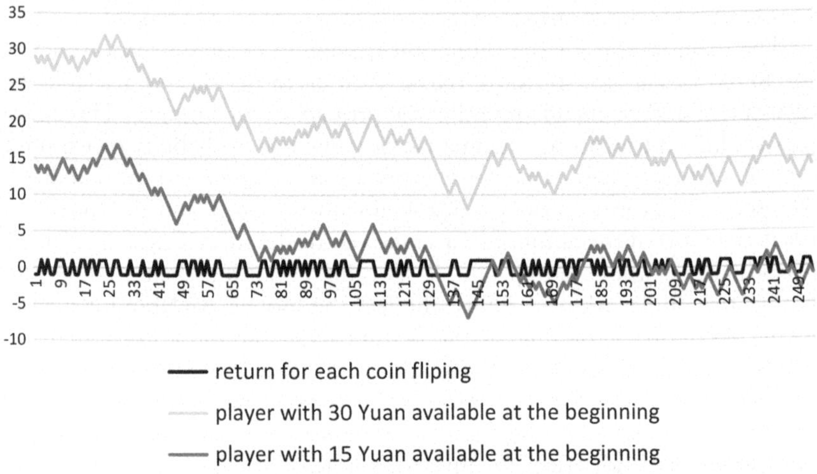

Fig. 10.7 Changes in total sum for different money available at the beginning

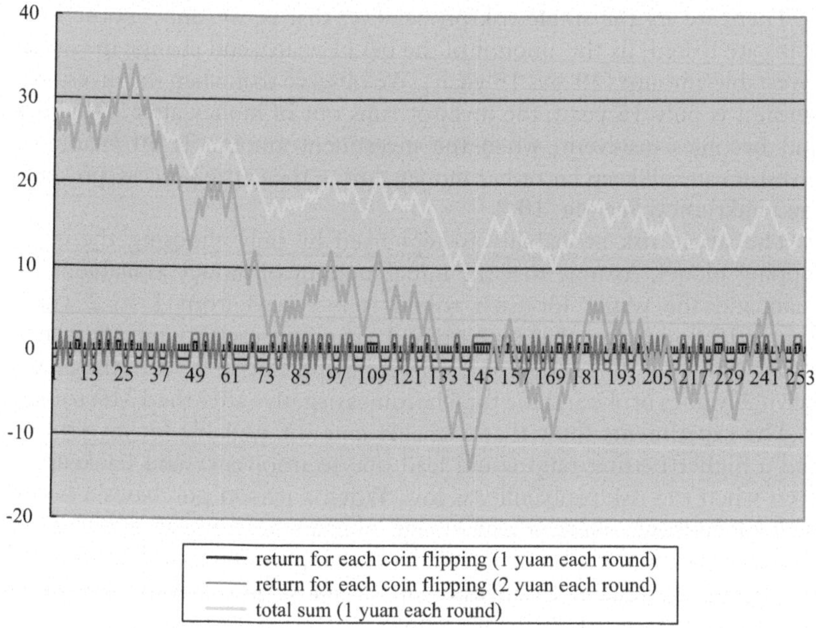

Fig. 10.8 Changes in total for different betting ratios

round). The single risk probability of coin-flipping is 1/2 or 50%, whereas that of dice-rolling is 5/6 or 83.3%. When flipping a coin, each win brings in 2 yuan, which is twice the input. For dice-rolling, the return for each success is 6 yuan or six times the input. The total changes after each round according to the spending and returns. The higher risk probability (dice-rolling) scenario shows that the total sum declines to less than zero (during the 180th round) and remains negative thereafter, indicating that the player is no longer able to make further investments and must quit for being cleaned out. If a portion of his or her money lost was borrowed, then he or she cannot repay it. This situation further demonstrates what was discussed in the first session; that is, with the same expected returns, higher single risk probability is more likely to cause actual losses given one's inability to continue his investment.

For the game with a lower single risk probability (coin flipping), the expected return for each win is small (2 yuan), but the total sum is mainly kept higher than 10 yuan—far from being bankrupt. See Fig. 10.6.

Then, we fix the single risk probability; that is, we only choose how coins are tossed, fix the amount of the bet (1 yuan), and change the initial investable amount (30 and 15 yuan). We observe that when the investable amount is only 15 yuan, the investor runs out of money after 131 times and becomes insolvent; when the investment amount is 30 yuan, the investor can still keep his or her money during the entire process, preventing bankruptcy. See Fig. 10.7.

The single risk probability is kept fixed by only choosing the coin-flipping model. Assume that the initial amount of money available is 30 yuan and the wager for each round is increased from 1 to 2 yuan. Figure 10.8 indicates that by putting 1 yuan into each round, the player always has some money at hand, whereas by putting in 2 yuan, the player inevitably goes broke and the total becomes negative after the 131st round.

The experiments show that a smaller amount available for investment and a higher betting ratio could lead one to insolvency and bankruptcy even when the risk probability is low. When a person purchases a house with a loan from a bank or a mortgage company by using all of his or her future income and the house as collateral, that person is spending all of his or her money available for investment. Even a small risk could make him or her unable to repay the loan on time.

From the viewpoint of financial balance for individuals or institutions, the meaning of risk is the risk of insolvency and bankruptcy or the "risk probability for bankruptcy." The factors affecting such risk include single risk probability—the amount of money available for investment and the betting ratio. This risk can be shown as follows:

Risk probability for bankruptcy = F risk probability amount available for investment betting ratio = risk probability × amount invested each round / mount available for investment

This equation indicates that the risk probability for bankruptcy is proportional to the single risk probability and the betting ratio and is inversely proportional to the amount available for investment. The risk probability = 1 − winning rate, and the single wager each round = betting ratio ∗ amount available for investment. The amount available for investment could be reflected by the betting ratio. When the total amount increases and the single wager stays unchanged, the betting ratio decreases and the equation is as follows:

Risk probability for bankruptcy = single risk probability ∗ betting ratio

Most people have their synthetic judgments on bankruptcy risks. People adopt investment strategies with different risk levels because of their different risk preferences. In the circumstance of a fixed risk preference, everyone has his or her acceptable risk probability for bankruptcy. If one believes that 5% is an acceptable bankruptcy risk probability, then his or her betting ratio should not exceed 0.0505 when investing with a 99% single risk probability. When the single risk probability is 10%, the person's maximal betting ratio is 0.5. When the single risk probability declines to lower than 1%, the maximal betting ratio increases to 5. A betting ratio higher than 1 suggests that one can turn to loans to cover an amount higher than the amount that he or she has available for investment, indicating that when the single risk probability is low, one might increase his or her betting ratio accordingly.

Both consumption and investment bring certain utility and are spending to obtain a certain type of "return." For consumption, the return is to enjoy in advance—receiving the time value of consumption utility with the characteristic of a zero-risk interest rate. In contrast, the "return" of an investment is compensation for "delayed consumption," which is reflected in the compensation for the value of time and is represented concretely as the discount rate. Investments sacrifice the present for the future, whereas consumption sacrifices the future for the present. Investments are worthwhile as long as the expected rate of return is higher than 1. Consumption brings immediate returns, turning the "future" into the "present"; therefore, from the perspective of consumption utility, advancing consumption through borrowing is very low risk. Once the individual fails to repay, he or she only loses current consumption—which did not exist before borrowing. Because of collateral, even if the price falls to lower than the value of the loan, the risk is borne by the lender. Therefore, people are willing to "buy" money or "sell" a financial asset called "borrowing" to engage in earlier consumption.

Assume that the bankruptcy risk probability for persons applying for a mortgage loan is accepted as 5% and that the value of the house serving as collateral has a fifty-fifty chance of both increasing and decreasing. As long as the loan institution's interest rate to the individual is 2.5% higher than that of the individual with a zero probability of bankruptcy risk, or half the possible default rate (5%), the expected return may achieve 1. These requirements are quite low, and if the lender only lends money that it owns, that is, to keep the betting ratio to no higher than 1, there is a serious problem. However, the low level of risk probability has convinced people that they can lend using borrowed money.

In reality, given this reason, house mortgage loans are refinanced. Frank Knight points out that people reduce their risk probabilities through "consolidation" and "specialization" (2006, p. 239). Consolidation reduces uncertainties through grouping, puts together items with the same type of risks, and turns risks of single items into risks for a category. In doing so, the risks of a linear distribution along the time axis are transformed into risks that coexist in parallel, making such risks more affordable to people with limited time and wealth. The consolidation of a significant amount of mortgage loans protected individual lenders from going bankrupt for a single bad debt and, instead, dilutes the loss into the large mortgage pool that affects the return probability for total revenue but not directly for any single investor. Furthermore, securitization based on this mortgage pool assigns the default rate of all mortgages to each security, and a certain amount of investable money can be invested in a wider range of mortgage pools. This situation is equivalent to reducing the actual single risk probability.

For instance, assume that the lender has 1 million yuan available for investment and it lends all of the money to a mortgaged borrower. The value of the collateral equals 100% of the loan, the borrower's default rate is 5%, and the probability that the house depreciates is 50%. If the value of the house declines to 500,000 yuan and the borrower defaults on the loan, the loss probability for the lender is 100% or 500,000 yuan. In this calculation, the actual risk probability is much greater than 2.5% (5%*50%). However, if the borrower invests by purchasing bonds based on mortgage loans, even if 5% of borrowers default and the home price plunges, his or her loss probability is only 5% or 25,000 yuan. Therefore, through securitization, the lender's single risk probability is significantly lowered.

However, reducing a single risk probability does not represent a risk reduction for society. When assessing an investment, people do not calculate its risk probability but the risk probability for their bankruptcy or "the benchmark of risk probability of bankruptcy." When the single risk probability is lowered, one's bankruptcy risk probability in this investment is remarkably lower than the level that he or she feels is acceptable, tempting him or her to raise the betting ratio and, ultimately, elevate the risk probability of bankruptcy to close to his or her benchmark. People invest more money into projects in which they have higher confidence. For investments with a very low single risk probability, the betting ratio increases—sometimes to higher than 1 (investing with borrowed money)—thus enhancing the development of refinancing. Therefore, the risk probability of bankruptcy is not reduced at the societal level. Different from the situation before consolidation and securitization, people put more money into various programs. Once these programs face problems, the reach is even broader.

The subprime mortgage crisis that started at the end of 2007 was, to a large extent, attributed to raising the betting ratio in society. The advent of subprime mortgage securities and multiple refinancings for a mortgage represent banks raising their betting ratios and allocating a significantly higher amount of funds into subprime mortgages than into traditional bank assets (capital base and deposits). In the fourth quarter of 2006, the percentage of subprime mortgages in the U.S. mortgage market surged from 2% in 1999 to 15%; the size of this market exploded from $81 billion in 2000 to $732.9 billion in 2006 (Research Group on the Sub-Prime Crisis 2008, pp. 75–77).

Defaulting coupled with the plummeting of housing prices leads to a higher risk probability of bankruptcy, causing serious losses or even collapse for many banks. According to IMF estimations, between 2007 and 2010, the loss suffered by U.S. and European financial institutions because of toxic assets and bad loans reached $2.8 trillion. Large financial institutions, such as Lehman Brothers, Citibank, Merrill Lynch, Bank of America, and many other giants, were severely influenced.

10.4 Greater Financial Risk Strengthened by the Negotiation and Lobbying Power of Financial Interest Groups

In general, higher risk in society indicates a larger income gap between different social classes. A society that rolls the dice (with a 1/6 winning rate) has a more even distribution of income than a society playing games with a 1/50 winning rate. See Fig. 10.9, in which dice-rolling stands for investments with lower risks, and a game with a 1/50 winning rate represents investments with higher risks.

When the expected returns are the same, the investment with higher risks has returns that fluctuate in a wider range. The winners get richer, and the losers get poorer, the number of rich is fewer, and the number of poor is greater. This phenomenon has already been proven in U.S. society as noted when we hear discussions over "the disappearance of the middle

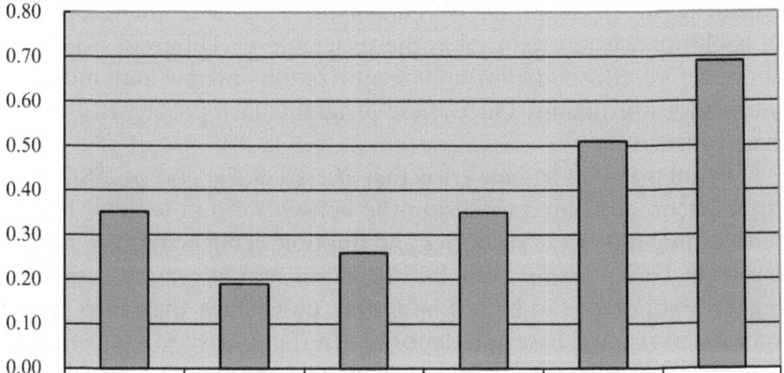

	coin tossing	dice rolling	1 for 50	1 for 100	1 for 200	1 for 100
■ Gini Index	0.35	0.19	0.26	0.35	0.51	0.69

Fig. 10.9 Gini index for games with different levels of risks. Note: The Gini index is calculated based on the model in Fig. 10.1, suggesting that the Gini index increases as the risk probability of the games increases, except for coin-tossing

class." When high-risk financial products are more frequently created and traded in society, the risk for the entire society increases and the beneficiaries are interest groups from the financial sector—not to say that they have better chances of winning fair competitions. They use the characteristics of high-risk financial products and transfer the risks of failure to other people while reaping significant profits regardless of how the investments turn out and do so even at the expense of other people.

Inside financial institutions, including investment banks and hedge funds, the incomes of management are directly linked to their performance. Incentives, often in the forms of the company's options and year-end bonuses, motivate them to develop and adopt new financial products and often through bolder strategies. On the one hand, after years of development, the demand for traditional financial products becomes saturated, and management cannot improve its performance by only adhering to existing strategies. On the other hand, option prices are more volatile than the prices of traditional instruments, such as stocks, and stock price volatility is magnified in the options market. Although the stock and the option on that stock are of the same expected returns, the management of financial institutions often prefers returns with higher volatility.

Higher volatility is desired because, first, the high-risk products that financial institutions introduce into the market are not for themselves to trade. They sell the products to others and charge commissions. Traders in institutions only need to market the products to the public, and the best way to do so is through a handful of successful cases that have brought in significant profits while playing down most of the failed cases. The public's attention is easily drawn to the high returns of successful precedents, and large losses are regarded as the inevitable collateral damage. This distribution of risks allows higher commissions for financial institutions, transfers the costs of the risk to the public, and only encourages institutions to create and sell products with even higher risks.

Second, management receives huge returns for their success but does not shoulder any responsibilities for their own failure. In fact, most of the losses are not borne by management but by the company's shareholders (Reed 2009, p. 95). The reason that management and operations teams receive such favorable terms when bargaining with shareholders is because of the characteristics of high risks, namely, the higher standard deviation for returns. If these riskier products turn out to be successful because of sheer luck, they bring much higher returns than low-risk products, but these returns are at the expense of losses from more cases of the same type of transaction.

Thus, in the financial sector, certain people are always touted as talent investors. However, general fund investors and investment bank shareholders do not know that probability is merely at work, and they blindly compete to recruit the so-called financial masters. Because a higher risk results in a lower winning rate and fewer successful players, these masters have become more popular and have increased their negotiating power with shareholders. They are not only given astronomical annual salaries and incentive arrangements but are often exempted from their symmetrical obligations, such as responsibility for losses. Therefore, on Wall Street, contract terms prevail with lucrative fixed salaries, extra rewards for better performance, and exemption from being responsible for the losses they create. This arrangement further motivates the management of financial institutions to pursue higher risks for developing and trading financial products.

When high-risk channels more wealth to fewer institutions and individuals, the market balance is destroyed. Financial upstarts with significant wealth obtain greater negotiation power, forcing their service suppliers to make greater compromises and even lying and counterfeiting for them. For instance, some securities rating institutions were proven to have interests in elevating the credit ratings for securities issued by some major financial institutions.

Financial exchanges are where financial products are traded, and their main form of income is from charging commissions. Thus, exchanges are not concerned about the risks of their products or the losses that the transactions might impose on the buyers. They only care about transaction volume. Because competition among exchanges is fierce globally and financial product and currency liquidity is high and can be transferred quickly among exchanges using modern technology, such as computers and the Internet, an exchange does not dare to strengthen its regulation of products even if it recognizes that the high risk can result in substantial losses and negatively affect society. Stricter regulations scare traders away and reduce the trading volume on exchanges, thereby reducing exchanges' income.

Therefore, as an interest group, financial institutions agree that financial products with higher risks are in their interest. In the political arena, financial institutions safeguard this collective interest. In the representative political system in the United States, interest groups can lobby the legislative body. According to "The Logic of Collective Action" by Olson, an interest group with greater benefits and fewer people is more motivated, more powerful, and more likely to influence Congress (1971). In this way, Wall Street is obviously among the most powerful interest groups in the United States.

Financial interest groups' lobbying muscle and opportunities increase as higher risks create a greater income disparity in society because a larger amount of wealth is channeled to even fewer people. Olson's theory suggests that financial interest groups are growing in interest but declining in terms of the number of members. Members in such a group receive a larger share of the profits for each successful lobbying effort and are, thus, more driven to act in unity. A decreasing number of people also make them easier to unite. A logical result of Olson's theory is that the political influence of financial interest groups on Wall Street increases as financial risks increase.

Therefore, the U.S. Congress faces increasing challenges when passing any act that can strengthen financial regulations and restrain interest groups on Wall Street. In contrast, Congress sometimes passes acts in favor of such groups. For example, hedge fund managers who already have unreasonably high incomes enjoy a reduction of 35% in income taxes and only pay a 15% capital gains tax (Krugman 2007, p. 191). When Wall

Street gave the bail-out money to their management teams as a bonus, it infuriated almost all of U.S. society. The House of Representatives immediately passed an act imposing higher taxes on bonuses, but eventually compromised to Wall Street's excuses to "honor the spirit of contract" and "prevent the outflow of quality employees." The management of financial institutions returned part of their bonuses, and the House of Representatives stopped passing similar acts. This situation represents strong evidence of the political muscle of Wall Street.

However, explicit statements have been made that financial interest groups should take full responsibility for the recent financial crisis, enhancing the political forces that require some discipline on Wall Street and strengthen financial regulations. President Obama proposed financial reforms, and the U.S. government indicted Goldman Sachs, which were important steps in restraining financial interest groups in the United States. However, whether the effort succeeds depends on the political contest between U.S. society and these financial interest groups.

10.5 Macroeconomic Policies Under U.S. Political Structure

The failure of the financial market did not necessarily lead to the financial crisis that started at the end of 2007 because taking excessive risks eventually harms the player in the long term. Particularly in societies that value family traditions, higher financial risks could do greater harm if viewed from the perspective that transcends individual lifespans. Regardless of how small the risk is for bankruptcy, once bankruptcy happens, the life of a family or an institution stops and any high expected turns become meaningless at that time. Therefore, in many societies, families and institutions live by the "culture of prudence" mostly in the form of prohibitions against gambling, speculating, or even entering the stock market. This cultural tradition has, to some degree, offset the failure of financial markets.

However, this cultural tradition could be interrupted by another force—that of the government. In America, citizens cast ballots for the electors, and these electors then cast direct votes for the heads of the government—basically, the direct election of the government. Thus, the will of the people is crucial for the government to make policy decisions. Although economic fluctuations without government intervention represent natural market adjustments, people always prefer faster economic growth and resent recessions. The general public often is incapable of judging what—the market or the government—should be responsible for a recession. A politician's evaluation is manifold, but the economy has always been the most important issue that can directly affect people's well-being. George H. W. Bush won the first Gulf War but lost his bid for a second term because of economic problems.

To win a presidential election, any president would select policies that stimulate economic growth—within his policy options. The president can directly adopt expansionary policies, such as increasing public expenditures. As Buchanan and Wagner pointed out, "in most electoral systems, considering fixed preferences and tax structure, the budget will grow as long as the majority prefer enjoying public services than paying taxation at the expenses of private goods" (1988, p. 96). For example, during the recent crisis, both the Bush Administration and the Obama Administration introduced stimulation plans in the hundreds of billions of dollars.

Although the Federal Reserve Board is said to have the decision power over monetary policies, pressure from the president and Congress cause it to follow a looser rather than a neutral monetary policy (Buchanan and Wagner 1988, pp. 120–122). For example, the monetary policies adopted by Alan Greenspan are always criticized as being responsible for this crisis.

Buchanan and Wagner (1988) once stated that Keynesianism provides the theoretical foundation and ideological weapon for the government to implement expansionary policies. To be fair, in the U.S. political structure, the government carries out only half of Keynesianism in that it adopts expansionary macro policies during recessions but does not tighten its policies during economic expansions. Presidents and Congress choose only half of Keynesianism that is conducive to economic expansions.

This "semi-Keynesianism" approach also suggests that, between the two macro-policy approaches, the government always prefers fiscal policies over monetary policies. This preference exists because, during economic depressions, expansionary fiscal policy can immediately expand the economy, whereas expansionary monetary policy does not always lead to direct expansion of the economy. Fiscal policies represent immediate government expenditures, whereas monetary policies issue more currency to households and companies; however, whether these expenditures are spent is not controlled by the government.

In contrast, fiscal policies, particularly large-scale increases in government expenditures, are proposed by the president and approved by

Congress, whereas the monetary policies are voted on by the Federal Reserve Board and do not require congressional approval. A characteristic of Congress is that it represents public opinions, which resent economic recessions and prefer booms and growth, indicating that Congress also prefers expansionary fiscal policies. Expansionary fiscal policy wins more support from Congress than a tight fiscal policy. The data show that, since 1945, U.S. fiscal expenditures have always increased and have no a period to decline obviously (see Fig. 10.10).

In contrast, without direct pressure from Congress, the Federal Reserve Board is able to decide flexibly whether to adopt expansionary or tight monetary policy. For example, whether to raise the discount rate or the reserve rate depends on the vote of the Federal Reserve Board. Although the Fed also prefers a loose monetary policy, sometimes it can still adopt tight policies. Therefore, monetary policy in the United States can still be adjusted in both ways. Figure 10.11 shows that, at least since 1994, the interest rate of the monetary base has had its ups and downs, with the highest being 16% (1981). Of course, the measure was tough against the serious inflation in the late 1970s.

Although the total supply of money showed a decrease during certain stages. See Fig. 10.12, in which narrow money (M1) declined from \$1160.3 billion in April 1995 to \$1066.2 billion in February 1998.

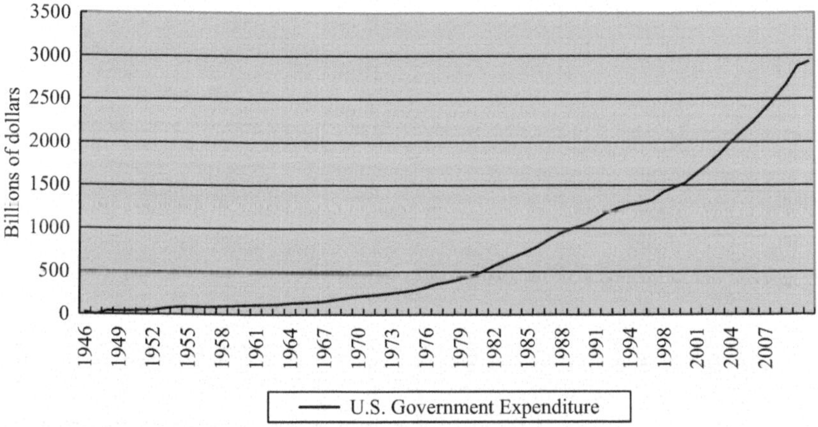

Fig. 10.10 U.S. government expenditures (1845–2009). Source of data: Bureau of Economic Analysis, U.S. Department of Commerce. Website: http://www.bea.gov/

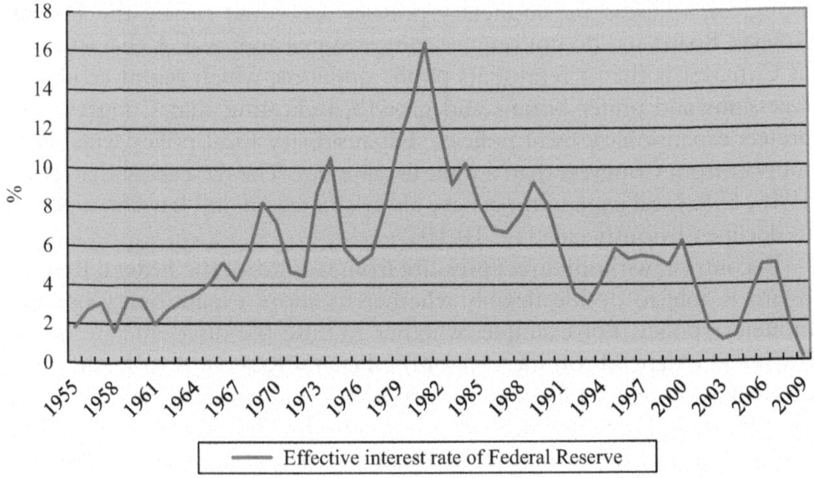

Fig. 10.11 Effective Federal Reserve Board interest rate (1954–2009). Source of data: Board of Governors of Federal Reserve System. Website: http://www.federalreserve.gov/

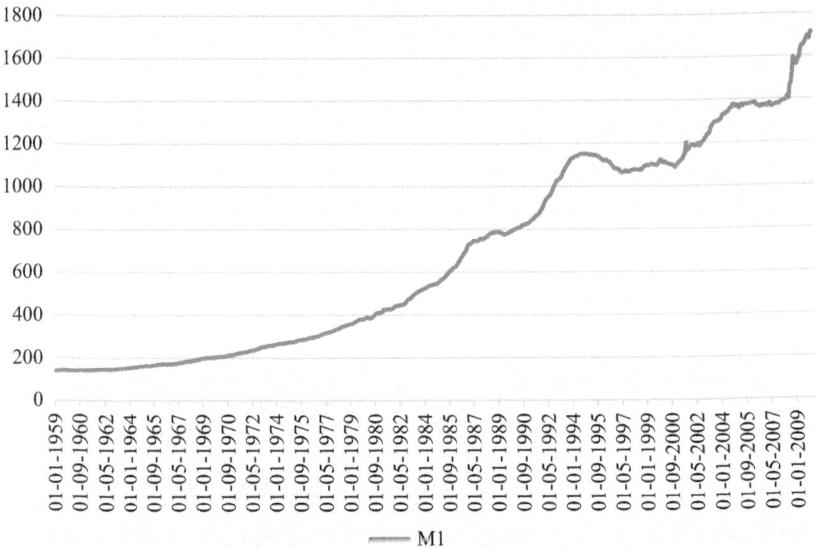

Fig. 10.12 US money supply (M1, 1959–2010). Data sources: Board of Governors of Federal Reserve System. Website: http://www.federalreserve.gov/

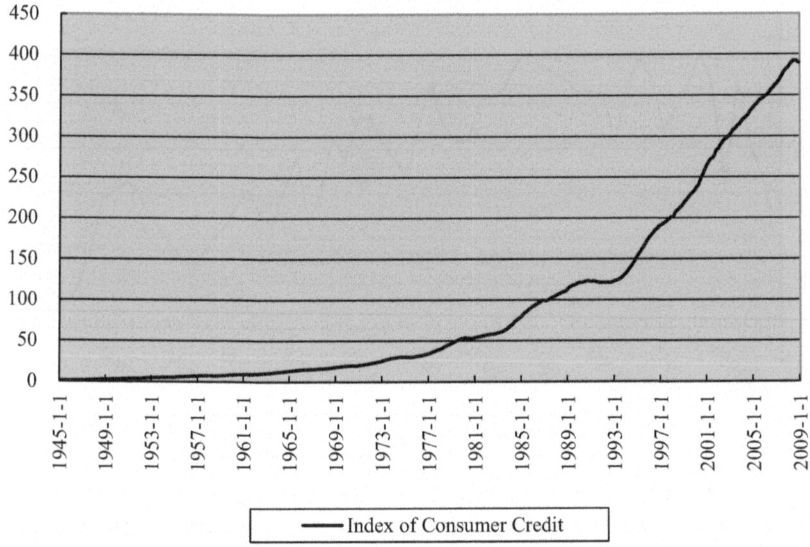

Fig. 10.13 Index of consumer credit in the United States (1945–2009). Data sources: Board of Governors of Federal Reserve System. Website: http://www.federalreserve.gov/

In addition to macroeconomic policies, the U.S. government also encourages direct consumption by supporting consumer credit. A positive approach would be to improve the legal environment of consumer credit and reduce transaction costs. A negative approach is for the government to directly involve itself in consumer credit activities. A typical example is the government's direct intervention in housing credit by founding Fannie Mae and Freddie Mac, two companies directly engaged in the home mortgage business. In general, the U.S. government's support for consumer credit often occurs in an economic recession or downturn and works as expansionary macroeconomic policy. However, when the economy is booming, policies to reduce consumer credit could not be adopted. Therefore, this policy is actually unidirectional. As Fig. 10.13 demonstrates, U.S. consumer credit has been increasing since 1945, except for a slight decrease from 1991 to 1994. However, from 1994 to 2009, U.S. consumer credit registered a sharp increase three times.

More importantly, policies that encourage consumer credit are at the expense of an increasing ratio of consumption to income. From 1945 to

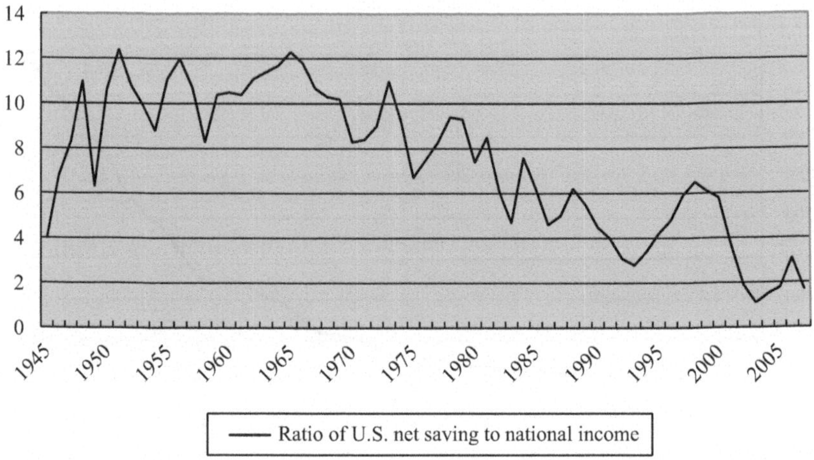

Fig. 10.14 Ratio of U.S. net savings to national income (%). Data sources: Bureau of Economic Analysis, U.S. Department of Commerce. Website: http://www.bea.gov/

2007, consumer credit soared 391 times, leading to a decrease in the net savings rate from 10% in 1945 to less than 2%. See Fig. 10.14.

From 1980 to 2007, the ratio of personal income saved to personal disposable income decreased from approximately 10% to less than 1%. See Fig. 10.15. This decrease resulted in expansionary policies that encouraged the end of consumer credit.

Semi-Keynesianism met some of the public's expectations. Since 1950, the United States has not suffered a recession as severe as the Great Depression, and seldom was there negative growth. The most serious situation was the 2% recession in 1982. See Fig. 10.16, which shows that economic fluctuations actually occur primarily in the upper half of a cycle. Generally, macroeconomic policy has a long-term expansionary trend rather than a countercyclical operation, as advocated by Keynes.

After the long-term implementation of policies that irreversibly encourages consumption, the government had no choice but to welcome consumer credit with higher risks after the saturation of the traditional consumer credit market. The government's policies encouraged consumer credit out of political considerations and the public confidence in the government that removed most people's concerns and led them to buy high-risk financial products such as subprime mortgage bonds. The trading of

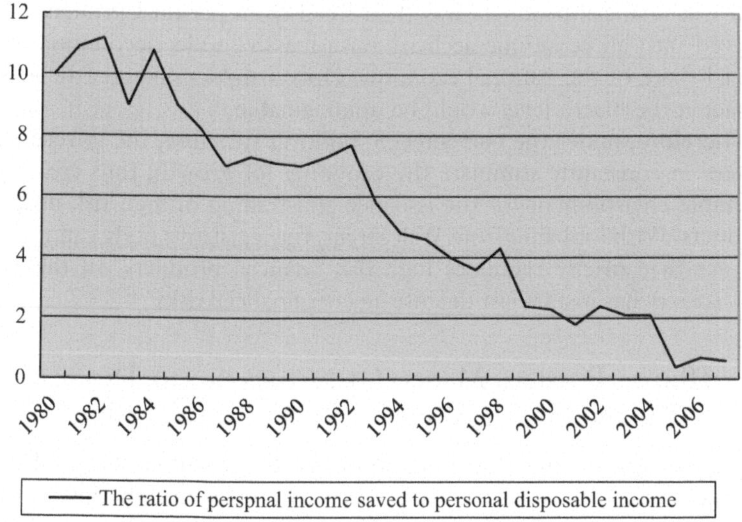

Fig. 10.15 Ratio of personal income saved to personal disposable income in the United States. Data sources: Bureau of Economic Analysis, U.S. Department of Commerce. Website: http://www.bea.gov/

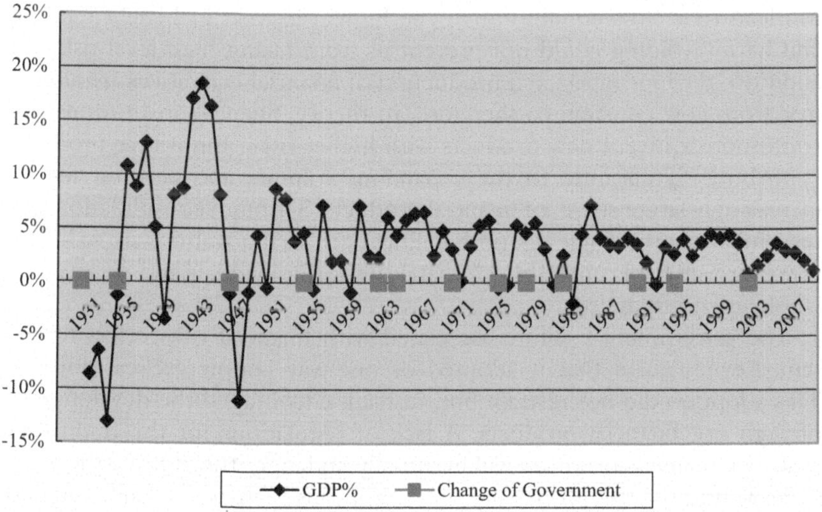

Fig. 10.16 Growth rate of U.S. economy and presidential transitions (1929–2008). Data sources: Bureau of Economic Analysis, U.S. Department of Commerce. Website: http://www.bea.gov/

high-risk financial products was then freed from personal prudence and evolved into an economic acclivity on a massive scale, accounting for a crucial share of the national economy. Once troubles emerge, the severe impact at the macro level would be unimaginable.

Therefore, under the current U.S. political structure, the government prefers to constantly stimulate the economy for growth, thus creating a favorable environment for the issuance and trading of high-risk financial products. With lobbying from Wall Street, the legislative body cannot pass any act that strictly regulates high-risk financial products. In this way, U.S. society has lost its last defense against financial risks.

10.6 Possible Macro Outcomes of the Double Failure of the Market and the Government

The analyses in the initial sections addressed the seven questions raised at the beginning of this chapter. A basic conclusion is that the institutions, including the market and the governmental institutions that could have prevented the financial crisis, both failed, thus making the financial crisis in the United States inevitable.

The market failure associated with financial risks is related to people conducting spontaneous financial transactions, and their rational decisions can lead to a "loss equilibrium." The human instinct of benefit-tending and harm-avoiding could not prevent us from taking high-level risks. In addition, the innovation and production of financial derivatives are almost free from cost constraints; therefore, in theory, financial institutions can continuously invent new products with higher risks. Innovative products contribute significantly to the expanding volume, and account for an increasingly larger share, of financial products. Through consolidation and securitization, the single risk probabilities of these innovations are reduced; however, the bankruptcy risk probabilities for individuals and society as a whole are not reduced.

The government's failure associated with financial risks refers to the semi-Keynesianism that it adopted or one-way countercyclical policies. This adoption did not restrain but, instead, encouraged the development of high-risk financial products. A lack of regulations for the trading of high-risk financial products will eventually endanger the entire society.

Lowering the risk probability through means such as consolidation and securitization is, in fact, distributing the risk to more people. This approach resembles the idea of insurance. However, the problem with insurance is that, when accidental losses are shouldered by the group, the insurer tends to be less motivated to prevent incidents from happening. Insurance turns a personal risk into a social one because the fire insurance that reduces the losses of individuals leads to an increased occurrence of fire accidents in society. Individuals increase their betting ratio in investments when faced with lower single risk probabilities, restoring the risk probability for bankruptcy to its normal level. However, for society, when everyone increases his or her betting ratio, the betting ratio of the entire society also increases. Different from individuals, although the amount of physical investment programs increases from financial innovation, the increase in the scale of investment projects is much less than the increase in the scale of financial products throughout society, causing more capital to be concentrated in fewer projects. The expected rate of return declines, driving up the single risk probability for the entire society as well as the risk probability for bankruptcy.

For instance, after securitizing housing mortgages, a lower single risk probability leads to a significant increase in funding supply, which then leads to lower interest rates for mortgage securities, further enhancing their demand. Because the loan offered by financial institutions is, in fact, supplying currency, the money supply then increases. When society realizes full employment, an increasing money supply creates inflation, which is when the financial authorities raise interest rates and tighten monetary policies—to stop or even lower the rising prices. When the housing price starts to decline, the default on mortgages increases, resulting in a rising risk probability of mortgage securities. When the financial institution fails to pay interest, it faces liquidation requirements by bondholders and eventually goes bankrupt.

In addition, as was mentioned, the disparity in income is greater in a society of higher risks. The haves become richer, and the have-nots become poorer. Most poor people are more vulnerable to economic fluctuations and more inclined to suffer losses or even go bankrupt. In contrast, because the expected returns of financial products are fixed, in a situation of extensive losses, a few people receive huge profits at the expense of the poor. Goldman Sachs went short on subprime mortgage bonds and reaped significant profits when the U.S. housing market plummeted. However, the high returns to a few could not compensate for the losses to the majority, and the widespread existence of losses has an impact at the macro level. In a society with smaller risks, the disparity is also less serious—the poor are more resilient to economic fluctuations, do not suffer severe losses or go bankrupt, and, thus, do not negatively influence the macro economy.

The significant amount of refinancing has increased the betting ratio of society, and securitization has attracted the inflow of large amounts of capital. Once the original loans defaulted, ripple effects occur that break the series of debtor–creditor relations. Because the currency is built using debtor–creditor relations as the monetary base, it is damaged when these relations are broken (Commons 1934, pp. 7–136) and then deflation occurs at a macro level. Deflation causes individuals' incomes to shrink, and they adjust their spending habits accordingly, which slows the rate of currency circulation and leads to further decreases in the amount of money in circulation. Through this vicious circle, society approaches an economic recession.

When facing economic downturns, the government's first reaction is to further implement expansionary macroeconomic policies, increase public investments, relax monetary policies, encourage public spending, and even provide direct support to financial institutions that are too big to fail. In doing so, the government constantly repeats its past mistakes, adopting excessively loose macro policies and stimulating commercial banks to increase consumer credit, all of which blurred the institutional reasons behind the financial crisis and allows parties that should be blamed for this crisis to escape without consequences. Such government behavior sends a misleading signal to the financial sector, which then adopts even more adventurous market strategies because it believes that the government will always bail it out. Such a belief leads to financial crises caused by institutional failures to be continually repeated.

10.7 Conclusion

This chapter makes the following conclusions.

1. Given the limited lifespan and wealth, people cannot take infinite or sufficient chances in an investment or game, the actual return of riskier financial products is lower than expected. However, because people have accepted the utility of expected returns, which is the possibility of obtaining higher rewards, they will accept the actual losses, leading to a "loss equilibrium" in society.
2. When all of the people accept the loss equilibrium and purchase excessively risky financial products, when losses occur, all of society experiences a financial crisis. Because people do not automatically stop when faced with losses, there exists a risk-associated market failure.

3. Because the development and production of financial products are subject to fewer cost limitations and individuals' demand for financial products is not influenced by diminishing marginal utility, the innovation of financial products could be endless, in theory. Such innovation could lead to a greater increase in financial product transactions than physical goods transactions, and financial products are being developed to have higher risks.
4. For both individuals and society, a significant risk index is the risk probability for bankruptcy. It is influenced by both the single risk probability and the betting ratio. When the single risk probability is lowered through financial approaches such as consolidation, specialization, and securitization, people tend to increase substantially their betting ratios—as is evidenced by the increase in refinancing activity. Thus, the risk probability for bankruptcy is eventually raised to the original level, at the same time increasing the risks in society.
5. The increase in the number of high-risk financial products and their risk levels leads to higher total risk for society and a larger income gap. By charging commissions, financial institutions ensure their profits and make others take risks. The coincidental success of certain managers and traders, coupled with the potential huge returns in high-risk conditions, gives them greater bargaining chips in negotiations with investors and shareholders of investment banks, enabling them to win contracts for only bonuses but shoulder no responsibility for any losses. These contracts drive management to engage in even more reckless behavior.
6. The U.S. government is directly elected by the people, and it—including Congress, administrative departments, and the Federal Reserve Bank—is inclined to loosen macro policies, encourage credit consumption, and tend to adopt long-term expansionary macroeconomic policies. Doing so drives people away from prudent principles and leads them to invest in high-risk financial products.
7. Lobby for legislation in the United States is legal, and Wall Street interest groups have been increasingly motivated and influential. Because higher risks channel more wealth into fewer institutions and individuals, the lobbying power of the Wall Street interest groups will continue to rise, making it more difficult for Congress to pass any legislation for stricter regulations of financial risks.
8. In summary, the financial crisis in the United States was caused by the double failure of the market and the government. Faced with

this crisis, the government continued its past mistakes and failed to fundamentally address the institutional problems that caused the crisis. Unless the United States calls for a constitutional reform, such as stronger representation in the political structure of the elites for their historical experience, amending a constitutional principle that requires a balanced budget for a fixed period (e.g., 10 years), identifying an appropriate risk level for society, and being able to stop right before reaching this level, the next crisis is inevitable.

References

奥尔森, 曼瑟, 《集体行动的逻辑》, 上海人民出版社, 1995. (Translated from: Olson, Mancur, *The Logic of Collective Action*, Harvard University Press; Revised edition (January 1, 1971)).

布坎南和瓦格纳, 《赤字中的民主》, 北京经济学院出版社, 1988. (Translated from: Buchanan & Wagner, *Democracy in Deficit*, Academic Press, Inc., 1977).

次贷风波研究课题组, 《次贷风波启示录》, 中国金融出版社, 2008. (Research group on Sub-prime Mortgage Crisis, *Sub-prime Mortgage Crisis*, China Finance Publishing House, 2008).

赫尔, 约翰, 《期权、期货和衍生证券》, 华夏出版社, 1997. (Translated from: Hull, John, *Options, Futures and Other Derivatives*, Prentice Hall; 3rd edition (June 28, 1996)).

康芒斯, 《制度经济学》, 商务印书馆, 1962. (Translated from: John R. Commons, *Institutional Economics: Its Place in Political Economy*, The MacMillan Company, New York, 1934).

克鲁格曼, 保罗, 《美国怎么了?》, 中信出版社, 2008. (Translated from: Krugman, Paul, *The Conscience of a liberal*, W. W. Norton & Company; First Edition (October 1, 2007)).

勒威, 哈姆; 萨纳特, 马歇尔; 《证券投资组合与选择》, 中山大学出版社, 1997. (Translated from: Levy, Haim; Sarnat, Marshall; *Portfolio and Investment Selection*, Prentice Hall (May 1, 1984)).

里德, 科林, 《金融危机经济学》, 东方出版社, 2009. (Translated from: Read, Colin, Global Financial Meltdown, Palgrave Macmillan; 1 edition (February 15, 2009)).

IMF, http://www.imf.org/external/pubs/ft/weo/2009/01/pdf/exesum.pdf.

Knight, Frank, *Risk, Uncertainty and Profit*, New York: Dover Publications, Inc., 2006.

CHAPTER 11

The Economic Logic of Specialized Markets

Contents

11.1 The Question

A very significant phenomenon exists in the rapid economic development in China: the development of specialized markets. The so-called specialized market is a market that sells only one, a few, or a small type of good, but its transaction volume is huge. In 2013, 3708 specialized markets existed in China that had sales higher than 100 million yuan, amounting to a total sales of 7.8087 trillion yuan (National Bureau of Statistics 2014), equivalent to 13.3% of last year's GDP.

Specialized markets are particularly common in Zhejiang Province. A famous case includes the bridge button market in Yongjia (永嘉), the

Translated from *Research of Institutional Economics* (《制度经济学研究》), Volume 50, Issue 4, 2015.

Sheng Hong, *Vision and Calculation*,
https://doi.org/10.1007/978-981-15-2898-9_11

electric appliances market in Liushi (柳市), the leather garment market in Haining (海宁), and the plastic furniture market in Taizhou (台州), not to mention that the Yiwu (义乌) small commodities market is made up of multiple specialized markets. In 2013, 530 specialized markets existed in Zhejiang Province, with total sales of 1.1606 trillion yuan (Trade Statistics Division of National Bureau of Statistics, Information Department of China General Chamber of Commerce 2014). In 2000, this figure was only 164.1 billion yuan (Trade Statistics Division of National Bureau of Statistics, Information Department of China General Chamber of Commerce 2001). These specialized markets promote the development of industries around, and further drive the economic development of, Zhejiang.

The question is why do specialized markets exist? This question can be transformed into, why are people willing to go to a more distant but more special market to buy goods? For example, many of the specialized markets in Zhejiang Province, such as the sweater market, cover the entire country. Why are people willing to travel far to buy a sweater?

Conversely, for investors, why is investing in a specialized market more profitable than investing in a less specialized market given the same amount of capital?

11.2 Why Is an Economic Individual Willing to Go to a More Distant But More Specialized Market?

When a person goes to the market to buy products, doing so is worthwhile as long as the transaction costs (expressed in distance) are less than his or her consumer surplus. When the person is buying lower-value items, on a proportional basis, the consumer surplus is less. Therefore, going to a more distant location and spending more on transaction costs is not worthwhile, meaning that for indispensable yet low-value daily consumption goods, consumers accept buying them from a convenience store adjacent to their community at a slightly higher price.

When buying higher value products that have a higher consumer surplus, such as televisions, accordingly, consumers are willing to go to relatively far electronics stores. If they own cars, they are willing to go farther afield.

Conversely, suppose that every consumer acts similarly. The scale of the farther market will be larger because more customers come from long distances. Such a distance is the customer radius of this market.

Larger and farther markets can have fewer varieties of products because the larger amount of each commodity sale (because of a higher number of customers) and higher prices enable these markets to reach a breakeven point.

Of course, a larger market (such as a supermarket) can have greater varieties, which reflects the economies of scope in purchasing. Given a scope economy in purchasing, a scale economy in purchasing also exists because one can buy a variety of goods such that the total value of the purchase and the consumer surplus are higher and going a longer distance is worthwhile. However, this topic is not the focus of this chapter.

11.3 The Utility of Variety of the Specialized Market

In turn, from the perspective of investors and considering these consumer characteristics, they could establish a specialized market with the same amount of capital. The so-called specialized characteristic could represent a large category of products, such as building materials; a small category, such as building ceramics; or one or a few types, such as ceramic tile. A product with fewer varieties is more "specialized." Features of this specialization are in the various brands or varieties, such as apparel and ceramic tile, and the varieties represent the values of the product. Similar to nature, there are no best flowers, only blossoms in a riot of color. The higher the number of varieties, the wider the consumers' selection scope, and for them to select products from varieties that they prefer becomes more possible. **Ceteris paribus, more varieties mean more consumer surplus.**

Assume that the capital scale is certain, and the unit price is the same. It can be proven that:

- A more specialized market has a greater consumer surplus than a less specialized one.
- Prices in the more specialized market are lower than in a less specialized one.
- The covering radius of a more specialized market is larger than that of a less specialized one; and,
- A more specialized market has more customers than a less specialized one (Fig. 11.1).

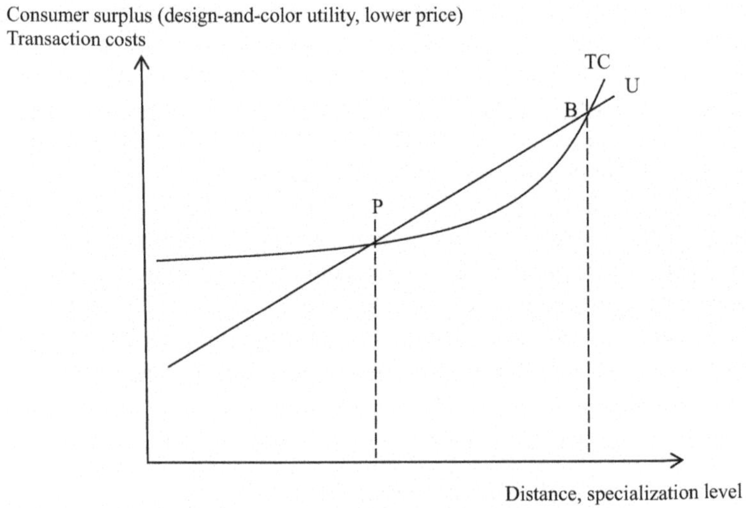

Fig. 11.1 Costs and benefits of specialized markets. Note: Assuming that a closer market is associated with a lower degree of specialization, a farther market is associated with a higher degree of specialization. Moreover, a more specialized market has a greater variety of the same commodity, and such a greater variety of the same commodity results in a higher consumer surplus, as shown by curve U in this figure. Transaction costs (TC) increase as distance increases, but in the beginning only increase in the same proportion as the increase in distance. After a certain distance, transaction costs increase rapidly. If the distance is too far to make a return trip on the same day, paying for accommodations is necessary

Going to a closer, smaller market is not worthwhile when there are fewer varieties and a lower consumer surplus. For example, one has very few choices, if any, when buying a TV in a small supermarket near the community. When going to a more distant (farther than P) electrical store with more varieties, the consumer surplus may be higher than the transaction costs. When the distance is father than b and transaction costs exceed the consumer surplus, going to that market is also not worthwhile.

However, if the purchaser is not an individual but a business, the quantity of each deal is much higher than that of individual purchases. If the commodity price does not change, the consumer surplus increases significantly and transaction costs do not increase proportionally. Therefore, companies can purchase products from a more distant place. Usually, companies purchase raw materials, such as a real estate decoration company purchasing large quantities of decorative building materials or a garment enterprise buying large quantities of buttons.

Furthermore, if the buyers are wholesalers, they may purchase on a large scale. Even if they cannot earn much money between the wholesale and retail prices of each product, the total gross margin for a transaction is very high from the large volume. Therefore, they can afford to travel to a farther, larger, and more specialized market.

Conversely, if many individuals, businesses, and wholesalers are willing to travel to farther and more specialized markets, they have their rationality of existence.

11.4 Why Could a More Specialized Market Be Larger, Ceteris Paribus?

If other conditions remain the same, such as regions, population density distribution, and market investment scale, a more specialized market can have a greater covering diameter and cover a larger crowd of people. Meanwhile, it can only provide potential consumers with smaller proportions of commodities given its specialization. The utility of variety is a function of the level of market specialization, as is the consumer spending ratio. That is:

$$\mathrm{Uk} = f(\mathrm{Sk});$$

$$\mathrm{Cr} = f_1(\mathrm{Sk});$$

Uk is the utility of variety;
Sk is the specialization level;
Cr is the consumer spending ratio.

If we describe the market specialization level using the ratio of expenditures for a particular type of product to total expenditures, then:

$$\mathrm{Cr} = f_1(\mathrm{Sk}) = \mathrm{Sk};$$

Here,

$$0 \le \text{Sk} \le 1; \text{Sk} = 0 \text{ indicates extreme specialization; Sk} = 1 \text{ indicates no specialization;}$$

$$0 \le \text{Uk} \le 1; \text{Uk} = 0 \text{ indicates one product has only one variety; Uk} = 1 \text{ indicates that there are full varieties; and}$$

$$0 \le \text{Cr} \le 1; \text{Cr} = 0 \text{ indicates that the ratio to total expenditure is } 0; \text{Cr} = 1 \text{ indicates that the ratio to total expenditures is } 100\%.$$

$$\text{Obviously, when Sk} \to 0, \text{Uk} \to 1, \text{and Cr} \to 0.$$

The market covering diameter is the function of the utility of variety and, thus, the complex function of the level of market specialization. That is:

$$R = f(\text{Uk}) = g(f(\text{Sk}))$$

Which means that when Sk→0时, R→∞.

We can assume the function as

$$\text{Uk} = 1 - \text{Sk}^{\rho} \tag{11.1}$$

P is the varieties preference coefficient; generally, $0 \le \rho \le 1$.

A smaller ρ indicates greater insensitivity to varieties. The following chart describes $\rho = 1$ (standard) and $\rho = 0.3$

As is shown by the blue line in Fig. 11.2, if people are equally sensitive to each degree of specialization, their utility of varieties steadily increases. More empirically, people are less sensitive to a tiny increase in variety; however, in a highly specialized market with large varieties, people's utility of variety increases significantly, as is shown by the red line in Fig. 11.2.

Put simply, assume that $\rho = 1$; then:

$$R = \text{Uk} / \text{tc} = (1 - \text{Sk}) / \text{tc} \tag{11.2}$$

Here, tc represents unit transaction costs, that is, transaction costs per kilometer. Because most other variables are in the interval [0, 1], the longest distance can be represented by a very long distance, such as 1000 km, as 1, then 1 km is 0.001. If the cost per kilometer is 10 yuan, the unit

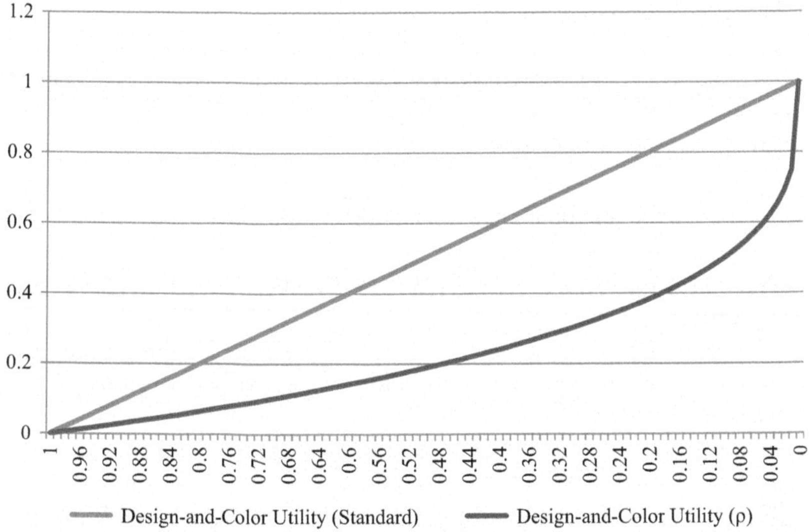

Fig. 11.2 The utility of variety and specialized level. Explanation: The vertical axis in this figure indicates the utility of the varieties, whereas the horizontal axis indicates the degree of specialization and left to right indicates that the degree of specialization increases; the blue line represents the varieties preference coefficient $p = 1$, and the red line represents $p = 0.3$

transaction cost is 0.01. We can also set tc according to the proportion of the actual unit transaction cost to the expected consumer surplus. If the expected consumer surplus is 1000 yuan, costs per kilometer are 10 yuan, and the unit transaction cost is also 0.01. These data should be adjusted according to the empirical evidence.

The market scale depends on income, which depends on population within the market covering diameter (N) and how much they spend on buying products in that market coverage. The latter depends on the average total expenditure for consumption (c) per person and the ratio of expenditure on products from this marketplace to total expenditure (Cr). That is:

$$\begin{aligned} I &= N * C * Cr = \left[\pi R^2 n\right] * C * Cr \\ &= \pi n * C * Cr * R^2 = \pi n * C * Sk * \left[(1 - Sk) / tc\right]^2 \\ &= \pi n * C * Sk * (1 - Sk)^2 / tc^2 = \pi n * C * Sk * \left(1 - 2Sk + Sk^2\right) / tc^2 \end{aligned}$$

N is population density.

$$I = \pi n * C * \left(Sk - 2Sk^2 + Sk^3\right) / tc^2 \tag{11.3}$$

The derivative of both sides is

$$dI / dSk = \pi n * C * \left(1 - 4Sk + 3Sk^2\right) / tc^2$$

The following figure describes ($Sk - 2Sk^2 + Sk^3$) in function (11.3) and its derivative.

Obviously, Fig. 11.3 shows that a market's degree of specialization is related to its benefits and that an optimum value exists depending on the varieties preferences.

When the rate at which the covering population increases given a more specialized market is higher than the rate at which the consumption ratio decreases, the covering radius of this specialized market continues to extend until the point at which the rate of increase in the population equals the rate at which the consumption ratio decreases.

That is,

$$dI / dSk > 0, \text{the market covering radius is likely to increase;}$$
$$dI / dSk < 0, \text{the market covering radius is likely to decrease; and,}$$
$$dI / dSk = 0, \text{the market covering radius reaches a balanced point.}$$

Then

$$dI / dSk = 0 = \pi n * C * \left(1 - 4Sk + 3Sk^2\right) / tc^2$$
$$3Sk^2 - 4Sk + 1 = 0$$
$$Sk_1 = 4 + \left(16 - 12\right)^{1/2} / 6 = 1$$
$$Sk_2 = 4 - \left(16 - 12\right)^{1/2} / 6 = 1/3$$

Substitute $Sk_2 = 1/3$ into function (11.3)

$$I = \pi n * C * \left(Sk - 2Sk^2 + Sk^3\right) / tc^2 = 0.148137 * \pi n * C / tc^2$$

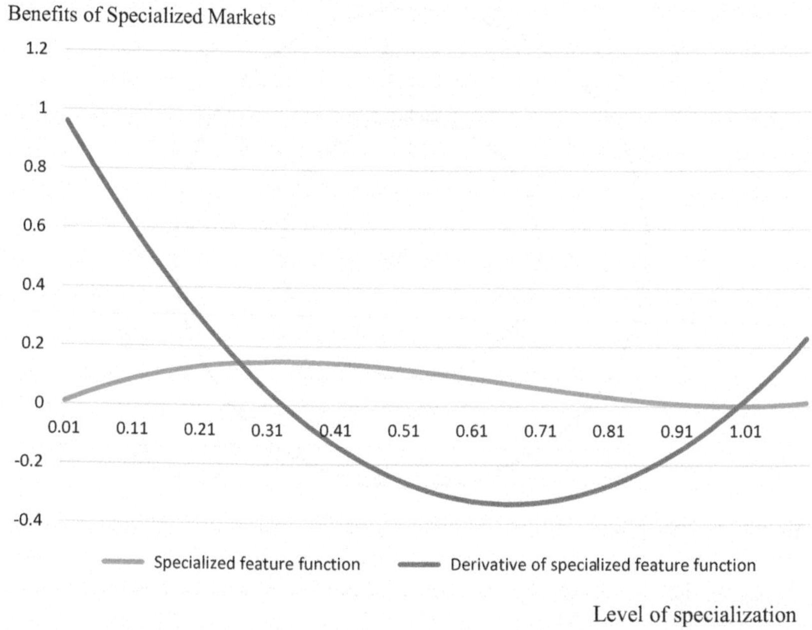

Fig. 11.3 Specialized feature function. Note: The vertical axis represents the benefits of specialization, and the horizontal axis shows the level of specialization. The value of 0 on the horizontal axis indicates the highest level of specialization, and 1 indicates no specialization. The area greater than 1 does not make sense

The value 0.148137 is the maximum value of the benefits when the specialization level is at its optimal. The specialized characteristic function is the blue curve in Fig. 11.5. With an increase in the degree of specialization, the value of the specialized characteristic function becomes higher, indicating that, in a certain range, a higher degree of specialization results in a higher utility of varieties, more consumers, and thus more revenue; its value peaks (0.148) until the degree of specialization reaches 0.33. After the peak, revenues decrease. **This finding proves that, within a certain range, a more specialized market can bring more consumer surplus and customers than less specialized ones.**

When $\rho = 0.3$, function (11.3) is represented by the red curve.

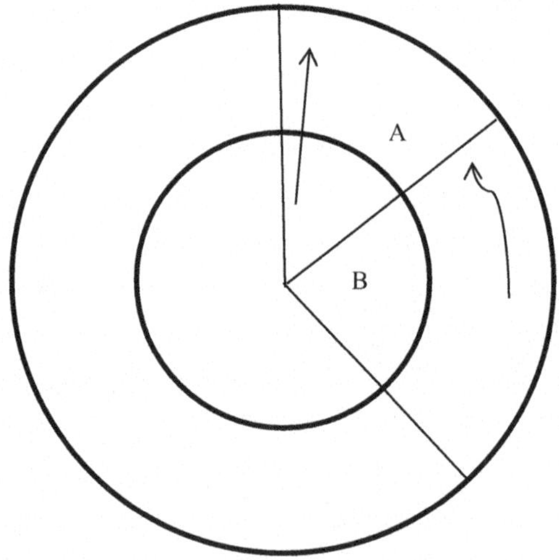

Fig. 11.4 Diameters of the specialized market and ratio of consumption to the total expenses in the market. Note: The round space represents the total expenses of the population covered by the market diameter. When the market becomes more specialized, the diameter expands and the ratio of consumption to total expenditures declines. In this chapter, when the market extends from a small circle to a big circle, area A is added, and area B is lost. When area A is larger than area B, the diameter of the market continues to expand until the two areas are equal

Multiply $\pi n * C/tc^2$ with the function of the red curve to estimate the market scale, as described in Fig. 11.6.

Change the coordinates:

$$R = \left(1 - SK^{\rho}\right) / tc$$

Assume that $SK^{\rho} = x$

When $\rho = 1$, $x = (1 - R * tc)$

When $\rho < 1$时, $x = (1 - R * tc)^{\rho}$

Substitute it into function (11.3)

$$I = \pi n * C * \left(\left(1 - R * tc\right)^{\rho} - 2\left(1 - R * tc\right)^{2\rho} + \left(1 - R * tc\right)^{3\rho}\right) / tc^2$$

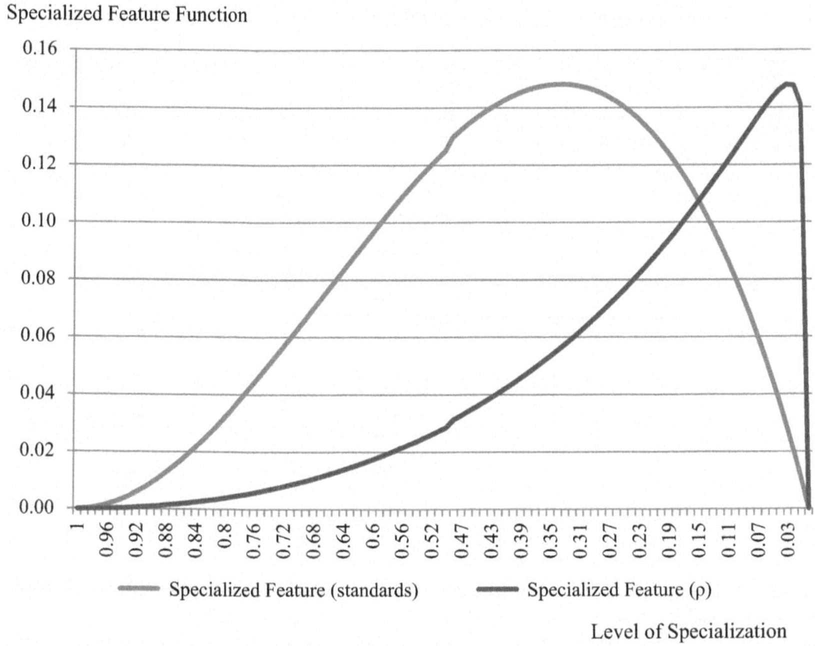

Fig. 11.5 Specialization level and benefits

$(1-R*tc)^{Á}-2(1-R*tc)^{2Á}+(1-R*tc)^{3Á}$ is the specialized characteristic function with the market radius as the x-coordinate, as described in Fig. 11.7.

In Fig. 11.7, $\rho = 1$ is the blue curve, and $\rho = 0.03$ is the red curve. In this case, the radius of the specialized market under the blue curve is approximately 67 km, and that under the red curve is 98 km. **Therefore, when people are less sensitive to a smaller increase in the varieties but very sensitive to significant varieties, a specialized market can be farther, or its market radius can be even larger.**

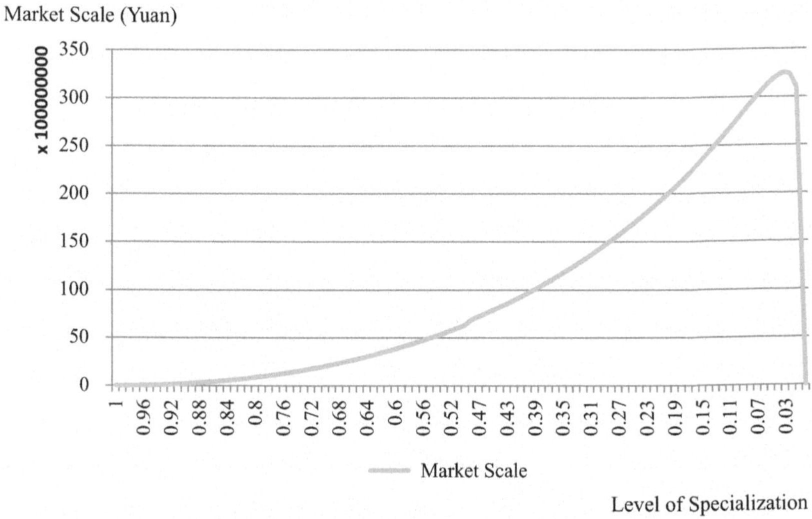

Fig. 11.6 Specialization level and market scale. In this case, when the degree of specialization is 0.02, the scale of the specialized market is approximately 32.4 billion yuan. The market scale is smaller if the degree of specialization is lower than or higher than this point. **This figure proves that, within a certain range, the scale of a more specialized market is larger than that of a less specialized one**

11.5 Conclusion

In the past, economics only talked about the market without reference to a specific time-space and lacked the specialization of time-space. When discussing the spatial agglomeration of human beings, space economics mostly focused on the agglomeration of production but less on the agglomeration of transactions. The discussion of a specialized market includes a market with a specific time-space for specialized transactions.

The specialization of production is shown to increase benefits by streamlining operations, increasing production volume, and facilitating machine production, whereas specialization of transactions increases consumer surplus by increasing the varieties of a certain product. Within a certain range, regarding the trading of products with many varieties, a more specialized market results in greater varieties and a more super-valued consumer surplus, which is the utility of variety.

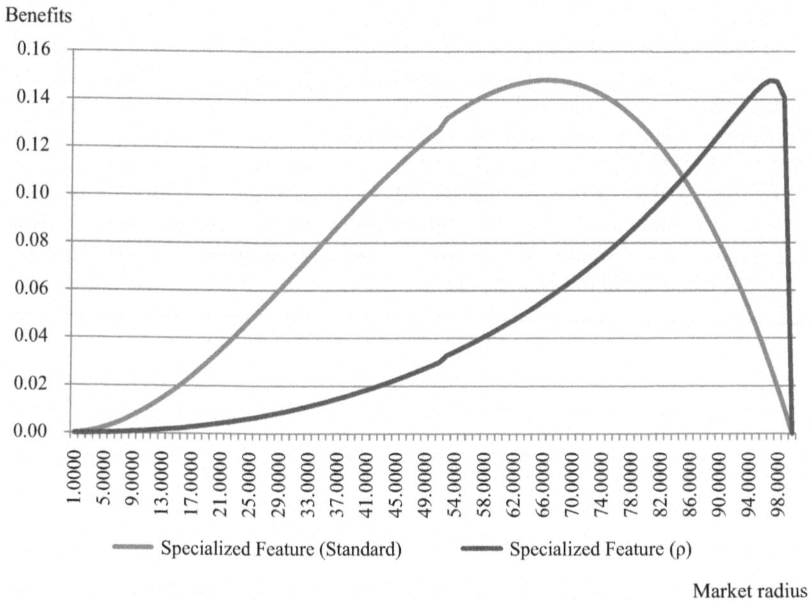

Fig. 11.7 Specialization level and market radius

People are willing to pay for a higher utility of varieties and go further, which is paying higher transaction costs, until their travel expenses offset the increase in consumer surplus from the utility of variety. Therefore, a more specialized market may have a larger radius, more consumers, larger-scale, and higher profits. Under the same conditions, a more specialized market has a larger market scale than a less specialized one, that is, a larger radius, more consumers, and higher profits.

Therefore, the specialized market has its economic rationality.

References

国家统计局, 《中国统计年鉴 (2014)》, 中国统计出版社, 2014. (National Bureau of Statistics, China Statistics Yearbook (2014), China Statistics Press, 2014).

浙江省统计局, 《浙江省统计年鉴 (2014)》, 浙江统计信息网, 2014. (Zhejiang Bureau of Statistics, Zhejiang Statistics Yearbook (2014), Zhejiang Statistics Information Net, 2014).

国家统计局贸易外经统计司，中国商业联合会信息部编，《中国商品交易市场统计年鉴—2001》，中国统计出版社，2001. (The Trade Statistics Division of National Bureau of Statistics, Information Department of China General Chamber of Commerce, *China Commodity Exchange Market Statistics Yearbook-2001*, China Statistics Press, 2001).

国家统计局贸易外经统计司，中国商业联合会信息部编，《中国商品交易市场统计年鉴—2014》，中国统计出版社，2014. (The Trade Statistics Division of National Bureau of Statistics, Information Department of China General Chamber of Commerce, *China Commodity Exchange Market Statistics Yearbook-2014*, China Statistics Press, 2014).

CHAPTER 12

A General Theory of Rent-Seeking: Rent Dissipating, Rent Keeping, and Rent-Seeking

Contents

Rent is a natural economic phenomenon that enables us to understand the value of scarce resources and to measure and judge this value. However, when people discover and grasp this value, they may take advantage of its nature to seize benefits. The method for seizing benefits may promote the effective use and efficiency of resources and may also seek benefits for themselves at the expense of harming the interests of others and society. This situation requires an in-depth discussion of the concept of "rent."

12.1 The Concept of Rent and Its Generalization

The concept of "rent" used in rent-seeking theory is an extension of the traditional concept of land rent. The term "rent" in terms of land rent mainly refers to the difference in the value of different resources used for

Translated from *Academics* (《学术界》), Issue 1, 2016.

Sheng Hong, *Vision and Calculation*,
https://doi.org/10.1007/978-981-15-2898-9_12

the same purpose, that is, differential rent. An extreme form is the difference between the value produced by a resource and that produced by the absence of such a resource, which is the so-called absolute rent or economic rent.

People will soon find that rent can also be produced by artificial means. If a technological monopoly is obtained through technological innovation, rent can be created by controlling production or directly setting the price. Another way is to impose a mandatory restriction on the supply of a resource or product through legal or administrative means. Of course, the former is productive, and the latter is unproductive.

Another concept of "rent" is the difference between the value of a resource's optimal use and suboptimal use. The difference from the previous concept of rent is that it is a choice between multiple uses of resources—different uses, different demand functions, different supply functions, and different incomes. For example, the demand function of a singer singing in a bar is different from that in an opera house, and the number of competent singers is different. These differences lead to different equilibrium prices, and the difference between the equilibrium prices for two uses is rent.

The number of singers for different purposes is different, and the supply function is different. The rent depends on the supply of resources. Economic rent is the difference between the value obtained by using the resource and that without it, and the latter is obviously zero. However, unlike economic rent, the "rent" here is the difference between the value of the best use and the value of the second-best use, and the latter is not zero. See Fig. 12.2a.

Even though they are different, the concepts of these two types of rents share common characteristics. First, they are all caused by the quantity limit of the resources supply. Second, they also affect the quantity of products or services produced by the resources. Therefore, the two concepts of rent can be generalized into one concept of rent.

Specifically, we can also assume that planting different crops on a piece of land produces different market values. We can also assume that different singers sing in the same opera house, and the audience is willing to pay different prices. The most general differential rent between one farming field and another is the difference in value between two fields when they are planting the most marketable crops. The differential rent between one singer and another is also the difference in remuneration between two singers who are singing in the place at which they receive the highest remuneration.

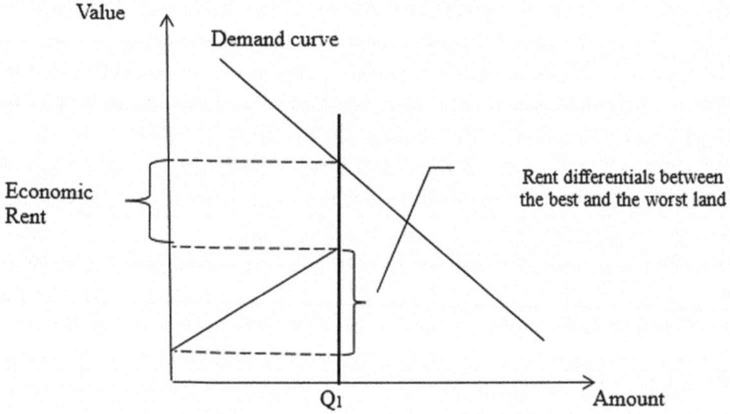

Fig. 12.1 Land rent. Note: Q_1 is the ceiling of the resource supply

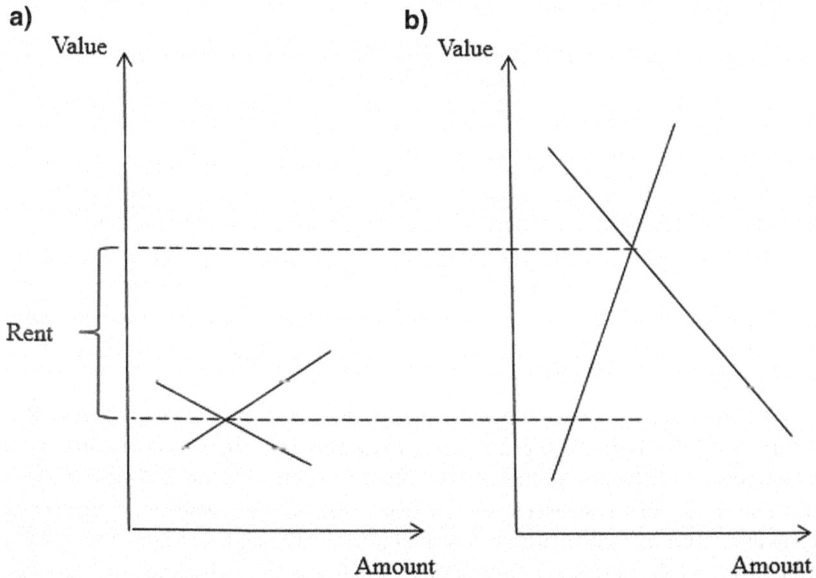

Fig. 12.2 (**a**) Singer's Supply and Demand Function in Bar. (**b**) Singer's Supply and Demand Function in Opera

Because a variety of resources have such a nature, rent has long been not limited to land rent but also applied to almost all resources.

More generally, because all economic resources are scarce in total for various reasons (natural or artificial), economic rent is more or less formed. Even with no scarcity in total, at least differential rent exists.

More strictly speaking, differential land rent is the scarcity caused by the limited quantity of better land. It is the cost difference between better resources and poorer resources of the same kind.

The cost function is matched by various resources, and each resource has its own quality differences that lead to different costs and differentiated rents. Moreover, all types of resources may be scarce in total for natural and human-made reasons, forming economic rents. Therefore, the producer surplus that is formed by the cost function's intersection with the demand function can also be broadly called "rent."

Thus, more generally, as Steven Cheung said, "rent" is almost equal to "income" (Cheung 1970).

12.2 Generalization of the Concept of Rent Dissipation

If we accept Steven Cheung's general concept of rent, the concept of rent dissipation is equivalent to the loss of social welfare. Therefore, the traditional and inconsistent concept of rent dissipation needs to be redefined. To date, roughly three scenarios exist concerning rent dissipation.

The first is the situation in which resources are limited for natural reasons. Steven Cheung pointed out that, in the case of economic rent from limited resources, if no exclusive property rights exist, the influx of entrants eventually reduces the rent to zero (Cheung 1970), as indicated in Fig. 12.3.

In this case, the so-called rent dissipation is only the decrease in the input–output rate of each person or the increase in the unit cost caused by an increase in fishermen, and the decrease in their income as a whole from the use of fishery resources, which does not affect consumers' interests. However, the loss of producers is also a loss of social welfare. Therefore, according to the most generalized definition of "rent dissipation," as previously mentioned, it is a kind of rent dissipation.

The second situation is that a limited resource supply is caused by the restriction of human factors on access to the supply of certain resources or

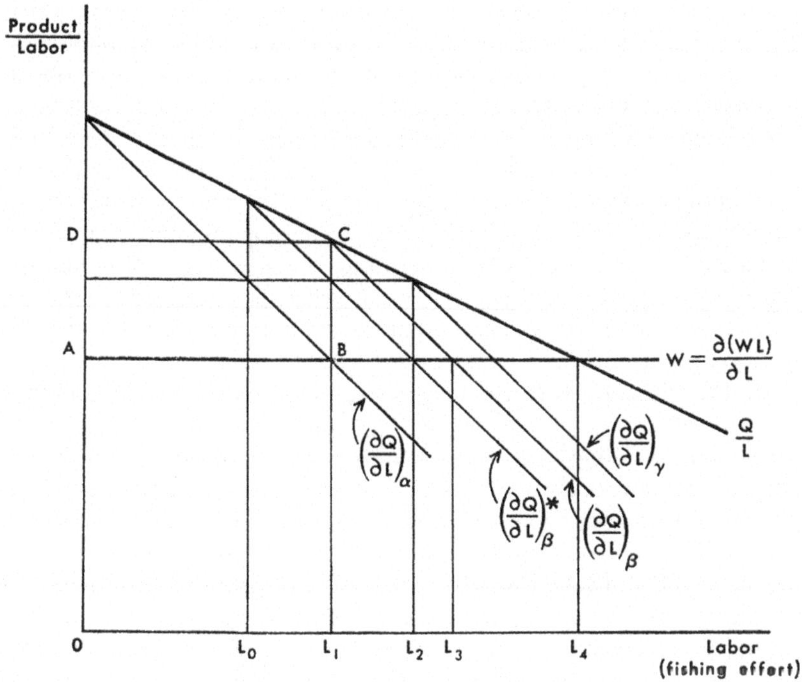

Fig. 12.3 Schematic diagram of rental dissipation of certain-scope fishing grounds
Source: The Structure of a Contract and the Theory of a Non-Exclusive Resource, Cheung 1970
Explanation: The assumption is that a certain range of fishing grounds exists, no exclusive property rights exist, and people can enter freely to obtain rent value. The vertical axis represents the amount of fishing per unit of labor, and the horizontal axis represents the amount of fishing or input. Because fishery resources are determined, when the number of fishermen increases and the amount of fishing per unit of labor decreases. The *w* in this figure indicates the marginal cost of the wage rate or labor factor. When the first person enters, the rent value is the area of rectangle ABCD; when the second person enters, the total rent value decreases; and when more people enter, the total rent value further decreases until it completely disappears (Cheung 1970)

products. This restriction can be divided into two situations. One is that enterprises invent new products or new processes through technological innovation, resulting in significant cost reductions. Enterprises obtain monopoly rights through patent protection, and other enterprises' entry is restricted, resulting in rent. As a result of new products or processes, new value has obviously been created out of nothing; therefore, although a monopoly exists, social welfare also increases. The rent formed by a patent monopoly is the return of the cost of technological innovation. When the patent period is over, other enterprises can enter freely. Although the enterprise's original rent disappears, social welfare has increased. Therefore, at this time, the disappearance of rent should not be regarded as the dissipation of rent value.

Another situation is that enterprises set up entry control by lobbying the government or conspiring with people within the administrative department, resulting in an increase in the scarcity of supply and, hence, rent. At this time, because of this kind of artificial entry control, supply is lower than that under competitive circumstances, resulting in the loss of social welfare known as the "Harberger Triangle" (equivalent to the light gray part of Fig. 12.4). Moreover, because lobbying the government or conspiring with officials requires resources, the maximum can be equivalent to the net present value of future rents. We know that the so-called rent here is not a newly created value but, instead, a transfer from consumers to producers through regulation. Therefore, the resources consumed for setting rent are the loss of social welfare and the dissipation of rent value. This part is called the "Turlock Rectangle" (see the dark gray part in Fig. 12.4). In this case, the sum of the "Harberger Triangle" and the "Turlock Rectangle" is the total amount of rent dissipation.

When the artificial factors of restricting entry are eliminated, the entrants increase and the price drops to the Sc level. The rent value originally formed by restricting entry disappears, and consumers gain this part of the benefit. The elimination of the "Harberger Triangle" means an increase in social welfare. Therefore, this deregulation process cannot be called rent dissipation.

The third case is the dissipation of rent value brought about by the government's price control. Steven Cheung offered many discussions about this situation. In his doctoral dissertation, *The Theory of Share Tenancy*, he pointed out that the "375 rent reduction" in Taiwan is equivalent to the price control of resources and that the reduced part of the rent is not exclusively granted to certain individuals. Therefore, tenants can

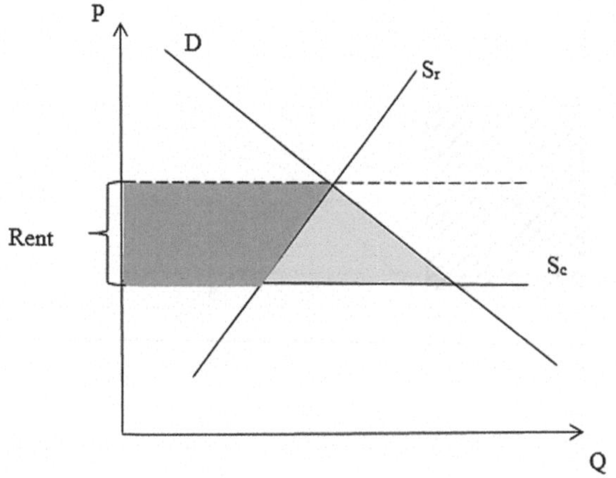

Fig. 12.4 Schematic diagram of deregulation of entry
Note: When free entry is available, the industry is completely competitive, and the supply curve is the horizontal line Sc; when entry is regulated, the supply curve is Sr and the rent value corresponds to the dark gray rectangular part. If there is no exclusive right to occupy this part of the rent, in order to obtain this part of the rent, people would consume this part of the rent in the competition. The equivalent part of the light gray triangle is the loss of social welfare. The latter is the loss caused by the pursuit of entry regulations, which is also the dissipation of rent. When entry control is abolished, a large number of enterprises enter, putting the supply curve back to the state of Sc. Then, the dark gray and light gray parts disappeared.

rent land competitively among themselves and landowners are willing to increase the labor force on a unit of land, which leads to excessive labor input and a decrease in marginal labor productivity. If the rent rate is reduced to zero, the marginal labor productivity can be negative (Steven Cheung 2000, pp. 166–169).

Subsequently, Steven Cheung pointed out in his article, "A Theory of Price Control," that as long as price control exists, the rent formed by the difference between the market price and the controlled price is completely offset by the reduced marginal productivity of labor.

To summarize, the rents generated by price controls are relative to those of consumers/demanders. If no one has the exclusive right to occupy these rents, they are inevitably dissipated (Cheung 1974), which is a pure loss of social welfare. Two specific cases also exist.

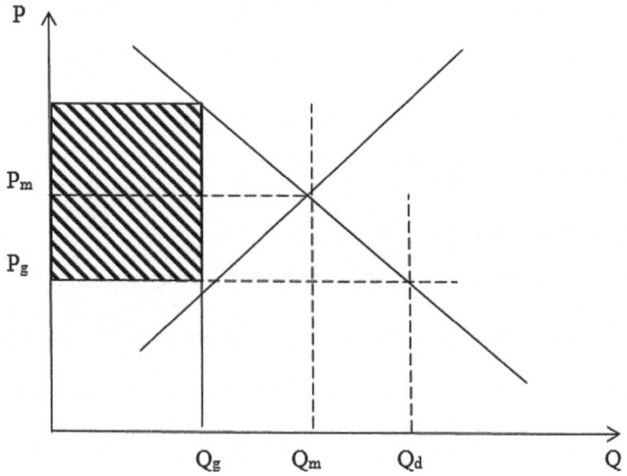

Fig. 12.5 Rent dissipation of consumers
Note: In this figure, the market equilibrium price is Pm. When the government lowers the price to P_g, the output decreases from Q_m to Q_g, and the demand increases to Q_d. In the case of a shortage, consumers compete in the form of queuing, and the total queuing time is the rental value consumed, as shown in the striped section. Of course, the part equivalent to the Harberger Triangle is also the rent dissipation part

One is the case by Steven Cheung, as previously described: the price controls of a natural resource leads to rents relative to those who use it. Because this part of the rent has no exclusive property rights, the rent value is dissipated in the competition among resource users. This situation is quite similar to the first case, in which rents are caused by a natural scarcity of resources. The results are similar regardless of the differences in causes. Rent dissipation occurs at the cost of reducing the marginal productivity of the resource (usually labor) owners competing for rent. A detailed discussion can be found in Steven Cheung's The Theory of Share Tenancy (2000, 152–157). Obviously, this situation is a type of social welfare loss and can be called "rent dissipation."

Another case is for pure consumers. For example, the government controls the price of certain consumer goods, such as medicines. The part of the regulated price that is lower than the market price is the rent relative to the consumer. However, because no consumer has the exclusive right to occupy the rent, a competition occurs among them to obtain the rent. Unlike competition among fishers, adopting technology and spending

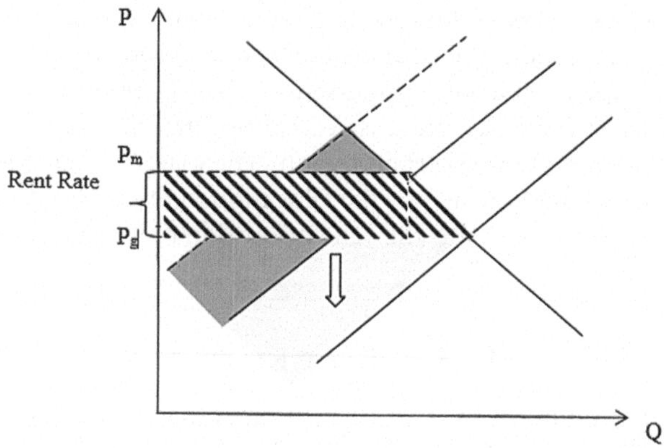

Fig. 12.6 Rent dissipation caused by moving to areas with higher rent
Note: This figure shows that a region that is given special preferential treatment by the government can obtain more service resources, such as medical treatment or education, than other regions. This situation lowers the actual price of services in the region (P_g, including consideration of reduced waiting) to under the average level (P_m), which obviously brings additional benefits to the population in the region (the white area in this figure). However, this price reduction occurs at the expense of reducing investments elsewhere. Therefore, the extra benefits in this area are offset by additional losses in other areas (the gray part). Moreover, because of the sufficient supply of services in the region and the low real price, people in other regions move to the region to consume related services. Such an influx brings about travel costs and reduces the additional benefits of the region. As a result, the rent dissipation brought about by the allocation of resources by the administrative department also includes the striped area in this figure.

labor to acquire such resources is not necessary; they can simply be bought. Under the controlled price, because the supply declines and the demand is much more than the supply, the fair way to obtain rent is to queue up. However, if queuing is regarded as a special kind of labor, the result is similar to that previously, which leads to rent dissipation.

Considering that the current government still has direct control over resources, a fourth situation exists in the formation of rent and the dissipation of rent value. For example, under certain geographical distributions of consumers, the government can allocate more supply resources to a certain region through direct allocation, resulting in rents that differ from those in competitive situations. At the same time, given the distorted allocation of resources, although they are naturally exclusive because of geographical separation, these "rents" for specific groups of people are still subject to competition from outsiders given that the population can move freely. Outsiders only pay the cost of transportation, accommodations, and so on for traveling to a certain region. The marginal maximum of this cost can equal the rent created by the allocation of resources by the administrative department, causing the rent of outside rent-seekers to dissipate at the same time.

12.3 Rent Keeping

An important condition for rent dissipation is that no exclusive property right to the rent exists. When people see that the rent is going to dissipate, they think about whether they can take some measures to retain the rent that will be dissipated. Of course, the simplest way is to establish formal exclusive property rights. However, the reason for rent dissipation is precisely because no formal exclusive property rights exist.

Therefore, in the absence of formal exclusive property rights, that people can consider various ways to exclude competition from others is logical and enables them to have some exclusive right to the rent to be dissipated. Excluding competition can be done in roughly two ways. One is the contract, and the other is the power of the government.

The so-called contract method is to avoid regulation and achieve rent keeping through the contract between the relevant parties. Of course, at this time, because government regulations do not allow such contracts, they are obviously informal contracts—at least not protected by the government—and may even violate the law. Because both parties consent to the terms of the contract, the reason that they can agree is that they have exchanged satisfactory goods with each other. More simply, one party may enter into a contract with the other party by paying in currency, which means that, in the presence of regulations, concluding contracts improves the allocation of resources and brings about efficiency improvements. At this time, the meaning of rent keeping is not only that some economic parties have obtained some rents that might have dissipated but also that all of society has reduced welfare losses through their rent-keeping activities. There are several forms.

First, complementary products depend on price-regulated products whose prices are unregulated. When consumers want to buy products with regulated prices, they must also buy complementary products at the same time. At this time, sellers can use the higher prices of complementary products as subsidiary products of regulated products to sell as compensation for the dissipation of rent caused by price controls. For example, Steven Cheung found that when rental building prices are regulated, the owner can set a higher rental price for furniture in the house to compensate for the loss of rent control, that is, to leave part of the rent (1974, p. 63). Similarly, medical services and medicines are complementary products. When the price of medical services is regulated, if the price of medicines is not regulated, doctors will use more expensive medicines to compensate for the loss from the price control of medical services.

Second, the adjacent contract. As Steven Cheung stated, when the Hong Kong authorities restrict the rental price of buildings, the owners evade price controls by subletting and installing rooftop wooden houses, thus retaining three-quarters of the rental value (Cheung 2000, F25–F28).

Third, private transactions between suppliers and demanders. For example, when the price of medical services is regulated, the patients' family members gave the doctor red envelopes. Because doctors provide services with their human capital, the quality of the services depends on their decisions. Price controls depress a doctor's income but fail to control the quality of his services. Patients' family members can mobilize the human capital input of doctors by using red envelopes.

Fourth, suppliers avoid price control areas and go to areas without price controls or with weak price controls to provide products or services. If a doctor goes to other hospitals where the price control of medical services is not strict, he or she can obtain a higher income than from his or her hospital.

Fifth, those on the demand side go to areas with many more human resources to obtain products or services. For example, patients go to big cities to seek medical treatment or "college entrance examination immigrants," and so on.

Sixth, products or services can be provided to regulated industries by signing contracts with consumers in different technological ways, such as Alipay and other Internet banking access to banking businesses.

Seventh, the right to enter an industry can be obtained by signing a contract with an enterprise that has an access permit. A joint venture with a telecommunications licensed enterprise is equivalent to entering the telecommunications industry.

Eighth, a contract can be signed with an entrance licensed enterprise to provide its upstream or downstream products or services and to obtain rent in part. If a telecommunication enterprise has an entry permit, it acts as an agent for its marketing business. Another example is signing a contract with a bank that has an entry permit to obtain a loan and transferring it.

Ninth, quota trading. In the field of quantity control, trading in quantity quotas can improve the allocation of resources and partly obtain rent value. Examples in the planned economy period include grain ticket transactions, later foreign exchange quota transactions, and now land-development-rights transactions.

Tenth, privately change the content of the contract. For example, during the "three-level ownerships and based on production team" period of the People's Commune, some production teams privately contracted with households on outputs, in fact, changing the contract of fixed working points into a fixed rent and tax contract.

Eleventh, alternative service contracts. That is, when people compete for rent nonexclusively, some people provide professional services to enable others to obtain competitive advantages at lower costs, such as vendors queuing professionally to buy and resell tickets, enabling buyers to save competitive costs. Of course, when tickets are improperly obtained, such as through the control of department or enterprise, this rent-seeking activity is another kind of rent-keeping activity.

Twelfth, retail licenses of institutions with entry permits. For example, publishing houses sell book permit numbers in the publishing industry, and its entry is regulated.

12.4 Rent-Seeking

Another form of rent keeping is to use government power to obtain certain exclusive rights in the competition for rent, which may be dissipated because of regulations, to retain rent value. This kind of rent keeping can be called rent-seeking.

Because this kind of rent-keeping activity relies on the government's power, a corresponding exchange may not necessarily exist, and specific economic parties take precedence over other parties to obtain rent value, which may not necessarily lead to the reduction of social welfare losses. Reducing, increasing, and remaining unchanged, which also take several forms, are possible.

First, in the presence of entry regulations, enterprises or individuals can obtain entry permits by paying money to administrative agencies or government officials. This so-called payment of money can be in a "legal" form to pay administrative fees or can be a private bribe to government officials. The former situation was very common in the 1980s and 1990s, when the registration and entry of enterprises into the market were subject to approval by the administrative department, which required the payment of management fees. In the latter case, we need to pay a significant amount to solve the problem, such as when wanting to obtain business licenses in some industries now. Such payments may lead to improving resource allocation under regulatory conditions and reducing social welfare losses.

Second, in the case of price regulations (low price) and excluding other competitors, relying on the power of administrative agencies or officials can provide preferential access to low-cost products or services. For example, during a competition to enter a school, some administrative departments adopt "coconstruction" with the school to obtain priority for their children to enter; other officials rely on "approval notes" to place some students in a good school. This form may not necessarily lead to a reduction in and may even increase social welfare losses because the students who are placed are not necessarily superior to other students.

Third, in the case of price regulations (low price), the relevant administrative departments and their officials can also sell their regulated products in batches on the black market to earn a profit. For example, in the case of low train fares, a large number of train tickets flow out of the railway department into the hands of scalpers. Whether this situation has improved the allocation of resources under controlled conditions is difficult to judge because railways are likely to deliberately restrict window ticket sales to obtain a black market price increase. However, if a real shortage of train tickets exists, the purchase of black-market tickets also improves the allocation of resources.

Fourth, when special rules exist for the access of the demanders, administrative departments can establish rules that are beneficial to themselves by influencing policies or regulations, allowing them to preferentially enjoy restricted services. When other people want to use this rule to enter, they can be charged a fee. For example, the "self-enrollment" policy at colleges and universities is conducive to the children of policymakers, whereas children of other groups can also enter by bribing officials.

Obviously, whether by power or money, this form leads to the deterioration of resource allocation.

Fifth, when prices of products or services are set by the administrative department, the enterprise can influence these prices by bribing people in the department. For example, officials in charge of drug prices in the Price Department of the National Development and Reform Commission (Zhao Chenxi, Gao Xin, 2014) were sent to jail because of bribery.

Sixth, in the case of quality and technology regulations, enterprises obtain quality or technology licenses by paying money to administrative departments or officials. For example, Zheng Xiaoyu, director of the Bureau of Medicine Supervision, accepted bribes and approved a large number of new drugs (Beijing First Intermediate People's Court, 2007). In this case, whether this rent-seeking has brought about improvements in resource allocation is also difficult to judge. On the one hand, the rent-seeking may shorten the process of approving new drugs but, on the other hand, may bring unqualified new drugs into the market.

Generally, rent-keeping activities take contractual or governmental actions to create some degree of exclusiveness without formal exclusive property rights and enable the parties concerned to obtain part of the rent value that otherwise may be dissipated. Through this process, we can conclude that the rent-keeping process has also brought about improvements in resource allocation if the contractual mode is adopted and that, if government means are adopted, we cannot judge whether resource allocation has improved.

Even if rent-seeking through government power may improve resource allocation under regulatory conditions, such actions cannot be said to be efficient because they are motivated to establish more regulations. In a word, rent-seeking is an undesired practice.

In a fully competitive market without market failure, the equilibrium price is determined by competition among multiple competitors on both sides of a transaction. At this time, the allocation of resources determined by the equilibrium price is efficient and fair.

The administrative department's intervention in such an equilibrium market, that is, setting rent, results in the aforementioned changes in resource allocation, which is inefficient. This intervention also results in the aforementioned changes in the distribution pattern, making it unfair.

Under the control and intervention of this administrative department, people or enterprises observe rent being dissipated in vain and take voluntary action by contract to retain this rent, that is, rent keeping. The rent is only partially restored, and resource allocation to a certain extent is returned to being determined by the market, making it efficient. At the same time, the distribution pattern is returned to the market-determined distribution pattern, which is fair.

In contrast, when the rent value is about to dissipate, using the public power that is in the hands of the government administrative department to make the department and its officials exclusively access resources or products in the regulated field—rent-seeking—may have a rent-keeping effect and may worsen resource allocation and distribution. Therefore, rent-seeking is generally inefficient and unfair.

According to Steven Cheung, no rent dissipation exists under the condition of the market equilibrium price (2014, p. 172). At this time, if no sufficient reason can be found to prove the existence of market failure, government intervention in the market, price controls, quantity controls, or access control or others will inevitably lead to rent dissipation in a broad sense, that is, loss of social welfare.

In our country, in the fields of education, health care, and land management, many types of intervention and control exist by government administrative departments that result in the destruction of the market price system and the dissipation of rent value.

Under this type of government control, people and enterprises adopt various ways to retain part of the rent through contracts, such as seeing doctors in big cities, sending red envelopes to doctors, immigrating for college entrance examinations, and "preoccupying classes" before going to school.

In contrast, the government and its officials also observe the rent to be dissipated. They use government or personal administrative power to obtain part of the rent in production and to exclude competition with others during consumption. This approach constitutes the basic characteristics of government behavior in the fields of education, health care, and land management.

The government will also prohibit people's and businesses' rent-keeping activities because this is what they should do when they set up regulations. Such a prohibition will affect their rent-seeking interests.

The core of the reform is not to change the form of government regulations but to cancel most of the regulations, which eliminates the conditions of rent dissipation and results in improvements in efficiency and the realization of justice.

References

Cheung, Steven, A Theory of Price Control, *The Journal of law and Economics*, Vol. 17, No. 1 (Apr., 1974), pp. 53–71.

Cheung, Steven, The Structure of a Contract and the Theory of a Non-Exclusive Resource, *Journal of Law and Economics*, Vol. 13, No. 1 (Apr., 1970), pp. 49–70.

Cheung, Steven, *The Theory of Share Tenancy*, The University of Chicago Press, 1969; (Chinese version: 张五常, 《佃农理论》, 商务印书馆, 2000).

北京市第一中级人民法院, "原国家食品药品监督管理局局长郑筱萸受贿, 玩忽职守案刑事判决书"(一中刑初字第 1599 号), 2007. (Beijing No. 1 Intermediate People's Court, "Criminal Judgement of Former Bureau Director Zhen Xiaoyu of Food and Drug Administration Taking Bribes and Dereliction of Duty", (No. 1 Intermediate Criminal No. 1599), 2007).

张五常,《制度的选择》(《经济解释》卷四), 中信出版社, 2014. (Cheung, Steven, The Choice of Institutions (Volume 4, Economics Explanations), Citic Publishing House, 2014).

赵晨曦, 高欣, "发改委系统落马官员已有19人, 价格司成最密集地",《法治周末》, 2014 年 10 月 8 日. (Zhao Chenxi, Gao Xin, "19 Officials Sacked in the NDRC System, Price Bureau Took the Heaviest Hit", Legal Weekly, October 8th, 2014).

CHAPTER 13

Medical Insurance Paradox: A Hypothesis on Medical Price Increases in Proportion to Copayment Rate Decreases and Verification in China

Contents

The content of this chapter is part of the research on the theoretical research, effect evaluation, and reform plan of China's medical system. The authors of this study, Zhang Lin and I, as participants, revised the previous sections into separate chapters.

Sheng Hong, *Vision and Calculation*,
https://doi.org/10.1007/978-981-15-2898-9_13

13.1 The Question Raised: Is the Increase in the Welfare of Medical Insurance Truly Greater Than Its Cost?

From a personal point of view, a person's illness or medical effect has the uncertainty that Knight stated, that is, the uncertainty of its probability distribution. As Knight stated, "it so rarely happens that a probability can be computed for a single unique instance" (1921, p. 234). However, Knight stated that, on the whole, "Uncertainties are less in groups of cases than in single instances" (p. 238). The probability distribution of a disease in a population is roughly predictable through statistical analysis and, thus, can be called a "risk" in the sense of Knight. That is, the uncertainty of the probability distribution can be predicted. Therefore, Knight suggested that "consolidation" and "specialization" should be used to deal with risks (p. 239). "Consolidation" means "reducing uncertainty through probability classification," and "specialization" means "reducing uncertainty by choosing someone willing to 'accept' uncertainty." This is the notion of insurance.

Kenneth Arrow stated that, because of uncertainty and because people are averse to risk, they tend to choose a certain return instead of a mean of returns around which actual returns fluctuate. Whether people get sick and whether the cost of medical services is more uncertain than the average product or service, so an insurance company or government provides insurance with a certain price but can fully pay for unexpected medical services. Such insurance increases benefits for everyone who is averse to risk. Because most people are risk-averse and insurers can pool the insurance premiums of many independent individuals to deal with the risks that are uncertain to the individual but that present a certain probability in society, the overall risk is significantly reduced such that the entire society also experiences a significant increase in benefits. This is the basic principle of medical insurance (Arrow 1963).

Then, the amount of income that medical insurance brings to consumers is generally estimated using an indirect method; that is, the benefits of medical insurance can be judged by the difference in consumption between insured and uninsured people.

In terms of an indirect estimation, some scholars' estimates (甘犁, 刘国恩, 马双, 2010; 臧文斌, 刘国恩, 徐菲, 熊先军, 2012; 朱铭来, 奎潮, 2012; 李晓嘉, 2014) indicate that households with medical insurance increase their spending on non-medical consumer goods. The ratio is between 7% and 13%. Bai Chongen et al. (白重恩, 李宏彬, 吴斌珍, 2012) found that medical insurance brought approximately 5.6% of non-medical consumption to farmers, deducting the income effect of government subsidies (17 yuan), and non-medical consumption increased by approximately 5%. Because Chinese farmers' income is relatively low, and the impact of insurance on consumption decreases as income increases, the estimates in Bai Chongen et al. may be more credible. However, their data are earlier and at the latest 2006, and we know that the insurance reimbursing payment rate is rising with the development of the new rural cooperative medical system. Therefore, we chose an intermediate value of 5–13%, with 9% as an estimate of the benefits of insurance. In 2014, per capita non-medical consumption expenditures of Chinese residents accounted for approximately 25% of per capita GDP. In addition to the reimbursement of medical expenses for consumers, medical insurance increased the certainty effect equivalent to 2.25% of per capita GDP for consumers, which is approximately 44.3% of per capita medical expenses.

In contrast, insurance also has its costs, including moral hazard, adverse selection, institutional costs, and buyer monopoly, that drive price increases and medical overtreatment (Martin S. Feldstein, 1973). A large body of literature discussed these costs, and we do not go into detail here. However, this issue is not the last one related to medical insurance. One of the most important issues is that, when people buy insurance, their payment methods change, and medical expenses are paid in whole or in part by insurance companies, causing consumers to lose their sensitivity to price. This lack of sensitivity not only promotes the demand for medical services in general. Prices continue to rise and the lack of dispersive selection and evaluation of different doctors, different medical services, and different medical products cannot price these doctors, services, and products, respectively, cannot form an effective market relative price structure, and cannot provide the correct price signal for the supply of and investment in these services and products. This situation results in a loss of resource-allocation efficiency.

From this point of view, this chapter puts forward the hypothesis that "medical prices are inversely proportional to the copay rate under insurance." That is, in the case of insurance, the macro results show that the higher the insurance payment rate for medical expenses, that is, the lower the copay rate, the greater the increase in the price of medicines. Can this hypothesis be established?

13.2 The Medical Insurance System Changes the Medical Demand Function

Because the basic demand by patients for medical services is to "heal," consumers have a certain expected effect on treatment for even more complicated diseases. To this end, patients do not increase their medical treatment and medications because of lower prices of medical services or drugs. This assumption has been confirmed. As Sherman Folland et al. pointed out, "most of the elastic values we get are in the range of inelasticity, that is, between −1.0 and 0.0" (2007, p. 188). The data on demand elasticity cited in their book, *Health Economics*, especially related to direct medical care, is closer to zero.

The patient's demand price is inelastic, indicating that the price of the medical market depends mainly on the market structure and the supply costs of the medical service provider. In addition, some studies have shown that patients' medical needs are more elastic given the existence of insurance. For example, RAND's insurance experiment found that the copay rate in insurance "has a considerable impact on average medical expenses": from a 95% copay rate to free or a zero copay rate, "the average family medical cost has increased by nearly 50%, from $679 to $982" (Quoted from Folland et al., 2007, p. 188).

Worth noting is that this elasticity of demand is the elasticity of the copay rate and not the price elasticity. After the consumer buys insurance, the cost already paid is equivalent to a sunk cost. When consumers get sick and are treated, they consider the marginal cost. In general, apart from the time spent on their medical treatment, the marginal cost mainly refers to the part of their payment under the insurance system. This part represents a portion of all medical expenses that we call the copay rate. However, after people buy insurance, they only focus on the copay portion. Even in the case of the same actual medical expenses, differences in the copay rate lead to different reactions.

We use data from the China Health and Retirement Longitudinal Study (CHARLS), which provides micro data on 4496 people in 2011, 2013, and 2015[1] and can obtain a conclusion similar to that of the Rand

[1] The data come from the sample of "Several visits to the clinic last month" in the 2011, 2013, and 2015 CHARLS surveys. Because the survey interval is two years, and the statistics of the previous month of the survey are recorded, only a small number of samples has been recorded in three consecutive surveys and should not be regarded as panels. Therefore, the

experiment previously described. The relationship between medical expenses and the copay rate can be expressed using the following equation:

$$C = 1419.4 - 902.95\alpha, \text{where } \alpha \text{ is the copay rate and } 0 \le \alpha \le 1.$$

According to this equation, if China's average copay rate is 50%, then people with insurance spend 87% more on medical expenses than those without insurance. The facts are clear and simple. However, we must note that the decline in the copay rate under the insurance system is not equivalent to the absolute price decline. From the viewpoint of the nominal price as a macro consequence, the absolute price of medical payment after insurance has increased, and the copay part of the price may be even higher than the original absolute price. This situation restructures the consumer's demand functions for medical services.

We continue to use the micro data provided by CHARLS to regress the linear demand function with or without insurance.[2]

When no insurance exists, $q = 3.86 - 0.00094\ p$, the average number of times is 3.71, and the average expenditure is 159.9 yuan.

When insurance exists, $q = 3.97 - 0.00066\ p$, the average number of times is 3.73, and the average expenditure is 369.4 yuan.

Figure 13.1 shows intuitively that medical insurance brings two important changes in the demand for individual outpatient services. The first change is that the entire demand curve shifts to the right, indicating an increase in income. However, this increased income cannot be used to purchase other commodities. The magnitude of the right shift is small, and the intercept on the horizontal axis is almost at the same point. In contrast, a small distance can be considered as an error. The second change is that the insurance demand curve turns to the right at an angle; that is, the slope decreases, and the price elasticity decreases.

mixed section method is used to process the data. The data sources and processing methods in this section are the same as used here.

[2] Here, the micro data on medical treatment in the clinic are used several times a month. For the sake of simplicity, price in the demand function is the second-average price, and number is the number of outpatients.

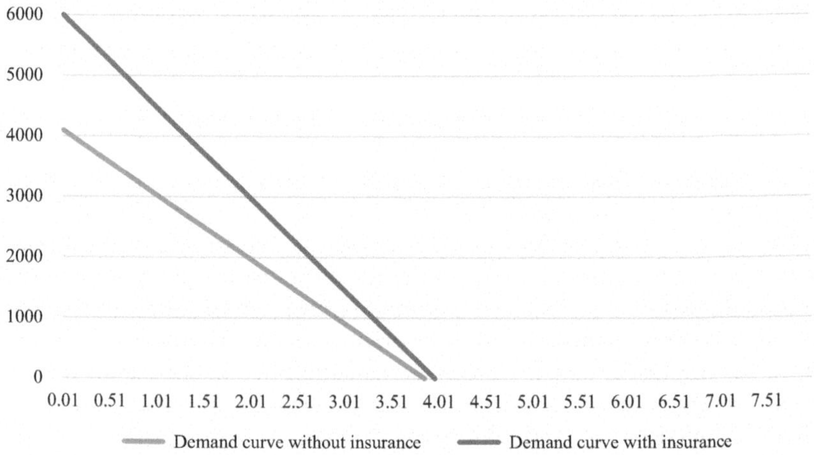

Fig. 13.1 Uninsured demand function and insurance demand function curve using CHARLS data

13.3 The Two Components of Insurance Utility

In the end, whether the actual price appears cheaper because of the insurance payment or that consumers believe that their income has increased from the insurance support seems difficult to judge. Here, we apply the Slutsky equation in an attempt to sort out the problem. Figure 13.1 and Slutsky's graph—used to analyze the change in the relative price of two commodities—are the same. As long as we consider price as a standard commodity, we can use the equation method in the analysis. The rotation of the insurance demand curve in Fig. 13.1 can be regarded as indicating more expensive medical services on the horizontal axis and cheaper currency on the vertical axis.

We can also use the Slutsky equation to estimate the substitution and income effects. According to the data from CHARLS with or without insurance, we use the average expenditure and average number of uninsured people as the equilibrium point and estimate the substitution effect according to the average insurance expenditure, which is approximately 2.11 times. Increasing the expenditure of 779 yuan is necessary to maintain the number of times medical treatment is sought without insurance; the income effect is 0.02 times, and the additional expenditure is 7.4 yuan. A total of 786 yuan in expenditures is required. In other words, the

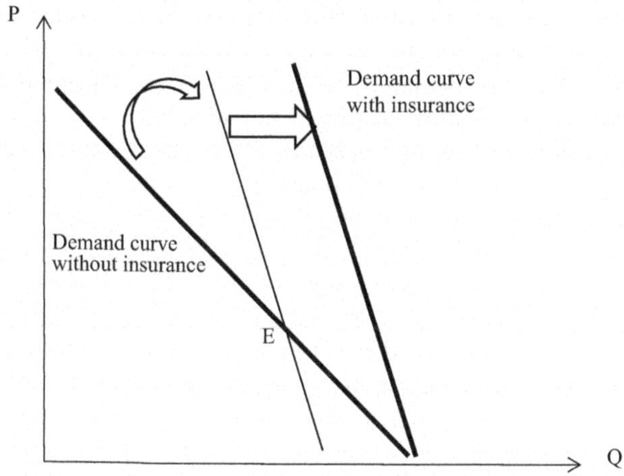

Fig. 13.2 Substitution effect and income effect of demand function with or without insurance

consumer increased his or her expenditure by 779 yuan for the demand curve to turn over to the right with the uninsured equilibrium point as the axis. Then, the expenditure increased by 7.4 yuan for the demand curve to move in parallel to the right. See Fig. 13.2 for details.

An increase in spending means that consumers need to increase their income to compensate for this increase. Therefore, in contrast, Slutsky's substitution effect and income effect need support from an increase in income. The so-called increased income under the insurance system is the result of the reimbursement of insurance companies—the "income illusion" caused by the decline in the copay rate. The reason for this illusion is that consumers regard insurance purchase expenditures that have already been paid as sunk costs and regard the current marginal cost as actual medical expenses. The price declines because of insurance company reimbursements, which is equivalent to an increase in income in the sense of the Slutsky equation. The reason it is called an "illusion" is that consumers have already paid for the reimbursement of insurance companies, not real income.

In fact, in the case of the insurance system, the situation is different from that described by the Slutsky equation. The latter is the effect on consumer choice after assuming a change in price; the former is that the consumer's income illusion causes a change in price and quantity. When thousands of consumers join the insurance system, the collective income illusion forms a strong force to change the market price. In 2016, Chinese residents received approximately 1478.3 billion yuan from the medical insurance system (including government subsidies). Consumers spend such a large amount of money as illusory "income," which may increase prices and quantities in the overall pharmaceutical market.

This type of income illusion can also be called "insurance illusion" or "insurance utility," which are the two types of consumer reactions to the copay rate, that is, two aspects of insurance utility. First, this type of income illusion increases the demand for medicine because of the perceived increase in income and is noted as U1. The second type is to note that the more expensive drugs have higher marginal benefits, making the consumer surplus much larger than that of less expensive drugs, and the amount of insurance reimbursement is higher than that of less expensive drugs, which is also a kind of utility—recorded as U2. Both U1 and U2 constitute insurance utility.

Regarding the first category, after people participated in insurance, they found that the amount of medical services or medicines purchased in the past to be "cured" is now partially or fully reimbursed by insurance. This reimbursement is equivalent to an increase in income, and they may be willing to buy more now that they can go to the hospital to cure "small illnesses" for which a hospital visit was not previously possible. Moreover, one can also demand more medicine for family backup or to relatives and friends. This increase in demand occurs without the relative price changing. See Fig. 13.3.

Regarding the second type of insurance utility, because medical expenses are partially or even fully reimbursed by insurance, people may choose more expensive services or products. At this time, the demand curve tilts upward as the copay rate decreases, and the price elasticity decreases. See Fig. 13.4.

In practice, these two types of insurance utility are comprehensively reflected; that is, at the same price, people with insurance tend to buy more than those without insurance. For the same quantity, people with insurance tend to buy more expensive than those without insurance. This judgment is supported by CHARLS data.

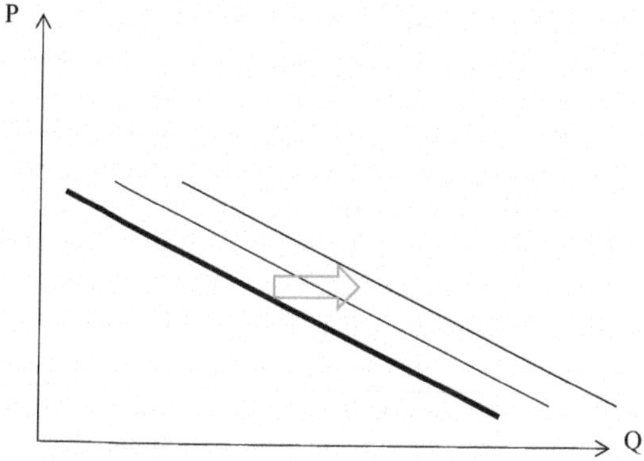

Fig. 13.3 Schematic diagram of the effect of copay rate change on utility curve (1). Note: In this figure, the thick line represents the demand curve when there is no insurance. After participating in insurance, the income effect caused by the decline in the copay rate made consumers willing to purchase more medical services or medicines at the same price

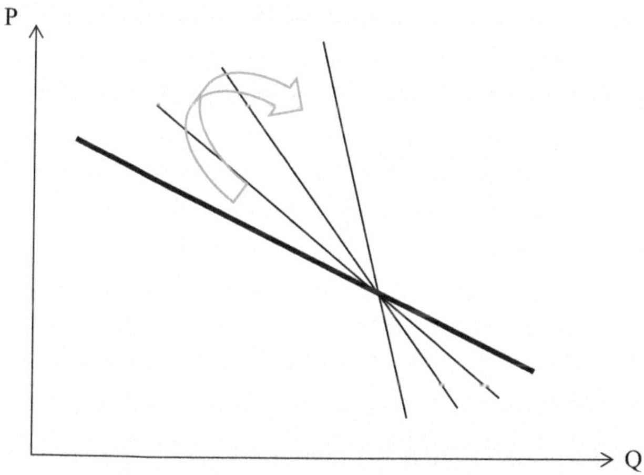

Fig. 13.4 Schematic diagram of the effect of copay rate change on utility curve (2). Note: After participating in insurance, people are willing to buy more expensive drugs because they are paid partly or wholly by insurance. A demand curve that rotates to the right and tilts upward is formed

13.4 The Hypothesis That Insurance Will Increase the Price Level Proportionally

Based on the discussion in the previous section, we can more generally analyze the changes in the consumer demand function resulting from the insurance system and the impact on the price and quantity levels of the overall market. Here, we propose an "insurance paradox" about price levels; that is, medical insurance increases the market price of medicine. The core factor describing the insurance system is the copay rate. Under a supply monopoly, the multiplier of the price increased by the copay rate is the reciprocal of the copay rate. We find that adding the copay rate to the demand function produces results consistent with the demand function of the previous CHARLS data regression and the situation described by the Slutsky equation.

Prove:

Assuming there are N consumers in the market, their individual demand function is as follows:

$$Q_i = \boldsymbol{a}_i - b_i P$$

where b_i is the slope and its relationship to point elasticity (E) is $b_i = E * Q/P$;

The constraints are as follows:

$$0.4I_i \geq Q_i P$$

Among them, Q_i contains Q_{0i}, which is the real inelastic medical demand of consumer i, and I_i is the income of consumer i. This equation indicates that the medical expenses of consumer i should not exceed 40% of his or her current income; otherwise, it will be regarded as exceeding his or her ability to pay.

The price function of the demand is as follows:

$$P = \left(a_i - Q_i\right) / b_i$$

Facing market prices, consumers make personal decisions and do not consider the impact of their choices on the market.

The demand curve of the market is the sum of that of individual consumers.

$$D = \Sigma q_i$$

In particular, when there is no insurance,

$$\Sigma Q_{0i} = Q_0$$

Among them, Q_0 is the accumulation of N people's inelastic medical demand.

Suppose the market supply function is

$$S = Q_0, \text{when there is no insurance;}$$

$$S = Q_0 + eP, \text{when there is insurance.}$$

The market price is a function of the market supply and demand,

$$P = f(D,S)$$

In the absence of insurance, when the market is balanced,

$$S = D = Q_0$$

$$P = c$$

Among them, c is the marginal cost under perfect competition and is expressed as a horizontal straight line.

Because we mainly discuss the problems of supply and demand under insurance conditions, we only use the supply function when $S \geq Q_0$.

$$S = Q_0 + eP$$

Its price function is as follows:

$$P = (S - Q_0)/e$$

Then, the market is described as follows:

$$Qi = ai - biP$$
$$D = \Sigma Qi = \Sigma(\text{ai} - \text{biP})$$
$$S = Q0 + eP,$$
$$P = f(D,S)$$

When the market is balanced, the market price is as follows:

$$P = (\Sigma Qi - Q0) / e$$

Assume that under the condition of medical insurance, the patient's copay rate at each price is α, $0 \leq \alpha \leq 1$, then the price function of the individual demand is as follows:

$$P_r \alpha = (ai - Qi) / bi \tag{13.1}$$

This function is equivalent to a price reduction to the level of α times the original price, that is, a value smaller than the original price. According to the Slutsky equation, this function can also be understood as an increase in income, which makes the elasticity or slope of the demand function without insurance smaller, as shown in the following equation. Because α is less than 1, αb_i is less than b_i.

$$P_u = (a_i - Q_i) / \alpha b_i \tag{13.2}$$

Because intuitively, $1/\alpha b_i > 1/b_i$, the former is $1/\alpha$ of the latter, that is:

$$P_u / P_r = 1 / \alpha$$

Here, P_u is the market price under the insurance system.

If every consumer participates in insurance, the market demand is the accumulation of their respective demand:

$$D = \Sigma Qi = \Sigma(\text{a}_\text{i} - \alpha\text{b}_\text{i}\text{P}_\text{u})$$

Assuming that:

$$A = \Sigma ai, i = 1,2,3,4,\ldots,N$$
$$b = \Sigma bi$$

The above equation can be rewritten as follows:

$$D = A - \alpha b P_u$$

When the market is balanced, $S = D$, then:

$$P_u = (A - Q_0) / (e + \alpha b) \tag{13.3}$$

Obviously, when e = 0, that is, when the supply is completely monopolized, the price is strictly determined by the reciprocal of the copay rate, $1/\boldsymbol{\alpha}$.

The ratio of the price level under insurance to the uninsured price level is as follows:

$$R_p = P_u / P_r = [(A - Q_0)/(e + \alpha b)] * [(e + b)/(A - Q_0)] = (e + b)/(e + \alpha b)$$
$$\text{that is,} \; r_p = (e + b)/(e + \alpha b) \tag{13.4}$$

Here, e is the slope of the supply function. When $e = 0$, the supply is completely monopolized. At this time, $rp = 1/\alpha$; that is, the ratio of the medical price after insurance to the original price is the reciprocal of the copay rate.

This statement is verified using the uninsured demand function $q = 3.86 - 0.00094$ p derived from the previous CHARLS data regression and $bi = -0.00094$. The sample of 4496 individuals is laterally added together to form the market demand function, and substituting into equation (13.3) results in the following:

$$A = 3.97 \times 4496 = 17355,$$
$$b = 0.00094 \times 4496 = 4.23,$$
$$Q_0 = 3.71 \times 4496 = 16680,$$

Assuming $e = 0$, there are the following:

$$P_u = (17355 - 16680) / (4.23\alpha)$$

Obviously, the price at $\boldsymbol{\alpha} = 0.25$ is four times that at $\boldsymbol{\alpha} = 1$.
Its derivatives are as follows:

$$P_u^{'} = -7500 / (47\alpha 2)$$

The meaning of Fig. 13.5 is as follows. Equation (13.3) shows that as the copay rate α decreases from 1 to 0, the price increases. This phenomenon is especially true when the copay rate approaches zero. See the solid line in the picture. The ordinate can be understood as the price in units of yuan. The derivative of equation (13.3), indicated by the dashed line in Fig. 13.5, shows that as the copay rate α approaches zero, the price increases faster. In particular, when moving to the left after the point at which $\boldsymbol{\alpha} = 0.5$, the price change accelerates and, after 0.25, the price increases sharply.

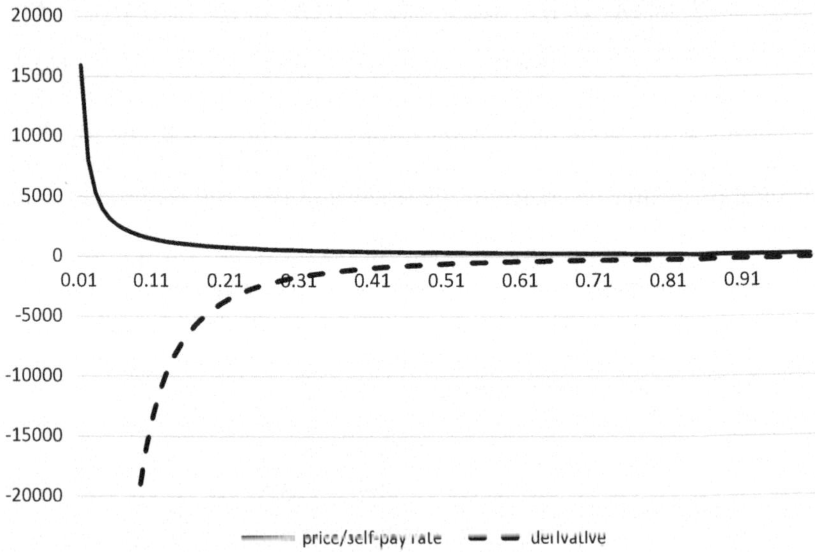

Fig. 13.5 Effect of copay rate (%) on price and its derivative

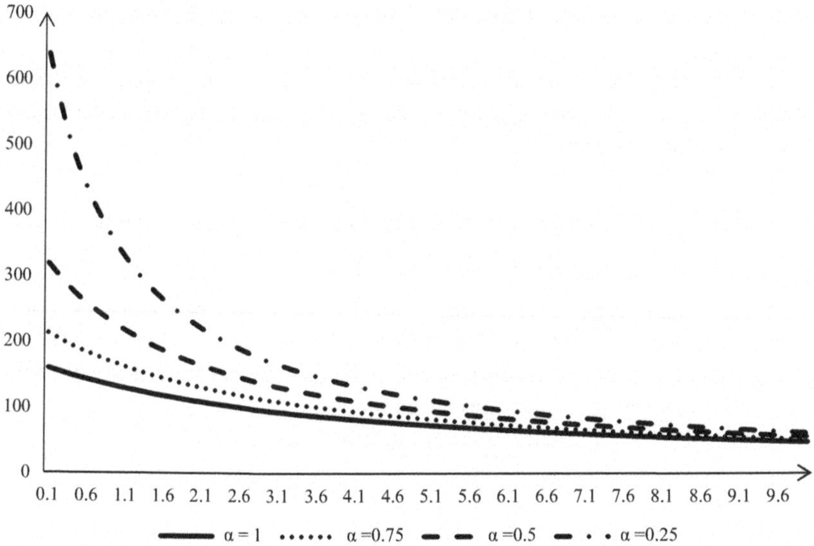

Fig. 13.6 Relationship between copay rate and price under different degrees of monopoly (e). Explanation: In this figure, the horizontal axis is the slope e of the supply function, $0 \leq e \leq 10$. The vertical axis is the price level

The slope e of the supply function reflects the degree of monopoly of the supply; a larger e indicates a higher degree of competition, and a smaller e indicates a higher degree of monopoly. Let us look again at the change in the slope of the supply function and the effect on the price at different copay rates.

Using the previous demand function and assuming that the slope e of the supply function varies between 0 and 10, the copay rate $\boldsymbol{\alpha}$ is 100%, 75%, 50%, and 25%, respectively. Then, varying the slope $\boldsymbol{e}$ of the supply function in the range of 0 to 10, the effect to changes within the price level is shown in Fig. 13.6.

Figure 13.6 shows that the closer e is to 0, the more monopolistic is the supply and the higher the price level; when $e = 0$, the price level is $1/\alpha$ times the copay rate $\boldsymbol{\alpha} = 100\%$. This result is consistent with the previous conclusions. When $\boldsymbol{e} > 0$ and gradually becomes larger, the phenomenon that the price level increases because of a decrease in the copay rate weakens, and the price level is equivalent to $1/\boldsymbol{\alpha} * 1/(\boldsymbol{e}/(\boldsymbol{\alpha} + b))$ times the price with the copay rate α = 100%. This relationship exists as long as $1/(e/(\alpha + b)) > 1$.

In contrast, this chart also shows that the lower the copay rate, the higher the price level brought by the monopoly. The lower the copay rate, the higher the price level.

13.5 Quantitative Analysis of Overtreatment Brought by Insurance

In the previous section, we assumed that, if the copay rate is lower, consumers are more inclined to "buy more," that is, seek medical overtreatment. We now analyze the amount of medical overtreatment according to the method developed in the previous section.

We already have demand and supply functions:

$$\text{Pr} = (\text{A} - \text{D}) / \text{b}$$

$$\text{Pr} = (\text{S} - \text{Q0}) / \text{e}$$

The insurance's copay rate α affects the demand function. This set of functions is as follows:

$$\text{Pu} = (\text{A} - \text{D}) / \alpha b$$

$$\text{Pu} = (\text{S} - \text{Q0}) / \text{e}$$

When the market is balanced, S = D, the equation of the upper group is rewritten as follows:

$$\text{Pu} = (\text{A} - \text{Q}) / \alpha b$$

$$\text{Pu} = (\text{Q} - \text{Q0}) / \text{e}$$

When the supply price equals the demand price and the market reaches equilibrium, there are the following:

$$(\text{Q} - \text{Q0}) / (\text{A} - \text{Q}) = \text{e} / \alpha b$$

This equation is rewritten as follows:

$$Q=((e/\alpha b)A+Q0)/(1+e/\alpha b) \tag{13.5}$$

Applying these parameters, the graphics are as in Fig. 13.7.

Figure 13.7 shows that, as the copay rate declines, in addition to causing price increases, insurance utility also increases demand, which can be considered excessive demand. However, the increase in demand caused by the decline in the copay rate is not very significant.[3] Similarly, demand under the insurance system is also affected by the degree of the supply monopoly. Because of content limitations, the analysis is not repeated in this chapter.

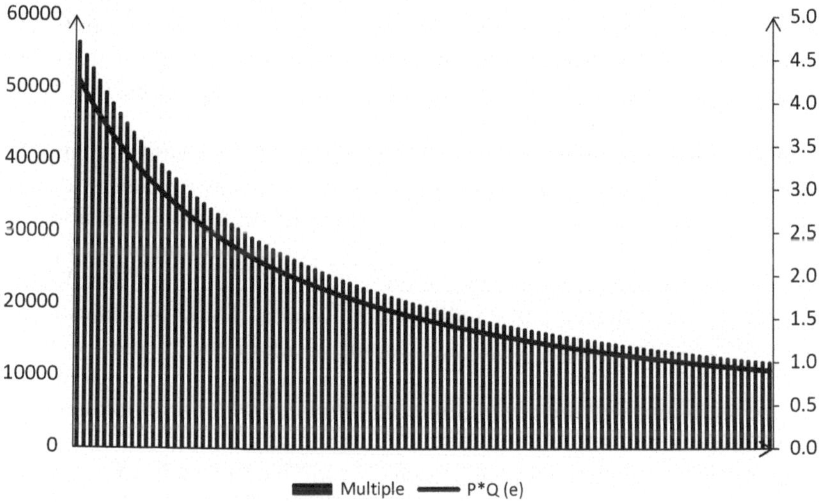

Fig. 13.7 Effect of copay rate on quantity, and multiples of quantity. Explanation: The black curve in this figure shows the effect of the copay rate on the quantity of medical demand. The left side is the total expenditure price; the black histogram shows that the demand quantity after insurance is the multiple before insurance, and the scale is on the right axis

[3] This result is consistent with some studies on "inducing demand," which is generally considered to be less serious in terms of oversupply of medical devices, drugs, and physician technical services. This chapter also yields similar results and further believes that oversupply, or excessive demand, is mainly characterized by price increases.

This analysis also indicates that, if insurance produces "insurance utility" and as the copay rate decreases and the supply monopoly increases, the demand and supply functions inevitably change, resulting in price increases and overdemand. Then, the moral hazard problem is inherent in insurance, and confrontational measures against moral hazards may be doomed as completely ineffective.

13.6 The Medical Market Under the Insurance System

As previously mentioned, two important variables exist under the insurance system: the copay rate (α) and the slope (e) of the supply function. The former affects the extent to which insurance results in price increases and medical care is excessive, whereas the latter determines the decline or growth between monopoly and competition and, thus, the amount that prices increase or excessive demand because of a copay rate less than 100%.

The copay rate (α) fluctuates between 0 and 1, and the slope (e) of the supply function theoretically varies between 0 and ∞.

These two parameters are adjusted to rotate the demand and supply curves. The copay rate (α) rotates from 1 to 0, gradually becomes steeper, and finally becomes a vertical line. The slope of the supply function (e) rotates from infinity to 0, causing the supply curve to rotate in the opposite direction to the demand curve and finally become a vertical line. When these two lines intersect, an equilibrium is formed. These two lines form many equilibriums when rotated, covering most of the medical market under the insurance system, including full payout and completely free, full competition and full monopoly, and all of the intersections between the two extremes.

According to equation (13.4), the price ratio with or without insurance is as follows:

$$\boldsymbol{R}_p = (e+b)/(e+\alpha b)$$

Because equation (13.4) does not include parameters such as price and the function intercept, we take $b = -1$ for simplicity. We can change e to between 0 and 100, and α varies from 0 to 1, giving us a matrix covering various market situations. We call this matrix $\boldsymbol{R}_p$. See Fig. 13.9. At both extremes, when the full monopoly (e) equals 0 and the copay rate (α) equals 1%, the price level will be 100 times the price during perfect competition (e = 100) and full copay (α = 100%). For any intermediate state during the period, as long as we specify the values of ***e*** and ***α***, we can obtain the corresponding price ratio (r_p) between prices with or without insurance.

Table 13.1 provides a simplified matrix of the price ratio matrix (Rp), with α in units of 0.05 from 0.05 to 1 and e in units of 0.1 from 0.0 to 0.9. Fortunately, the parameters involved in this study can be found in this table.

This matrix improves the convenience of the analysis. We understand that a particular insurance system (with a defined copay rate) and a given supply structure (described by the slope of the supply function) must have an equilibrium. We only need to analyze this particular situation to obtain a certain amount of judgment. For example, in Fig. 13.8, the demand curve determined by the specific copay ratio is D2, the predetermined supply structure determines that the supply curve is S1, and the two intersect at B. The price determined by this point multiplied by the quantity is the medical cost, which is obviously much larger than the medical cost of O (no insurance, competitive supply).

In addition to a static analysis, we can analyze changes in a certain parameter in preparation for institutional reform. If the supply structure is

Table 13.1 Brief table of matrix of price ratios with or without insurance

	e									
α	*0.0*	*0.1*	*0.2*	*0.3*	*0.4*	*0.5*	*0.6*	*0.7*	*0.8*	*0.9*
0.05	20.00	7.33	4.80	3.71	3.11	2.73	2.46	2.27	2.12	2.00
0.10	10.00	5.50	4.00	3.25	2.80	2.50	2.29	2.13	2.00	1.90
0.15	6.67	4.40	3.43	2.89	2.55	2.31	2.13	2.00	1.89	1.81
0.20	5.00	3.67	3.00	2.60	2.33	2.14	2.00	1.89	1.80	1.73
0.25	4.00	3.14	2.67	2.36	2.15	2.00	1.88	1.79	1.71	1.65
0.30	3.33	2.75	2.40	2.17	2.00	1.88	1.78	1.70	1.64	1.58
0.35	2.86	2.44	2.18	2.00	1.87	1.76	1.68	1.62	1.57	1.52
0.40	2.50	2.20	2.00	1.86	1.75	1.67	1.60	1.55	1.50	1.46
0.45	2.22	2.00	1.85	1.73	1.65	1.58	1.52	1.48	1.44	1.41
0.50	2.00	1.83	1.71	1.63	1.56	1.50	1.45	1.42	1.38	1.36
0.55	1.82	1.69	1.60	1.53	1.47	1.43	1.39	1.36	1.33	1.31
0.60	1.67	1.57	1.50	1.44	1.40	1.36	1.33	1.31	1.29	1.27
0.65	1.54	1.47	1.41	1.37	1.33	1.30	1.28	1.26	1.24	1.23
0.70	1.43	1.38	1.33	1.30	1.27	1.25	1.23	1.21	1.20	1.19
0.75	1.33	1.29	1.26	1.24	1.22	1.20	1.19	1.17	1.16	1.15
0.80	1.25	1.22	1.20	1.18	1.17	1.15	1.14	1.13	1.13	1.12
0.85	1.18	1.16	1.14	1.13	1.12	1.11	1.10	1.10	1.09	1.09
0.90	1.11	1.10	1.09	1.08	1.08	1.07	1.07	1.06	1.06	1.06
0.95	1.05	1.05	1.04	1.04	1.04	1.03	1.03	1.03	1.03	1.03
1.00	1.00	1.00	1.00	1.00	1.00	1.00	1.00	1.00	1.00	1.00

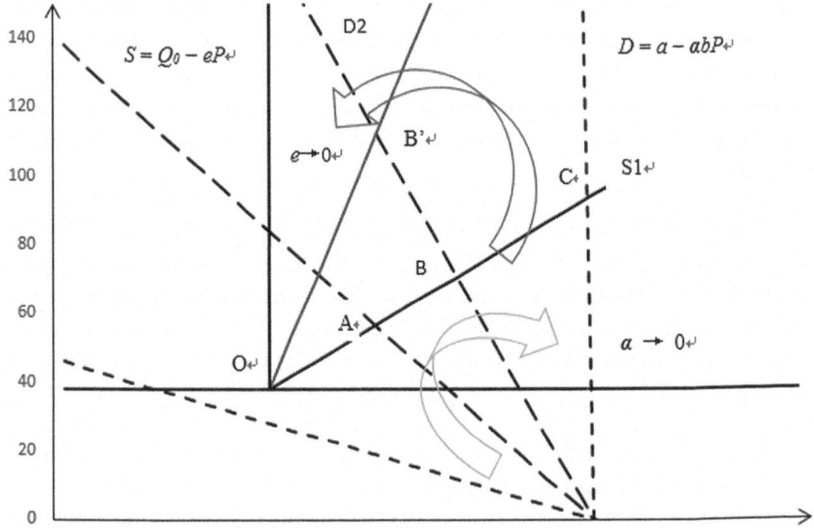

Fig. 13.8 Changes in copay rate (α) and degree of monopoly (e) cover the entire market situation. Note: In this figure, the black dotted line represents the demand curve, $D = A - \boldsymbol{\alpha} bP$, and rotates from the lower left to the upper right as the copay rate ($\boldsymbol{\alpha}$) decreases from 1 to 0. The solid black line representing the supply curve, $S = Q_0 - \boldsymbol{e}P$, rotates from the lower right to the upper left as the supply function slope ($\boldsymbol{e}$) decreases from ∞ to 0

assumed to be constant (this is at least more realistic), the out-of-pocket rate under the insurance system is changed. This change is equivalent to fixing supply curve S1 in Fig. 13.9, changing the copay rate ($\boldsymbol{\alpha}$) and letting the demand curve rotate along S1. Then, the intersection of the supply and demand curves also slides along S1. In Fig. 13.9, the intersection points pass through three points A, B, and C—all on the straight line of S1. Obviously, as the intersection points from A to B to C, the price and quantity are increasing and, thus, medical expenses increase as the copay rate decreases.

Conversely, fixing the demand curve and turning the supply curve represent similar situations. If the fixed demand curve is D2, the supply curve is rotated, and the intersection of the two curves slides along D2 in the direction of B to B'. Any intersection gives a pair of price and quantity

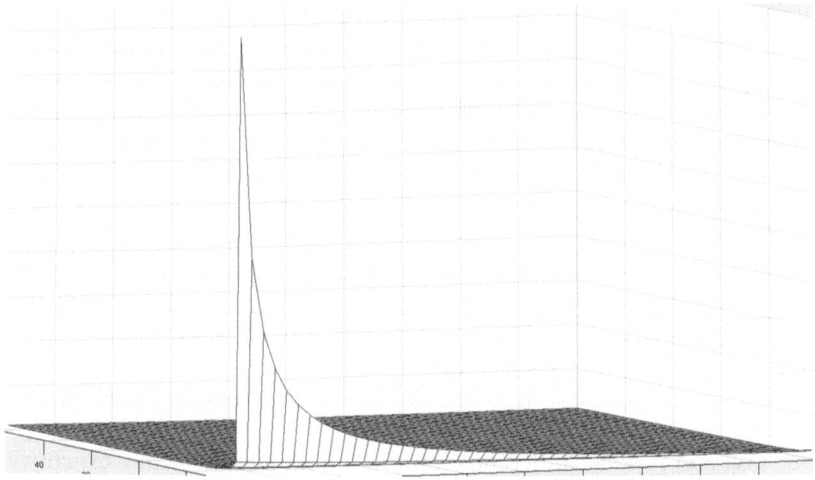

Fig. 13.9 Space view of matrix of price ratios with or without insurance

values, which are multiplied with each other to determine medical expenses.

Because we have a matrix ($\boldsymbol{R}_p$) of the price ratio with or without insurance, we can obtain the number of insurance ratios according to the supply function:

$$\boldsymbol{R}_q = \left(1 + \left(\boldsymbol{e} / Q0\right) Pu\right) / \left(1 + \left(\boldsymbol{e} / Q0\right) \mathrm{Pr}\right)$$

For simplicity, let us make Pr – 1. Then, Pu equals the corresponding rp; let Q0 = 1, or the average amount of demand per person without insurance. Therefore, there is the following equation:

$$\boldsymbol{R}_q = \left(1 + \boldsymbol{e} * rp\right) / \left(1 + e\right) \tag{13.6}$$

We obtain Rq, that is, the number matrix with or without insurance. As long as we know the determined $\boldsymbol{\alpha}$ and $\boldsymbol{e}$ values, we can find the corresponding quantity ratio with and without insurance, that is, the amount of medical overtreatment. By multiplying $\boldsymbol{R_p}$ and $\boldsymbol{R_q}$, we can obtain the ratio of medical expenses with or without insurance, which we call $\boldsymbol{R_c}$.

Referring to the $\boldsymbol{R_p}$ space view and the matrix profile, we can obtain the spatial view and matrix summary table of $\boldsymbol{R_q}$ and $\boldsymbol{R_c}$.

The analysis indicates that after the insurance system came out, the medical market as a whole experienced a significant expansion. This expansion occurred mainly because of the insurance utility brought about by the insurance system, which makes people tend to buy more expensive and more medical services and products.

On the supply side, given the fundamental change in demand characteristics, people tend to buy expensive, and only an increase in the monopoly level and product differentiation can induce people to buy expensive services or products. Therefore, suppliers of medical services or products are motivated to increase the degree of monopoly.

Because people's incomes do not increase simultaneously with an increase in medical expenses, the ratio of medical expenses to people's incomes is rising. In particular, because of the significant increase, the cost to treat major diseases may break through the affordability of people's incomes and, in contrast, increase their financial risk.

In particular, we must also consider that if certain diseases are major, characterized by high medical prices and monopolistic supply, then the demand side will have no excessive demand because, even if a reimbursement system exists, consumers will still face very high prices after reimbursement. At this time, the "cheap" effect is offset by the high copayment price, and consumers are not willing to overconsume; that is, the demand curve is close to a vertical state.

Furthermore, for major diseases, patients have a maximum consumption line given their incomes. The cost of exceeding this line is unacceptable to patients, and patients choose to give up treatment. In the extreme, the effect of "taking advantage of insurance" is so great that the entire demand curve has no near-vertical part, and insurance can only be above the highest consumption line to avoid market distortions caused by insurance utility. However, that this result has been contrary to the original intention of establishing an insurance system should be emphasized.

Although insurance companies and managerial medical organizations have motives to curb price increases and overtreatment, their efforts are rather weak given the strong trend that all economic entities in this medical market have motives to drive up medical costs.

13.7 The Insurance System's Push on China's Pharmaceutical Price Levels and Excessive Medical Care

Regarding the insurance system's push on China's medical prices and overtreatment, we can use the previous two methods as an estimation tool. One method estimates the presence or absence of the insurance demand function based on the regression of CHARLS clinic data. We know that the cost of insured people per visit is 369.4 yuan and the average without insurance is 159.9 yuan or smaller than the former by 2.3 times, and the average number of medical treatments with or without insurance is 3.73 and 3.71, respectively, or the former is 100.5% of the latter. Considering the price and quantity together, the average medical cost with insurance is 2.32 times that without insurance. This method provides a very intuitive way to tell us that insurance has brought about a significant increase in medical expenses.

Because we have obtained a price ratio (r_p) of 2.3, we have obtained the slope of the demand function without insurance, b = 0.00094, and substituted it into equation (13.4), $r_p = (e + b)/(e + \alpha b)$, resulting in $e = 0.47$. This result provides an indirect reference for us to estimate the degree of monopoly in the pharmaceutical supply market. Of course, two limitations to the CHARLS data still exist. One is having only 4496 samples, and the other is that only outpatient data are sufficient and the hospitalization data are small.

In this way, we must analyze our country's specific situation by focusing on the general methods that we developed in the past. According to the market structure and specific situation of medical services and medicines in China, because slope b has meaning only when compared with the copay rate (α) and, for the sake of simplicity, $b = -1$ is still defined. The copay ratio varies according to different groups of people. We know that the price is not determined by the average but is determined at the margin. Therefore, we still select the copay rate for outpatient expenses for urban workers of 25%; the insurance payment for hospitalization expenses is 90%, that is, the copay rate is 10%. Considering that there are still approximately 21.4%–27.2% of self-funded drugs, the median value is

24.3%, the insurance payment range is 75.7%, the average insurance payment rate for hospitalization expenses is 68.1%, and the copay rate is 31.9%. The outpatient insurance payment rate is 56.8%, and the copay rate is 43.2%

$$\text{When } \boldsymbol{e} = 0.47, \alpha = 0.43, r_p = 1.63; \text{when } \alpha = 0.32, r_p = 1.86.$$

According to data from the China Health Statistics Yearbook, the average per capita expenditure on minor (outpatient) and major (hospitalization) diseases accounted for 57% and 43% of average per capita medical expenditures, respectively. On a weighted average basis, the insurance system pushed up the price of medical services and medicines by 73%.

According to the same method, we use the quantity ratio matrix (Rq) with or without insurance and provide a quantitative description of the loss from medical overtreatment. Then:

$$\text{when } \boldsymbol{e} = 0.47, \alpha = 0.43, r_q = 1.20; \text{when } \alpha = 0.32, r_q = 1.28.$$

Considering that under the starting line of reimbursement for outpatient expenses, patients generally do not undergo excessive medical treatments, which account for approximately 20% of total outpatient expenses, a slight amendment is made, $r_q = 1.16$. On a weighted average basis, the insurance system makes consumers buy 21% more medical services or medicines.

The data on price increases and medical overtreatments were substituted into the mean model of this study. Using 2017 statistics, we found that when per capita medical expenses under the insurance system are approximately 3081 yuan, medical expenses without an insurance system are approximately 1432 yuan. That is, under an insurance system, people pay 115% more in medical expenses, or approximately 2.3 times, than when they do not have insurance. These figures are calculated using CHARLS data and can be mutually verified. Under the existing insurance system, the total medical expenses of individuals in the country are estimated to be 4282.6 billion yuan. In the absence of insurance, the total medical expenses of individuals in the country should be 1991.9 billion yuan. In other words, insurance increases medical expenses by 2290.7 billion yuan.

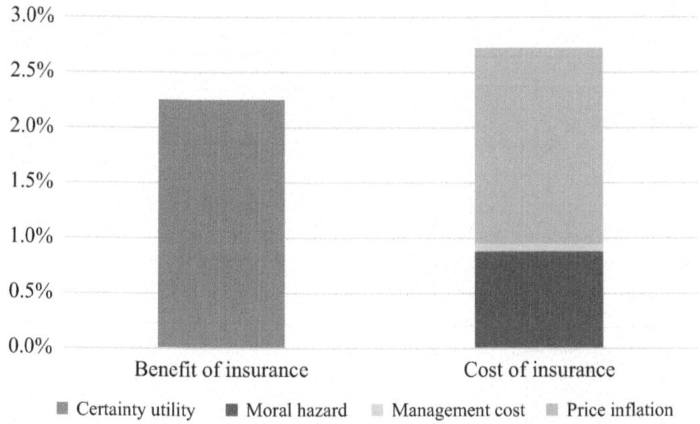

Fig. 13.10 Comparison of insurance advantages and disadvantages, unit: % of GDP per capita

Compared with a GDP of 59,201 yuan per capita, the 3081 yuan that is higher than 1432 yuan represents 2.78% of per capita GDP; excluding medical expenses outside of the insurance system, this figure mainly refers to pharmacy sales (approximately 7.6% of the medical expenses for minor illnesses), which is approximately 2.69%. If we reconsider the certainty utility of insurance (estimated in this study as 2.25% of GDP per capita), we can conclude that, if this utility is deducted, the figure is revised to 0.44%. Multiplying this adjusted value by 82,075.4 billion yuan of GDP in 2017 results in approximately 361.1 billion yuan. That is, although we consider the certainty utility of the insurance system, this system still brings about a loss of static efficiency of approximately 361.1 billion yuan, which is a pure negative value.

Therefore, a judgment of only the role of medical insurance makes such insurance seem not worthwhile. See Fig. 13.10.

13.8 Reform Solution: Increasing Copay Rate, Increasing Competitiveness and National Fund for Serious Disease Relief

To solve the problem of rising medical expenses, the problems caused by the insurance system must first be solved. According to the previous analysis, the two most important variables are the copay rate (α) and the degree

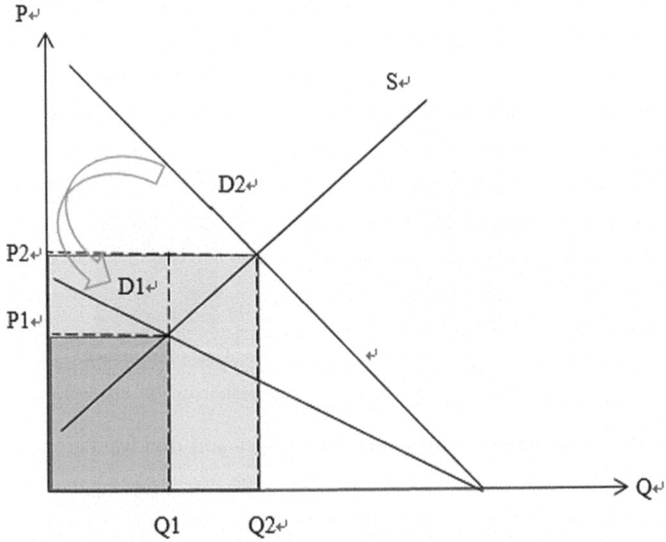

Fig. 13.11 Schematic diagram of canceling the outpatient insurance effect. Explanation: For minor illnesses (outpatients), because insurance was canceled by our proposed reform plan, the copay rate increases to 100% and people's demand for insurance disappears. The demand curve in this figure returns from D2 to D1, and the price declines from P2 to P1. The demand declines from Q2 to Q1

of monopoly (*e*) under the insurance system. Our research finds that the lower the copay rate, the higher the price of medicines and medical expenses. Therefore, increasing the copay rate is an important measure.

In contrast, our research also found that the increase in medical expenses is greater because the degree of monopoly of the supply side in the medical market is higher. In addition, in the case of low copay rates, a monopoly amplifies the negative effects of price increases and excessive medical care. Therefore, another key point of reform is reducing the degree to which supply is a monopoly.

Specifically, for minor illnesses (outpatients), attaining complete copaying is basic, which is represented the copay rate being increased to 100%.

Consumers can decide for themselves this part of the medical treatment without insurance at all. If we consider the low elasticity of medical service demand, we can at most consider the establishment of personal accounts for minor illnesses. On average, 0.9% of personal income is enough.

Individual accounts can be used for outpatient payments or for pharmacies to buy drugs. Unused money in an account can be inherited by future generations. Moreover, setting up a personal account for minor illnesses is not needed because the individual can make direct payment. Even considering the differences among different people, the cost of a minor illness is generally not high enough to make a person unable to afford it.

Our proposed major illness (hospitalization) insurance reform is to cancel the starting line and adjust the copayment rate from 10% to 50% or 70%. Moreover, from the first yuan of medical expenses, 30% will be paid by insurance.

According to the with-or-without-insurance price ratio matrix $\boldsymbol{R}_p$, we only need to find the price ratio corresponding to the copay ratio.

$$\text{When}\, b = -1, e = 0.47, \alpha = 1, rp = 1; \text{when}\, \alpha = 0.7, rp = 1.26.$$

At this time, the per capita cost of minor (outpatient) and major (hospitalization) illnesses accounted for 57% and 43% of per capita medical costs, respectively. On a weighted average basis, this system pushes up the price of medical services and medicines by 11% compared with the system without insurance. Compared with the existing insurance system in which the price of medical services and medicines has increased by 73%, the proposed program has the downside power to curb price rises by 62% and save 1404.9 billion yuan according to 2017 data, or 1.7% of GDP. Of course, this saving does not necessarily lead to price declines because the reform is gradually realized and directly manifested in the inhibition of the annual rise in medical prices.

Reforms that increase the copay rate will not only curb the rise in pharmaceutical prices but also reduce excessive demand in terms of quantity.

$$\text{When}\, \alpha = 1, r_q = 1; \text{when}\, \alpha = 0.7, r_q = 1.082.$$

On a weighted average basis, the quantity demand increased by 3.5% relative to the absence of insurance, which was approximately 17.5% lower than the 21% increase under the current insurance system, equivalent to a savings of 397 billion yuan according to 2017 data or approximately 0.48% of GDP.

Use of the previous method is continued in the medical cost ratio matrix:

$$Rc = Rp * Rq$$

The corresponding medical expense ratio is selected.

$$\text{When } \alpha = 1, r_c = 1; \text{when } \alpha = 0.7, r_c = 1.359.$$

The weighted average of outpatient and inpatient costs is approximately 1.15. That is, the reform plan we propose is 15% more medical expenses than without insurance; however, medical costs in the existing insurance system, which are 215% of that without insurance, are reduced by 100%.

In contrast, we must break the monopoly in the field of pharmaceutical supplies and increase the competition. This approach is manifested by an increase in the slope (***e***) of the supply function. According to our model, if the slope is increased from the existing 0.47 to 2, they are compared.

$$\text{When } \boldsymbol{e} = 0.47, \alpha = 1, \text{rp} = 1; \text{when } \alpha = 0.7, rp = 1.26, rq = 1.082, rc = 1.359.$$

$$\text{When } \boldsymbol{e} = 2, \alpha = 1, rp = 1; \text{when } \alpha = 0.7, rp = 1.12, rq = 1.074, rc = 1.193.$$

An increase in the level of competition (e = 2) has no effect on a full self-payment situation (a = 1); that is, it has no effect on outpatient expenses after the reform and has an effect on a situation with a copay rate of 0.7, making the price increase multiple of 1.12 compared with a situation without insurance 14 percentage points lower than that when the monopoly level is high but has little effect on the quantity—only 0.8 percentage points lower than that when the monopoly level is high. Overall, the increase in competitiveness further reduced hospitalization costs by 16.6 percentage points, resulting in a saving of 127 yuan per capita.

According to our model, the reform of increasing the copayment rate results in per capita medical expenses of approximately 1671 yuan, and the reform of improving the level of competition further reduces per capita medical expenses by 127 yuan to 1544 yuan, which is higher than 1432 yuan without insurance but much lower than 3081 yuan under the existing insurance system. That is, each person saved 1537 yuan in medical expenses, approximately 2.59% of GDP per capita. Multiply this percentage by 1.39 billion population results in 2136.4 billion yuan in medical expenses saved.

In the case of an uneven distribution of income and medical expenses, one of the key points of this reform plan is to improve the sharing of medical expenses among poor and sick groups. Because commercial insurance cannot redistribute wealth, the support for these people mainly depends on financial funds. First, we need to estimate the size of such groups and the amount of financial funds that they will use.

If we consider the fluctuations in income and health status distributions, the previous assumption based on averages cannot be fully realized. In addition, the author simulates the fluctuations in income and consultation distributions using a general Monte Carlo model and estimates that if the proposed reform is carried out, the copayment ratio of medical expenses of major illnesses (hospitalization) is 70%. We narrow the scope of our consideration to those who self-pay medical expenses that are more than 40% of their incomes in that year. According to the aforementioned model, these people account for approximately 2.45% of the total population or, multiplied by 1.39 billion, approximately 34.06 million people. If medical expenses exceed 40% of one's annual income in that year, the subsidy ranges from 5000 to 13,000 yuan. On average, if a national fund for major illness relief is established, its scale will be approximately 250 billion yuan with a standard deviation of approximately 30 billion yuan or approximately 0.3% of the country's GDP.

13.9 Summary

The reform proposals put forward in this chapter mainly include:

1. Cancelation of insurance for outpatient medical expenses; payment may be made in the form of self-payment or from a personal account;
2. Increase the copayment rate of hospitalization medical expense insurance to 70%; and,
3. Establish a national fund for the relief and protection of serious illnesses and grant subsidies to those who paid more than 40% of their annual income for medical expenses of serious illnesses (hospitalizations) in that year.

According to the model in this study, the following estimations are made.

1. The reform will bring about a downward force that restrains 62% of the price increase, saving approximately 1404.9 billion yuan or 1.7% of GDP.

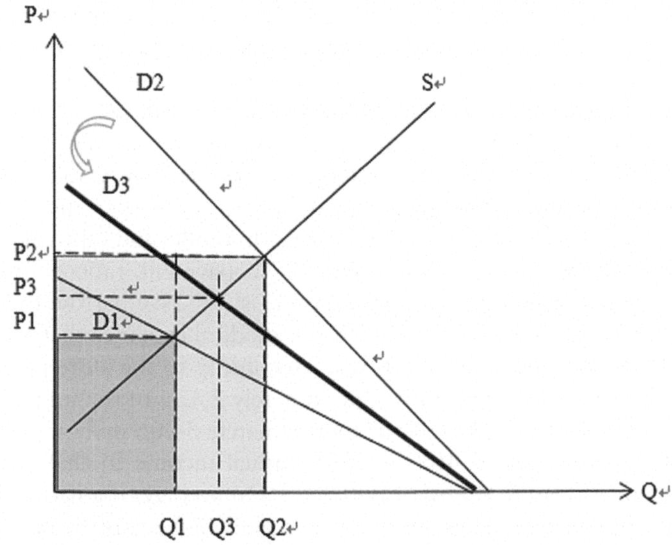

Fig. 13.12 Effect of abolishing the starting line of hospitalization medical insurance and improving the copay rate. Explanation: Because the proposed reform program cancels the starting line of medical expenses for serious illnesses, insurance institutions can reimburse medical expenses from the first yuan, but the copayment rate increases to 70%, which reduces insurance demand. The demand curve in the graph moves from D2 to D3 but has not completely returned to D1

2. The reform will bring about a downward force of approximately 17.5% to restrain medical overtreatments, which is equivalent to saving 397 billion yuan or approximately 0.48% of GDP.
3. To further break the monopoly and encourage competition, that is, to change the slope (e) of the supply function from 0.47 to 2 will further save 127 yuan per person in medical expenses, or a total of 176.5 billion yuan will be saved nationwide.
4. Medical expenses per person saved will be 1537 yuan, which is approximately 2.6% of GDP per capita, resulting in 2136.4 billion yuan saved nationwide.
5. In that year, people for whom the self-paid part of their total medical expenses exceeded 40% of their annual income account for approximately 2.45% of the total population; if a national fund for major illness relief is established, its scale would be approximately 250 billion yuan or approximately 0.3% of the national GDP.

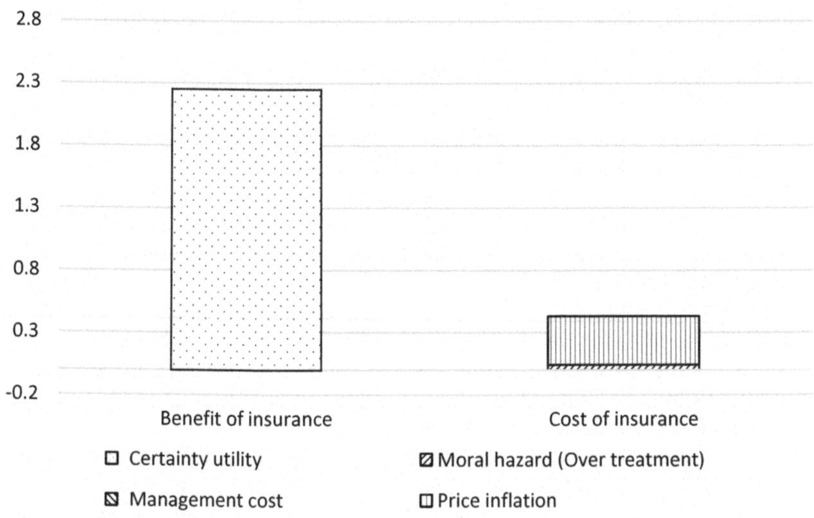

Fig. 13.13 A schematic diagram of the reduction in insurance premiums caused by the reform plan in this chapter

6. When the rise of medical expenses is restrained, the certainty utility of insurance will emerge again. See Fig.13.13.
7. Overall, the reform plan will reduce medical expenditures per person from 5.2% to 2.6% of GDP per capita, a reduction of 49.9%.
8. This reform plan will also reduce the medical expenses covered by insurance from 3.3% of GDP per capita to 0.4%, or 87%. If expressed in terms of medical insurance deduction of existing urban workers, the insurance deduction will be reduced from 9.5% to 1.2% of total wages, which also significantly reduces the burden of enterprises.

References

Kenneth J. Arrow, Uncertainty and the Welfare Economics of Medical Care [J], The American Economic Review, 1963, (53): 941–973

Martin Feldstein, The Economics of Health and Health Care: What Have We Learned? What Have I Learned?, The American Economic Review, Vol. 85, No. 2, January 6–8 (May, 1995), pp. 28–31

Folland, Goodman, and Stano, Economics of Health and Health Care, 5th Edition, Pearson Education Inc., 2007.

Knight, Frant, Risk, Uncertainty and Profit, [M], Houghton Mifflin Company, 1921.
白重恩, 李宏彬, 吴斌珍, "医疗保险与消费:来自新型农村合作医疗的证据",《经济研究》, 2012 (2):41–53. (BAI Chongen, LI Hongbin, WU Binzhen, "Medical Insurance and Consumption: Evidence from New Rural Cooperative Medical Care", Economic Research, 2012 (2): 41–53).
甘犁, 刘国恩, 马双, "基本医疗保险对促进家庭消费的影响",《经济研究》, 2010 (s1):30–38. (GAN Li, LIU Guoen, MA Shuang, "The Impact of Basic Medical Insurance on Promoting Household Consumption", Economic Research, 2010 (s1): 30–38).
李国锋, 刘黎明, "个税起征点改革对纳税能力的影响:基于居民收入分布的估算",《数量经济技术经济研究》, 2015 年第 8 期. (LI Guofeng, LIU Liming, "The Impact of the Reform of Taxation Starting Point on Taxpaying Capacity: Based on the Estimation of Residents' Income Distribution", Journal of Quantitative and Technical Economics, No. 8 (2015)).
李晓嘉, "城镇医疗保险改革对家庭消费的政策效应—基于CFPS微观调查数据的实证研究",《北京师范大学学报(社会科学版)》, 2014 (6):123–134. (LI Xiaojia, "Policy Effect of Urban Medical Insurance Reform on Household Consumption—An Empirical Study Based on Microscopic Survey Data of CFPS", Journal of Beijing Normal University (Social Science Edition), 2014 (6): 123–134).
臧文斌, 刘国恩, 徐菲, 熊先军, "中国城镇居民基本医疗保险对家庭消费的影响",《经济研究》, 2012 年第 7 期. (YAN Wenbin, LIU Guoen, XU Fei, XIONG Xianjun, "The Impact of China's Urban Residents' Basic Medical Insurance on Household Consumption", Economic Research, No. 7, 2012).
朱铭来, 奎潮, "医疗保障对居民消费水平的影响—基于省级面板数据的实证研究",《保险研究》, 2012 (4):103–111. (ZHU Minglai, KUI Chao, "The Impact of Medical Security on Residents' Consumption Level—An Empirical Study Based on Provincial Panel Data", Insurance Research, 2012 (4): 103–111).

CHAPTER 14

Zero Marginal Cost and Virtual Rent

Contents

14.1 Marginal Cost Pricing

In China, the most typical business models for the Internet trading platform are the Alibaba and Tencent model, that is, Taobao, QQ, and WeChat are the main forms of the business model.

The most puzzling part of this model is the issue of zero marginal cost pricing. Specifically, this model first requires significant funds to build a huge infrastructure, namely, a platform for online trading or to make friends. Once established, given its large scale of supply, its variable

When writing this chapter, I received assistance from Qian Pu, who organized the questionnaire investigation on people's online purchasing behavior.

Translated from ***Research of Institutional Economics*** (《制度经济学研究》), Volume 61, Issue 3, 2018.

Sheng Hong, *Vision and Calculation*,
https://doi.org/10.1007/978-981-15-2898-9_14

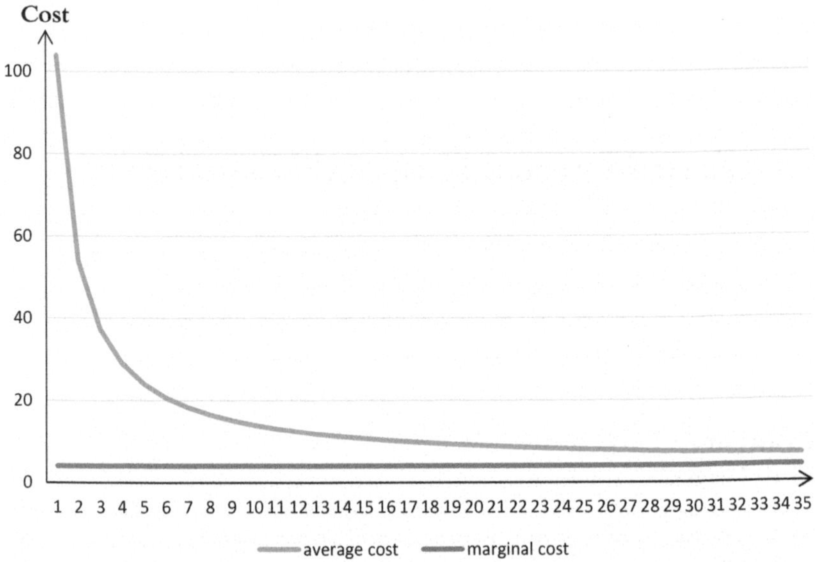

Fig. 14.1 Average and marginal costs of high fixed-input network services

cost—the marginal cost—is almost always zero. That is, increasing product or service volumes does not increase costs. According to the pricing principle of microeconomics, resource allocation is optimal when price equals marginal cost. However, this principle only applies to the situation in which the marginal cost is increasing. When the marginal cost is constant or decreasing, according to marginal cost pricing, the fixed input cost cannot be covered and, thus, the company will suffer a loss. A zero marginal cost is obviously an extreme situation. If the pricing is zero, there will be no income (Fig. 14.1).

This situation has created a discussion in the economics community. Professor Coase wrote a dissertation called "Marginal Cost Controversy," which discussed this issue. When faced with the problem of high fixed-cost inputs and constant lower marginal costs for utility companies, Hotelling argued that, in this case, the total cost exceeds the total revenue and should be borne by the government. Coase countered that doing so would be equivalent to using taxpayers' money to subsidize public utilities used by only some people, which is neither fair nor efficient. Coase suggested adopting two-layer pricing methods, namely, that consumers should pay both the marginal cost and the average fixed fee (Coase 1946).

Coase seems to have been correct. Currently, a large number of utilities are using two-layer pricing. For example, consumers pay for every cubic meter of gas (marginal cost or variable cost) as well as an initial installation cost of the gas pipeline (i.e., average fixed cost). Other public utilities actually use two-layer pricing that is not as intuitive, such as for tap water and electricity. Ordinary consumers do not feel that they have to pay for the initial installation of tap water and electricity because these costs are paid by the housing developer first and then are included in the price of the house.

However, this pricing approach does not seem to work for the Internet. Originally, we could distribute equally the massive fixed asset investments of the online trading or friend-making platforms to each consumer. However, the problem is that once this is done, it will hinder the entry of consumers, and the trading or friend-making platform will lose money from not having enough consumers. Public utilities do not face this problem because the services that they provide are necessities and have low elasticity, and consumers have to pay the initial installation fees.

Another difference between Internet trading and friend-making platforms and public utilities is that when a platform of sufficient size is established, the marginal cost of using it is almost zero. If you have already invested in the platform's fixed assets, those funds represent a sunk cost. Adding a consumer at this time will not increase the platform provider's cost.

The general logic is that online trading and friend-making platforms have the nature of public infrastructure, and it is easy for action to be in accordance with Hotelling's solution—investments by the government. However, in various countries, such platforms are created through private investments. For example, in China, the platforms Alibaba and Tencent have discovered a new model for solving this problem that is neither the Coase model nor the Hotelling model. This model is based on zero marginal cost pricing, which is a zero price. For example, the friend-making platforms QQ and WeChat are free to enter; Taobao is also free for consumers and individual businesses to use.

14.2 Agglomeration and Market Network Externalities

The question is, how does a zero price make money? How are costs offset? When Coase discussed the issue, he assumed that a central market existed where people went to buy things, and they hired porters to carry the goods home. Here, the number of porters is fixed, and they always listen to the customer's call—similar to fixed input. Coase stated that one person must pay for the purchase of goods but also pay for porters. In this way, the cost can be compensated. The mystery of the online trading platform model is precisely the nature of the central market that Coase ignored. This cluster is formed when people go to the central market to buy things.

We know that when a population gathers, it brings about the market's network externalities; that is, people's agglomeration leads to a disproportionately rapid increase in the possibility of transactions between people. The relationship is as follows:

$$\mathrm{ME} = kn(n-1)/2$$

Among them, ME is the market network externality, n is the population density, and $0 < k < 1$ is the transaction possibility when people come into contact with others. The formula indicates that, for a certain population density, the market network externality is the combination number. Of course, in general, this is a trading possibility (k). Assume that $k = 0.01$. For example, the market network externality with a population density of 10 is 0.45, and the market network externality of 100 is 49.5. The key is that as long as this coefficient is positive, market externalities increase at a faster rate when population density increases. If the population density increases from 10 to 100, ME is 110 times the original; when population density increases to 1000, ME is 11,100 times the original. Obviously, it is increasing dramatically.

Market network externalities have grown more rapidly as population density has increased. In the real physical world, a crowded externality exists that increases at the same time; that is, as the population density increases, the cost of congestion increases. However, after these two opposing forces are combined, a certain amount of gain still exists. We call this gain the "aggregation rent." We can imagine that if a person exists who owns the central market's land and provides free transportation services to attract people to the central market to buy things, the increase in trading opportunities from the clustering of people will increase the value of the land in the central market. The owner charged rent to cover the cost of providing a free porter service. This is the mystery of the online trading platform, which prices at zero but can compensate for its costs and has a surplus. Of course, cyberspace is a virtual world, and the resulting rent can be called a "virtual rent."

However, several important differences must be noted when using this method in the Internet environment. First, in the real world, geographical location is important, that is, a certain point on the Earth is more superior or less favorable than other points. In the virtual world created by the Internet, any point is not better or worse than other points—all points are equal. Second, in the real world, if someone owns a piece of land, it is exclusive and others cannot occupy this land at the same time. The land on the Earth is limited; in the virtual world, no one point occupies the actual space and *vice versa*—the space of the virtual world is almost infinite. The two natures of the Internet that distinguishes itself from real space preclude natural inequities and monopolies in competition, thus making competition purer.

If the Internet is analogous to the New World, online trading or friend-making platforms are cities in the New World. The difference between this "city" and a city in the real world is that it is a city without congestion. Obviously, without the cost of crowded externalities, there will be no major cost to offset the externalities of the market network. Virtual cities will become very large. For example, in 2016, there were approximately 3.2 billion Internet users worldwide, which is equivalent to the population of the Virtual New World. China's 730 million Internet users can be viewed as the "China" population in the virtual world.

Taobao, QQ, or WeChat are all equivalent to cities in the New World. Because there is no cost of crowded externalities in the city, one "city" can almost contain "one country." For example, Taobao users are said to have reached 600 million in 2015, and QQ users have already reached 1 billion. In contrast, the largest cities in the real world, such as Shanghai and Beijing, are just over 20 million in population. If only those who visit the shops in the city center are counted, there will be fewer people. For example, the daily average flow of people in the Xidan Commercial District in Beijing is only 320,000. In 2015, Taobao's average daily traffic was between 60 million and 70 million and was 110 million during the double 11 period, to which real cities and their commercial centers are far from comparable.

For the inference of virtual rent, we must also consider two characteristics of the Internet. First, the agglomeration on the Internet is a virtual agglomeration that, in turn, makes the agglomeration more prominent. Therefore, the significance of agglomeration is not the proximity of people to people but the information that their desires can communicate with each other. Thus, the agglomeration on the Internet is manifested as the mutual delivery of information. When an online shop enters Taobao Mall, it encounters consumers who have "gathered" through its search engine; some of these consumers will also "enter" the shop to look around as online customer traffic. At this time, the degree of agglomeration can be measured by the customer traffic per unit time.

Second, people's agglomeration on the Internet is different from the city's agglomeration in reality. The latter mainly resides, whereas the former mainly gathers in commercial centers or public communities, simplifying the agglomeration nature of the existing Internet. In particular, the agglomeration of commercial centers is more inclined to trade, and the possibility that agglomeration causes market externalities is higher.

Because we discuss virtual rent, we should classify differential rent and absolute rent. In a virtual city, centers and edges obviously exist that simply do not appear in the physical space but can be described by the degree of virtual agglomeration, that is, the number of page views per unit time or browsing density. For example, customers who buy a certain type of product will browse one online store more than other online stores. Many factors exist, one of the most important being the "position" of an online shop in a virtual city, that is, where the Taobao Mall page falls in the ranking. Obviously, the first shop on the first page is in the most advantageous position. Because the cost of browsing on a web page is very low, the different positions of the same page are not much different. Different pages may differ, and the latter page is viewed by fewer people than the previous page. We can also say that the previous page has more virtual rents than the next page.

We can imagine a virtual space in which the most central point is the hypothetical highest point of agglomeration. This first page is where people engage in trading or making friends on the Internet. Intuitively, this is the first desktop that we boot, which we assume is done instantaneously. Everyone sees this desktop at first sight, giving it the highest concentration in the virtual world. If the goal is to trade or make friends, then the next step is to find the appropriate platform and click into it, such as Taobao Mall.

On the front page, we can see the category list on the left, and on the right and the bottom are various commodities. The top of these displays may be the most expensive place, and the merchandise display is a loop of four or five commodities. Obviously, this place has the highest degree of agglomeration. People generally search the search engine directly for what they want to buy. Some people search for products by classification. If one does not browse the homepage content, going from the homepage to another page may take a few seconds—but just a few seconds—which makes the degree of aggregation significantly lower than the homepage. Moreover, people may also be attracted by the content of the homepage.

A specific product, such as women's handbags, has approximately 100 pages. People generally follow the default order (called "comprehensive sorting" on Taobao). Looking from the first page, consumers turn pages back in order until they find one or two more satisfactory products and then no longer turn back. With approximately 60 merchandise displays per page, it may take a few minutes to read one page, and it may take twenty minutes to see a few pages. Obviously, the page views of the behind page are lower than those of the front page; that is, the rear page is less concentrated than the previous page. Through this difference, we may see differences in the transaction volume of different pages.

According to our questionnaire on online shopping behavior (the questions are provided in the appendix), this behavioral pattern is proven to exist. Approximately 81.2% of people directly search for the required products on the platform website and 59.3% search by product category because it is "multiple choice," and the sum of the two is more than 100%. That most people adopt these two methods can be imagined, indicating that they go straight toward their goals. Approximately 37.2% of people browse a product by sorting (by default) and approximately 39% browse by sales volume, and there is a large overlap between the two. A total of approximately 76% of people browse pages in the order outward from the "city center" formed already, and 99.1% of people look from the first page. In addition, fewer people view pages when they turn pages forward. The desktop and laptop computer situation is illustrated in Fig. 14.2.

Because mobile phone users account for 81% of terminal devices, understanding how to shop online using a mobile phone is more important. See Fig. 14.3.

Figures 14.2 and 14.3 show that people use either the desktop/laptop computer or the mobile phone and are more concentrated in the "city center" (first page/screen).

Obviously, this situation can constitute a graded sequence of virtual rents. The main influencing factor is the time at which people arrive downtown. Although these times are much shorter in the virtual world than in the real world, the key is not the absolute time but the different platforms, different product categories, and relative arrival time of different pages of the same product. A page arrived at a shorter time than another page is

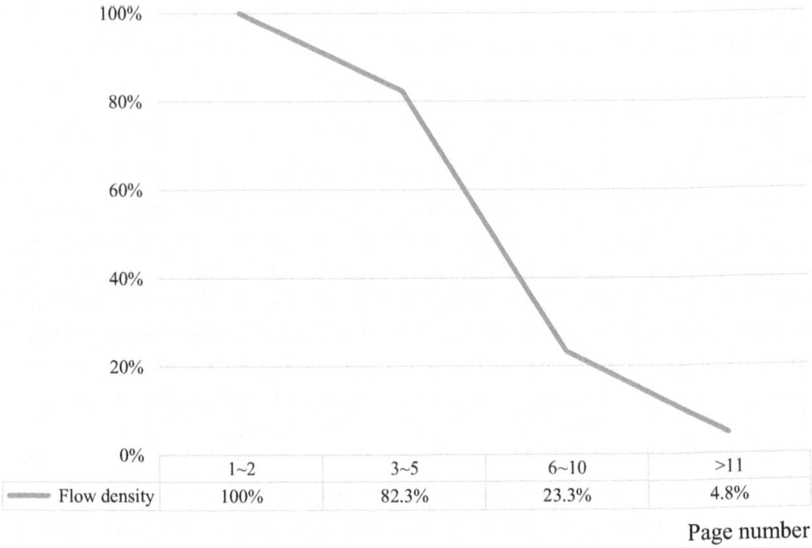

Fig. 14.2 Distribution of online shopping traffic on pages (desktop and laptop). Explanation: The horizontal axis represents the number of trading platform pages

equivalent to a competitive advantage, that is, more visits and a higher degree of agglomeration. In this way, what we see is a conical virtual city that is similar to a single-center city in reality. The city center is the place with the highest degree of agglomeration. As the distance from the city center increases, the degree of agglomeration continues to decline. From this, we can use the existing method of spatial economics to analyze virtual cities.

For simplicity, we assume that the average price per transaction is 100 yuan. The average number of page views per day is the agglomerative degree, which can be called a virtual population density. The combination of population density times the probability (k) (less than 1 and greater than zero) represents market network externalities. Market network externalities are multiplied by the transaction bonuses of the corresponding transactions to estimate how much social welfare value the virtual space can provide. If only the producer surplus is calculated, GDP can be approximated; then, labor and other material costs are deducted. The value and distribution of virtual rents are derived. As long as we know the

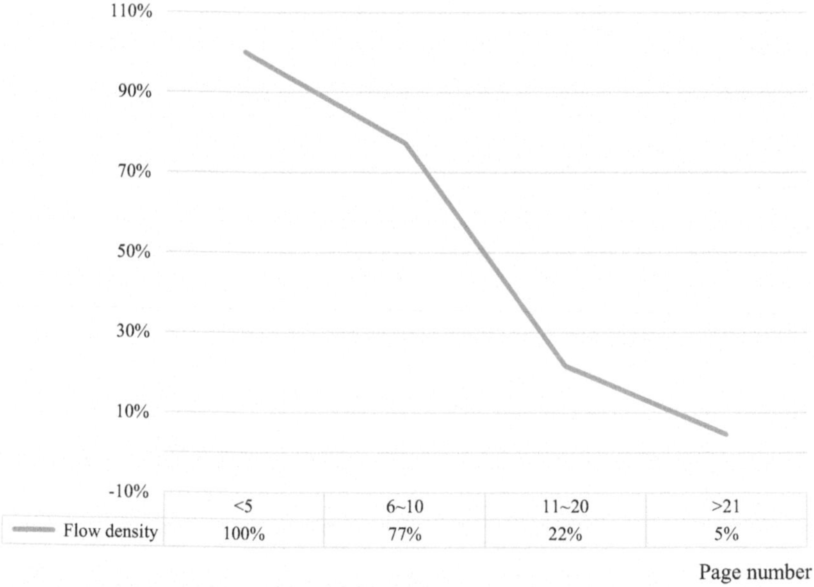

Fig. 14.3 Distribution of online shopping traffic on screens (mobile). Note: The horizontal axis represents the screen number of the mobile phone

various factors that affect the density of the virtual population, we may establish a mathematical model to analyze and evaluate the virtual space, such as the Internet platform that exists in practice.

14.3 The Existence of Virtual Rent and Its Characteristics

We can also retrieve data from existing trading platforms to verify our virtual rent. Figure 14.4 illustrates the product of the price and number of transactions (16:07 on June 20, 2017) of the 12-inch tablet PCs that we searched for on the Tmall trading platform, which is the amount of income. First, this amount is smoothed in 60 data points, and then data on 60 shops per page are averaged. Thirty total pages are arranged from left to right in the order of first, second, third, …, thirty. The scatter plot is observed in Fig. 14.4, which is regressed to obtain the regression curve shown. The regression equation is as follows:

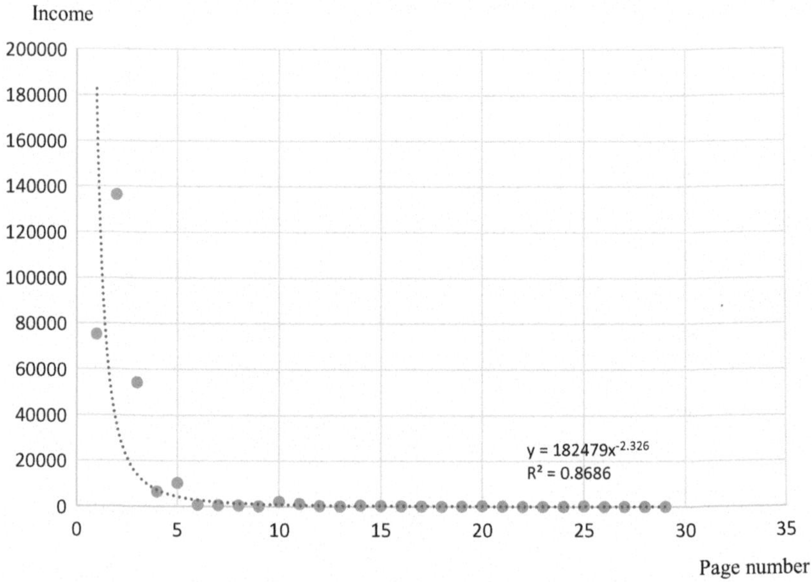

Fig. 14.4 Pages and earnings of 12-inch tablets

$$y = 182479x - 2.326$$

$$R^2 = 0.8686, \text{indicating a good fit.}$$

$$\text{Will } y = 182479x^{-2.326}$$

Find the derivative:

$$Y' = -212223077 / \left(500x^{(1663/500)}\right)$$

The graph is as follows (Fig. 14.5).

Here, the meaning of the derivative is that, as the page number decreases, that is, the closer to the "city center," the larger the grade difference in differential rent.

Regarding rent, apart from differential rent, there is absolute rent. Absolute rent is the value resulting from the scarcity of the total resource supply. In the trading platform here, the so-called total scarcity is

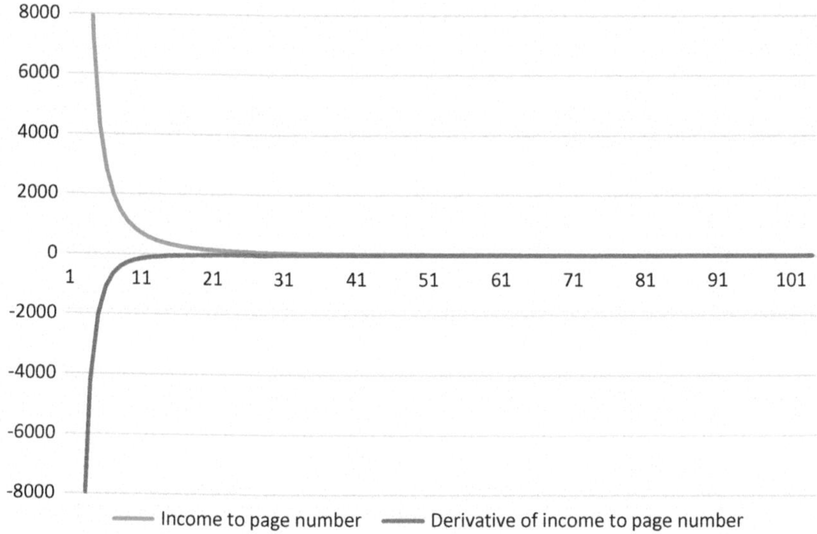

Fig. 14.5 Derivative of the relationship between the number of pages in a 12-inch tablet and the income amount

measured by the scarcity of the resources available to invest in the platform, and the value of resource scarcity is the market price of the total investment—in short, the total fixed investment. Therefore, the so-called virtual rent indicates differential rent and absolute rent. In theory, the absolute rent per user is the average fixed cost, which is relatively simple. We discuss this topic later. Here, we mainly discuss differential rent. The derivative of the income regression equation means differential rent, but it is negative when expressing the relationship with the page number (a smaller page number results in a larger number), we only need to change the sign from negative to positive as differential rent. See Fig. 14.6.

As the seventh page, the amount of income is only less than 2000 yuan. Pages after this page can be ignored, and we only consider the situation before the seventh page. As shown in Fig. 14.6, the part under the orange line is differential rent, and total income is under the blue line. The two are divided by approximately 24.4%. That is, in the estimation of the previously presented data, the theoretical differential rent can be up to 24.4% of the total income.

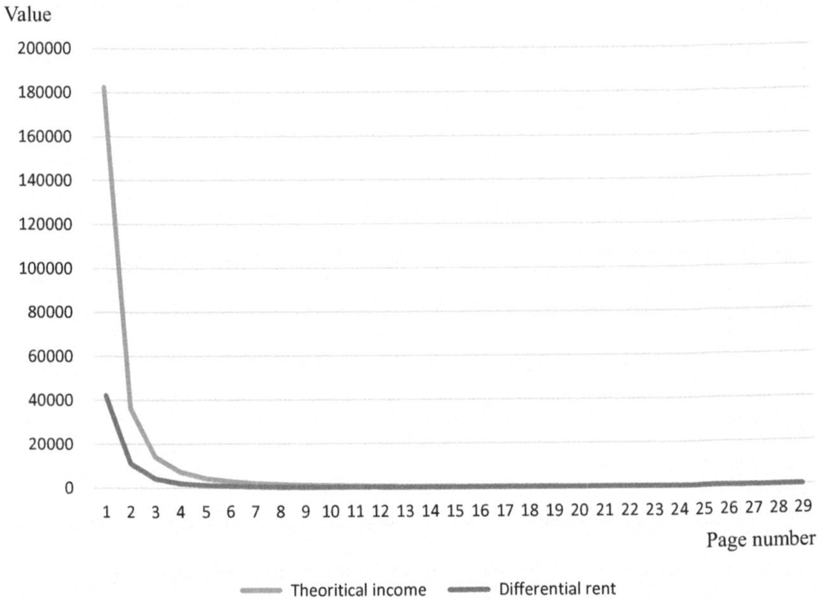

Fig. 14.6 Virtual differential rent for 12-inch tablets

Another example is as follows. We collect data on price and monthly sales of women's handbags from Tmall. The product of the two is the monthly income, smoothly averaged on a per-page basis and then averaged for each page, yielding 100 average monthly income data points. The first to the 100th page are arranged from left to right as scatter plots. The regression curve is indicated in Fig. 14.7, and the regression equation is as follows.

$$y = 1e + 06x^{-0.983}$$
$$R^2 = 0.8063, \text{indicatinga better fit.}$$

The derivative is as follows:

$$y' = -983000 / x^{1983/1000}$$

This regression equation is the monthly income with respect to the position of the web page and indicates that the closer one is to the first

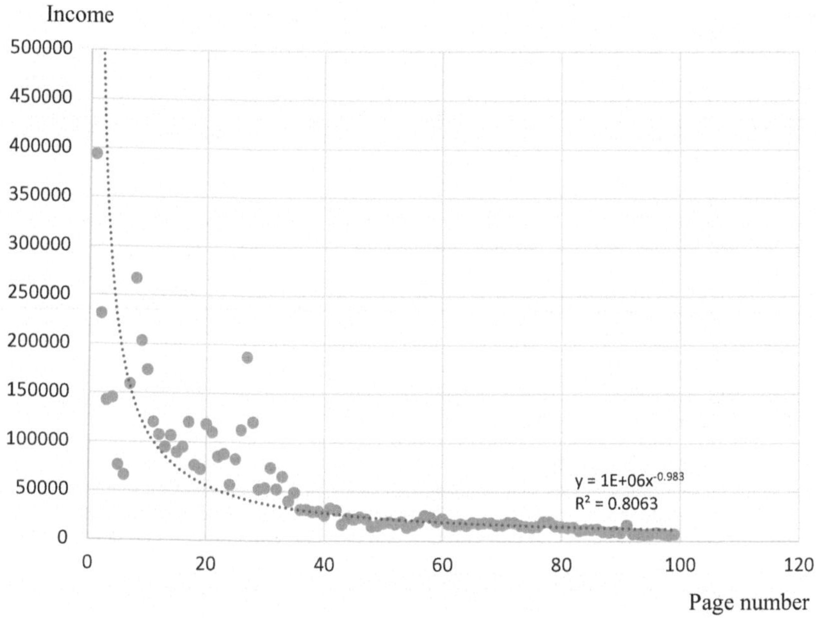

Fig. 14.7 Page number and income of women's handbags

page (i.e., the "city center"), the higher—and accelerating—the monthly income. By subtracting from the monthly income of the first page to that of the second page, we can develop a virtual differential rent between the two pages. By analogy, we can arrive at a differential rent sequence, as shown in Fig. 14.8.

The total monthly income of this 100-page shop is divided by the sum of the differential rent, which is 12%. That is, the virtual rent rate is approximately 12%, which represents a significant difference from the previous example and shows that the virtual rent rate for different commodities is different.

Regardless of the amount of virtual rent, these two examples at least indicate the existence of a virtual rent, which is the case when companies providing Internet trading platform services can receive returns on investments and services by charging virtual rents. The clustering degree and the externality of the market network in the virtual city are extremely high; the "rent" that Taobao or QQ and WeChat can receive is a significant

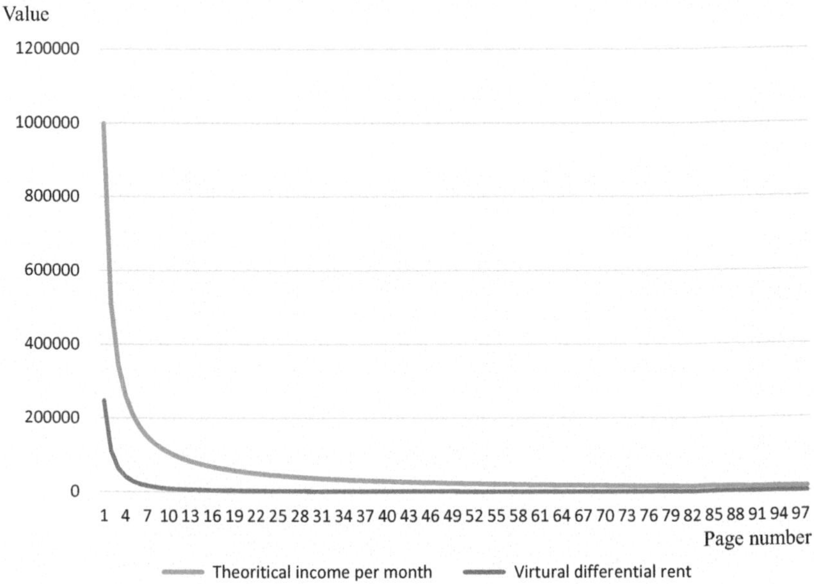

Fig. 14.8 Virtual differential rent for women's bags

amount. The problem is that people do not seem to see the word "rent" in the financial statements of Alibaba or Tencent. Of course, because it is in the virtual space, people do not realize the existence of rent, and Alibaba and Tencent do not use the word "rent" when collecting rent. Of course, to open a store in Taobao, one also needs some costs, such as webpage production and consumer deposit costs, but these do not reflect the concept of rent.

In fact, entering the Taobao Mall does not necessarily sell well because it is divided into the "center" and the "periphery," similar to a physical city. Of course, in the virtual space, the center and the edge are not in a specific physical space but are determined by the conspicuity, accessibility, and coverage of the information. In Taobao, when we search for a specific product, there will always be a page, which is the first page of the product arrangement, and a second page, third page, ..., and nth page. The general default "comprehensive sorting" rule is a more complex formula that includes indicators such as popularity, sales, reputation, and price. On the right and bottom sides of each page are shops called "Shopkeeper Hot" purchased through a "through train." Approximately 15 shops are on the right, and 5 shops are at the bottom. These locations are obtained through a pay-per-click auction. In general, the higher the bid, the higher the rank.

In the middle of the page are approximately 60 more business locations. On the surface, although they are not directly related to the bid, the indicators make it appear as if they contain higher sales and popularity (including page views and reservations), and they are obviously related to the appearance on the first few pages, which is related to the "through train." Therefore, when calculating the click-through payment of a "through train," the merchant must not only consider the direct income from the top position obtained by the bid but also the indirect revenue, that is, from the appearance of the first few pages—the benefits of moving forward the position of the merchant in the comprehensive ranking. Whether direct profit of the "through train" or indirect profit, it is definitely a virtual rent. The purpose of the "through train" is to appear on the first few pages. Its indirectly driving of commodities toward the overall ranking is also moving toward the "city center." Therefore, intuitively, bidding for rank is paying for virtual sites that have a higher degree of agglomeration and a higher market network externality. The existence of virtual rent should be proven.

The next question is, what is the actual rate of rent? We know that virtual rents, which appear as "through train" bids, exhibit extremely strong grade differences. As shown in Fig. 14.9, the marginal differential rent rate decreases rapidly from the first page to the second and third pages. On the first page, the marginal differential rent rate is approximately 25%, on the second page it is approximately 22%, the third page approximately 18%, the fourth page approximately 16% ... the ninth page is approximately 10%. Conversely, when a merchant is bidding the "through train," he or she attempts to determine the degree to which the bid is appropriate or even optimal.

One of the simplest strategies is that the merchant's cost for a "through train" is equal to the additional direct income that he receives. For example, a commodity has a price of 100 yuan and a cost of 50 yuan. When a "through train" is not used, only 100 can be sold per month, indicating a monthly income of 5000 yuan; when using a "through train," the assumed cost is 10,000 yuan. An additional two hundred can be sold each month, and income increased by 10,000 yuan. Intuitively, the costs and benefits are equal; however, because of the potential for higher sales and popularity, this product will move forward in the overall ranking, increasing

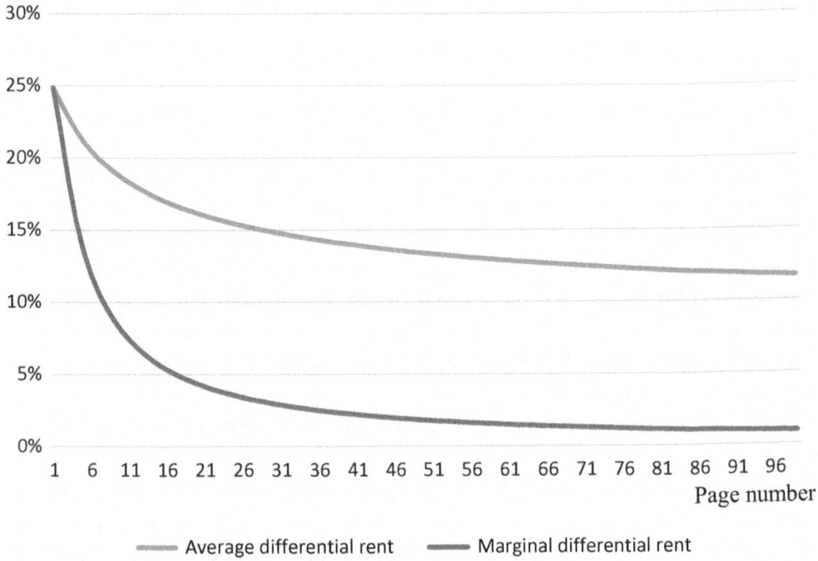

Fig. 14.9 Differential rent rate

consumer traffic and market network externalities—and revenue. This situation shows that this strategy has "extra income." However, this strategy may not last long because some people will find that a higher bid is ranked higher even though the cost is not covered by direct income but by earnings from moving toward in the overall ranking. This outcome is acceptable as long as the total income increase is equal to the total cost of the "through train."

However, as a result, we have discovered that the trend of "through train" bids causes merchants to pay differential rents; that is, the price formed by the auction is extended to the left along the marginal rent curve, which is of course the income of Alibaba.com. However, as a result, the benefits of the Internet trading platform to merchants—the increase in revenue generated by the increase in the degree of agglomeration—have all been taken away by the platform company. What benefits does this offer to merchants? The actual bidding can be said to have not completely absorbed the differential rent, and part of the differential rent has been enjoyed by the merchants because an Internet trading platform, such as Taobao, is not entirely monopolized. Taobao faces other platforms, such

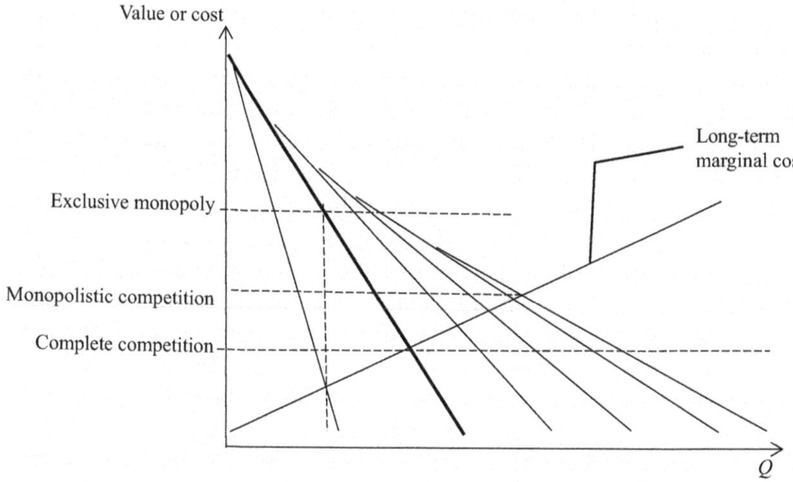

Fig. 14.10 Competition between trading platforms determines platform price. Explanation: The demand curve of the trading platform is assumed to be a cumulative summary of demand curves for each platform. The thick solid line is the demand for the Taobao platform. If there is only the Taobao platform, it sets a monopoly price and removes all virtual rents. However, given competition from other platforms, the actual price is set as the price of monopolistic competition

as Jingdong, Suning, Yigou, No. 1, Gome Online, Amazon, Dangdang, Paipai, and so on. Once the cost of Taobao becomes too high, businesses move to other trading platforms. Therefore, the differential rent in a trading platform will not be entirely grabbed by the platform company (Fig. 14.10).

If we assume that only Taobao is an online trading platform, it is equivalent to an exclusive monopoly situation. It can monopolize pricing and, naturally, grab all virtual differential rents. However, if there are multiple online trading platforms competing, any one merchant will consider which is better: to be on Taobao to pay the costs of offsetting all differential benefits, open a store on another platform, or operate a physical store. Any online trading platform is in competition regardless of whether the price is determined by the platform or whether competition among demanders results in a price lower than the monopoly price, that is, the price of monopolistic competition. In the long run, this price reflects the point at which the long-term marginal cost equals the long-term average return and may be a price higher than the average cost, that is, a certain amount of profit will exist.

If we think that the main income of the online trading platform is virtual rent, we can estimate this virtual rent from their income. Jingdong's data show that, in 2016, the third-party market business achieved GMV 281.8 billion yuan; thus, Jingdong's operating income obtained was 22.2 billion yuan (JD 2017). This income can also be regarded as the total rent paid by third-party companies to Jingdong. The rental rate is 7.9%. Alibaba Group (including Taobao, Tmall, Ali 1688, and others) had a 2016 platform turnover of RMB 30,924 million and operating income of RMB 101.1 billion (excluding cloud computing and other revenues) (Alibaba 2017). The total rental rate was approximately 3.3%. Because Jingdong's income may include logistics revenue, we use Ali's data that are, obviously, much lower than the previous estimate of 12% or even 24.4% based on specific commodity data. Competitive factors exist that affect the matter.

14.4 Several Forms of Virtual Rent and Their Combinations

In fact, in addition to the "through train," Alibaba and other platform companies also use other methods to collect virtual rent, including the following.

(1) A fixed fee may be charged. The name may be reflected in the membership fee, such as Ali's 1688 platform charges of 6188 yuan/year; a technical service fee, such as Tmall's charge of 30,000–60,000 yuan/year, or platform use fees, such as Jingdong's charge of 500–1000 yuan.
(2) Volume or turnover commission, such as Tmall's commission of 0.5–5% on turnover or the commission rate charged by Jingdong, which varies according to different commodities but is generally less than 10% and has a median value, is approximately 5%.
(3) Security deposits are collected. For example, Tmall receives a security deposit of 50,000–150,000 yuan, whereas Jingdong receives a margin of 30,000–100,000 yuan. Although the deposit is returned to the merchant at the time of withdrawal, under normal circumstances, the merchant does not withdraw, and the deposit becomes the platform's income with a value that can be assessed from its interest.

In general, although these methods of charging fees differ, they actually charge virtual rents. For example, regarding the platform usage fee, obviously, when the platform was built and became very popular, realistic virtual rent will be formed. Merchants are willing to pay for this differential benefit. For example, Tmall was set up after Taobao became a trend, the consumer population density on Taobao already reflects the reality of market network externalities, and the potential benefits of this reality have already been presented. Therefore, charging a platform usage fee is a form of a fee that explicitly acknowledges the existence of "land rent." The form of the commission collected based on volume or turnover is charged after a differential benefit has been realized. This differential benefit is not only charged on the basis of the benefit from the differential advantage but also without any error (as opposed to, e.g., the so-called conversion rate of a nonstop train), making it a very simple and very straightforward way to charge virtual rent (Fig. 14.11).

$$\text{Generalizing the 12-inch sales function } y = 182479x^{-2.326}$$

$$\text{Sales}: y = A / x^{B}$$

$$\text{Bidding cost}: p = -y'$$

$$\text{Commission}: c = r * y$$

$$\text{Platform usage fee}: f = C$$

where x is the number of pages, and A, B, and C are constants.

The platform fee f can be understood as the average fixed fee, which is the total fixed fee divided by the number of users. According to the previous discussion, this fee is absolute rent. In fact, the usage fees of current online trading platforms are not based on the average fixed asset costs of all merchant users. Analyzing the usage fees of Tmall, JD.com, and 1688 shows that this fee is charged to places near the city center after a huge virtual city has emerged. For example, Tmall is based on Taobao. Previously, Taobao was basically free to enter, which enabled it to attract millions of businesses in a short period, quickly gather the popularity of consumers, and bring huge market network externalities and related benefits. On this basis, the differential benefit of the virtual city has already apparently appeared. Developing a "high-grade commercial area" (Tmall) near the "city center" and collecting the platform usage fee is realistic.

Jingdong's model is slightly different from that of Taobao-Tmall. Jingdong is a virtual city built on a self-employed basis. It attracts

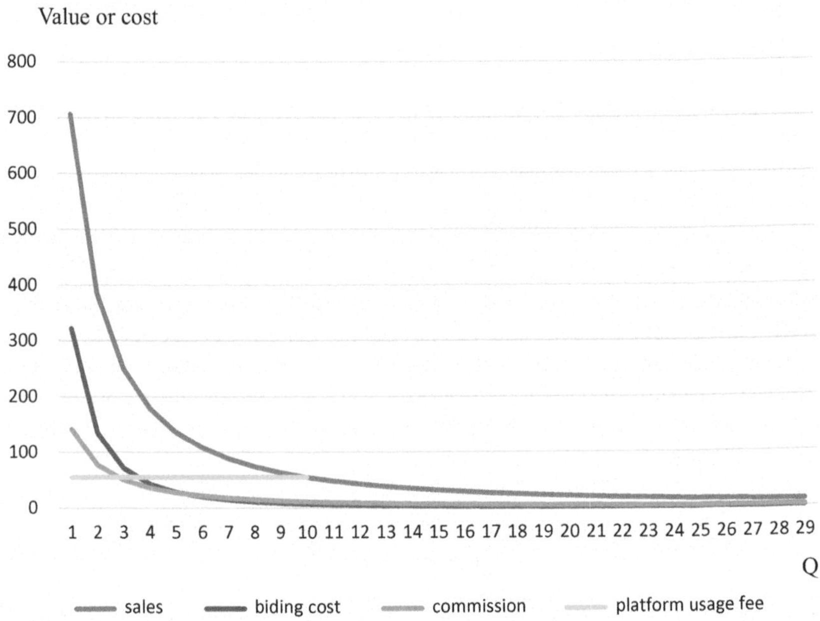

Fig. 14.11 Several forms of collecting virtual differential rents

consumers through its multiple products, thus forming a virtual agglomeration point with significant differential benefits. At this time, charging the merchant a platform usage fee will provide real value as a return.

1688 and other online wholesale trading platforms are of another nature. Because the demand for wholesale comes from retail sales, as long as retailers form a cluster and successfully attract a large number of consumers, demand for wholesale will exist. Therefore, the success of the 1688 platform depends on the success of Taobao. Taobao has brought significant demand from retailers. The 1688 platform as a subsidiary of Ali naturally receives many purchases from Taobao retailers. Therefore, the 1688 platform fee collection can be said to have not left the basic mode of an online trading platform, that is, zero price entry, gathering popularity, forming a virtual city, and bringing huge market network externalities.

That is, in theory, the platform's fixed fee should be paid by all users as an average fixed fee for the payment of absolute rent to cover the total fixed fee. However, in reality, given the zero marginal cost characteristic of the online trading platform, by the rule that price equals marginal cost, for the platform to charge all users is impossible. Because of the market network externalities formed by the platform's aggregated consumer traffic, a virtual rent is then formed, and the platform charges users in the vicinity of the central location for rent in the form of differential rent. It is possible and, therefore, it contains the content of absolute rent. That is, by collecting differential rent from a portion of users, the collection of absolute rent has been completed.

Judging from the fixed investment of platform companies, platform usage fees are a type of compensation for capital investments; from the perspective of network platform businesses, these fees represent the purchase of differential benefits, that is, the payment of differential rent. The two are not contradictory. Because virtual space is not naturally generated, it is an artificial space that requires capital investment. Therefore, virtual land is a capital investment, and the return on virtual land is the return on a capital investment.

We slightly modify the regression equations of the aforementioned sales of network platforms and the average fixed-cost equations of the trading platform to form a system of equations:

$$R = p = -y' = -(A / xB)'$$
$$AFt = F / x$$

Among them, R is virtual differential rent, which is theoretically equal to the price of the ranking bid and is also equal to the derivative of the sales volume. x is the number of platform merchants; however, in the sales regression equation, x is the number of businesses sorted from the first page's first position. F is the fixed investment total, and AF is the average fixed cost per user (Fig. 14.12).

Of these two functions, one is a first-order equation and the other is a multiple-order equation. Obviously, their trajectories are different, where one is steeper than the other, which also indicates that an intersection must exist between them. The solved x value, x', is this intersection, which indicates that the R value corresponding to this point, that is, the platform usage fee or the average fixed cost, is the level at which the platform fixed fee is fully compensated. At the price of this platform usage fee—at the margin—a merchant at least earns back the platform usage fee that he or she paid from sales, whereas many merchants (i.e., businesses ranked

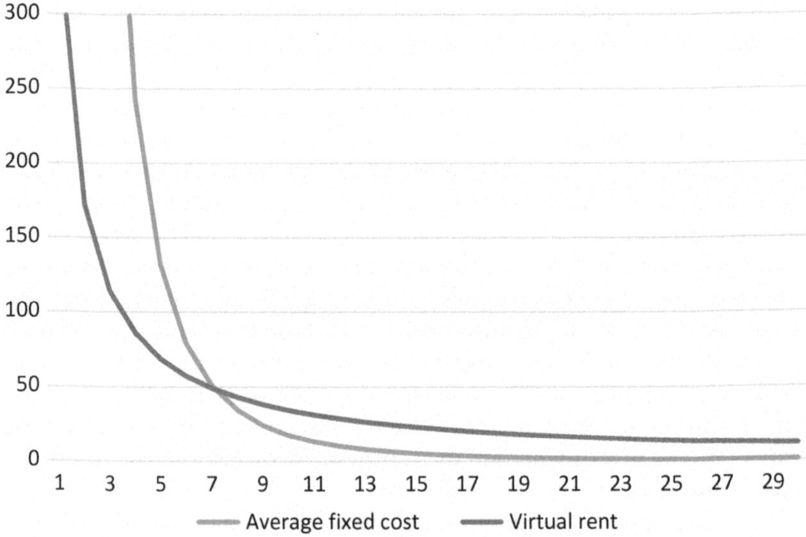

Fig. 14.12 Intersection of average fixed cost and differential rent

before x') receive a higher sales return. This finding shows that an online platform may collect usage fees from some users rather than from all users, that is, it can impose the platform usage fee on only some merchants (those ranked before x') but not on merchants ranked after x'. To do so, all fixed costs invested in the trading platform can be covered. For those businesses that are ranked after x's, they still enter the trading platform at zero prices, similar to Taobao.

We use the data in Alibaba's annual report to simulate the platform (Fig. 14.13). Here, we have to make some amendments to the previous equations because many types of commodities exist on a trading platform, and we can think of them as three-dimensional. We use Alibaba's 2016 annual cost of 34.35 billion yuan as the fixed cost of the platform for the year, and annual sales were 3.1 trillion yuan (Alibaba 2017). The proportion of total sales based on page 1 is approximately 71%. One page of sales was estimated at 2201 billion yuan. The parameters of the regression equation apply that of the 12-inch tablet.

$$AF_{2016} = 343.5 / x$$

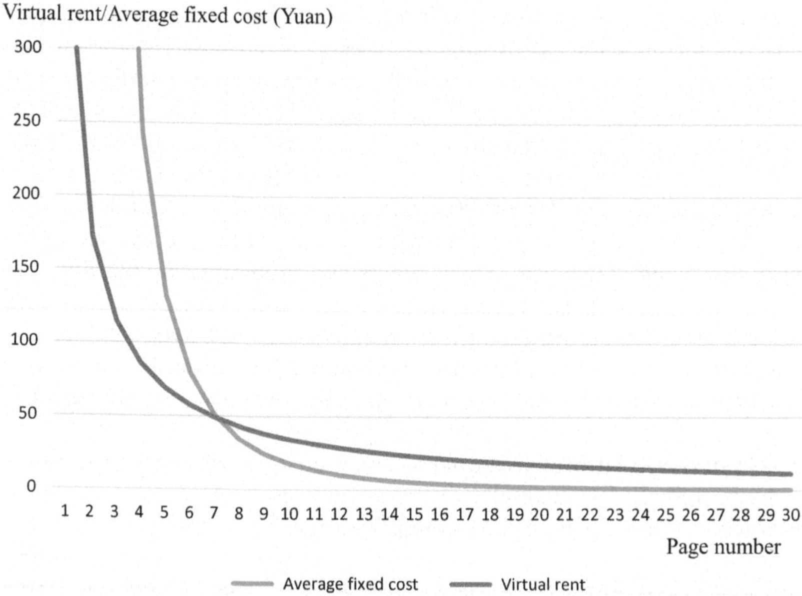

Fig. 14.13 Simulated equilibrium between average fixed cost and virtual differential rent (Alibaba platform, 100 million yuan). Explanation: The blue line in this figure represents the average fixed cost, and the orange line represents the virtual rent

$$y = 22010 / x^{2.326}$$
$$R = -y' = 2557763 / \left(50 * x^{1663/500}\right)$$

When $AF_{2016} = R$,

$$x \approx 8.7$$

X equals 8.7, which means that page 8.7 is the equilibrium point where the average fixed cost equals the virtual differential rent. Platform companies can compensate for their fixed investment as long as they charge the platform usage fee equivalent to the average fixed fee to the merchants before page 8.7. Available data show that 9.4 million sellers are on Taobao with approximately 100 pages for each product type. In other words, 8.7% of the merchants, or approximately 818,000 merchants, pay for the use of the platform, which can cover Ali's fixed costs. Substituting this number into the formula for calculating the average fixed cost (AF) results in 42,003 yuan. That is, if each annual platform usage fee (AF) is set at 42,003 yuan, approximately 818,000 merchants will consider it worthwhile to pay, indicating that the fixed costs of Ali's platform are covered.

Of course, the actual data are that the usage fee of the Tmall platform is approximately 30,000–60,000 yuan, and another 50,000–150,000 yuan in security deposits are equivalent to the platform usage fee previously estimated. However, Tmall sellers are approximately 60,000, and the number of merchants is much lower than that previously estimated because other factors are at play in market practice, such as people's habits, competition from other platforms, and being still in a transitional process that has not reached equilibrium. What is important is that Alibaba also does not fully rely on the idea of using platform fees to recover full costs. In addition to platform usage fees, Tmall charges sales commissions of between 0.5% and 5%, as well as a "nonstop-train," which partly compensates for the fixed costs of the trading platform.

If the platform usage fee corresponds to a fixed cost, the sales commission may correspond to a variable cost. Because the variable cost varies according to the number of products or services provided, the unit variable cost does not change. The sales commission also has such a nature, but the sales amount is the benefit realized from enjoying the service and is proportional to the number of services and, thus, also approximately corresponds to the amount of services. To charge according to sales using a certain percentage is to charge according to the amount of services. Obviously, the optimal commission rate should equal the variable cost of the services that realize a unit of sales and, of course, also contain reasonable profits. The key is that we need to obtain data on variable costs. Generally, the cost of an online trading platform is believed to be mainly a computing cost. Whether or not a calculation is provided, the cloud computing platform always needs to stand by and consume various operating costs. Therefore, the variable cost (marginal cost) is at least close to zero. Other reasons exist for receiving positive sales commissions, such as compensating for fixed costs.

Pay-per-click has two properties. First, this bidding process is for virtual space allocation that makes the allocation more effective and brings more benefits. It is beneficial to both buyers and sellers and platforms. First, the return caused by virtual agglomeration brings about virtual rent, and this type of agglomeration with urban characteristics has a certain level of monopoly. In fact, when we talk about differential rent, it means that "good land" is limited; otherwise, no differential rent will exist. The so-called differential indicates that different virtual spaces have different "passenger flow" and, thus, different "markets." There is a "page market" on a page of the online trading platform with limited and clear borders. The market size is determined by the volume of traffic on this page. The number of sellers accommodated is limited. Other sellers cannot access this "page market" unless they pay a higher virtual rent and squeeze out the same number of other sellers. Because this "page market" is limited, it is not completely competitive.

At this point, we must distinguish between two pairs of different transactions on the trading platform. A pair is a transaction between a seller and a platform, and another pair is a seller-to-buyer transaction. The first pair of transactions is that multiple companies compete for the entrance to the limited "page market." In contrast, only for a platform company—a one-to-many deal—will pricing obviously benefit the platform side and, thus, pay-per-click bidding will reach a considerable height. If no other platforms exist, the platform side can grab almost all differential rents. Therefore, it should be said that the pay-per-click revenue generated by the platform is monopolistic in nature. Therefore, the pricing principle is not marginal cost pricing under perfect competition but pricing under monopolistic competition. This type of monopolistic nature of fees should also be a typical business model of trading platform companies because the initial investment in the platform means the establishment of a virtual city, the formation of virtual agglomeration, and the harvest of virtual rent.

The other pair of transactions in the "page market," namely, the buyer's and the seller's transactions, have a monopoly given the limited number of sellers, but there may be no monopoly pricing. As long as the number of sellers exceeds three, there will be effective competition and no monopoly-competition pricing. However, there may be a monopoly on the costumer resources of a specific "page market," which is reflected in higher sales volume and, thus, higher selling revenue. This situation can be called "low-price monopoly" or "customer flow monopoly."

When economists talk about "rents," they imply that resources are scarce; monopoly increases from supply scarcity increases in a particular platform space. Therefore, the virtual rent of the online trading platform contains a monopolistic, certainly not competitive price. This type of monopoly is also a result of the investment of platform investors and, thus, their income is reasonable.

14.5 Analysis of Incentive Effect of Several Types of Virtual Rent

When we consider platform usage fees as virtual rents, we find that it is one type of land rent, that is, fixed rent. Economics traditionally believes that fixed rent is an efficient form of rent because, under fixed rent, 100% of the income generated by all of the new inputs of tenants becomes the income of tenants, and landowners do not increase their income accordingly. This situation offers strong incentives for tenants who will not only invest more time in labor but also continuously improve the fertility of the land and invest in land-matching equipment. When the time is long enough, as in a permanent tenancy system, the increased land productivity of the tenants results in additional land rents. The tenant also has the right to transfer this part of the land benefit to others and to obtain land rent and become the owner of some land property rights, that is, the owner of the "surface right of farming land" (盛洪 2014). This nature also exists on Internet trading platforms. Only now do platform companies adjust the platform usage fee from time to time, which is equivalent to a shorter lease term. When the platform extends the lease period of the determined platform usage fee, such as by ten or twenty years or even longer, the aforementioned incentive effect on permanent tenants will appear. At that time, we will also see businesses that continue to provide input to the "land" of an online platform and the resulting new virtual rents. These businesses can even sell these new differential benefit rights and become owners of the online "surface right of farming land."

If the platform usage fee is fixed rent, the commission represents sharing land rent, and only their share ratio is fixed. Previous economic theories considered that sharing rent was inefficient because it reduced the incentive for tenants to invest in labor and capital. However, Steven Cheung's "The Theory of Share Tenancy" proved that sharing rent is efficient. He pointed out that because agricultural products face harvest risk, and harvests in different years fluctuate greatly, "share tenancy may then be regarded as a device for risk sharing" (2000, p. 68). Here, Cheung assumed that the landowner focused on the interest of property rights rather than improving the land or land allocation. However, in the context of online trading platforms, platform companies have incentives to improve platform services and platform space allocations because of commissions—a kind of sharing rent. This is because, given that sellers' revenue can be shared, the revenue generated by platform improvements also partially flow into their pockets, and the platform has the means to improve platform services and platform space allocation. In the former, the efficiency of the platform operation is improved and a user's transaction costs are reduced. The latter is to improve the position of different sellers in the platform space, enabling more effective sellers to be in a more favorable position, thereby maximizing the benefits of the entire platform.

Therefore, what is an appropriate rate of sharing rent? We found that the commission rates of different commodities are different for the Tmall and Jingdong platforms. Is this difference related to the degree of risk of different commodities? Steven Cheung pointed out that "as long as higher transaction costs can be compensated at least by the benefits of diversification of risks, people choose sharing contract rather than a fixed-rent or wage contract" (2000, pp. 100–101). In the online trading platform, the operation of determining the revenue and dividing it into the agreed-on proportion is almost at a zero cost. Therefore, the transaction cost of the sharing contract is very low, and other reasons may exist that affect the proportion of shares. The first reason is the degree of risk of the product. According to Cheung's theory, the higher the degree of risk, the more it needs a sharing contract. Does this affect the share ratio? It should be said that the degree of risk will have no effect. The proportion should be a reasonable rate of rent averaged over many years and should equal the corresponding fixed rent rate. For example, the fixed rent rate is 100 jins, the average of a multiyear harvest is 200 jins, and the sharing rent rate is 50%. In financial economics terminology, the means of sharing rent and fixed rent are equal, but the variance is not the same. The variance of fixed rent is zero, and the variance of sharing rent is positive. A large variance means large fluctuations and high risks.

Therefore, what is an appropriate commission rate? Among various platforms, we found that only Dunhuang.com does not charge platform usage fees but only commissions, which is a relatively pure form of a commission. According to the different products, commissions are charged at three levels, and each level reduces the commission rate according to the increase in the sales amount of each order (Table 14.1). This practice of decreasing the commission rate by sales amount slightly flattens the total commissions charged by some platforms, which is closer to platform usage fees maintaining a horizontal state.

Therefore, what are the different commission rates for different categories? In the previous discussion, we found that different commodities have different agglomeration levels, different market network externalities, and

Table 14.1 Dunhuang website commission rate

	0–300	*300–1000*	*1000–5000*	*5 K–10 K*	*>10 K*
A	8.50%	4.00%	2.00%	1.00%	0.50%
B	12.5%	4.00%	2.00%	1.00%	0.50%
C	15.50%	4.00%	2.00%	1.00%	0.50%

Source: Dunhuang Website (http://seller.dhgate.com/promotion/xzjiedu.html?d=f-4xzsxgg)

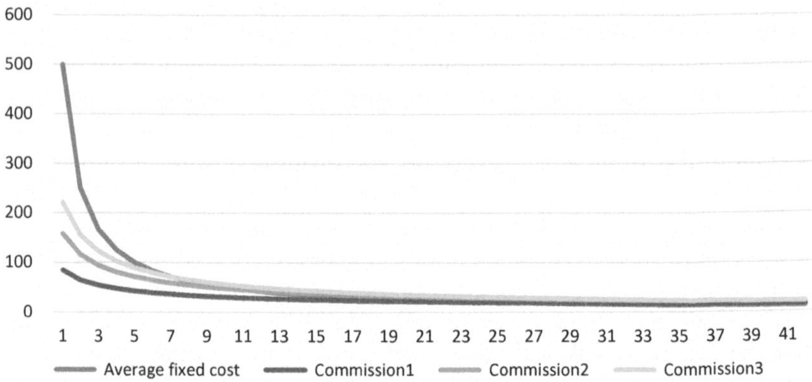

Fig. 14.14 Breakeven point for different commission rates. Illustration: In this figure, the horizontal axis represents the number of transactions, and the vertical axis represents the amount of income or average fixed cost per transaction

different specific functions of differential benefits. Different levels are needed to consider commission rates that cover all costs.

In Fig. 14.14, the average fixed cost is the same for different commodities, where an average fixed cost curve represents three average fixed costs for three commodities. Commission 1, commission 2, and commission 3 represent the commissions that the three types of goods receive at different sales commission rates. The commission rates for these three types of commodities are different. The higher the sales, the lower the commission rate, which decreases with an increase in sales, as seen in the previous example of Dunhuang.com. The specific degrees of agglomeration and differential benefit of different commodities differ, and sales are different. However, because the cost of the platform is based on the number of transactions rather than turnover, the transaction should be charged according to the number of transactions. However, it cannot be fully charged according to the number of transactions, which will reduce the number of goods sellers with smaller sales, thus reducing the variety of commodities traded on and the scope economy of the platform. Therefore, because the commission rate with relatively small sales is higher, and the commission rate with relatively large sales is slightly lower, the final commission for goods with three different sales amounts is roughly the same.

As previously shown, commissions for different types of commodities intersect with the average fixed-cost curve in different positions. On the margins of these three points, the commissions of merchants that sell different products offset the average fixed fee. The commission rate determined on these three points is equivalent to platform usage fees that equal the average fixed costs. If the number of transactions is lower than these three points, the commission rate is lower than the equilibrium commission rate. For a higher volume in each transaction, however, the commission is higher than that at equilibrium. The higher part is the portion that merchants regard the platform deserves, given its risk sharing with them, and it is considered worth paying. When the number of transactions exceeds these three points, the commission rate is higher than the platform usage fee at equilibrium, and merchants may be attracted to other platforms. Therefore, the highest commission rates for these three commodities do not exceed the three equilibrium points.

The trading forms of other trading platforms, such as Tmall and Jingdong, are commissions grafted on platform usage fees and are a composite form, assuming that the platform usage fee does not achieve the goal of fully reimbursing the fixed cost. Because commissions are a type of supplement and not very pure, I am not discussing them further.

However, regarding platforms that have the incentive to improve the seller's allocation in platform space under the form of a commission, it is necessary to continue discussing the bidding mechanism, which is the aforementioned pay-per-click auction. This mechanism is for a broader view of land rent. In an ideal land market system, tenants bid on different lands. In general, farmers who are more able to farm have higher prices for better land; that is, they are willing to pay higher rent rates. Assume that there are two farmers, A and B, and there are two pieces of land, good land and bad land. B's labor productivity is E, A's labor productivity is $E + \Delta E$, the land productivity of the bad land is R, and the good land's productivity is $R + \Delta R$. Then, there are four combinations. See Table 14.2.

The combined productivities of the four combinations are as follows:

Table 14.2 Combination of two farmers with good land and **bad land**

	Farmer A	*Farmer B*
Good land	$(R + \Delta R) \times (E + \Delta E)$	$(R + \Delta R) \times E$
Bad land	$R \times (E + \Delta E)$	$R \times E$

$$\text{Farmer A farming good land} = RE + R\ \ E + \ \ RE + \ \ R\ \ E$$

$$\text{Farmer B farming good land} = RE + \ \ RE$$

$$\text{Farmer A farming bad land} = RE + R\ \ E$$

$$\text{Farmer B farming bad land} = RE$$

That the overall productivity of farmer A farming good land is intuitively the highest, combined with farmer B farming bad land, which is also a combination of the highest productivity of society, that is, the optimal allocation of resources. If the status quo is farmer A farming bad land, farmer B farming good land, changing farmer A from farming bad land to good land, and farmer B from farming good land to bad land, then society will have a $\Delta R \Delta E$ wealth increase, and farmer A will have a $\Delta RE + \Delta R \Delta E$ wealth increase, but farmer B will have a loss of wealth of ΔRE. At this time, if farmer A increases his bid by at least ΔRE for good land, farmer B has no incentive to compete with farmer A for good farming. Of course, landowners also obtained more rents (ΔRE).

The principle of the online trading platform is the same. Sellers with better product quality, broader sales, and better service are in a better position, that is, closer to the "city center," which leads to higher overall productivity and social welfare. Therefore, a better position for the seller to obtain a higher price is an improvement in the resource allocation of the platform space, which is beneficial to society, enables better sellers and platforms, and does not harm poorer sellers. For this reason, the current online trading platform adopts a pay-per-click bidding method. As previously mentioned, given the existence of competition among trading platforms, this bidding method does not absorb all of the platform's differential benefit but enables the merchant to obtain a partial differential benefit, enabling platform companies and merchants to share together the market network externalities and their virtual rent.

14.6 Conclusion

1. Because the online trading platform requires a significant fixed investment and the marginal cost of providing services is almost zero, the pricing principle that the price equals the marginal cost seems unable to make up for its investment.
2. Because the online trading platform has greatly gathered businesses and consumers and has formed a high market network externality, the resulting virtual rent of the cyberspace has become the main source of income for network platform companies that price at zero marginal cost. The problem of zero marginal cost pricing is resolved.
3. The webpage of each product on the online trading platform presents a phenomenon in which the degree of agglomeration is significantly reduced when moving from the first page ("city center") to the second page, the third page, and so on, thereby forming a virtual city image. This image proves that a virtual differential rent exists.
4. The network platform company collects virtual rents in the form of platform usage fees, sales commissions, and ranking bids.
5. Given the existence of multiple network trading platforms, monopolistic competition exists between them, making it impossible for platform companies to obtain all virtual rents.
6. Because the virtual rent is mainly located near the center (first page) part, the platform company can only charge merchants near the center part with the virtual rent to meet the goal of covering all costs while maintaining the zero price for the "edge" merchants. The existence of the latter is an important factor in the formation of a significant agglomeration.
7. The form of the platform usage fee is equivalent to a fixed rent, which has a significant incentive on businesses. However, only if the cost is stable over a long period can it play a greater role; the form of a commission is equivalent to sharing rent, which plays the role of an incentive for businesses and platforms. Ranking bidding is equivalent to bidding for land rent, which helps improve the space allocation of businesses on the platform, thereby improving the efficiency of platform trading.

References

Alibaba, Alibaba Group Holding Limited Index to Financial Statements, 2017. https://www.sec.gov/Archives/edgar/data/1577552/000104746916013400/a2228766z20-f.htm.

Coase, The Marginal Cost Controversy, Economica, New Series, Vol. 13, No. 51 (Aug., 1946), pp. 169–182.

JD.com, Inc. 2017. http://ir.jd.com/phoenix.zhtml?c=253315&p=irol-irhome.

Steven Cheung, *Theory of Share Tenancy*, Arcadia Press, 2000.

盛洪, "永佃制的经济性质", 《制度经济学评论》, 2014 年第 4 期; (Sheng Hong, "The Economic Nature of Permanent Tenancy", Review of Institutional Economics, No. 4, 2014)

CHAPTER 15

Religious Person and His or Her Implication in Institutions

Contents

15.1 Issue Raised

The observation of institutional structure determines that no institution in a heteronomy can satisfactorily restrict individuals or organizations from impinging on others' interests. For instance, if there are problems of externality, public goods, and monopoly, the market system will fail. One solution to overcoming market failure is to establish a government. However, solving this problem causes a bigger problem because differences among individual traders in the market are not enormous. Enterprises may have different sizes but no differences in rights. Once a government is established, it can be enormous and can monopolize power. Such power is a force of dominance supported by public violence, which is stronger than

Translated from *The Review of New Political Economy*, Volume 28.

Sheng Hong, *Vision and Calculation*,
https://doi.org/10.1007/978-981-15-2898-9_15

rights because it can limit rights. Once a government fails, subsequently solving problems will be more difficult.

One solution is democracy; that is, all citizens have the right to determine their legal and governmental leaders through voting, thus restraining the government's cross-border expansion. However, democracy may fail sometimes. For instance, in Condorcet's majority of a cycle, Borda mentioned that elections might select out the least-welcome people. Regarding Arrow's voting paradox, Buchanan noted logrolling and the tyranny of the majority; Olsen noted that minority interest groups are more powerful; and so on. As a result, once a government leader is elected, he or she may use his or her real power to change the existing law to obtain more power (such as Hitler or Chavez). Even though the expansion of personal power is restrained, the government's expansion is still difficult to avoid (such as Europe and the United States after Second World War). More importantly, even if democracy fails, stakeholders cannot fade out society just as they did in an existing market, because doing so means to be displaced.

According to Hayek, the solution to the failure of democracy is the rule of law rather than the rule by men. The ultimate form of the rule of law is constitutionalism, that is, restraining power through constitution. However, the rule of law is still the rule of law by men. Paradox thus comes: if you want to restrain power, especially the supreme power or the de facto supreme power (such as military power), is there a need for a greater power to restrain the supreme power? If not, according to the Economic Person hypothesis, how could those in power consciously restrain themselves? If there is such a greater power, who is going to master it?

More generally, these questions can be classified as a failure of the individualistic assumption. If we assume that society is full of individuals who only attempt to pursue their maximum interests, having a range of institutional arrangements designed for the nature of the Economic Person will be impossible for effectively restraining all people in society from crossing their right or power border and violating or impinging on other's rights, especially the rights of citizens in general. That is, within the scope of economics, namely, assuming that people are rational Economic Persons, no institutional structure can solve the problem of power restraint. We can guess that constitutionalism, which used to be considered the power restraint, is not only to take advantage of human instincts to favor benefit and avoid cost but also has some other contributing factors.

In fact, economists have realized this problem. Santa Fe Institute has pointed out that society will collapse eventually if there is only a self-interested Economic Person; even if there are some weak reciprocators, this destiny cannot be avoided because selfish people cannot be stopped from violating covenants for their interests. Only if strong reciprocators are evolved out and do not hesitate to pay extra to maintain the market order and contract principles can social survival and development be achieved (Bowles and Gintis 2004). However, no one has the answer to how these strong reciprocators evolved.

Buchanan concluded that "a unanimous constitution is the best constitution." After this, he asked another question: Who drafts the constitution? Economics cannot answer this question. A good constitution can benefit not only the contemporary people but also the future generation. How can drafters obtain rewards from the future generation? Therefore, Buchanan used ethics to explain, that is, let those who have "ethics of constitutional citizenship" draft the constitution (2008, pp. 153–205). Subsequently, he summarized his theory in "The Economics and Ethics of Constitutional Order." However, Buchanan did not answer this question: Where did those who have "ethics of constitutional citizenship" come from?

In this regard, our question is, if heteronomy institutions based on individualism cannot provide satisfactory functions to restrain power, then self-disciplined individuals and corresponding institutions become necessary. What do these self-disciplined institutions look like? Where do these self-disciplined people come from? Even for people who are self-disciplined, are they strong enough to resist the great temptation of power?

15.2 Religious Person

Here, a Religious Person is a general concept that also applies to economics. The term Religious Person includes not only the current followers of religions or the noble men and women who comply with religious culture but all who believe the existence of a Heavenly course or the highest justice that is above individual interests. These people are willing to sacrifice their personal interests to fulfill the Heavenly course or the highest justice. In economics, "Religious Person" can be used as a counterpart to "Economic Person." An Economic Person only does things for his or her benefit, whereas the Religious Person may do something against him or herself but that he or she believes benefits others.

More specifically, a Religious Person can jump out of his or her interests to view relationships with others on a neutral stand; these individuals even can perceive things in a holistic (social and universal) manner. Therefore, when encountering a conflict of interests with others, they can put themselves in others' shoes to consider these issues and not just see things from their perspective. Thus, they can be more just when dealing with conflicts. When a choice is favorable for the entire society but has no good for himself or herself, the Religious Person is still able to make such a decision.

Apparently, a Religious Person is different not only from self-serving people (shortsighted economic individuals) but also from weak reciprocators (economic individuals with long-term vision). Augustine stated that free will can lead people to choose to live morally because it is impossible for everyone to lead an immoral life without being harmed, but harm can be avoided if everyone chooses to lead a moral life (quoted from Huang Yusheng 2008, pp. 110–111). This "moral life" is nothing but a long-term vision of the economy's choice, and these people are very similar to the Economic Person described by Adam Smith in "Theory of Moral Sentiments." From the comparison of longer-term costs and benefits, the conclusion can be made that following moral principles can benefit themselves. However, people can only follow these principles to a certain degree. Once the costs related to following them outweigh the benefits, these moral principles are no longer followed.

Even regarding some behaviors that seem altruistic, Smith would still say that they are from "self-love," "a love for their own good character" (p. 137, quoted in Coase 2010, p. 118). This self-love is, of course, not limitless. Coase once interrogated Adam Smith's metaphorical assumption of "hundreds of millions of Chinese people's life and his little finger" to say: "would a humane person be willing to sacrifice his little finger if it can save millions of Chinese life?" He then followed: "if not to lose the little finger, but the arm or thigh, and he can only save 100 Chinese people, rather than 100 million, the decision probably would be made differently." Sympathetic behavior is the same as other ones: "to which degree to practice them depends on the price which has to be paid" (page 118).

However, it is not so with Religious People. When they do what they think is right, they do not care too much about whether or not to bear the price. Of course, a different price could be borne by different Religious Persons according to their different "religiousness," which can mean thinking lightly of fame or money (such as the Joy of Kong and Yan, 孔颜之乐) or sacrificing their life (such as the crucifixion of Jesus). Religiousness is individual thinking of a holistic situation, and the word "holistic" includes the entire space and eternal time. Differentiating from the weak reciprocators, the wholeness of a Religious Person is limitless, whereas the vision of the Economic Person is limited regardless of the long-term sighted vision that they have. When things are viewed from a holistic approach, the situation is more accurate and comprehensive than having been viewed through a limited vision.

Then, how to become this Religious Person? Confucius said: "those who are born to know are the best, and those who learn to know are secondary" (生而知之者上也, 学而知之者次也). This statement implies that some persons are naturally born with religious awareness. However, they are rare, and most people have to obtain such awareness through learning and religious inspiration. Thus, becoming a Religious Person from an Economic Person is a process, which was usually called the process of conversion or self-refining. This converting process is not an insignificant shift and is not just a change in a person's ideas—it is a psychological change, a fundamental transformation of basic human nature. It is not a wonder that the exploration of how this transformation happens is one of the key topics of research in Religious Psychology.

The reason Economic Persons can become Religious Persons is because every human heart harbors religious awareness or, as Mencius said, "good source." Why does an individual who is self-interested have this good source? It is because each individual, from the very beginning, is part of the whole. During hundreds of millions of years of interaction with the whole as an individual, he or she must contain some sort of "wholeness." Precisely because of such wholeness—similar to how the individual feels about the costs and benefits—can the complex creature and society constituted thereof be evolved.

However, religious awareness was usually buried deep in a person's heart, and only through a heuristic process can it be stimulated. In general, religion means not only religious classics (texts) but also a set of heuristic religious ceremonies and often an organization. This heuristic process of religion or of a good source has been spoken in different religious or cultural traditions. Wang Yangming's metaphor is that this religious awareness or good source is similar to a mirror, and the heuristic process to stimulate this good source is the process of polishing the mirror. However, the rust on the mirror is "human desire," that is, the flesh desire. Thus, Wang Yangming said: "Once flesh desire ends, Heavenly justice begins." In other words, once we go beyond personal interest, we see the

Heavenly course or God's justice. Such metaphors can be found in the Christian Bible, the Koran, and the Buddhist scriptures, among others.

15.3 Psychological Description of Becoming a Religious Person and Its Significance

Modern Western psychology of religion provides many cases of a religious conversion experience. In the book, "The Varieties of Religious Experience," many psychological experiences were quoted, such as the following.

Stephen Bradley:	*"My heart continues to accelerate, and soon I was convinced that it is the Holy Spirit compelling me." (James, 2012, p. 144)*
S. H. Hadley:	*"I sat there contemplating, feeling a great and extraordinary thing appearing to me ... later I learned it was Jesus." (James, 2012, p. 145)*
David Brainerd:	*"I went into the thick woods; an indescribable glory seemed suddenly being revealed and was comprehended by my soul." (James, 2012, p. 156)*
Alan:	*"Suddenly, the redeeming love flowing from the chanting verses pierced into my soul, so strong that my whole heart was melt in love." (James, 2012, p. 163)*
Alphonse Lahti Hobsbawm:	*"When I left church, a full of brightness filled eyes ... as if a man born blind suddenly opened his eyes and saw the bright daylight." (James, 2012, p. 169)*
Aylward, famous in China:	*"One night, for some reason I cannot explain, I attended a religious gathering, where I first realized God has a calling for my life, so I accepted Christ Jesus as my Savior." (Gladys, 1974, p. 1)*

Through this psychological process, people completely changed, including as follows.

T. W. B.:	*"When my consciousness becomes alive again, I was kneeling down, praying not for myself, but for others ... the care for myself seemed completely lost, giving way to the concern for others." (James, 2012, p. 157)*

Alan:	*"I am eager to fulfill the cause of Christ. ... I have completely lost the interests in worldly pleasures, worldly partner, so it is possible for me to stay away from them." (James, 2012, p. 216)*
A correspondent of Professor Liu Ba:	*"I submitted myself entirely to God, and firmly convinced that my own self would be destroyed and He would take everything from me, but I am willing to do so." (James, 2012, p. 219)*
Alphonse Latisbon:	*"I only know I was changed, and I believe I have become another self. I was looking for myself within me, but never succeed." (James, 2012, p. 221)*

After the conversion, their behaviors changed.

Alan immediately became a Christian missionary. "He dedicated his whole life to public affairs and his position responsibilities, which made him qualified enough to be ranked among the most pious saints. Although he obtained his happiness in hard work, he never tasted worldly pleasures any longer" (James 2012, p. 216).

Regarding the correspondent of Professor Liu Ba, he once was a heavy smoker and drunkard but completely quit after conversion (James 2012, pp. 219–220).

Aylward subsequently read an article about China and then was determined to go to China as a missionary. During China's Anti-Japanese War, she adopted and rescued more than one hundred orphans and escorted them through the mountains all the way from the Yangcheng of Shanxi Province to Xian (Gladys 1974).

If we think carefully about these cases of conversion, it is not difficult for us to see the religious conversion process and its result, which is to reduce or even cancel concerns for personal interest and transform them into caring for others, for all of society, and for all human beings. This result was specifically embodied as awe and obedience to God, who is the divine existence on behalf of the entire universe. This result could also be illustrated from the perspective of economics: a common Economic Person transforming into a Religious Person. Thus, economics as analyzed on the premise of the Economic Person would be no longer valid.

This spiritual orientation of obeying God, that is, obeying the overall interests while ignoring one's interests, makes economic analysis ineffective because it enables religious people to choose to abandon completely their personal interests, that is, even in the face of death, it will not change.

As Voith Sarkozy said: "If any harm comes, they are willing to endure, for the Lord is their protector; if not by the Lord's will, nothing would happen. If this is the Lord's will, then even harm is to them, a blessing, not calamity" (James 2012, p. 271).

Of course, "The Varieties of Religious Experience" is only for Christianity studies. In other religious and cultural traditions, no mature research exists, only some records, such as the information on Wang Yangming's "Longchang Wudao" (龙场悟道, Realizing the doctrines of Confucianism at Longchang in Guizhou Province) as recorded in "Wang Yangming Chronicle" as follows.

Being pursued by Liu Jin, he came to know that those things like honor or dishonor, gains or loss, are nothing, only life and death are incomprehensible. So, he sat by a stone and said to himself: "I will leave my life to God's disposal!" From then on, he barely speak to anyone and remained silent for days and nights so as to have pure thought and heart; after a while, He felt his heart being brightened and was at peace with himself. But his accompanies were very ill, so he make[s] [a] fire and got water to cook food for them; being concerned that they may be distressed, he then [sang] for them; but it did not make them happy, so he [sang] their hometown songs and telling them jokes. This has made them [forget] their sickness and sufferings. Wang then said to himself: "If the saints were in my shoes, how would they feel?" One night, he suddenly rose up from bed, feeling someone was speaking to him about Confucian thoughts: to observe things and to know the wisdom behind, and immediately being enlightened. His accompanies were woken up by his excitement. He then realized that to look for justice from outside is wrong, but to find peace within self is the right answer.

Wang's Longchang Wudao can be viewed as a process of forgetting self-interests and understanding the Heavenly course by heart.

In fact, the distinction between a gentleman and an ordinary person has long existed in China. In this context, the ordinary person is the Economic Person, and the "gentleman" is the Religious Person. Confucius said: "the gentleman sees righteousness; the ordinary person sees profits." This statement means that the gentleman thinks highly of righteousness (heavenly righteousness) and thinks little of self-interests. Mencius said: "To live is what I desire, while to be righteousness is also my desire. If one cannot have both, then sacrifice life for the righteousness." This statement indicates, for the sake of heavenly righteousness, that he is willing to sacrifice his life. However, in addition to the way of knowing the heavenly course through self-enlightenment, such as Wang Yangming, another way is self-refinement, that is, becoming a noble man or woman by reading sacred books. Many studies exist on this topic, but we need to carefully extract and refine them.

After all, after a religious conversion or understanding the heavenly course, people come to a new psychological balance. William James, the author of "The *Varieties of Religious Experience*," called this balance "attributes of saints," which includes the following:

Feel like living a life in a broader sense, detached from the little personal interests of this world ....
Feel the power desired is connected with our own lives ....
Extreme excitement and freedom, as if the boundary of self-restraint was melted away ....
For those demands beyond self-willing, emotion-centered decision making turned to love and harmony .... (James 2012, pp. 267–268)

Apparently, a distinctive difference exists between the attributes of saints and Economic Persons, and the latter emphasizes shunning harm and inclining to benefits, making decisions for self-benefits, and opposing things that are disadvantageous to themselves. However, the former (the saints) has no such thoughts at all. They go beyond self-interests and demand "denying self" (Points 1 and 4), connecting self with the heavenly righteousness (the "ideal power"). That is why he or she feels the boundary between himself or herself and society or the entire universe being melt away (Point 3). However, a Religious Person with the attributes of a saint is not completely against the Economic Person. His or her happiness does not only come from forgetting self-interests and its concerns attached but also from society and themselves. A mutually beneficial relationship exists between the whole and the individual, and we can say that a Religious Person does not deny the Economic Person but goes beyond that person.

If we are convinced that such Religious Persons exist, then it is natural to think that, because of the differences they have with Economic Persons that go beyond personal interests, the paradox of how to restrain the greatest power in political structures raised in the first section might be solved.

15.4 United States: Case Study

Generally, American constitutional democracy has been believed as successful for the result of the check and balance mechanisms contained in such a system. This outcome is good from a general point of view. However, this general view obscures a more important fact that such a system cannot achieve a perfect balance in all aspects. In contrast, this view makes people mistakenly think that once you have this mechanism of checks and balances, moral self-discipline is not necessary, and its role in the institutional structure is not important at all.

However, facts do not reflect this belief. An example is the establishment of the United States, which we know is not just a well-designed secular political structure but is filled with ideal Puritan moral passion, and the latter is an important pillar of the American constitutional framework. John Eidsmoe, author of *"Christianity and the Constitution: The Faith of Our Founding Fathers,"* pointed out the following: the Puritans emigrated from England to North America who primarily wanted to build a "City of God" in North America, which is a Christian utopia described by Augustine. Some people even called Calvin the true father of the United States (2010, p. 4).

Is there any significance of the Christian vision to the American constitutional system? This issue is indeed significant; however, given space limitations, it cannot be discussed in detail here. As an alternative, we only conduct a simple discussion through two stories and the Christian background of the American founding fathers.

The first story takes place during the American Constitutional Convention of 1787 in Philadelphia. Delegates of all states were at loggerheads. The convention came to a deadlock, and many of them were about to go home. On June 28, Ben Franklin, at that time 81 years old, stood up and said that human intelligence is limited, and we need the wisdom of God and "God is in charge of man's affairs." Franklin suggested asking pastors to lead the prayers before the General Assembly every day. His proposal was not immediately accepted by most people, but pastors did the prayer eventually after several compromises. Importantly, these formal and informal prayers made people place and reexamine secular issues in God's view. "A harmonious spirit eventually returned to the General Assembly. Delegates reached a broad agreement on most issues, and reconciliation was achieved on other ones" (2010, pp. 321–322). Thus, the U.S. Constitution came into being.

If this story is true, it at least tells us that in cases without religious factors, people only act based on economic logic to approve the choices that are to their advantage and oppose those that are against their interests. In the market, issues exist for which no agreement can ever be reached, but people can just walk away and leave these issues unresolved. However, in public affairs, disputes caused by conflicts of interest cannot be solved simply by walking away and leaving each other in a stalemate. If Religious Person means to weaken or even give up one's interests, doing so will lead representatives to avoid disputing over minor differences, and they may reach an agreement. As Benjamin Franklin said, "I agree to this Constitution because I could not expect a better one, also because I'm not sure this is not the best. Concerning some places which I think are wrong, I am willing to give up my own opinion for the sake of public interest" (Quoted from Eidsmoe 2010, p. 324).

The second story is that, in 1783, after the end of the War of Independence, a group of young army officers attempted to launch a mutiny to overthrow the Continental Congress because of unrealized payments. As soon as Washington learned of this plan, he went to the barracks and persuaded them to give up. Those officers took Washington's advice, and an important tradition in the United States was formed: the military serves under civilian control. At the end of the same year, Washington, after a great victory, returned the military power of commanding the army to the Continental Congress, thus creating a constitutional precedent in the United States, that is, America's military is subordinate to civilian authority. I must say that this is the most important principle of a constitutional government because mastering the army in fact means possessing the power of the de facto use of public violence. Once the army was put into private use and no one can stop it, the constitutional structure would have no guarantee.

I must say that Washington made a crucial contribution to the American constitutional system, for "A triumphant general in Washington's position might have tried to seize power, but Washington returned to private life" (National Museum of American History). What force drove him to give up such a great temptation in the eyes of the Economic Person? Obviously, that force was the moral force in his inner self. Then, where did this moral force come from?

In the book, "Christianity and the Constitution: The Faith of Our Founding Fathers," the author Eidsmoe clarified the founding fathers' religious beliefs. Obviously, Washington was a man who believed in God.

Because of political considerations and the caution in fighting among interreligious denominations, he rarely stated the specific religious denomination to which he belonged, but he never minded saying that he believed in God. When responding to a pastor's sermon, he showed his agreement: "(1) God wants people to live among civil society; (2) God has set a ruler for the people; therefore, (3) rulers have the right to be respected; but (4) rulers are also under the governance of God; (5) rulers are under God's judgment; and (6) God makes the rulers cease to be" (Quoted from Eidsmoe, p. 105).

If Washington knew that government was set up by God for the benefit of the citizens and rulers can only stay in power when they observe God's justice, then although Washington firmly believed that political power can be held and maintained even by the use of the army and that if he violates God's justice, he will step down. Even if he stayed on the stage, he would have lost the legitimacy to govern with no positive meaning and sooner or later would have stepped down. Therefore, using the army to gain political power was not within his choice.

In addition to Washington, most of the other founding fathers also have strong religious beliefs, such as Madison, Hamilton, Adams, Jefferson, and Franklin, among others. Among them, Adams and Jefferson were the two typical ones. Although Thomas Jefferson put greater emphasis on rationalism and not as much on Christianity, he certainly believed in God. In the "Declaration of Independence" that he drafted, he mentioned the following:

"… the separate and equal station to which the Laws of Nature and of Nature's God entitle them …";
"… all men are created equal, that they are endowed by their Creator with certain unalienable Rights …"; and
"… with a firm reliance on the Protection of Divine Providence …."

John Adams was a pure Puritan or an orthodox Calvinist. He believed that truth can only be revealed by God; reason alone is not enough. The Bible is the revelation of God. Because Adams had the vision that transcended himself, although he advocated for the American Revolution, he defended British soldiers who fired in the Boston Massacre and he opposed the French Revolution. What motivated him to proceed with American independence were not just secular interests but the religious fervor of Christianity. He compared himself to Moses: "Moses said, 'Who am I?

Can lead this great nation?' Whenever I think, in the past those great events and even greater ones in rapid development, I might have played a key role in springing the toggle or pushing the pinion, my heart was filled with indescribable awe" (Eidsmoe 2010, Chapter XV).

Eidsmoe mentioned two professors, Ronald Lutz and Charles Hyneman, who sorted out 2200 types of American literature between 1769 and 1805 and found that the most cited literature source is the Bible, by up to 34%. The cited proportions of various resources are listed in Table 15.1.

Table 15.1 also shows that the founding fathers of America were basically believers in religion, or were Religious Persons. Their religious beliefs made them believe the following:

...

4. Men are not perfect, and this must be considered in government theory.
5. The Government is ordained by God to restrain the sins of humans.

...

8. Human law must be consistent with divine law and natural law. Human laws that are against the higher law are invalid and should not be observed but be resisted.

...

Table 15.1 Studies cited by the founding fathers of the United States in 10-year increments

	1760s	*1770s*	*1789s*	*1790s*	*1800–1805*	*Percentage of the total*
Bible	24	44	34	29	38	34
Enlightenment literature	32	18	24	21	18	22
Whigs	10	20	19	17	15	18
Common law	12	4	9	14	20	11
Classics	8	11	10	11	2	9
Contemporaneous literature	6	2	3	6	5	4
Others	8	1	1	2	2	2
Literature numbers	216	544	1306	674	414	3154

Source: Donald S. Lutz, The Relative Influence of European Writers on Late Eighteenth-Century American Political Thought, *American Political Science Review*, 1984, pp. 189–197. Cited from Eidsmoe, 2010, p. 38

10. Life, liberty, and property are the inalienable natural rights given by God, included in divine law and natural law.
11. The establishment of the government is for the protection of human rights based on the contract or agreement of the people.
12. The government enjoys the power granted by the people in such contracts**Error! Bookmark not defined.** or agreements; once it attempts to usurp the powers not granted by the people, the government becomes illegal and should be resisted.

... (Eidsmoe 2010, pp. 60–61)

We know that these principles are the foundations of the U.S. Constitution, which is more likely to be alert to the problem of abuse of power by the government than any other human law in the past—abuse of power is why the system of checks and balances was designed. However, this set of constitutional principles must go through a due process to be effective and must be agreed on by the majority of the representatives in the constituent assembly. At this time, for religious reasons, Franklin called on the delegates to adopt a broader view, to reduce the battle for self-interests and compromise respectively to reach a majority agreement to enable these principles of the U.S. Constitutions to be written into the text.

However, the constitutional text has to be implemented and practiced by individuals. Washington, as the highest military officer, consciously abided by the basic constitutional principles, becoming an example for subsequent political and military leaders. Then, each subsequent U.S. president, if not Christian, was at least a man who believed in God and has gone through a different conversion process. Thus, by some measure in most cases, they were Religious Persons. Their religious beliefs made them consciously abide by the constitution and ensure the success of the American constitutional system.

15.5 Conclusion

If we confined our minds only to the Economic Person assumption, we would be unable to address the issue of restraining the supreme power (or de facto power). The history of humankind has told us that people can be converted to Religious Persons and comprehend the Heavenly course through self-enlightenment and self-refinement. Religious Persons are different from Economic Persons. They go beyond personal interests and consciously abide by the constitutional principles, even in the absence of external constraints. Therefore, the problem of no restraints for the supreme power might be solved, and the constitutional system could thus be established.

In modern times, people believe too much in the function of violence, of heteronomy institutions designed according to human beings' instincts to shun harms and incline to benefits but to ignore the role of thousands of years of religious and cultural traditions in the institutional structure, consequently resulting in significant defects in this structure. In China in particular, many people only limit ways to improve society through democracy or violence but fail to see the important role that religious and cultural traditions played in the constitutional structure. The result might be the swing between democracy and violence, and a truly effective constitutional system cannot be established. If we realized the institutional implications of Religious Persons, we would reexamine Chinese cultural traditions and foreign religious resources, making it possible to form a mature and effective constitutional system.

References

艾兹摩尔, 《美国宪法的基督教背景: 开国先父的信仰和选择》, 中央编译出版社. 2010. (Translated from: John Eidsmoe, *Christianity and the Constitution: Christianity and the Constitution: The Faith of Our Founding Fathers*, Baker Book House Company, 1987).

Bowles, Samuel, and Gintis, Herbert, The evolution of strong reciprocity: cooperation in heterogeneous populations, *Theoretical Population Biology* 65.1(February 2004).

布坎南, 2008, 《宪法秩序的经济学与伦理学》, 商务印书馆. (Translated from: James M. Buchanan, *The Economics and the Ethics of Constitutional Order*, University of Michigan, 1991).

黄裕生, 2008, 《宗教与哲学的相遇: 奥古斯丁与托马斯·阿奎那的基督教哲学研究》, 江苏人民出版社. (Huang Yusheng, *Religion Meets Philosophy: Christian Philosophical Study of Augustine and Thomas Aquinas*, Jiangsu People's Publishing House, 2008).

科斯, 2010, 《论经济学与经济学家》, 格致出版社. (Translated from: Ronald H. Coase, *Essays on Economics and Economists*, University of Chicago Press, 1994).

詹姆斯, 威廉, 2012, 《宗教经验种种》, 华夏出版社. William James, *The Varieties of Religious Experience*, Longmans, Green, And Co, New York, London, Bombay, Calcutta, and Madras, 1917.

CHAPTER 16

On the Theological Coordinates of Economics

Contents

Economics has always implied two reference systems. One is man's frame of reference, and the other is God's frame of reference. The human reference system is based on the hypothesis of economic man. The so-called economic man is a person who considers interests. People have advantages and disadvantages because they exist in limited space and time. Limited space-time represents the coordinates of human beings.

In contrast, economics imagines an overall optimal situation. In the imagination, economists assume that not only themselves but also all economic agents have all information, unlimited rationality, and zero transaction costs. At this time, limited space-time disappears. Economics imagines according to God's frame of reference.

The problem is that economists often use these two coordinates without being aware that they are doing so. For example, Marx observed that markets had costs but assumed that there were no institutional costs in his ideal communism. This assumption has led to a catastrophe of the planned economy. Another example, Neoclassical Economics, studies economic

Sheng Hong, *Vision and Calculation*,
https://doi.org/10.1007/978-981-15-2898-9_16

man with zero transaction costs and infinite rationality assumptions and cannot explain why there are still enterprises and other non-market organizations now that the market is effective.

The purpose of this chapter is to make it clear that economics has a purely theological coordinate, which can be used as a standard to reflect the position of human coordinates and to establish the relationship between human coordinates and the coordinates of God. When an economist changes coordinates, he or she clearly realizes that he or she is changing coordinates, not because of not realizing that coordinates have been changed, resulting in confusing conclusions.

16.1 The Concept of God in Economics

According to human imagination, the so-called God means transcendence, wholeness, and infinity, omniscience and omnipotence, the best, and the most beautiful. In addition, a "human" is concrete, partial, and limited.

The so-called transcendence is a realm that concrete people cannot imagine because of the dimension of the human physiological structure. Just as two-dimensional animals cannot imagine three-dimensions, human beings as three-and-a-half-dimensional animals cannot imagine a more than four-dimensional universe. The so-called three-and-a-half-dimensional refers to three-dimensional space and limited time. Therefore, the human limitation is limited in dimensions.

Conversely, God's infinity is the infinite dimension and not just the infinite four-dimensional space-time.

The so-called whole means that there is no omission, which is the greatest without an outsider and the smallest without an inner. It is an infinite whole.

This infinity also means the infinity of perception, information, and ability. That is, God itself is an infinite whole and, in its view, any part of the whole is instantaneously perceived by it, similar to people's perception of each part of their body. Alternatively, from a local point of view, the whole's perception of the part takes time, but because the whole God is infinite in time, time is meaningless—similar to "instantaneous perception." From the perspective of human beings, a distance exists between one part of the universe and another part, and the life span of human beings is limited. It takes at least time as a cost to perceive another part.

The costs of interactions between individuals can be called transaction costs. However, in terms of the form of the perception and consciousness of the whole to the individual, the interaction between God as a whole and the individual is beyond the distance, that is, there is no need to wait for a time lag because time is infinite and cannot "feel" the time lag. Therefore, God has no transaction costs.

Because all parts of the universe are part of God's entity, God can exist as a whole consciousness of all parts of the universe. This holistic consciousness does not come from the extraordinary brain isolated from wise creatures in the universe but from the sum of the rationality of all of these wise creatures. Although we can distinguish different brain cells, the consciousness in our brain is not the result of the combination of these cells but the result of their existence as a whole.

Economics, in terms of its characteristics, is the study of how to allocate scarce resources effectively. It is an effort to communicate individuals and the whole, starts with a limited number of individuals, and moves toward overall efficiency. What economics does not realize is that the whole is infinite. Economics generally believes that the whole is limited, such as a people, a country, and even the world. In the abstract concept of theory, the whole is infinite. Once economics realizes this, it can build itself on theological coordinates. In economic terms, all infinite beyond the finite is God's measure; if we measure the finite by the infinite, we can see the location and degree of the finite and can understand the finite more deeply and compare the different finite.

16.2 Why Does the Infinite God Set Scarce Rules?

Because God is infinite, he does not feel scarce. There is a lack of neither time and space nor resources and information in space and time. Therefore, why is God's rule for the universe based on scarcity?

The answer may be that, although the universe is infinite, every part of it is finite. If a part is infinite, it contradicts what is called a "part." If the part is infinite, then it is a universe itself, and there is no need to be a part. If it is an infinite part, it contradicts the concept of the whole because the whole in its original meaning is bigger than the part, and if the part is smaller than the whole, then the "infinite part" cannot be infinite. Therefore, the part is limited. Proof completed.

If the part is limited, resources are limited. Limited resources may generate and nurture intelligent organisms. Wisdom creatures must be limited; otherwise, they are gods. Among the various resources for generating and nurturing intelligent organisms, there must be scarce resources relative to the population of intelligent organisms. If not, these resources are infinite, which contradicts the precondition of limited resources. Because some resources are bound to be limited for these intelligent creatures, they are scarce, and the rules of the scarce world are reasonable.

Therefore, how do these limited parts connect with the infinite universe? If there are infinite finite parts, we can form an infinite universe. That is, the sum of infinite finite is infinite. Here, the finite and the infinite run through.

The further question is, is it better to have a whole summed up infinitely by better local parts than a whole summed up infinitely by poorer local parts? In mathematics, a finite number regardless of size multiplied by infinity equals infinity. There is no point to how big this finite number is. However, the whole is composed of innumerable individuals or parts. If we only consider the whole without individuals or parts, the whole will be abstracted and nihilist and thus will be meaningless. Of course, focusing only on the limited parts is also meaningless. Therefore, having an infinite whole with better parts is meaningful.

Therefore, how can a whole be judged as "infinite and made of better parts"? This is to treat the part as "the part of the whole." How can a part become "the part of the whole"? If a local situation can instantaneously affect the "feeling" of the whole, it is "the part of the whole"; if all parts are "**any part of the whole**," they are "the part of the whole." That is, if the God representing the whole randomly extracts a part—not a specific part, but any part may be extracted—then all parts are any part of the whole. When the extracted part is better than any part of the other whole or the other moment of the whole, the whole is "infinite and consisted of better parts"; if not, it is "infinite and consisted of worse parts."

Therefore, the local good or bad is related to the whole. Thus, creating rules about scarcity in various parts of the infinite universe is meaningful. In addition, because the part that affects the whole is "any part," this rule about scarcity must be the rule that runs through the whole universe, that is, the rule without exception.

Because of scarcity, competition is needed; the rule of competition is that species that use scarce resources more efficiently can win. This makes more efficient material structures and species stand out. The so-called more efficient refers to more inorganic or organic matters with specific structures that can be formed and supported, given both quantitative substances and energy. It is more efficient because these objects or species adopt more orderly and complex structures. In the extreme, there will be life, consciousness, and even wisdom. In a local part, that there is life, consciousness, and wisdom is "better" than if there is none of them because the infinite whole feels "better." Similar to a person, if the cells of all parts of the body are full of vitality, he or she is also full of vitality.

16.3 Natural Order in Theological Coordinates

Specifically, what are the "rules of the scarce world"? It is a relationship between an individual and an individual. Individuals form a relationship between them through interactions, including competition and exchange, to enable them to use scarce resources more effectively. This relationship can be "group" (economies of scale), "symbiosis" (economies of scope), "division of labor" (specialization), "reference" (e.g., price system formed through exchange and competition), or "exchange" (information exchange). Because of this relationship, the individual is no longer an isolated individual but part of a larger whole. In other words, how an individual saves scarce resources generally takes the form of a larger whole.

Therefore, the so-called better universe is one in which individuals form a larger whole. Here, the so-called forming a larger whole can generally be expressed by "more complex" (such as complex systems), "more orderly," "higher degree of organization," "higher negative entropy," and "more information." Such expression will lead to the result that parts of the universe will be more closely linked, more such as a "universe." Conversely, without the rules of the scarce world, there is no need for individuals to form a larger whole. The universe is a universe in which innumerable individuals have no connection. It is not "one universe" but "innumerable universes."

Would God be more willing to accept the consequences of the rules of the scarce world? Is it more labor-saving to manage one universe than to manage countless universes? The question is, if God is infinite in time and space in terms of energy and information, will it "care" about saving divine power? Similarly, with the relationship between the whole and the part, although God is infinite, in every part of time and space, God's input cannot be infinite because the limitation of time and space also limits the input of God's power. If God invests infinite divine power in limited space-time, is it not equal to saying that God is incompetent? God's input in a part must be less than its input in multiple parts and much less than its input in the whole. The so-called less than an infinite quantity must be a finite quantity. There is no "larger infinity" or "smaller infinity." Because God's input is limited, it makes sense to save it and make it more effective. Thus, from the perspective of God's more effective governance, a scarce rule is also necessary.

At all times, at home and abroad, people look up to and explore the Tao of Heaven or natural order, which is mainly the scarce rules. However, when people refer to the Tao of Heaven or the natural order, they also imply the belief that the evolution of the interaction of natural things will naturally lead to a good result, which is often expressed as an invisible hand. This is clearly the understanding in human coordinates.

Since the Cambrian bioexplosion, especially since the birth of mammals, scarce rules have brought mainly good results on Earth. After the rise of human beings, especially after the development of human civilization in the recent thousands of years, they have been sailing smoothly. Basically, no major natural disasters have occurred. Therefore, in human memory, the result of the natural order is good. However, if we extend the time axis of human coordinates from thousands of years to hundreds of thousands of years, tens of millions of years, or billions of years, the result of the natural order does not always seem to be good.

For example, geological archaeologists believe that two snowball periods occurred on Earth between 2.45 billion years ago and between 800 million and 600 million years ago. Around this time, life emerged 2.5 billion years ago, and the Cambrian biodiversity emerged 550 million years ago (Peter Ward and Donald Brownlee 2003, p. 114). During the snowball period, the Earth's temperature ranges from minus 20 degrees Celsius to minus 50 degrees Celsius (Peter Ward and Donald Brownlee 2003, p. 115). Without plant growth, there can be no living conditions for animals. Of course, human beings cannot survive. In a longer time dimension, we see the benefits of natural order only because the solar system is located in the galaxy just in an area suitable for human survival, which astrophysicists estimate is only approximately 4 billion years old (Peter Ward and Donald Brownlee 2003, p. 17). On a large scale, it is just a white foal crossing the gap. Do we still believe in the natural order when the Earth's environment is no longer suitable for human beings?

From the perspective of God's coordinates, the rules of the scarce world always lead to saving limited resources through the formation of larger entities in the universe, but this process is not straightforward. It may be tortuous and periodic. From the point of view that the rules of the scarce world lead to more complex and orderly development, whether human beings are present or not, it will promote the development of the universe toward the birth of human beings. Therefore, the result of this natural order is also "good." For some fluctuations in the process of forming a larger whole, they are also very normal, just as there are days and nights and four seasons. The morning dew cannot see the sunshine at noon. The locusts do not know another spring after the winter. The longer periods in the universe are similar to days and nights, and seasons. Only in the long winter of the universe, life takes the form of surviving a severe winter to preserve itself, such as seeds. During the snowball period when humans and even most animals cannot survive, if some single cells can survive, they, as "seeds" of humans and other animals, will help us tide over the difficult time. When the environment gets better, single cells will develop advanced animals and even humans. Therefore, from the perspective of God's coordinates, the natural order is still good.

16.4 Man in Theological Coordinates

Western economics' view on natural order comes from deism, which is the theory of the rational interpretation of God. This theory absorbs the resources of Christianity and Greek rationalism at the same time. Deism imagines a God different from that of the apocalyptic religion. This God did not have to do anything personally but set up a natural order in Genesis and then went back to sleep. With natural order and corresponding rewards and punishments, the universe automatically works.

It should be said that a condition should also be added that there are people who can know and understand the natural order, act in accordance with the natural order, and bear the consequences of action. This requires that people have self-consciousness, wisdom, and free will. Augustine discovered free will from the original sin theory of Christianity. Adam opened his eyes and felt ashamed to see himself naked, which meant that he had self-awareness. The so-called self-consciousness means that the individual is separated from the whole and humans from God. He and Eve stole the forbidden fruit and became wise. Because of wisdom, we can choose freely; that is, we have free will. Because of their free will, they will bear the consequences and be punished for their actions against God's will. Of course, if it conforms to the natural order, it will be rewarded.

Because of such people, God can go back to sleep after setting up the natural order. Of course, this is a metaphor. It means that God is more energy-efficient in governing the universe and can have a better universe. In fact, this is the most extreme result of the rules of the scarce world. To make more effective use of resources on the limited Earth, human beings form the largest whole and global unity through groups, symbiosis, division of labor, reference, and communication. Any animal with less intelligence than human beings, even the smartest, has no larger interindividual union than a natural group. For God, humans represent a good and inexpensive species. Their autonomy saves God's input, and they are the best part of the universe.

However, from God's point of view, human beings are only superior to other species, but there are still many limitations. Strictly speaking, the natural human is only a two-and-a-half dimensional creature. The so-called two-dimensional refers to space. In most cases, people walk on the ground, moving approximately in two-dimensional space. Many people like climbing because they want to add a dimension. Confucius said, "Benevolent person enjoys mountain," that is this meaning. However, on God's scale, it is only two-point-one-dimensional. On the large scale of the universe, the people standing on top of the mountain are also approximately standing on the two-dimensional plane. Furthermore, with the help of science and technology, people have realized their dream of flying; that is, they have made greater progress in the third dimension. Perhaps only when we reach the edge of the solar system can we truly count as three-dimensional organisms.

From the perspective of God's time, because the human life span is limited, they have only half a dimension. However, in accordance with the natural order, people form a large whole through the relationship between individuals, which extends in the dimension of time. People form families and extend their being via reproduction, and nations and societies made up of people through institutions and cultures exist for a much longer time. However, families, nations, and societies are not sufficient to enable human beings to go far in the fourth dimension. They would all perish eventually. Therefore, religions were created. Religion, through the theory of soul and the theory of afterlife, gives people the idea of eternity in time, and that they also live as if life were infinite. Through science, technology, and religion, a human being becomes a four-dimensional organism.

The economic man to whom economics usually refers is generally a two-dimensional organism in the spatial dimension. In the temporal dimension, it can be extended from the individual with a limited life span to the individual who has a family and society and has an eye over generations. Because of different time horizons, economic man may be short- or long-sighted. However, in economics textbooks, economic man generally refers to the former. They only respond to current information and generally do not think about things for too long a time, such as five or ten years. However, under a market system, these short-sighted economic men can synthesize an efficient society through interactions.

This is because, through the interaction, trading, and competition among economic men in the market, a price system has been formed. Price information is concentrated, convergent, and simple. By responding to a price, a short-sighted economic man can basically produce and live efficiently, and the whole society prospers.

Unfortunately, more generally, the market system depends on the system of individualistic choice of interests and cannot cover all places and occasions. Therefore, the short-sighted economic man may not master where the market fails, where there are externalities, and where resources are allocated by politics. These places happen to be complementary to the market system, such as property rights, the judicial system, and others. At this time, the visionary economic man has important significance.

This kind of economic man is an intellectual elite. They depend on the reading of historical documents and have a time horizon beyond their life span. They also often stand in the perspective of family or society and temporarily surpass their personal interests. In the absence of market signals, they can also predict the future outcome of certain actions; in the absence of intuitive information, they can also think of the impact of certain actions on others who do not appear to be present. As a result, these visionary economic men can avoid some less intuitive threats to themselves; in society, they can provide institutional rules to remedy market failure or even individualism failure and actually assume the responsibility of maintaining these institutional rules.

Although these two types of people are economic people, they can be distinguished according to the time horizon from the coordinates of God. In addition, this distinction is very important. Economists usually come from visionary economic man. However, they often fail to see the difference between themselves and the short-sighted economic man and confuse the difference between themselves and the coordinates of God, thus confusing the difference between man and God. When they think about efficiency, they think that there is the best realm from the perspective of the whole society and even the whole universe as if they are gods, and then assume that other economic people are gods. Their contacts are without distance. They know each other as to know the hands of themselves and, thus, there is no transaction cost, that is, the hypothesis of "complete information" and "zero transaction cost." This has thrown economics into chaos because the proper meaning of the topic of "economic man" is "limited" but becomes "infinite" in interaction.

The other type of human is ignored by economics, even though they are everywhere. This is the human who enriches the dimension of time by believing in a certain religion or cultural tradition, which I call "religious man." This kind of person has a nearly infinite time horizon because of the theory of soul or the theory of afterlife, and a nearly infinite space horizon because they connect themselves with God; therefore, they hardly consider the current interests of the individual and their behavior cannot be explained using the concept of the economic man. For this reason, their existence can make up for the problems that economic man cannot bypass and maintain the necessary order of individualism where individualism fails.

Finally, although human beings have the wisdom to understand the natural order, they still have limited rationality and some aspects that do not understand the natural order. The so-called limited rationality means that the dimensions are limited; in other words, they are doomed to fail to understand high-dimensional things. Therefore, the scope of autonomy granted by God to human beings is limited. When humans' free will choices violate the natural order, God warns by befalling a catastrophe on all of humankind. However, this warning may be the end of humanity. Therefore, the smartest thing to do with man's limited wisdom is to know the infinity of God and the limitation of man to avoid being wise in vain but to adopt an attitude of obeying the natural order. This theological interpretation offers why the mainstream of economics emphasizes the philosophy of the natural order.

Reference

Peter Ward and Donald Brownlee, *Rare Earth*, Copernicus Books, 2003.

Index[1]

[1] Note: Page numbers followed by 'n' refer to notes.

Sheng Hong, *Vision and Calculation*,
https://doi.org/10.1007/978-981-15-2898-9

C

The manufacturer's authorised representative in the EU is Springer Nature Customer Service Centre GmbH, Europaplatz 3, 69115 Heidelberg, Germany. If you have any concerns regarding our products, please contact ProductSafety@springernature.com

Printed and bound by CPI Group (UK) Ltd, Croydon, CR0 4YY
25/09/2026
02222881-0009